Enabling the New Era of Cloud Computing:

Data Security, Transfer, and Management

Yushi Shen
Microsoft Corporation, USA

Yale Li
Microsoft Corporation, USA

Ling Wu
EMC² Corporation, USA

Shaofeng Liu
Microsoft Corporation, USA

Qian Wen
Endronic Corp, USA

A volume in the Advances in Systems Analysis, Software Engineering, and High Performance Computing (ASASEHPC) Book Series

Managing Director:	Lindsay Johnston
Editorial Director:	Myla Merkel
Production Manager:	Jennifer Yoder
Publishing Systems Analyst:	Adrienne Freeland
Development Editor:	Austin DeMarco
Acquisitions Editor:	Kayla Wolfe
Typesetter:	Lisandro Gonzalez
Cover Design:	Jason Mull

Published in the United States of America by
Information Science Reference (an imprint of IGI Global)
701 E. Chocolate Avenue
Hershey PA 17033
Tel: 717-533-8845
Fax: 717-533-8661
E-mail: cust@igi-global.com
Web site: http://www.igi-global.com

Library of Congress Cataloging-in-Publication Data

Shen, Yushi, 1978-
  Enabling the new era of cloud computing : data security, transfer, and management / by Yushi Shen, Yale Li, Ling Wu, Shaofeng Liu, and Qian Wen.
       pages cm
  Includes bibliographical references and index.
  Summary: "This book discusses cloud computing as an emerging technology and its critical role in the IT industry upgrade and economic development in the future"-- Provided by publisher.
  ISBN 978-1-4666-4801-2 (hardcover) -- ISBN 978-1-4666-4802-9 (ebook) -- ISBN 978-1-4666-4803-6 (print & perpetual access) 1. Cloud computing. I. Title.
  QA76.585.S54 2014
  004.67'82--dc23
                                                    2013027879

This book is published in the IGI Global book series Advances in Systems Analysis, Software Engineering, and High Performance Computing (ASASEHPC) (ISSN: 2327-3453; eISSN: 2327-3461)

British Cataloguing in Publication Data
A Cataloguing in Publication record for this book is available from the British Library.

All work contributed to this book is new, previously-unpublished material. The views expressed in this book are those of the authors, but not necessarily of the publisher.

For electronic access to this publication, please contact: eresources@igi-global.com.

Advances in Systems Analysis, Software Engineering, and High Performance Computing (ASASEHPC) Book Series

Vijayan Sugumaran
Oakland University, USA

ISSN: 2327-3453
EISSN: 2327-3461

MISSION

The theory and practice of computing applications and distributed systems has emerged as one of the key areas of research driving innovations in business, engineering, and science. The fields of software engineering, systems analysis, and high performance computing offer a wide range of applications and solutions in solving computational problems for any modern organization.

The **Advances in Systems Analysis, Software Engineering, and High Performance Computing (ASASEHPC) Book Series** brings together research in the areas of distributed computing, systems and software engineering, high performance computing, and service science. This collection of publications is useful for academics, researchers, and practitioners seeking the latest practices and knowledge in this field.

COVERAGE

- Computer Graphics
- Computer Networking
- Computer System Analysis
- Distributed Cloud Computing
- Enterprise Information Systems
- Metadata and Semantic Web
- Parallel Architectures
- Performance Modeling
- Software Engineering
- Virtual Data Systems

IGI Global is currently accepting manuscripts for publication within this series. To submit a proposal for a volume in this series, please contact our Acquisition Editors at Acquisitions@igi-global.com or visit: http://www.igi-global.com/publish/.

Titles in this Series

For a list of additional titles in this series, please visit: www.igi-global.com

Enabling the New Era of Cloud Computing Data Security, Transfer, and Management
Yushi Shen (Microsoft, USA) Yale Li (Microsoft, USA) Ling Wu (EMC, USA) Shaofeng Liu (Microsoft, USA) and Qian Wen (Endronic Corp, USA)
Information Science Reference • copyright 2014 • 329pp • H/C (ISBN: 9781466648012) • US $195.00 (our price)

Communication Infrastructures for Cloud Computing
Hussein T. Mouftah (University of Ottawa, Canada) and Burak Kantarci (University of Ottawa, Canada)
Information Science Reference • copyright 2014 • 583pp • H/C (ISBN: 9781466645226) • US $195.00 (our price)

Organizational, Legal, and Technological Dimensions of Information System Administration
Irene Marie Portela (Polytechnic Institute of Cávado and Ave, Portugal) and Fernando Almeida (Polytechnic Institute of Gaya, Portugal)
Information Science Reference • copyright 2014 • 321pp • H/C (ISBN: 9781466645264) • US $195.00 (our price)

Advances and Applications in Model-Driven Engineering
Vicente García Díaz (University of Oviedo, Spain) Juan Manuel Cueva Lovelle (University of Oviedo, Spain) B. Cristina Pelayo García-Bustelo (University of Oviedo, Spain) and Oscar Sanjuán Martinez (University of Carlos III, Spain)
Information Science Reference • copyright 2014 • 424pp • H/C (ISBN: 9781466644946) • US $195.00 (our price)

Service-Driven Approaches to Architecture and Enterprise Integration
Raja Ramanathan (Independent Researcher, USA) and Kirtana Raja (Independent Researcher, USA)
Information Science Reference • copyright 2013 • 411pp • H/C (ISBN: 9781466641938) • US $195.00 (our price)

Progressions and Innovations in Model-Driven Software Engineering
Vicente García Díaz (University of Oviedo, Spain) Juan Manuel Cueva Lovelle (University of Oviedo, Spain) B. Cristina Pelayo García-Bustelo (University of Oviedo, Spain) and Oscar Sanjuán Martínez (University of Oviedo, Spain)
Engineering Science Reference • copyright 2013 • 388pp • H/C (ISBN: 9781466642171) • US $195.00 (our price)

Knowledge-Based Processes in Software Development
Saqib Saeed (Bahria University Islamabad, Pakistan) and Izzat Alsmadi (Yarmouk University, Jordan)
Information Science Reference • copyright 2013 • 296pp • H/C (ISBN: 9781466642294) • US $195.00 (our price)

Distributed Computing Innovations for Business, Engineering, and Science
Alfred Waising Loo (Lingnan University, Hong Kong)
Information Science Reference • copyright 2013 • 369pp • H/C (ISBN: 9781466625334) • US $195.00 (our price)

www.igi-global.com

701 E. Chocolate Ave., Hershey, PA 17033
Order online at www.igi-global.com or call 717-533-8845 x100
To place a standing order for titles released in this series, contact: cust@igi-global.com
Mon-Fri 8:00 am - 5:00 pm (est) or fax 24 hours a day 717-533-8661

Table of Contents

Section 1
Cloud Computing Overview

Chapter 3

Yushi Shen, Microsoft Corporation, USA

Yale Li, Microsoft Corporation, USA

Ling Wu, EMC² Corporation, USA

Shaofeng Liu, Microsoft Corporation, USA

Qian Wen, Endronic Corp, USA

Section 2
Data Management and Data Security

Chapter 4

Yushi Shen, Microsoft Corporation, USA

Yale Li, Microsoft Corporation, USA

Ling Wu, EMC² Corporation, USA

Shaofeng Liu, Microsoft Corporation, USA

Qian Wen, Endronic Corp, USA

Chapter 5

Yushi Shen, Microsoft Corporation, USA

Yale Li, Microsoft Corporation, USA

Ling Wu, EMC² Corporation, USA

Shaofeng Liu, Microsoft Corporation, USA

Qian Wen, Endronic Corp, USA

Section 3
Data Storage and Big Data

Chapter 9

Yushi Shen, Microsoft Corporation, USA

Yale Li, Microsoft Corporation, USA

Ling Wu, EMC² Corporation, USA

Shaofeng Liu, Microsoft Corporation, USA

Qian Wen, Endronic Corp, USA

Section 4
Networking in the Cloud Era

Chapter 10

Yale Li, Microsoft Corporation, USA

Yushi Shen, Microsoft Corporation, USA

Yudong Liu, Western Washington University, USA

Chapter 11

Yushi Shen, Microsoft Corporation, USA

Yale Li, Microsoft Corporation, USA

Ling Wu, EMC² Corporation, USA

Shaofeng Liu, Microsoft Corporation, USA

Qian Wen, Endronic Corp, USA

Chapter 15

Yushi Shen, Microsoft Corporation, USA
Yale Li, Microsoft Corporation, USA
Ling Wu, EMC² Corporation, USA
Shaofeng Liu, Microsoft Corporation, USA
Qian Wen, Endronic Corp, USA

Foreword

by Howard A. Schmidt

Few can argue that "the cloud" gives us tremendous capabilities and efficiencies that are like nothing we have seen before. Governments, businesses, academia, and all other organizations that embrace cloud computing are achieving competitive advantages from the better utilization of IT resources and faster services for their customers. The US government has adopted a "cloud first" policy, and this supports better fiscal responsibilities, so we can achieve necessary spending cuts without cutting into essential services. Cloud also makes the government more responsive to the needs of its citizens and increases the collaboration and coordination between agencies. Through data.gov, recovery.gov, and other related .gov projects, cloud has demonstrated its capability for increased interactions with the public, allowing for more feedback and easier contact with interested parties. New cloud datacenters use power more efficiently than the traditional IT infrastructures, while supporting the same workload. This can dramatically reduce the carbon footprint and encourage the society's move into the green IT era.

Many of us talk about the challenges to privacy and security in the cloud. Much of this can be enhanced with good planning, requirement setting, and full understanding of the environment. Taking the US government as an example again, federal and state CIOs need to report to the legislators on how data is being kept private and secure in the cloud. Data is often handled by many departments and agencies with varying levels of sensitivity, such as the intelligence and law enforcement reports, the citizens' personally identifiable information, and a host of other types of data. The security and privacy protection requirements are complex and varied; therefore, a cloud environment must be well understood in order to achieve the above goals in the cloud and in parity to what we have done for an on premise environment. Strategic planning will help us to achieve the goals in a coordinated effort.

The book, *Enabling the New Era of Cloud Computing: Data Security, Transfer, and Management*, comes at a critical time when existing markets need to keep the cloud adoption momentum, and emerging markets want to land in the cloud in the right way. Indisputably, data is the core asset, and we should understand how it can be secured, transferred, accessed, and managed in the cloud. I am impressed that all of the authors have shared their insights in this book from the different perspectives through their unique experiences.

Howard A. Schmidt
SAFECode, USA

Howard A. Schmidt *brings together talents in business, defense, intelligence, law enforcement, privacy, academia, and international relations gained from a distinguished career spanning 40 years. He currently serves as a partner in the strategic advisory firm, Ridge Schmidt Cyber, an executive services firm that helps leaders in business and government navigate the increasing demands of cybersecurity. He serves in this position with Tom Ridge, the first secretary of the Department of Homeland Security. He also serves as executive director of The Software Assurance Forum for Excellence in Code (SAFECode). Mr. Schmidt served as Special Assistant to the President and the Cybersecurity Coordinator for the federal government. In this role, he was responsible for coordinating interagency cybersecurity policy development and implementation and for coordinating engagement with federal, state, local, international, and private sector cybersecurity partners. Previously, Mr. Schmidt was the President and CEO of the Information Security Forum (ISF). Before ISF, he served as Vice President and Chief Information Security Officer and Chief Security Strategist for eBay Inc., and formerly operated as the Chief Security Officer for Microsoft Corp. He also served as Chief Security Strategist for the US-CERT Partners Program for the Department of Homeland Security. Mr. Schmidt also brings to bear over 26 years of military service. Mr. Schmidt holds a master's degree in organizational management (MAOM) from the University of Phoenix, and an Honorary Doctorate degree in Humane Letters. He was an Adjunct Professor at GA Tech, GTISC, Professor of Research at Idaho State University, Adjunct Distinguished Fellow with Carnegie Mellon's CyLab, and a Distinguished Fellow of the Ponemon Privacy Institute.*

Foreword

by Aloysius Cheang

I was truly excited and honored when Yushi and Yale approached me to write the foreword for their new book, *Enabling the New Era of Cloud Computing: Data Security, Transfer, and Management*. It could not be more appropriate, as the world begins to embrace the Cloud, amidst some global controversy over data protection and privacy issues. Cloud computing heralds the coming of a new era, where IT, in taking on the mantle of a public utility, signals its true harmonization with business. The security of data within the cloud is essential in ensuring that businesses can meet their strategic goals. Indeed, a data-centric approach towards cloud security is one of the key concepts highlighted in the Cloud Security Alliance's Definitive Security Guidance for Critical Areas of Focus in Cloud Computing.

The Cloud Security Alliance or CSA's mission is to promote the use of best practices for providing security assurance within Cloud Computing and education on the uses of Cloud Computing. It also aims to secure all other forms of computing. As a truly global organization that is instrumental in building a trusted and secure cloud eco-system, CSA operates over the following key regions: Americas, Europe, Middle-East and Africa (EMEA), and Asia Pacific (APAC). It is powered by over 200 member organizations and over 48,000 individual members worldwide in 64 chapters.

Yushi and Yale are respected cybersecurity experts who are trusted advisors to some of the largest corporations in the world. Thus, it has come to me as no surprise that they are sharp and on target (once again!) in identifying the key security concerns that inhibit the ascension of cloud computing and providing the appropriate treatment to ensure trustworthiness of data within the cloud – any cloud, anywhere, anytime, and anyplace. Furthermore, their extensive experiences, taking them halfway around the globe and back again to their roots, must offer insights that are unparalleled and valuable to those who are looking at entering the lucrative Chinese market.

There is no doubt that this high-profile book will significantly improve our understanding of this most important phenomenon, bringing IT to the mainstream and into the boardroom. It will tremendously promote the growth of the cloud industry worldwide, especially in emerging markets such as China.

Aloysius Cheang
Cloud Security Alliance, Singapore

Aloysius Cheang *is currently the Managing Director APAC of Cloud Security Alliance. He also heads the Standards Secretariat. Mr. Cheang brings to the Alliance extensive experience gained from running business units and multi-million enterprise security and technology programs for Global 500 organizations worldwide in his previous roles as a CSO for a Telco and APAC practice leader with leading management consulting firms. He is an active community leader, having founded and mentored various information security projects, forums, groups, and associations in Singapore and many parts in APAC. He is also active in standardization and was most recently a co-editor for ISO/IEC 27032 "Guidelines for Cybersecurity," having contributed towards many other security standards such as ISO/IEC 24762 et al. in the past. Mr. Cheang holds a B.Sc (Hons) and Master's degrees in Computer Science from the National University of Singapore and is currently a doctorate candidate. His professional certifications include CISA, CISSP, and GCIH. His views are valued by global media, such as Times, Wall Street Journal, and CIO Magazine as a trusted independent source of specialist opinion over the last decade.*

Preface

Over the years, Cloud Computing has been one of the most popular topics in the IT industry and beyond. Cloud Computing is deemed the main trend of IT development for the coming decades, and it is to have a profound impact on the development of the human society and the world economy.

Cloud Computing is not only a technical terminology but also a marketing terminology that aims at providing computation, software, data access, and storage services, which do not require end-user knowledge of the physical location and configuration of the system that delivers these services. In other words, it is the delivery of computing as a service rather than a product, whereby widely shared resources, software, and information are provided on-demand.

It is becoming increasingly clear that we are moving from the era of personal computers to an exciting new era of personal computing. The integration of a wide range of devices, cloud services, and natural experiences that span the technology ecosystem and enable truly personal computing – nothing is to work in isolation, and everything is to work for the client.

Cloud Computing is not something that has suddenly appeared overnight: in some form it can be traced back to a time when computer systems remotely time-shared computing resources and applications. The lack of common understanding has been a big issue, as IT leaders try to reach a consensus on how to best approach Cloud Computing. In July 2009, the National Institute of Standards and Technology (NIST) released their first draft definition of Cloud Computing, and in October 2011, after sixteen rounds of revisions, they published the "final" definition in the NIST Special Publication 800-145. For the most part, the debate over the definition of Cloud Computing is over, at least for a period of time. Recently, Cloud Computing extended to cover applications, servers, as well as the network infrastructure and business solutions. Many companies, such as Microsoft, Google, Apple, IBM, Amazon, and Salesforce.com, have been delivering business from the cloud, and are starting to generate some revenues.

According to the official NIST (n.d.) definition: "Cloud Computing is a model for enabling ubiquitous, convenient on-demand network access to a shared pool of configurable computing resources, such as networks, servers, storage, applications and services, that can be rapidly provisioned and released, with minimal management effort or service provider interaction." In short, Cloud Computing is described as a pool of abstracted, highly scalable, and managed computer infrastructures capable of hosting end-customer applications, and its clients can be billed by consumption.

Cloud Computing allows for the sharing and scalable deployment of services as needed from almost any location, and for which the customers can be billed based on their actual usage. Cloud Computing has a variety of characteristics: shared infrastructure, dynamic provisioning, network access, and managed metering.

SHARED INFRASTRUCTURE

Being in the "cloud" with virtualization technology, Cloud Computing enables the sharing of physical services, storage, and networking capabilities. The cloud infrastructure, regardless of deployment model, seeks to make the most of the available infrastructure for a number of users.

Shared infrastructure also makes Cloud Computing device and location independent. It enables the users to access systems using a Web browser regardless of their location or the device they are using.

DYNAMIC PROVISIONING

Scalability and elasticity via dynamic (i.e., "on-demand") provisioning of resources are some important characteristics of Cloud Computing, which allows for the provision of services based on user requirements.

This is achieved automatically using software automation, enabling the expansion and contraction of service capabilities as needed. This dynamic scaling needs to be done while maintaining high levels of reliability and security.

NETWORK ACCESS

Cloud Computing requires broadband networks, including both wired and wireless, for a broad range of devices such as PCs, laptops, and mobile devices. Deployments of services in the cloud include everything from using business applications to the latest application on the newest smartphones.

MANAGED METERING

This characterizes Cloud Computing from the business point of view. Cloud Computing uses metering to manage and optimize services and provide reporting and billing information. In this way, consumers are billed for services according to the amount of computing resources they actually use during the billing period.

In general, each company can choose its cloud service and deployment model based on the specific business, operational, and technical requirements. The NIST have listed three service models of Cloud Computing: Software as a Service (SaaS), Platform as a Service (PaaS), and Infrastructure as a Service (IaaS). Thereafter, IT companies and organizations have also introduced other service models such as Security a Service (SECaaS), Monitoring as a Service (MaaS), Communications as a Service (CaaS), and XaaS or "Anything as a Service."

SOFTWARE AS A SERVICE (SaaS)

With SaaS, consumers can purchase the ability to access and use an application or service that is hosted in the cloud. Users do not have to install or maintain the SaaS application. Software is running on a cloud infrastructure belonging to the provider, and a user can access it via a Web browser.

The SaaS model can save companies costs on hardware, software, and maintenance. A benchmark example of this is Salesforce.com, where necessary information for the interactions between consumers and services are hosted as part of the services in the cloud. Microsoft is also expanding its involvement in this area, and as part of the Cloud Computing option for Microsoft® Office 2010, its Office Web Apps are available to Office volume licensing customers and Office Web App subscriptions, through Microsoft's cloud-based Online Services.

PLATFORM AS A SERVICE (PaaS)

With PaaS, consumers purchase access to platforms, which enables them to deploy their own software and applications in the cloud. The operating systems and network access are managed by the provider instead of the consumer.

The PaaS services provide a great deal of flexibility, allowing companies to build their PaaS environments on demand with no capital expenditures, and enable companies to develop applications more quickly and efficiently in a cloud environment using the programming languages and tools supported by the provider.

INFRASTRUCTURE AS A SERVICE (IaaS)

With IaaS, consumers control and manage the systems in terms of the operating systems, applications, storage, and network connectivity, but they do not control the cloud infrastructure.

IaaS enables companies to deliver applications more efficiently by removing the complexities involved with managing their own infrastructure. IaaS enables fast deployment of applications and improves the agility of the IT services by instantly adding computing processing power and storage capacity when needed.

OTHER CLOUD SERVICE MODELS

SaaS, PaaS, and IaaS are the three primary service models of Cloud Computing, and there are other service models such as Security as a Service (SECaaS), Monitoring as a Service (MaaS), Communications as a Service (CaaS), and XaaS, or anything as a Service.

SECaaS is a business model in which a large service provider integrates their security services into a corporate infrastructure on a subscription basis. It is more cost effective than most individuals or corporations can provide on their own when the total cost of ownership is considered. These security services often include authentication, anti-virus, anti-malware/spyware, intrusion detection, security event management, and others.

MaaS provides an option to offload a large majority of monitoring costs by having it run as a service as opposed to fully invested in-house tools. So, for example, by logging onto a thin client or central Web-based dashboard, which is hosted by the service provider, the client can monitor the status of their key applications regardless of location.

CaaS is one subset of the model used to describe telephony services. It enables the client to utilize Enterprise-level VoIP, VPNs, PBX, and Unified Communications without the costly investment of purchasing, hosting, and managing the infrastructure by themselves.

Finally, XaaS, or Anything as a Service, is the delivery of IT as a service through hybrid Cloud Computing and is a reference to either one or a combination of SaaS, PaaS, IaaS, and so on. XaaS is quickly emerging as a term being readily recognized as services that have been previously separated on either private or public Clouds but are becoming increasingly more transparent and integrated.

Deploying Cloud Computing can differ depending on requirements. The NIST have also listed four primary deployment models—briefly discussed below—each with specific characteristics that support user demands.

PRIVATE CLOUD

The cloud infrastructure is deployed, maintained, and operated for a specific organization (such as a company, a university, or a government sector).

COMMUNITY CLOUD

The cloud infrastructure is shared among a number of organizations with a similar set of interests and requirements.

PUBLIC CLOUD

The cloud infrastructure is available to the public on a commercial basis by a cloud service provider. For example, Google online search is a public cloud service.

HYBRID CLOUD

The cloud infrastructure consists of a number of clouds of any type, and these clouds have the ability to move data and/or applications from one cloud to another through their interfaces. This can be a combination of private and public clouds, supporting the requirement to retain data in an organization and also the need to offer services in the cloud.

As discussed, Cloud Computing is about moving services, computation, and data offsite to an internal or external location-transparent and centralized facility or contractor. It makes data easily and ubiquitously accessible, often at much lower costs. It increases information value and enables opportunities for enhanced collaboration, integration, and analysis on a shared common platform.

Some of key benefits of Cloud Computing are:

- **Cost Savings:** Organizations are able to reduce their capital expenditures and use operational expenditures for increasing their computing capabilities. It provides a lower barrier of entry and also requires fewer in-house IT resources;

- **Scalability and Flexibility:** Cloud computing provides a smooth scalability path for organizations, which can start with a small deployment and grow to a large deployment fairly rapidly, and then quickly scale back if necessary. Cloud computing is also flexible enough to allow organizations to use extra resources at peak times, enabling them to satisfy fast-changing consumer demands;
- **Reliability:** Services using multiple redundant sites can support business continuity and disaster recovery;
- **Low Maintenance:** Cloud service providers perform the system maintenance, and access is through APIs that do not require application installations onto PCs, thus further reducing maintenance requirements;
- **Ubiquitously Accessible:** Mobile users enjoy increased productivity due to systems accessible in an infrastructure, available anywhere and anytime.

There are also some notable challenges associated with Cloud Computing. Most of them can provide opportunities if resolved with due care and attention in the planning stages. For example, some of well-known challenges include:

- **Security and Privacy:** The most challenging issues surrounding Cloud Computing are relate to storing and securing data and monitoring the use of the cloud by the service providers;
- **Lack of Standards:** Clouds have documented interfaces; however, no common standard exists with these clouds, and thus, most clouds are expected to have interoperability issues;
- **Continuously Evolving:** User requirements are continuously evolving, as are the requirements for interfaces, networking, and storage. This means that a "cloud," especially a public one, does not remain static and is going to be continuously evolving;
- **Cloud Abuse:** With privately purchased hardware, crackers posing as legitimate customers can purchase the services of Cloud Computing for nefarious purposes. This includes password cracking and launching attacks using the purchased computing resources.

Through these challenges, several inevitable technology trends are going to be critical in driving the IT industry into a new cloud era, transforming the global technology scene, the enterprise sectors, and the society as a whole. They all serve the purpose of increased mobility, more social networking and interactions, the development of cloud computing, and the growth of big data. These are inter-dependent trends having an influence amongst themselves. Here, we would like to briefly touch on the three major trends:

- **Big Data:** Today, we are generating massive amounts of data, often called "big data." At the same time, we are developing some exciting new ways to analyze data, which can help us see patterns or relationships that have been previously hidden. All these generate valuable insights. To tap into the latent value of big data, we need machine learning technologies that can learn from experience;
- **Natural User Interfaces:** Cloud computing, which encompasses voice, vision, gesture, multi-touch, and so on, is becoming more prevalent. Computing systems are gaining human-like perceptions, such as a better ability to see, hear, and understand. Combining this enhanced perception with big data and machine learning, these systems are beginning to understand our intent and context. This makes it possible for computers to really help us and even work on our behalf;

- **Blending of Two Worlds:** The digital world and the physical world are starting to blend together. The associated opportunities and means to collaborate are rapidly evolving, taking advantage of low-latency broadband networks and more natural computing interactions. When we blend the digital and physical realities together, we get something completely new. In the future, neither the human physical world nor the digital world will be sufficient all by itself.

As a result, we see more and more connected devices in a wider array of form factors changing the way we do business and conduct our lives. As the line between our work and personal lives blurs, people expect to apply the tools and advantages from one sphere to seamlessly blend with another. Therefore, we see new social tools in the workplace connecting colleagues and customers, as well as family and friends, all on whatever device we use at that time. Our users expect this. This of course is being enabled and accelerated by Cloud Computing, with its advantages of always-on connectivity and instant scalability, meaning that new apps and services are not only possible but have attractive economics. As these apps and services proliferate, so does the information that they capture and use, and this creates exponential growth of data, which is an enormous opportunity for deriving better insights for businesses and society.

Cloud Computing can creatively empower traditional businesses. The current economic climate is encouraging the IT departments to evaluate Cloud Computing as a clear path to cost reduction. Nearly everyone that consumes Cloud Computing is to enjoy cheaper alternatives to the on premise models. Although Cloud Computing can surely help reduce operating costs, the real promise of the cloud lies in its ability to help us fashion what we call the "real-time enterprise" – one that demands faster application development, a constant stream of data, and a responsiveness to business needs that is just not achievable with planning and refresh cycles being dragged out for years. Thus, the shift to Cloud Computing is not just a shift in the way storage is handled, or where computing tasks take place, it is a shift in the fundamental ways in which applications are designed and delivered. These "cloud-designed" applications require more than a simple collection of cloud-based services.

These trends are also fueling more advanced developments in e-commerce. Consumers expect to have device-specific experiences with applications, multiple-form factors, switching from a desktop PC and a browser to a slate type device and to smart phones. Consumers expect their experiences to be consistent but modify themselves contextually in an appropriate way. What we are finding out is that the buying experience is becoming more and more device centered, and the channel to reaching through to these market places is also where we deliver our first-party products. The destination is really an integrated buying experience on whatever device the consumers carry, and once they buy something, they want to know that it is going to transition and flow to all the other experiences they have. These are some very dramatic changes that all come back to this notion that the people have multiple devices, and the devices and people are more socially connected and/or interconnected, thus significantly changing the way we do commerce.

Cloud computing is opening new opportunities for entrepreneurs and innovators. It is revolutionary for startups and small businesses. Such companies typically have very little money for capital expenditures, and the cloud provides an affordable model that enables these companies to pay-as-they-go. The cloud offers opportunities to fuel entrepreneurship, job creation, and new venture creations by giving small-and-medium-sized enterprises easily scalable automated business processes and advantages. This enables more entrepreneurs to be able to easily translate their ideas into reality and enjoy their full potential building the next global business.

We need to also pay attend to Cloud Computing in emerging markets, especially in China – the center of gravity in the world not only economically but also in terms of innovation. Our world is shifting from what we call "the West"—North America, Europe, and a few other places—to "the East," and China accounts for a huge share of this shift. With an existing strong talent base, the leading market for PCs, servers, mobile devices, and Internet users, the possibility for cloud development, with positive impacts on China's economic growth, represents a significant area of opportunity. China's leaders are well aware of all of the challenges before them and believe very strongly that to spur investment in innovation and technology is the clear path to successfully overcoming these challenges. China as a nation has five-year planning stages, and we are now in the 12th iteration. In that plan, China is committed to changing its model of economic growth toward a more innovation-driven economy, growing strategic industries including IT, and improving lives through sustainability, along with a number of other different initiatives. The government has explicitly embraced the cloud in their national policies, seeing it as a new area for economic growth, and they have already taken the steps to encourage the development of Cloud Computing in China.

Our book gives a comprehensive high-level overview of Cloud Computing, data management and security, data storage and big data, and some of the latest research results in networking aimed at satisfying the network demands in the cloud era. Finally, in the Appendix we discuss the development of cloud computing in China, which covers strategies that are most suitable for the Chinese society and culture.

With our book, we hope to help familiarize the readers with some key concepts of cloud computing, the available cloud technologies in the areas of big data and data security, communication networks, and also to become well aware of the direction of the IT development in the world. In this, we hope to help them in terms of making better informed short term and long term IT decisions for their enterprises and organizations.

Finally and most apparently, the information world is entering a new era, which is both driven by and enabled by Cloud Computing. Let's be well prepared to embrace this new era!

Yushi Shen
Microsoft Corporation, USA

Yale Li
Microsoft Corporation, USA

Ling Wu
EMC² Corporation, USA

Shaofeng Liu
Microsoft Corporation, USA

Qian Wen
Endronic Corp, USA

REFERENCES

NIST. (n.d.). *Cloud computing definition*. Retrieved from http://csrc.nist.gov/publications/nistpubs/800-145/SP800-145.pdf

Acknowledgment

Although we are responsible for writing and organizing this book, it would not have been possible without the support of many people. We would like to express our deepest appreciation to all those who have provided us the support and helped to complete this book.

Our sincere gratitude goes to Professor Howard Schmidt, Retired Special Assistant to the President, Cyber Security Coordinator at the Executive Office of the President, White House, and Mr. Aloysius Cheang, Managing Director at CSA APAC. They have shared their broad vision and pioneering opinion about cloud computing with the authors.

A couple of chapters in this book are based on the collaborative research efforts with our CSA colleagues. Our thanks go to Jairo Orea, Marlin Pohlman, Yaron Levy, Dan Logan, Price Oden, et al., for Chapter 4 ("Trusted Cloud Initiative Reference Architecture"), and to Jens Laundrup, Andrea Bilobrk, Moshe Ferber, Robert Gutcho, Bernd Jager, and Roshan Sequeira for Chapter 5 ("Security Information and Event Management Implementation Guidance"). We also appreciate the support from Dr. Yudong Liu, Assistant Professor at the Department of Computer Science, Western Washington University, and Kevin Zhang, Software Engineer at Microsoft Corporation, on Chapter 6 ("Enterprise Security Monitoring with the Fusion Center Model").

We would like to acknowledge the EMC^2 Education Services for supporting us with books and training materials. We could not have written the chapters on big data without their assistance.

A few chapters of the book are based on original work together with Tom Defanti and Jurgen Schulze, distinguished scientists at Calit2, California Institute for Telecommunications and Information Technology. They have largely contributed and supported the work about cross-stream coding for parallel data transfers.

Furthermore, many thanks go to Mr. Zheng Li, Sr. Director of the Public Sector Group at Microsoft China, Dr. Tayfun Keskin, Professor at the Business School of the University of Washington, and Mr. Jie (Jason) Yang, Sr. Finance Manager at Microsoft Corporation. They have contributed tremendously in the research on the comparison of cloud computing ecosystems in the USA and China, as well as the future trend of IT in China. This work has been included in the Appendix.

Last but not least, we would also like to acknowledge with much appreciation Dr. Ya-Qin Zhang, the Corporate Vice President of Microsoft Corporation, Mr. Jim Reavis, the Co-Founder and Executive Director of Cloud Security Alliance (CSA), and Mr. George Yan, the General Manager for Cloud and Enterprise of Microsoft Corporation, who were abundantly helpful to us in their support and guidance for the completion of this book.

Yushi Shen
Microsoft Corporation, USA

Yale Li
Microsoft Corporation, USA

Ling Wu
EMC² Corporation, USA

Shaofeng Liu
Microsoft Corporation, USA

Qian Wen
Endronic Corp, USA

Section 1
Cloud Computing Overview

Chapter 1
Cloud Computing Overview

Yushi Shen
Microsoft Corporation, USA

Ling Wu
EMC² Corporation, USA

Yale Li
Microsoft Corporation, USA

Shaofeng Liu
Microsoft Corporation, USA

Qian Wen
Endronic Corp, USA

ABSTRACT

Cloud Computing is deemed the main trend of IT development for the coming decades, and it is to have a profound impact on the development of the human society and the world economy. In this chapter, the authors examine the history of cloud computing, the technical and business models, and the global implications of cloud computing's development in the near future. Finally, the market demands for cloud computing and the foreseeable developmental stages are explored.

THE HISTORY OF CLOUD COMPUTING

Cloud computing was not born overnight. The concept of the Cloud in reality had encompassed the entire history of business machines and the Internet. In as early as 1961, when the first manned space craft was launched into space, a computer scientist and Turing Award recipient, John McCarthy, predicted: "Like the public telephone networks, the future of computing will be organized in such a way that it will be offered much like public resources and utilities. This will bring about a whole new industry." In 1964, an American inventor, Douglas Engelbart, did research in the area of human-computer interactions, which brought the rise of computer mice, links and network machines. During the same period, the ARPANet inventor, J.C.R. Licklider, had foreseen grid computing in the form of global network delivery. In the 1990s, grid computing was very popular and extremely similar to cloud computing, in that access for computing power became as easy as plugging into the electricity grid. (Baidu Encyclopedia, 2013)

Microsoft had been quite closely related to cloud computing. It could be said that the Cloud operating system was a Microsoft invention.

DOI: 10.4018/978-1-4666-4801-2.ch001

The former President of Microsoft Platform and Services group, Jim Alchin, while working on his Ph.D., at the Georgia Institute of Technology, published a paper titled: "An Architecture for Reliable Decentralized Systems," describing the world's first cloud operating system architecture as "the clouds distributed object-oriented operating system."

One major contribution due to the birth of Cloud computing was that it brought the world a brand new business model. Two things that happened in the 1990s were considered landmark initiatives: First in 1991, CERN broadened the use of the Internet from a limited research tool to its popular uses in all walks of life. Secondly in 1995, Microsoft's global Internet data center realized the concept of cloud, by making its applications available to hundreds of millions of users around the world. This "cloud" was the MSN Internet service, and its associated "terminals" were supported by the simultaneous release of the Windows 95 operating system. The core application, connecting this "cloud" and its "terminals," was the IE (Internet Explorer in Windows Plus), where its home page was http://www.msn.com.

In 1997, an American professor of Indian descent, Ramnath Chellappa, who specialized in the area of Information Systems, first coined the term - "Cloud Computing." A cloud shape was generally used to represent the Internet in textbooks and design diagrams. In his lectures, Chellappa defined Cloud Computing as: a computing paradigm where the boundaries of computing will be determined by the economic rationale rather than technical limits alone.

From the economic and business model point of view, Salesforce.com and Amazon were pioneers in cloud computing. In 1999, Saleforce.com introduced the concept of delivering enterprise applications through its web site. In 2002, Amazon launched the Amazon Web Services. The year of 2006 was deemed the first year of the modern cloud computing era: Google Docs appeared in the public view; Amazon's EC2 (Elastic Comput-

ing Cloud) started formally providing services for small businesses and individual users, where client applications were run on the established Amazon website servers; Microsoft launched the Red Dog Cloud platform, a predecessor to Windows Azure. David Cutler, father to Windows NT, developed the Red-Dog OS Kernel from the Windows operating system kernel. In November 2009, Microsoft's Windows Azure cloud platform officially began commercial services after a long trial period.

In 2008, the IT industry had widely recognized that the biggest challenge to Cloud Computing was computing security. Jim Reavis and et al., created a global Cloud Security Alliance (CSA). In January of 2008, Nicholas Carr published the book "The Big Switch: Rewiring the World, from Edison to Google", where he used an example of switching the power station from small to large generators to illustrate the cloud computing concept from the various perspectives of history, economics, technology, development prospects and its impact on society. Numerous articles and publications had come into play to define and give guidance on the subject areas related to cloud computing; the following being some generally recognized classics:

- **Academia:** University of California, Berkeley, "Above the Clouds: A Berkeley View of Cloud Computing." This article gave cloud service providers a profit formula, ten technical challenges and opportunities;
- **The Government:** U.S. National Bureau of Standards (NIST), in "The NIST Definition of Cloud Computing," presented the industry-recognized SPI cloud model, where the cloud computing service models were classified into three categories: IaaS (Infrastructure as a Service), PaaS (platform as a service) and SaaS (software as a service). The cloud computing deployment model was divided into the public, private and hybrid clouds;

- **Industry Associations:** Cloud Security Alliance (CSA), "The Security Guidance for Critical Areas of Focus in Cloud Computing." In this article, critical areas of cloud security had been classified and guidance provided;
- **Private Companies:** Microsoft (Microsoft), "The Economics of the Cloud." In this article, economic benefits brought by Cloud Computing were profoundly expounded with large amounts of data and graphics. It provided enterprise IT leaders a vision and strategy for the cloud transformation.

CLOUD COMPUTING MODELS

A Technical Model of Cloud Computing

Currently, Cloud computing is supported by virtualization and management technologies.

Virtual machine technologies directly promote the rapid development of cloud computing. The emergence and maturation of virtual machine technologies have made possible the remote and fast reconfiguration of computer systems. With the support of this technology, high market demands for IT services in areas of the fast implementation of network services, network storage and the convenient management of these services have led to the formation of today's cloud computing. Currently virtualization technologies are divided into three camps: Microsoft Hyper-V, VMware by ESX and Citrix's open source Xen.

To characterize cloud computing, the U.S. National Bureau of Standards (NIST), the Cloud Security Alliance (CSA) and other agencies have come up with three service models, four deployment modes and five characteristics.

On the abstract level, the computer provides two basic functions: computing and storage. The computer structure can be roughly abstracted into three levels. From low to high, they are the hardware, the operating system and applications. The

Figure 1. The three service models, four deployment modes and five characteristics of cloud computing

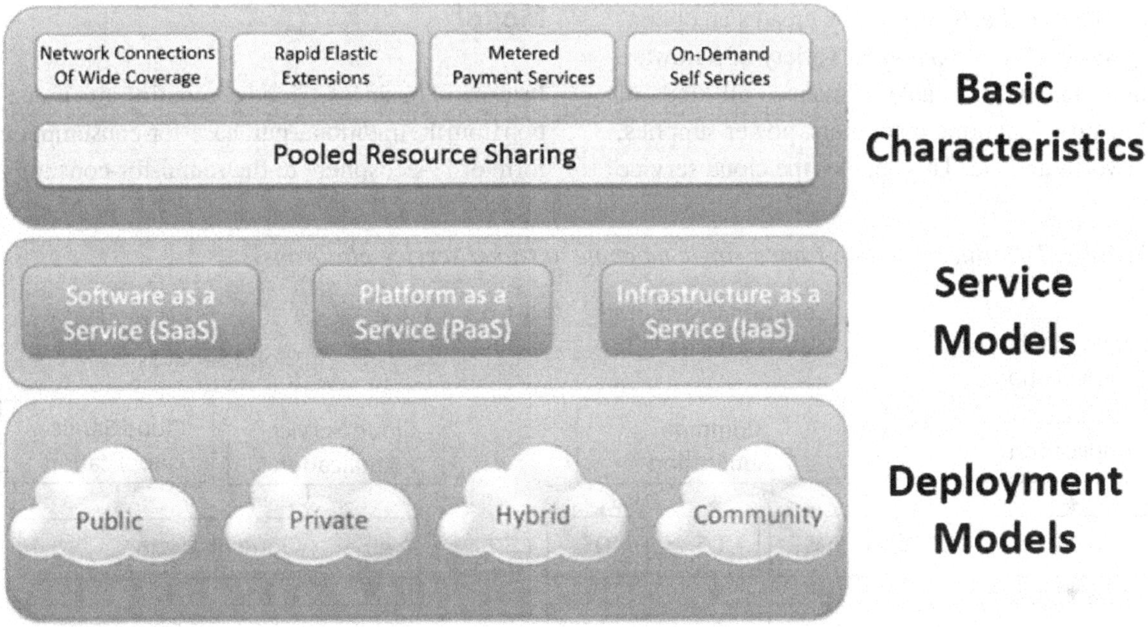

computer hardware is responsible for the actual computing and storage operations. The operating system is responsible for the management of hardware resources, and providing the application programming interface for applications. An application is written by software developers, and is responsible for the realization of business functions, such as computing and storage by the end user.

In the stand-alone machine case, the operating system provides some convenience that an application software developers does not need to participate in the management of system hardware. However in many cases, with the huge demand for computation and storage capacities by end users, a single machine is able to fully meet these needs. Also, customer demand for network services may vary seasonally: in the case of an e-commerce site, throughput during the holiday season may rise sharply, or even reach blowout levels. Server systems built on the basis of fixed hardware are inevitably going to become inadequate at times, and the extra capacity may get wasted at other times. These issues have been problems that needed to be addressed in the initial stages of the cloud development.

Also known as the cloud platform, Platform as a Service (PaaS) in essence creates an operating system based on a great variety of hardware environments. It is able to manage all kinds of hardware, including computers, power supplies, networks and etc. This enables the cloud service

developers to concentrate on doing their own service development, without having to worry about the underlying hardware management issues. Similar to the stand-alone machine, cloud platforms also provide two basic functions, and they are computing services and storage services.

In addition to the realization of full service cloud hardware management by the platform as a service (PaaS), the main goal of Infrastructure as a Service (IaaS) is to be fully compatible with all exiting cloud service applications. In order to achieve this, the IaaS service providers no longer fully manage the operating systems, and the application runtime environment no longer join. Instead, it simply provides users with virtual machines. It retains the self-healing function for services (service healing), at the same time allows the user to freely choose an operating system.

Software as a Service (SaaS) cloud service providers directly pass the application form of cloud services to a user, the user can get a complete end-to-end service experience, without the need to be involved in the management and development of any system. The relationship between IaaS, PaaS and SaaS can be seen in Figure 3.

The Cloud Computing Business Model

In terms of business, Cloud computing is to transition from the traditional purchase-for-consumption form of IT-ecosphere to the rental-for-consump-

Figure 2. The transformation from a single machine to Cloud service platforms

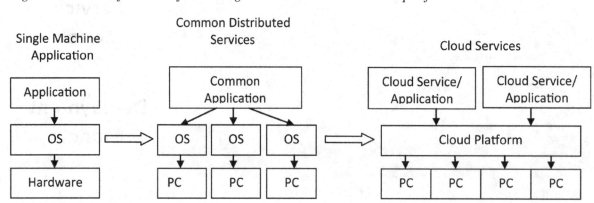

Figure 3. The relationship between IaaS, PaaS and SaaS

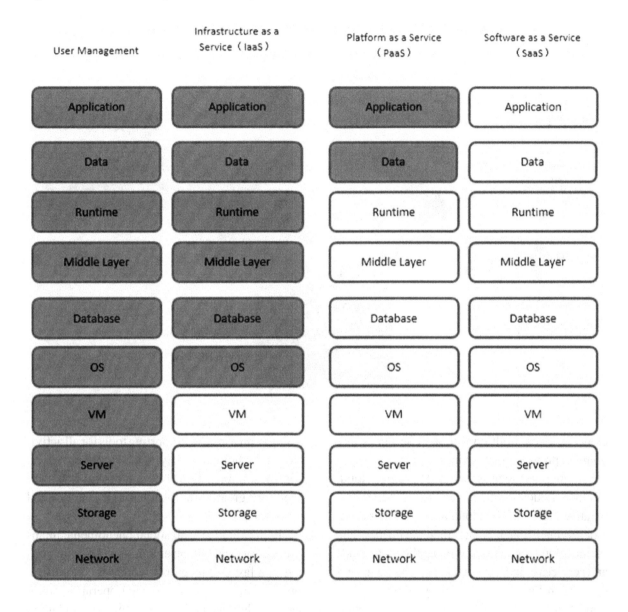

tion ecosphere. Cloud platforms are to provide just the basic cloud operating system, while the majority of cloud services, cloud solutions and cloud applications are the real value potential in the new cloud business model. User demand for material may be limited, but the emotional and services demands can be unlimited. The cloud industry is going to be able to inspire and meet the needs of people anytime and anywhere. In this new biosphere, the industry's value chain is to re-

shuffle. Established companies and employees that are incompatible with the new model are going to be eliminated. Those innovative companies and employees, who can stay ahead of the game, are going to see much growth potential.

In the cloud computing business model, cloud data centers and cloud platforms, belonging to those large cloud vendors such as Microsoft, Amazon, Google and etc., are supporting nodes of limited business value. A variety of large-scale

Figure 4. The Cloud Computing ecosphere

Opportunity: Cloud Platforms -> Industry Chains -> Ecosphere

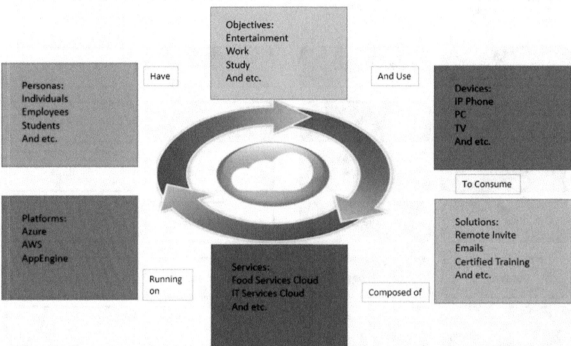

cloud services, built on top of these nodes, are going to provide great business opportunities for the community: such as food and beverage cloud, IT cloud, Education cloud, medical cloud, administrative cloud, traffic cloud and etc. Their combined value is much greater than the former. The various cloud segments, such as application clouds and services clouds, are quickly springing up and thriving in the cloud. The list goes on, such as remote invitation, video conferencing, e-mail, certified training, photo retouching, and product exchanges etc. The human material, emotional, and value-added services can be limitless.

These cloud services through a variety of cloud terminal devices such mobile phone, computer, TV and etc., are to reach all user groups such as individuals, employees, and students etc., for their various purposes of use such as entertainment, work, study and many more. Cloud computing is

going to provide the supporting tools for all activities of the human society, such as crowd control, logistics, information flow and capital flow, and therefore greatly improve people's material and spiritual lives.

In the cloud era, all social phenomena, intangible assets and human emotions can be transmitted in a fast and mega manner. In the cloud era, profit margins, the commercial operation space and the human ability space may be enlarged countless times across time and space. Humans are to cross the boundaries of time and space. The virtual and real worlds are to facilitate each other. The potential value in smart information, and the people's capabilities in innovation, are going to be uncovered to a greater extent. The information industry and even the history of human development indicate that there exists the possibility and inevitability of explosive growth for the cloud business. The cloud and the associated new technologies are going to bring about radical changes to the world economy and the various human lifestyles.

The public cloud is a cloud service on the Internet. It allows maximum utilization of its resources. It can lower prices and provide quality services to the majority of users, in order to create new business values. Public cloud as a core can also be able to integrate upstream service providers, such as value-added services and advertising, and downstream end-users, to create new value chains and ecosystems.

A private cloud is a cloud service in a private environment, such as those established within the data centers of businesses, governments and organizations, or hosted and constructed by the operators. It is used by a single customer, thus providing the most effective control over data security and the quality of services. A private cloud gives high levels of control over the use of cloud resources. At the same time, it also provides the required expertise for the establishment and operation of such environments.

A hybrid cloud is a mixture of public and private clouds. Some users have built a private cloud, but have insufficient resources, such as computing power and/or storage space. They have to dynamically apply to the public cloud resources, to supplement their own private cloud. Also because of security and control reasons, some public clouds must place their sensitive corporate information in a private cloud.

THE WAVE OF CLOUD TRANSFORMATION IN THE GLOBAL INFORMATION INDUSTRY

The information industry (IT) is a knowledge, technology and information-intensive industry that belongs to the tertiary sector of the economy. It is an important driving force for today's global social economic development, and the strategic,

fundamental and guiding pillar industry of national economies, and it plays an important role in promoting social employment, stimulating economic growth, adjusting the industrial structure, changing the mode of development and maintaining national security.

Since the last century, the rapid development of the information industry has caused its implications to change and expand accordingly. Today, a broad definition of the information industry refers to all industries that can turn information into some form of commodity. It not only includes software, databases, a variety of wireless communication services and online information services, but should also include the publication of traditional newspapers, books, movies and audio-visual products. There is no doubt that in the future, the information industry of the cloud era is to be redefined on a continuous basis.

The information industry's developmental history is full of innovation and constant changes. It is also about constant discoveries, mining and continued efforts to meet demands by the human society in terms of production and livelihoods. In this field filled with fresh air of innovation, we can find many ambitious entrepreneurs and investors, and the endless supply of wacky novelty ideas and products.

History shows that the development of the information industry has never been straightforward, nor uniform, but comes in waves of innovation, one "wave" after another. Over one hundred years have passed, some companies are fortunate enough to have guided or caught up with the technology wave for a certain period, either consciously or unconsciously, to have rapidly risen to become a global technology empire, and to dominate their own industry.

Table 1 lists the basic data for some IT companies mentioned in this chapter, with the hope to familiarize the readers with a general knowledge of their operation scales and company profiles. Despite the different origins of these international IT giants, one common denominator is that they

Table 1. An overview of basic data of the well-known global IT companies

Company	Industry	Year Founded	Employ-ees (2012)	Market Capital (2012/11)[1]	Income/ Income Ratio (Billions) (2012/09)	2011 Brand Value (Global Ranking)
Microsoft	software	1975	94,000	$233.14	$15.71 21.71%	4.5812 (#3)
Apple	hardware	1976	72,800	$537.61	$41.73 26.67%	7.0605 (#1)
Google	Internet	1998	53,600	$219.49	$10.56 22.20%	4.7463 (#2)
Amazon	Internet	1994	69,100	$108.66	$0.040 0.07%	2.8665 (#10)
IBM	Hardware	1911	433,400	$218.63	$16.26 15.53%	3.9135 (#4)
Facebook	Internet	2004	3,540	$51.99	$.524 6.28%	-
Intel	Chipset	1968	100,100	$98.13	$11.90 22.13%	2.1908 (#20)
Qualcomm	Communi-cations	1985	21,200	$107.58	$5.33 31.95%	-
AT&T	Telecom	1984	252,330	$195.16	$4.44 3.49%	2.8379 (#11)
Cisco	Networks	1984	66,640	$99.87	$8.36 17.9%	1.2865 (#66)

have been or are still in a field dominating the IT industry's development (branddirectory.com, 2012). Perhaps the most important aspect, that they all have in common, is that they are to potentially become either allies and/or competitors in all areas of the information industry, on the industry playing field of the cloud computing era. The entire information industry is facing an overall reshuffle and integration.

After years of continued research and consolidation, cloud computing has become a mainstream focus for today's global IT industry. The cloud era architecture includes the three main themes: the Cloud Hub (cloud computing), cloud networking and cloud terminals. Three levels of cloud services include software as service (SaaS), cloud platforms as service (PaaS), and cloud infrastructure as service (IaaS). Presently, competitors on the current cloud computing playing-

field can be broadly divided into five major categories: telecom operators, data center IT giants, chip and server manufacturers, software companies that specialize in providing platforms, as well as numerous application service companies. These categories cover the entire ecosphere, including the innumerable products and services in cloud applications, cloud platforms and cloud infrastructure, where the cloud concepts and possibilities are endless. The boundaries between these categories and the competitive relationship cannot be clearly defined, and the formation of large and small alliances represent some very intricate relationships.

Facing this tidal wave of cloud computing, the great change, integration and reshuffling of the traditional information industry, the traditional IT giants have to either choose to fundamentally restructure or take the exit, with no other alternative available! In the recent years, some global leaders in the Information Industry have all had their original business scope extended, further developed and re-defined. By the analysis of the past trajectory of their strategic development and expansion, some common characteristics are revealed. One important feature is that all enterprises start from their traditional place of advantage, then transition from the "ground" up into the "cloud", and through vertical or horizontal integration, gradually search for the right development opportunities on all three levels of application, platform and infrastructure, or rather, they decide to make large and comprehensive developments on all levels.

The following are a few examples of multinational companies which we are most familiar. Their developmental trajectories are briefly discussed.

- **Microsoft:** Microsoft's cloud expansion path is to take advantage of its original product lines that already have very wide coverage. Cloud versions of all of Microsoft's original software products that have been on the "ground" are developed in its entirety, such that cloud computing is realized in all areas of its business. Microsoft's cloud services are deployed across the entire SaaS, PaaS, and IaaS. Its strategic thinking is the so called "three screens and a cloud" and "all in on the cloud". Microsoft has also pioneered the emphasis on a combination of hardware and software development strategy, with the terminals supporting the cloud, the cloud maintaining the terminals, where terminal hardware and software products such as WP Phones, Surface, Xbox, and Skype are to play vital roles.
- **Google:** Google has a large number of individual users to its advantage. Services on the SaaS level such as Gmail and Google document (Google Docs) are provided for free to its users. Then Google Apps have

completed a smooth transition from the individual customer base to the SME customer groups, to becoming a major provider of SaaS. Down-stream, Google has continued on to launch the Google Apps Engine, a network application platform that is developed and run on the Google system. Its services are free for small users, and appropriated fees are charged for its merchant users, aiming to expand their businesses and services.

- **Amazon:** Amazon initially takes advantage of its online shopping platform, intending to uncover the additional values in its infrastructure built by previous investments. Presently, Amazon's Web Services (AWS) has become an independent cloud strategy, specifically designed for developers and service providers wanting to expand on their existing infrastructure. The main products include scalable cloud computing server and storage, database services, web hosting, web pages and e-commerce solutions and so on, thus forming a distinctive expansion path from IaaS to PaaS.
- **VMware:** VMware is a pioneer of the virtual platform, from the very beginning of cloud computing. It provides infrastructure solutions, and then gradually begins to provide a full range of other services. Using VFabric, Java developers enjoy an open development platform that provides PaaS. It has since then acquired Zimbra to provide e-mail and user cloud collaboration, and thus moving into SaaS.

The following figure summarizes the cloud transformation path for some of the major players in the IT industry. It also shows how they have used their own advantages to achieve their strategic expansions into the entire cloud.

Cloud computing is a trend in the information industry, and continued cloud developments are currently underway. The essence of cloud comput-

Figure 5. IT Industry leaders' development paths into the cloud

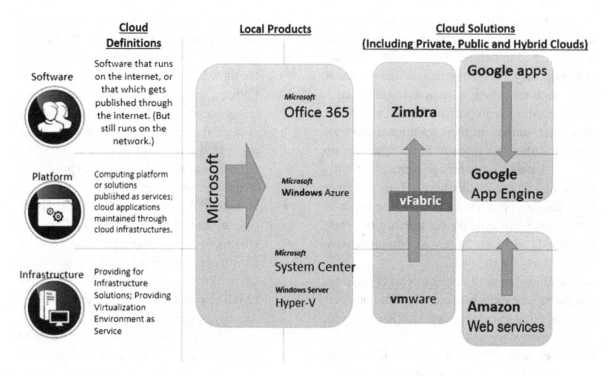

ing is the re-integration and re-allocation of information resources, and it is again a brilliant new round of technological revolution for the information industry. Broadly speaking, the concept of the "cloud" is the integration of many of information resources, in forming a modern high-tech production and service system. The purpose of which is to satisfy all human information needs.

Cloud computing itself embodies a more advanced computing model, an economic model and a model of transformation in terms of productive relationships. But in the end, major companies and industry experts today cannot agree on how such a new model of cloud computing is to be developed. In the end, it is even more confusing and difficult to try to determine who represents the more advanced model of the cloud era. Historical development, however, is always the inevitable hidden in random chances, and certainty coming from uncertainties. Right before the birth of a new global civilization, the present is a "chaotic period" of industry-wide debates, from which the

cultivation of a foundation for the most robust new civilization is quietly taking place!

An Era of Global Cloud with Emphasis on China's Cloud Development

Presently, almost all the world's leading IT companies are going all out in order to fully realize cloud computing, such as Microsoft, Apple, Google, Amazon, Facebook, IBM, Cisco, Salesforce.com, Oracle, Hewlett-Packard, Dell, Fujitsu, Huawei, Alibaba, Baidu, Tencent and so on. Cloud computing brands continue to emerge, such as Microsoft's Windows Azure Platform, Microsoft Office 365, Amazon Web Services, Google Apps, Salesforce.com, VMWare ESX, Citrix XenServer, IBM Smart Business/Cloudburst, Cisco newScale and Apple iCloud.

Most of the world's enterprises have begun to recognize the benefits of cloud computing, and are starting the transmigration into the enterprise cloud. Most business users in the United States have been more or less using cloud computing. Microsoft's Azure cloud-platform already has a client base in tens of thousands. Microsoft's enterprise itself is a typical case of cloud transformation. After its first enterprise software migrated into the cloud in 2009, Microsoft has established the enterprise cloud transformation strategy and road map. Currently dozens of Microsoft's enterprise software are running in the cloud. In the future, the pace of enterprises transmigrating to the cloud is going to become increasingly faster.

In the United States, the U.S. government plays a key advocacy role in promoting the cloud computing concept. It has established a series of national cloud standards, including the cloud architecture and the cloud development roadmap. The US Federal government and governments of all levels are leading the large-scale use of cloud services from early stages. Through NASA, the national government's private cloud, named Nebula, has been established. The U.S. government plans to spend 25% of its information and communication technology budget on cloud services. U.S. colleges and universities are also making great efforts to cultivate talents for cloud computing, to meet the needs of the industry's development. For instance, the University of Washington, together with the government security agencies, have established cloud fellowships, where research projects and programs are to be opened soon.

Currently, the U.S. leads the world in the development and application of cloud computing, but many countries are also catching up. The Japanese government plans to set up a cloud computing special zone, aiming to build the largest database in Japan. The amount of investment is not to exceed fifty billion yen. Experts estimate that Japan's cloud computing market size in 2014 is expected to reach two trillion yen. Recently, the British government has announced that it is to embrace the Government Cloud Strategy (G-Cloud), where the government is to invest £60 million to build a public cloud services network.

By the year 2015, at least 50% of the British IT resources can be acquired through the public cloud services network, savings £340 million pounds in IT expenditure. In an effort led by Germany's Ministries of Economy and Technology, and with the extensive participation by experts from the business sector, the scientific community and government agencies, a plan of action on Germany's cloud computing development is being jointly developed. It outlines a series of actions to be taken by the German government on its cloud computing development efforts.

The well-known IDC recently released a research report on Microsoft. It says the global "cloud computing" expenditure for the year 2011 has incurred a total cost of $28 billion, while expenditures for traditional IT services and products are $1.7 trillion. Cloud computing has created many remote jobs, where employees can work remotely through computers, smart phones, tablet computers and other information equipment. In 2011, cloud computing with an investment value of only $400 billion has helped to create 1.5 million jobs. In 2012, cloud computing related jobs are to increase to 6.7 million, and it is to exceed 13.6 million by the year 2015. Among which, China and India are to add 6.75 million cloud-related jobs, while Europe, Middle East and Africa are to add 2.07 million jobs, and 1.17 million in North America.

Being a traditional manufacturing country, China is going to experience much change from its Internet and high-tech industries, with the emergence of a number of internationally famous businesses, such as Huawei, Lenovo, Tencent, Baidu and Alibaba. Cloud computing in the future, like today's mobile Internet is to enable the reshuffling of industries. Nations and businesses that overlook this trend are going to be left behind or even eliminated. Those that seize the opportunities are to rise with the trend. If China's cloud computing industry can successfully achieve leapfrog development, not only can it greatly contribute to the domestic economy, but it is also to play a significant role in the global IT marketplace. The Chinese can more than satisfy China's domestic service demands, which can also provide for the many foreign high-end services, such as software development, security testing, business intelligence and so on.

Different Countries' Policies toward the Development of the Internet of Things [2] (IOT)

The IOT is an integral part of the strategic new emerging industries. It plays an important role in the accelerated transformation of the economic development model.

An important characteristic of the development of the IOT is that it is under the government guidance or being directly promoted by governments. Presently, many countries in the world have developed many applications in the cloud for the IOT, and certain achievements are noteworthy. Especially the United States and Europe, as well as the Japanese and Korean governments and enterprises, all of them have proposed various strategic plans for the revitalization of the IOT. The U.S. media is calling for "Today, the Internet, -- Tomorrow, the Internet of Things." In 2009, President Obama foresees new energies and the IOT as the two major areas for economic revitalization. In Asia, Japan and South Korea have put forward the Ubiquitous Network Strategy in as early as 2004, and even earlier, the "E-Japan", "I-Japan" and "U-Korea" strategies have been proposed. In 2009, a report titled "I-Japan strategy 2015," released by the Japanese IT Strategic Headquarters, says that by 2015, Japan is determined to achieve a wide use of digital technology in all aspects of its social and economic lives, like air and water everywhere. Japan hopes that the realization of this environment is to help the Japanese people to have fair, convenient and secure access to necessary information, in order to build rich lives and make convenient social contacts. In 2009, the Korean Communications

Commission has adopted the "Internet of Things – Basic Infrastructure Construction Planning," and also established in 2012, the goal of "the creation of a super first-class ICT powerhouse that has achieved a future fusion of broadcasting and communications fields, by building the world's most advanced basic infrastructure for the IOT."

The Chinese Government has always attached great importance to the development of the Internet of Things (IOT). In as early as 2009, Premier Wen Jiabao proposed the vigorous use of network technologies in the Distributions Industry, especially the IOT technology, in order to achieve distribution modernization. On March 5, 2010, Premier Wen Jiabao for the first time, during the annual session of the National Political Congress and the Chinese People's Political Consultative Committee, has stressed the importance of the development of the IOT. Former Minister of Industry and Information Technology Li Yizhong has also authored articles that promote the combining of the Internet with the development traditional industries. On November 28, 2011, the Ministry of Industry and Information Technology published on its website, "the Internet of Things 12th Five-Year Development Plan," which is the first planning of the IOT in the history of China's five-year plans. This "Plan" states that by the end of the 12th Five-Year period, China is to achieve a preliminary completion of the industry's system structure, to form a relatively complete industrial chain of the IOT, to nurture and develop 10 industrial enclaves, to form more than 100 backbone enterprises, to build a number of "highly disciplined, highly refined, highly specialized, highly up-to-date" small and medium business enterprises, to construct public service platforms with wide coverage and strong support, and to form a preliminary industrial system of the IOT with a complete range of applications, reasonable layout, and optimized structures. At the same time, the "Plan" proposes the nine major applications of the IOT: including intelligent manufacturing, intelligent agriculture, smart logistics, smart transportation, smart grid, smart environmental protection, smart security and defense, smart medicine and smart homes. Many provinces and municipalities such as Beijing, Shanghai, Tianjin, Fujian, Hangzhou and Wuxi have independently formed their own development plans for the IOT. (China Ministry of Industry and Information, 2012)

Currently, the IOT is a very hot topic in China's IT sector. Meetings and seminars on the Internet of Things are being held almost every month. It is clear that the IOT is on the rise in China. Industry reports state that "with a large number of industrial applications, the popularity of the Internet and the growth of smartphone sales, China's Internet of Things will be on a fast track development." We believe that with the government support and corporate investments, the China's IOT is entering a golden age. Below are several of our recommendations for the development of the IOT in China:

1. Pay attention to facts, act based on local conditions, and plan for the entire country and economy. We must not have unrealistic expectations, rush on the project with irrational exuberance and misallocation of investment funds. In this regard, many countries in the world have had their share of lessons in the past. China has a vast territory, the situation in the various localities are very different, and so are the levels of economic development and the availability of technical staff. The IOT's development must take the local situation into consideration, with its applications to be developed in a steady pace, and with the deployment of only mature technologies. The development of the IOT is a long-term process, where vanity projects like that of the "Great Leap Forward" should be avoided.

2. Correctly handle the relationship between the Chinese government and enterprises in the development of the Internet of Things. The release of the "12th Five-Year Development Plan of the Internet of Things" shows that the development of the IOT in China has risen to the level of its national strategy. The development of the IOT, however, cannot solely rely on the government policies, nor should it cause the government to go beyond its intended roles. The development of the IOT should mainly be corporate-driven. In 2010, Microsoft's senior vice president Dr. Yaqin Zhang has pointed out that basically the United States does not have a so-called national strategy; instead people see an industrial strategy that is mostly enterprise-driven. Strategies are not formed first, then enterprises find their positioning in accordance, but rather, R&D activities are started from the demand for new applications, followed by marketing and expansions. The government exercises its influence in basic research, and the development of the industry mainly relies on businesses. Dr. Yaqin Zhang also clearly points out that the government and enterprises should play their respective roles, that livelihood projects related to the construction of urban infrastructure should be led by local governments, business applications should rely on businesses, and projects related to the building of fundamental infrastructures such as transportation should rely on the central government.

3. Vigorously develop cloud computing. Cloud computing is the core of the Internet of things. Without cloud computing, the Internet of Things is to lose the basis for its existence. In the end, the success of the Internet of things is determined by cloud computing. Dr. Yaqin Zhang also states: "a consensus is formed that a new generation of information technology, the Internet of Things, mobile computing and so on, will depend on cloud computing as the nerve center. Especially, the cloud-based application platforms are to possess strong regional and local characteristics. It is believed that the Chinese enterprises have a tremendous

opportunity in this area. Our technical teams are working closely with our partners in the local ecosystems, leading the cloud industry forward, actively making the effort to ensure the development of the cloud industry is in a more rational and prudent direction, and hoping to broadly share the fruits of the future. "

4. Vigorously promote innovations. Innovation is the life force of enterprise development. Chinese enterprises should seize the opportunity to develop the IOT's new technologies and products: Radio frequency identification technology, sensor technology, intelligent technology and nanotechnology, the four key technologies for the applications of the IOT. China should vigorously develop the four aspects of the technology, and strive to gain intellectual property ownership rights to these technology products. If the Chinese enterprises can take the lead position in any one of these technical areas, huge market potentials are sure to follow.

5. Emphasize on the social problems brought about by the IOT, establish and improve the laws and regulations for the IOT, ensure the IOT's security and protect user privacy. As the IOT is to bring people more convenience, we need to pay attention to the risks in security and privacy protection: from the daily small information leaks, to the more serious threats to people's lives and property, or even more seriously, threats to national security and social stability. In addition to the use of technical means to address these two aspects of the problem, such as the establishment of firewalls, encryption technology, we need to also establish and improve on relevant laws.

Exploring China's Road of Smart Urban Development

Let's look at the current international trends on urbanization. On one hand, with global urbanization entering into the mid and late stages, the metropoli-

tan sizes keep increasing. Urban infrastructures are becoming increasingly complex. Urban business innovations are picking up the pace of development. Urban management becomes increasingly more scientific and fine-tuned. More attentions are being paid to green ecological environments and environmental protection. On the other hand, with the development of information technology such as cloud computing, mobile internet and the internet of things, municipal production and life styles are beginning to see some revolutionary changes taking place. Following the industrialization, electrical revolutions, and the information technology revolution, the intelligence based urbanization is deemed another new wave of urban development. (Wang, 2009)

Urbanization in China has become the main engine of its economic development. With focus shifting from industrialization to urbanization, the growth model that has been mainly investment-driven is shifting to sustainable development. Clearly stated in the national "12th Five-Year Plan", China is to further the integration of industrialization with information technology. Urbanization, together with the transformation and upgrading of information technology, is to further promote China's industrialization process. The new concept of the smart city provides a timely new path for China's urban development.

There is no universally accepted or a specific definition for the smart city concept. It is generally believed that the smart city concept is an advanced form of urban development, supported by a new generation of innovative environment, based on a new generation of information technology and knowledge-based society. Its basic features include thorough perceptions, broadband ubiquitous internet, smart fusion applications, as well as people-oriented sustainable innovations. In this regard, technical experts mostly emphasize that the smart city concept is inevitable, due to the development of a new generation of information technology. Experts in the humanities are focused more on the sustainable urban development, relating to the smart city and urbanization concept. In short, the smart city concept requires urban planning, city building, city management, municipal services and urban development, to be done with high levels of intelligence.

Taking into the consideration of China's present conditions, the essence of the smart city concept is a more advanced stage of city information technology. In the cloud era, it is to build a "city cloud" with Chinese specific characteristics. From the philosophy of social development, the fundamental requirement of smart urban development must be people-oriented and based on scientific developments. In the development of Chinese smart cities, we need to learn from, but not copy the Western models. We must take the path of a sustainable and low-carbon eco-road with Chinese specific characteristics.

The core of the smart city concept is in the deep fusion and integration of the physical world and the virtual world. It means an in-depth integration of the information technology, industrialization and urbanization. When the integration of traditional industries and IT can directly contribute to the generation of new industries, it is to also indirectly promote the upgrading of the city's traditional pillar industries. This not only enhances the urban management service levels, but also becomes a point of the development effort to promote independent innovations, guides China's industrial structure adjustment and transformation, and provides a comprehensive and sustainable economic growth momentum.

The above is an introduction, and some recommendations for the government policy and the route of smart urban development suitable for China. Guidelines refer to the direction and the target problem to be solved. The path taken is for the discussion of ideas, and ways to find solutions. With set targets and the guidance of a principle route on the strategic level, a "master plan" is then developed. On the tactical level, an "implementation plan" needs to be proposed. Both the planning and solutions are issues in relation to methodology that need to be addressed.

The scientific development process of city information technology is: "workflow standardization → digitization → networking → intelligence", referred to as the "four modernizations". The essence of process standardization is in the standardization, i.e., urban construction, management and services must be done in accordance with a standardized workflow, which is the basis of digitization. Digitization turns all kinds of acquired original information about urban construction, management and services into digital formats, and this includes the selection of information and data, pre-processing, standardization and so on, so as to realize computerized information and data management. Networking is to resolve the problem of information "islands" or information isolation, to further integrate information, in order to achieve value-added information processing. Intelligence means making full use of the most advanced cultural philosophy, and the most modern means of science and technology, to realize the two advancements in human information needs: from data to knowledge, and from intellectual to emotional information applications. All these are to realize intelligent applications of information, making possible that all of the people can participate in the innovation process of the future urban development.

The major problem of the construction of smart cities in China lies in the leadership's ideas and insights. First of all, it is an ideological issue, especially among the municipal leaders, industry sectors and user groups. Secondly many management issues are involved, especially the necessary reforms and innovations needed, in order to meet the requirements of the information technology. The current administrative system, work-flow mechanisms and business models need to be updated. Thirdly, technical problems are unavoidable challenges in the cloud era, which may involve open technical cooperation and independent innovation in core areas. Finally, with regard to the legal and ethical issues, smart cities are expected to cause an in-depth integration of the physical and virtual worlds, which changes all aspects of the government, the society and people's lives. Change must be accompanied by sound legal and moral adjustments. This is already a very realistic problem that "smart cities" are to collect large amounts of social, corporate and personal information. How to keep the information confidential, ensure ethical private and public use of the information, are issues to be addressed.

Specifically how to build a smart city? We recommend the following principles and paths: the overall planning and step-by-step implementation, leadership by example and breakthroughs in key areas, capitalizing on key trends, and finally the full-fledged development.

- **The Overall Plan and Step-by-Step Implementation:** Intelligence building is a continuous process that deepens with technology development, and changes by demand. A master plan is based primarily on the overall qualitative analysis, with focus on the business needs analysis. Proposed implementation programs are going to be under the guidance of the overall plan, and based on quantitative analysis, with focus on the analysis of the actual status and future expectations. Overall plan has to establish itself from the commanding heights of development and must be forward-looking. Implementation programs have to be practical and realistic. China's social management system and working mechanisms need a lot of reform and innovation, but experiences have shown that this cannot be done in haste, that slow pace means stability and fast pace brings chaos. Relatively practical solutions basically do not change the existing institutional mechanisms for the moment. It is first to promote the application of advanced scientific and technological applications. After full brewing and fermentation, reforms can be deepened in accordance to the advanced

concepts, in a timely and reasonable manner. Developments are to progress steadily, healthfully and sustainably.

- **Leadership by Example and Breakthroughs in Key Areas:** Differences in China's various regions, different cities, or even in the same city, the different industries or different government agencies, the construction of the information technology infrastructure, environmental conditions, and even developmental stages can vary widely. This implies that "intelligent" solutions cannot be the same for all situations. In the intelligence building process, each city should firmly root itself in its actual developmental stage and reality, focus on the most urgent needs and the most concentrated businesses, rely on the most knowledgeable leadership, and start with organizations that have the best fundamental conditions. At the same time, we must also select projects with the greatest political impact, and departments with the strongest influence within the government, as starting point to make a typical demonstration project. Examples are smart police, intelligent transportation, digital city management and etc. These implementations have the potential for major political breakthroughs, and therefore can be catalyst for global development. What are the extents of key breakthroughs? How deep? This depends on the specific circumstances of the various municipalities. Under the guidance of the overall plan, uniformity in terms of development is not to be expected.
- **Capitalizing on Trends and Full-Fledged Development:** Experiences are gained through breakthroughs in key areas, and with good and effective demonstrations, we can then gradually promote the solutions to the various agencies, within the government or other sectors. Intelligence building process should be continuously

tracked, and close attentions are paid to the types of problems encountered during the development process. Implementation plans are to be improved along the process. We need to capitalize on the digital trend, and fully carry out the smart city concept to making it a reality.

In addition, for future development, the smart city concept is to be gradually expanded to "smart province", "smart China", and even "smart of Earth".

In China, people's social activities can be divided into two major types: they are social management and social life. Social management includes national administration, party, government and military affairs, industrial and institutional management. The so called social life includes business activities such as market transactions or business services, people's livelihood and services. These activities relate to all aspects of politics, economy, finance, industry, customs, taxation, industry and commerce, civil affairs, culture, education, energy conservation, environmental protection, health care, sanitation, food, health, public safety, traffic control and housing construction. The respective levels of information management, corresponding to the various cloud applications both large and small, can be represented on a plane with vertical and horizontal axes:

- **Horizontally:** Sorted according to the centralized scale of data and in increasing order, city cloud (including counties and districts) → provincial cloud (including departments and bureaus) → regional cloud (including several provinces) → national cloud (including ministries and commissions) → global cloud (including different countries)
- **Vertically:** Sorted according to the number and types of business services and in increasing order, individual business/service cloud (such as police and security in-

telligence analysis, etc.) → single industry integrated services cloud (such as police and etc.) → cross-industry comprehensive business cloud (such as government affairs) → industry-wide total cloud .

These "clouds" are responsible for all aspects of social responsibilities in varying degrees. The corresponding architecture of the smart city is to include the two major types of social activities, and therefore "smart government" and "smart livelihood", which embodies the eight major systems: party affairs, government affairs, military affairs, business affairs, civilian affairs, industry affairs, business affairs and individual affairs, and the various sub-systems that fall under these eight major systems.

The overall functionality of the smart city generally consists of four major parts:

1. The city operating center portal functions;
2. The city event management service functions;
3. City operation and maintenance management services;
4. Knowledge discovery and decision support functions.

Building a smart city can be started with the three sub-systems of the government affairs system (Administrative cloud): public safety, intelligent transportation and urban management. Through the city emergency command platform and operation management centralized linkage platform, we can achieve four key unifications of the city's social activities: all unified management, coordination, command and actions. This linkage command platform is to collect the day-to-day management information of the municipal departments, such as police, urban management, transportation, communications, first aid, electricity, water, gas, civil air defense and civil affairs. The information is to go through a unified analysis, management, scheduling and command system. In the day-today work situation, the system provides managers with general city information, and the data support for decision-makers. In the case of sudden emergency, strong technical support is provided for unified command, and dispatch operations that are cross-regional, cross-sectorial, cross police and military forces, in order to realize a unified city operation and emergency response. In such cases, the city's response system is to transition from a passive response system to a proactive protection system, and the strategic transition from a traditional experience based system to empirical based management system. This helps the government to fully complete and improve its service systems, and realize the full force of the innovation mechanisms. In such a way, the city's intelligence on the overall emergency command, as well as the day-to-day management, can be raised to higher levels.

To contemplate along the development patterns of the human society, including both the economic and social developments, China's current urbanization rate is about 51%, which is at a critical node of accelerated growth. For the coming decades, urbanization is to become the most important strategic opportunity, and core driving force for sustainable economic development. This provides for the smart city concept a vast stage and a great historical opportunity.

Urban development calls for more intelligence, and intelligence determines the future directions. We should establish ourselves in a global stand point, and a long-term development strategy of the nation. China needs to catch on with the historical trend of the new urbanization process, in order to find a smart city development path that's suitable for itself. We firmly believe that the development of the smart city is expected to effectively promote better practices of Chinese cities, to implement the scientific concept of development, thus strongly support China's strategy of harmony, development and transformation. We look forward to playing an active role in the rejuvenation of China as a great nation of the world.

Consequences

This era of great historical opportunity belongs to the world, and also to China. On seizing this opportunity, after the popularity of the Chinese cloud, "Made in China" is going to become "IT Services in China", a new core driving force of China's national economy.

With the rise of cloud computing, the Internet of Things and so on, China is facing a golden opportunity. How to seize the opportunity, follow or even lead this wave of change? The challenge is to be faced by the Chinese government and Chinese enterprises. Comparing with China's situation during the previous waves in IT development, China has since made considerable progress in the areas of soft and hard power, trained a large number of IT talents, and has many excellent IT enterprises. China today participates more actively on the world's political, economic, scientific and technological stage, more so than any period in its previous history. In this context, China should take a more proactive stance, take the initiatives to contribute to this wave of information-based cloud computing development, and also take this opportunity to promote deeper administrative and economic reforms throughout the country, in order to achieve all-round political and economic developments. Microsoft is very proud to participate in China's rapid development, be part of this historical process, and continues to make contributions to China's future development.

EXPLORING THE CLOUD ERA MARKET DEMAND

The cloud era brings about new changes in areas that include culture, science and technology, value system, economic structure, social rules, the legal system and the world view. It also brings a historic opportunity for businesses. However, history tells us that disruptive new technologies can be a double-edged sword to the commercial market.

In the resource rich cloud era, from a business point of view, the information industry's tasks are to explore an ocean of business models and new market demands!

The business value of cloud computing does not simply come from moving user data and software from the terminal to the cloud. Much greater value can be found in the utilization of high information processing capacity, network accessibility and coordination capacity, in providing more application services that are more complete, having wider coverage in terms of space and time, and more optimized in terms of functionalities, than the standalone PCs and existing wired / wireless network can ever provide. Most importantly, the cloud can make up for the gaps in the traditional PC and Internet technologies, and in the market place, providing unprecedented new services that have commercial value.

The main applications of the cloud era information industry are not simple add-ons or natural extensions of application services for the existing Internet, wireless communications and PC technologies. Instead, a brand new "blue ocean market" is to be opened up. It is based on an intellectual business market, with its foundation being built on the intelligent analysis of large data; and also the emotional business market is to be based on a full range of film and television content, including high-quality real-time video communications, experience and consumer industry.

The Law of Scientific and Technological Revolution

Represented by the progress of human history, the scientific and technological revolutions are like any other objective matter that has its inherent laws of development. For example, the breakthrough of a revolution in science and technology is often the result of two driving forces, the inherent contradictions of the powerful economic and social demands, and the technological system. Another example, the scientific and technological revolu-

tion in essence is a kind of "negation," under the premise of development, namely development on the basis of inheritance, and negation on the basis of development. Also, a sudden breakthrough in scientific and technological revolution often occurs on the basis of a long and gradual accumulation of mild changes.

The emphasis here is a law relating to the revolution in science and technology, market demand and economic development. Namely, the huge role that the scientific and technological revolution plays in the economy is mainly reflected in the new markets. It brings in a whole new level of existence for the human society, rather than the higher efficiency it might bring to the traditional and existing markets. In fact, it is precisely because the scientific and technological revolution bringing high levels of improvements to the traditional industries and the society as a whole, in terms of efficiency and progress, and if new markets of sufficient scale and commercial value are not created in a timely manner, traditional industries are going to be severely injured. In this sense, a disruptive new technology is veritably a double-edged sword!

Looking back in history, such examples are numerous: The invention of gunpowder brought in the era of hot weapons, and steam engines brought in the industrial era, at the same time cold weaponry and manual production have been marginalized and put into extinction. Another example in the information industry, that happened not too long ago, is the popular use of internet telephony. Before the advent of internet telephony, long-distance telephone services are expensive and yet people cannot live without this service. Such a profitable business created AT & T's brilliant century. Towards the end of the last century, internet telephony appeared in the market place. The industry has been very excited, and internet telephony has being highlighted as much as cloud computing today. But telephone charges dropped much faster than the growth in consumer usage and call volumes. Total call volume has quickly saturated. In just five years after the advent of the internet telephony, the total revenue of the entire long-distance telephone industry has started on a rapid decline, causing the Nasdaq (NASDAQ) to collapse. Long-distance telephone markets have been marginalized because of the challenges of the new market, AT&T has to restructure, while many superstar companies have gone bankrupt.

Like the above, how can the laws of the technological revolution be reflected in the changes in cloud computing? Today, IT departments are an integral part of businesses in the various industries. But also for the vast majority of businesses, the homogenization of the IT department not only fails to provide a competitive advantage, but has become a big burden. Once cloud computing becomes more popular, corporate IT departments are to experience large-scale migration to the extremely efficient cloud platforms. This is to streamline the IT departments, and cause effective sharing of resources. Also, it is to significantly reduce the operating costs, and cause a substantial increase in productivity. These are all undoubtedly great contributions of cloud computing, but the information industry, including the traditional PCs, server and enterprise software industry and so on, are going to face a serious recession.

Just like the internet telephony has brought in the popular use of long distance telephones, but not the new prosperity of the communications industry, is cloud computing to experience similar regressions in the industry? The information Industry, the instrumental industry and the cloud computing vision, once achieved, are going to undoubtedly provide cheap and on-demand supply of virtually unlimited processing power and communication ability, to communicate in all walks of life and the entire community. This for the whole society is to bring about higher productivity, life efficiency, and broader development space of the productive forces. The problem is whether IT is still important in the future? What will cloud computing bring for the information industry? Will it usher in the great prosperity as we all eagerly anticipate, or a great recession for the IT industry?

The answer to this question lies in whether we can find new demands and new markets, with explosive commercial value, that can largely consume the inexhaustible cloud era basic resources. If there exists such a thing like the new demands and new markets, where can we find it?

Two Types of Information Industry Markets

Data are the basic element of the information industry, and according to the nature of its contents, can be classified into two categories: "intellectual" and "emotional" content. Intellectual content, such as text descriptions, is an abstract description of a fact or phenomenon, which contains a large amount of information, where the accuracy and usefulness of the information are stressed. Emotional content, such as multimedia content, and from the perspective of information, belongs to redundant data, and its purpose is to enhance the human experience. Therefore emphasis is in making the user experiences pleasant, and to pay attention to the audio-visual processes.

Based on the data content being processed or transmitted, being either intellectual or emotional, market operations of the new information society can be divided into two categories: "intellectual" business and "emotional" business. Because the abstract intellectual content does not require a large amount of data, intellectual business generally is a narrowband service that has low resource requirements. This business is easy to integrate and expand, such as the Twitter business space can quickly extend from the Internet to wireless terminals. Emotional business generally falls under the broadband business. It has high resource requirements, and the requirements of human experience such as the sound quality, music enthusiasts' requirement for audio quality, digital cameras and high-definition TV. In such, the demand for resources is almost never-ending. In the current situation, the intellectual business includes air ticket and hotel room booking, information services and funds transfer. On the other hand, perceptual businesses include film appreciation, dynamic games, real-time communications and multimedia services.

New explosive market demands for the information industry are to materialize in both the intellectual business market and the emotional business market. The intellectual business market is based on the intelligent analysis of large data, decision support and artificial intelligence, which is to lead the entire human society into the big data era. In the emotional business market, high-quality real-time video communications and virtual reality are leading humanity into the entertainment economy and experience economy era. The former core technical requirement is the enhancements in the nature of the information processing capabilities in the cloud information hub. The latter's core technical requirements are the fundamental improvements in the information transmission and exchange capacities for the cloud communication networks.

Let's first look at the intellectual business market. With the popularity of cloud computing, Internet of Things and so on, data resources from the various fields regardless of academia, the business community, governments or persons, are to be widely collected. Quantized data with associated background becomes complete information, and through the comparison in the relationships within the large amounts of information, knowledge is formed and laws are distilled. These knowledge and rules being used to guide our social practices bring in new intelligent analysis and new social values. In the era of big data, the need for intellectual information sharing and interaction has become saturated. High-capacity data integration, analysis, mining and support, that can enhance decision-making capacities based on limited human rationality, can create new market demands with unprecedented depth and breadth!

Big data is not a simple increase in the amounts of data, but a change in the nature of data. Big data's impact on human society can be compared with the impact on the human understanding of our physical world, by the inventions of the microscope and the telescope, as both inventions advanced the human observation and measurement capabilities respectively to cellular and celestial levels. Big data has become our next "microscope" in the observation of human social behavior, the next "dashboard" for monitoring nature, and the next "telescope" for forecasting laws of future developments. In this sense, the bigness in the data, not only refers to the amounts and extent of data being obtained, but also means that every piece of data is to take on its own life in the cloud era, that can produce intelligence, exude in vitality and radiance. As the information technology serves the role of basic tool in society, big data is bound to be a game changer for the various industries and the lives of the general public, and thus brings about a sea of new demands for the information industry.

Secondly, let's look at the emotional business market. High-quality, safe and real-time video communication has been in demand since the most ancient times, but has not yet been fully realized. With near-perfect solutions to the data and voice communications in the cloud era, the consumer market, including the desktop, the living room and hand-held terminals, is going to enter the new market mainly dominated by video communications. This new market consumes little of the material and energy resources, produces virtually no environmental pollution, can provide a lot of service job opportunities, and therefore it is a truly green and sustainable market.

Of course, popular use of video communications is also to experience the process of a gradual change, and finally reach an abrupt breaking-through stage. In as early as the 1960s, AT&T has successfully achieved visual communications, but decades followed without any large-scale development. In fact, anything new in its early development can often encounter various doubts and setbacks. Just as in the past, horse riding masters have doubted the practicality of a train. In the era of horse-drawn carriages, people are not going to push forward the demand for automobiles out of thin air. Edison's invention of the electric light has been "scientifically" proven to be not as good or practical as gaslight.

Video communications mainly bring experiences or feelings that are auxiliary to information, if the market does not popularize universal video communications, consumers are not going to automatically create demand. Poor videos, expensive videos and difficult-to-operate videos do not embody value. However, upon the arrival of high-quality, secure and real-time video communications, the user habit once formed, surely is going to become the basic elements of our daily lives, and thus a whole new demand-driven market. Built on this foundation, the human-machine natural interface, virtual reality, intelligent recognition, auto-piloting and highly realistic online games are going to be fully realized. The human society is entering the era of entertainment economy and experience economy, and thus the overall quality of life is to be raised.

The Three Stages of the Cloud Era

The economic attributes backing up the cloud era designates, that cloud computing is to become an entirely new productive force. The cloud era social life and commercial activities are going to be very different from that of the industrial economy. We predict the future of the cloud era is to go through three stages of development:

The Primary Stage

The core features of the initial stage of the cloud era are the physical concentration of information resources. The effects of which is the convenience and efficiency brought in by the economies of scale.

At this stage, information resources, including computing, storage, communication, control and etc., are going to be inexpensive, stable and safe, and provided to the users according to their needs. The cloud lets its users integrate all these resources into one at any time, any place and on any device. Users no longer have to worry about re-installation of IT products and services, updates, virus scanning and data backup. The main driving force that helps to promote cloud computing, in this initial stage, comes from the ease and efficiency of use. In fact, the soul of cloud computing is the "concentrated and focused" computing.

In the present, Microsoft, Google, Apple, IBM, Amazon and other large international companies have their own unique cloud computing strategies. This inevitably leads to many of the "cloud" services. Examples can be classified by the modes of operation, including private cloud, community cloud, public cloud, hybrid cloud and etc. Also reflected in the initial stage of cloud computing, centralization appears on different levels, such as software as a service (SaaS), platform as a service (PaaS) and infrastructure service (IaaS). But with the intensified concentration of computing power, the above boundaries of many of these cloud computing classifications are gradually becoming more blurred, and starting to converge.

The Intermediate Stage

The core features of the intermediate stage of the cloud era are the "chemical reactions" caused by big data. The effect is based on the intelligent analysis of big data to assist in decision-making, and to solve large-scale business, government and social problems.

At this stage, the concentration of data leads to "enhanced value" of the information. Through in-depth processing and mining, also knowledge forming and law discovering, the decision support stage gets finalized. Under the influence of positive feedback mechanisms, and the so-called black hole effect, many small clouds are to combine into a large cloud, and the centripetal force is continuously causing the strengthening and eventually the forming of social information hubs. This effectively changes the present situation of "data flooding and lack of knowledge," to promote the new business model of operation and decision-making in all walks of life.

The information center at this stage is to greatly expand in terms of the breadth (data set) and depth (data mining) of information services. However, it is in essence still stuck in the field of information services. In other words, the intermediate stage of cloud computing is mainly reflected in the deepening and integration of the intellectual business market, which includes the internet of things, on top of the information service platforms. This can also be referred to as the "small integration."

The Advanced Stage

The core features of the advanced stage cloud era is represented by a "genetic mutation" of the virtual world. The effect of which is to produce a large number of new market applications and services based on high-quality videos and multimedia intelligence.

At this stage, we are going to see the "reality environment" within the online world to be the results of a lot of human creativity, with both long-term accumulations and rapid new developments. Real-time multimedia contents are to experience in-depth processing. Cloud computing is to change from the information processing stage to the multimedia intelligent interpretation stage. Major breakthroughs are going to be in applications mainly based on Multimedia with added Artificial Intelligence. Examples include highly realistic online games, virtual reality and auto-piloting. New markets for intelligent pets and intelligent robots are to develop rapidly. Intel-ligent robots are not only expected to recognize human faces, but also be able to interpret facial expressions, understand human expressions or even catch the intent of a person.

Obviously, in the advanced stage of the cloud computing development, the original primary and secondary application services are not going to disappear. However, the perspective of resource consumption is to become relatively insignificant, and relegate to become ancillary and incidental functions of more advanced applications. In other words, the advanced stage of cloud computing is mainly reflected in the further integration of the communication, media and entertainment platforms based on the information service platform. This can also be referred as the "great integration."

The major trend of the cloud era industry is the continued centralization of resources, such as computing and storage, due to the nature of the cloud computing model. In its advanced stages, the source of this centripetal force comes from the ever changing cloud computing, the sharing and fermentation of intelligent products accumulated over time, which includes information, ideas, film and television content, intelligent algorithms and so on. Its effectiveness is to far exceed the convenience and efficiency of the cloud computing in its initial stage, or the value upgrading in the intermediate stage.

The development of cloud computing is also expected to face some resistance. This is mainly due to the traditional vested interest groups and different cultural groups. The real bottleneck, in terms of promoting large-scale cloud computing, does not come from the field of information services, nor is it in the novel computer systems, but rather the ecological environment of the entire network, which includes the network's integrity system. Looking to the future, the competition between the driving force (centripetal force) and resistance are to show a general trend: the gradual increase in terms of driving force, and the gradual weakening of resistance. This is to lead to the continuous integration between clouds. Multiple clouds are going to be merged into a large cloud. Of course, the path leading to a unified cloud is still going to be a lengthy one.

CONCLUSION

Throughout history, from the Stone Age, the Bronze Age, to the Iron Age, from an agricultural society, the industrial society, to the information society, new environments have always been brought about by the discovery of new resources, thus promoting overall social progress. Moreover, the development of science and technology has never been straight forward. It has always been a process of enlightenment, in the middle of which, there might be a brief turbulent period of quick changes.

The characteristics of information technology can be described as affecting a very wide area and easily replicable. The information revolution process from birth to maturation is becoming shorter. We believe that in the near future, mankind is to complete cloud computing's development, from its initial stage to the intermediate stage, and finally the transition to the advanced stage. This starts from the centralization of information resources, transitioning to the "small integration" of information service platforms, which is to include the internet of things, and finally transitioning to the "great integration" of the four platforms, which includes information services, communications, media, entertainment and emotional content. The latter is expected to be an extended long period of stable growth.

Today, we are on course and experiencing a fast paced period of change in the development of cloud computing. This is bound to nurture non-traditional theories and technologies, and new non-traditional markets and services! The future cloud technologies are not going to be a simple extension of the existing IT cloud services, nor a simple sum of applications and services, coming from the existing PC and the three networks.

Obviously, by fully grasping the theoretical and technological innovations, one is to take control of the cloud business for further stable development down the road. This can thrust the human society into the information society of the cloud era in the truest sense!

REFERENCES

Baidu Encyclopedia. (2013). *Information economy*. Retrieved from http://baike.baidu.com/view/62984.htm

Baidu Encyclopedia. (2013). *Electronic information economy*. Retrieved from http://baike.baidu.com/view/2302817.htm

Branddirectory.com. (2012). *Global 500 2012 – Find out what the world's top brands are in 2012*. Retrieved from http://brandirectory.com/league_tables/table/global-500-2012

Chandler, A. D., & Cortada, J. (2000). *A nation transformed by information: How information has shaped the United States from colonial times to the present*. Oxford, UK: Oxford University Press.

China Ministry of Industry and Information. (2012). *Internet of things – 12th five-year development plan*. Retrieved from http://www.gov.cn/zwgk/2012-02/14/content_2065999.htm

Yu-Gang, W. (2009). *Enjoy the blessings of the internet of things, but we do have privacy?* Retrieved from http://news.xinhuanet.com/mrdx/2009-06/21/content_11575947.html

ENDNOTES

[1] Hoovers Online

[2] The technical concept of the Internet of Things is to be extensively covered in Chapter 2.

Chapter 2
Main Components of Cloud Computing

Yushi Shen
Microsoft Corporation, USA

Ling Wu
EMC² Corporation, USA

Yale Li
Microsoft Corporation, USA

Shaofeng Liu
Microsoft Corporation, USA

Qian Wen
Endronic Corp, USA

ABSTRACT

Cloud-era Information Technology (IT) contains three main themes: The information hub (cloud), network communications (pipes), and intelligent terminals. In this chapter, the developmental stages of these three main components of cloud computing are discussed, with emphasis on future development. The Internet of things is also examined, which is expected to thrive as a direct result of the development of cloud computing.

CLOUD ERA INFORMATION HUB

The information hub occupies the center position. Its fundamental tasks are to construct the cloud storage and computing systems, and complete the cloud era tasks of ultra-large scale and ultra-high complexity.

Originally referring to the main part of the human nervous system, the so-called hub or nerve center has the following major functions: stores and processes information, produces a variety of mental activities, and controls all aspects of the human behavior. In the personal computer (PC) and the internet age, a computer can be the information hub of a person or an enterprise that realizes information storage and computing functions. In the cloud computing era, cloud computing data centers are to replace personal computers, and become the new information hub that lowers costs and improves on the efficiency, in satisfying the human demands for massive information storage, computing and security.

DOI: 10.4018/978-1-4666-4801-2.ch002

Microsoft's Senior Vice President Yaqin Zhang has pointed out: "Cloud computing is the engine and the nervous center for the next generation of the Internet, Internet of Things and mobile Internet." It is very true, that cloud computing is, in essence, the central nervous system of the cloud era. Presently, this fact has been mainly reflected in the cloud data centers. Various kinds of cloud terminals are connected through the various communication networks, to interact with the end users as well as the physical world. In this sense, the relationship between the "cloud" and the "terminals" may be compared with that of the spirit and matters, or the soul and bodies.

In the coming years, the world is to be populated with tens of billions of network-enabled devices, billions of network users, and countless cloud applications and services. It is not difficult to foresee that in this cloud era, there is not going to be a lack of devices and end users, nor applications and services. However, a smart "nerve center" that can resolve highly complex tasks is going to be in high demand. The development of cloud computing is not to be limited to commercial activities, nor is it going to be a simple update of the IT application model. Instead, the cloud computing development is likely to be a contest and competition, between the various cloud era nerve centers.

Computing System Based on the Conventional Architecture

Of human invention, a computer is a tool used mainly for the purpose of information processing. If other man-made tools are considered extensions of the human limbs, then a computer can be considered an extension of the human brain.

Although quite different from the modern day computers, the first computer has already possessed the basic components of a modern computer: the arithmetic unit, controller and memory. Modern computers are based on either the von Neumann architecture, first proposed in 1945 by von Neumann (Neumann, 1958), and

also known as the Princeton architecture, or the Harvard architecture. The von Neumann computer architecture has the following basic components: a memory, a controller, an arithmetic unit, input and output devices. The computer systems designed to take advantage of this principle are collectively referred as the von Neumann machines. One other computer architecture is the Harvard architecture. Its basic characteristics are similar to the von Neumann architecture. The difference is that the storage of program instructions and data are separate. Most of the CPU processors are based on the von Neumann architecture: a representative example is the Intel (Intel) x86 microprocessor (Yang, 2011).

With the von Neumann architecture, one can achieve simplicity and low cost. However, when running at high speeds, simultaneous instruction and operand fetches are not possible with this architecture, thus a performance bottleneck exists for data transmission. On the other hand, the most representative examples that use the Harvard architecture bus technology are DSP and ARM. With the Harvard bus architecture, program space and data space are separate inside the chip, which allows simultaneous instruction and operand fetches, thus greatly increasing computing power. However the Harvard architecture is more complicated in that it requires high processing power and high-speed connections for its peripheral devices, and also it is unsuitable for external memory expansion. Modern processors have unified the two architectures with the help of CACHE storage.

For the PC, that is in essence designed based on the von Neumann or the Harvard architecture, their patterns of behavior can be called: "independent hardware and independent software to constitute a usable system," i.e., serial processing CPU hardware and onion-like layered software. The system functionality is limited to a single application software, and the system size is limited to a single piece of hardware.

Traditional hardware and software systems that are primarily designed for stand-alone machines and personal use, on a desktop environment, are called desktop computing. Prior to the cloud computing era, the computing model has experienced the transformation from the host computer to the client/server. The associated application characteristics and the load model have undergone tremendous changes, and the computing model has evolved from centralized to distributed computing. The computing load has also shifted from the host machine to the server. The current cloud computing is still in its early stage development: major emphasis is still on the business model, and technical innovations are far and few, where mostly existing technologies are given new names. The currently available super PC and data centers have fundamentally expanded on the complexity of its hardware and software, but the cloud processor architecture is still the continuation of either the von Neumann or Harvard architectures. Essentially, it is the natural evolution of the multi-core technology, the virtualization technology and parallel processing technology based on the original PCs.

The current cloud computers have largely utilized virtual machines, but the underlying physical machine processors are still based on the conventional microprocessors: such as Intel and AMD 64-bit microprocessors. The speed performance of such a computer processor in the very long run follows the Moore's law, first proposed by Gordon Moore in 1965, i.e. the performance of a microprocessor or the integrated circuitry on an IC chip are to double every 18 months. When the CPU clock frequency becomes saturated, the performance of microprocessors can continue to improve by increasing the number of cores, and decreasing the on-chip crystal element size, as well as the optimization of parallel computing algorithms.

However the von Neumann and Harvard architectures require super computing power, massive data processing capacity, as well as a huge amount of network throughput capacity, which may not necessarily be the best architectures for cloud computing. With the popularity of cloud computing, and the arrival of big data, the development of the cloud data centers are experiencing a growing challenge, with increasingly larger data centers requiring even higher performance and greater power consumption. Additionally, the traditional data communication traffics are mainly between the server and internet outlets that are for external use only. However for the cloud data centers, the vast majority of traffics are within the data center itself, while only about 30% of data transmissions are between the data center and other external elements. This is due to more effective data management, demand for data the processing collaborative and other reasons. This means that the three cornerstones of the cloud data center: server performance, storage and network interoperability, need to be greatly enhanced.

There are also physical limitations to computing power. The physical size of on-chip components cannot decrease ad infinitum, and therefore the number of components per unit area that can be integrated on a chip is to eventually reach a limit. In addition, with the increase in the silicon line density, chip complexity and error rates are to grow exponentially, which makes the comprehensive and thorough testing of the on-chip circuitry almost impossible. Once the on-chip line width reaches the nanometer (10^{-9} meters) orders-of-magnitude, the equivalent to only a few molecules in size, the physical and chemical properties of the material are to experience qualitative changes, and the resulting semiconductor devices are not going to work normally, with the current processing technology. Soon Moore's Law is no longer going to hold, and the future growth of the microprocessor speed and performance is to eventually reach a limit.

The scalability of a cloud computer is achieved by increasing the number of virtual machines. With a sharp increase in the number of users or data processing tasks, the cloud computer is to increase the corresponding number of virtual machines, in response to the increase in the required computing power. This extension is called the horizontal expansion, which requires that the computing tasks of those virtual machines stay mutually independent and unrelated to each other. The dynamic characteristics of a virtual machine also require that session states not to be saved. Horizontal expansion is still valid at the present stage, for websites with a large number of users, e-commerce, big data or parallel processing. However, problems such as databases with high read and write requests, and overall supercomputing tasks with a high level of coupling, can only be resolved by scaling up. This can be clearly demonstrated in the case of an aircraft carrier, when it is required to serve a combat mission, a number of destroyers cannot be considered a viable alternative. By utilizing virtual machines, with the present cloud data center model, and in the situation of longitudinal expansion, computing resources are surely to be stretched thin.

Even more seriously, with the increase in computing needs in the new cloud era, the evolution, along the path of the traditional von Neumann computer architecture and also in making the computer to adapt to people's communication habits, is to inevitably lead to more complex hardware and software. The complexity in hardware is seen as huge data centers getting ever larger, and also the increase in energy consumption. The complexity in software is leading to another software crisis, also called "the third software crisis" within the software industry. Even though good programming and strict management practices can help to improve on software quality, the nature of the software crisis is to challenge the limits of the human intellect, also to challenge the laws of nature, and therefore further improvements in this area may not be as optimistic.

New Computing Systems Based on Non-Traditional Architectures

Today, the entire computer industry is based on an assumption, that cloud computing is an evolution and extension of the traditional PC technology.

However, any successful and innovative practices are often guided by innovations in theory first. The development of human science and technology can be better described, as revolutionary changes continuously overcoming vast legacy systems. The cloud era technology may not necessarily be a continuation of the PC technology, as the PC technology has not been a continuation of the central mainframe technology – a large-scale power plant cannot be built, by the accumulation of tens of millions of small Edison generators.

Today, the vast majority of computers are making the effort to achieve the same goal: building super and complex computer hardware and software. This in essence is still based on the traditional PC architectural building blocks.

The natural law of evolution means minimization of energy, i.e. the system becomes more and more efficient, rather than increasingly more complex. The more complex the architecture, the less adaptable it becomes. On the contrary, small, simple and most elegant solutions can serve a world of functions. Perhaps, the real goal of the cloud computing hub should be designed as simple as possible to accomplish more tasks more effectively; this approach may not necessarily be limited to the traditional architectures.

Today, the "people-oriented" design concept has helped to achieve the many glories of the PC era. The cloud central computing system, based on the traditional architecture, also naturally inherited this gene. Cloud computing information hubs require fully automatic operation, where the personal operating environment is no longer necessary. "People-oriented" design becomes extra and burdensome. The cloud design concept, likewise, should be transitioning toward a "computing-oriented or machine-oriented" design mentality, which includes decomposition of complex processes, cutting out unnecessary elements, and focusing on the naked information. Of course, from a terminal and application service perspective, "people-oriented" is always correct, but this has nothing to do with the cloud tasks!

In short, the central nervous system of the cloud era should not be the evolution and extension of PC technology. A new computing system, based on non-traditional architectures, is to become the main supporting theme, for the future of the cloud era information hub technology.

Over the years, many people's ideas have transcended Neumann, but are only partial improvements to the original, while a systematic approach is still lacking. In recent years, a new direction is based on a new neural network computing architecture, which has gone beyond the traditional separation of computer hardware and software architecture, in order to achieve the integration of software and hardware and the integration of computing and communications. The neural network theory has made some achievements, but not complete, in the sense, that its performance ignores the various shapes of the different parts of the neuron, the innate biological instinct of the neural network, and the biological resistance to foreign intrusion, such as immune and self-healing capabilities (Haykin, 1999). Therefore, the study of neural networks should not be confined to the brain, but should be inclusive of the whole organism; should not be limited to imitating the details, but should also learn from the entire organism. On this basis, the theory puts forward four elements: the neural network neuron structure, the conduction agreement as innate instinct, immune and self-healing, and self-learning capabilities. Dedicated hctcrogeneous neurons, based on this new theory, are to replace the traditional universal machine. The new system is to be a new cloud computing element, based on the anti-von Neumann architecture. Through the rational use of existing resources, the new system can quickly obtain huge amounts of computing power in the cloud, and resolve the software crisis through sustainable means.

As we get closer and closer to the performance limits of the traditional computer processor technology, scientists are continuously seeking new breakthroughs from other perspectives, such as new materials, new transistor design methods, and molecular-level computing technologies. Presently, there are at least four new technologies that are gaining widespread notice, and require in-depth examination: they are photonic computers, biological computers, quantum computers and Nano-computers. Although these studies are still in the laboratory stage, they all possess the great potential to a new revolution, but the likelihood of success in the marketplace is yet difficult to predict.

Implications of the New Cloud Information Hub

History is always interesting, that it undulates back and forth between contradictions and unifications of opposites. After a time of unification, separations are sure to follow, and a time of separation is to lead to unification. In the history of the computer, two prophecies by industry celebrities are considered classic, and later deemed ridiculous, and now become close to correct. One from IBM's founder, Thomas Watson: "I think there is a world market for five computers." The other is by Microsoft's founder, Bill Gates, namely "640k ought to be enough for anyone."

With the arrival of the cloud era, many phenomena of the PC era have been reversed. When the consumer groups become huge, their needs greatly converge, that is the number of consumers is to greatly exceed the type of demands. The popularity due to network connectivity is going to promote the rearrangement of resources in the direction of maximizing value. Cloud computing, that dominates by size and concentration, signifies a return to old Thomas Watson. Similarly, with the development of cloud computing, computing, storage and management capabilities, and so on, are re-distributing, leading to large amounts of in-the-cloud computation and storage, the terminal is to be greatly simplified: Bill Gates' prediction of a light PC again proves correct.

With the breakthrough in the cloud computing data center development, as well as the integration of new technologies with neural networks, natural human-machine interfaces, super-computers, new computing forms such as quantum computing, cloud computing is going to eventually bring in a new smart computing age.

CLOUD ERA COMMUNICATION NETWORKS

The communication network is the pipe that connects cloud services with the users, and directly determines the depth and breadth of those services. The communication network is the important infrastructure, which determines the popularity of the cloud model.

In the recent years, the rapid development of cloud computing is largely due to the development and integration of the Internet and the wireless communication technologies. The overall trend of the current communication business is moving from voice-centric to data-centric. In the future, video content and real-time information processing are going to gradually increase proportion wise. The driving force behind this change is no other than networks with broadband communications, and especially the development of the wireless broadband technology. While cloud computing is definitely a major trend, but the network environment is the key factor determining the success or failure of cloud computing. The great abundance of communication resources is the material foundation, for the future popular market acceptance of the cloud model.

Most experts agree that user experience depends on the terminal and content. Currently, Apple, Google and Microsoft are all focused on the intense competition for cloud computing and the end products that include hardware, software, services and fashion elements. This is certainly good, but one cannot overlook the fact, that between the cloud hub and terminal devices, there needs to be a network! In fact, the network determines the quality of content and services to be delivered: a second-rate terminal on top of a first-class network can easily surpass a first-class terminal on top of a second-rate network. Concurrent with the innovations in cloud computing and the terminal, if the network does not deliver, it is bound to hinder the effective transfer of information, which can restrict the development of cloud computing.

On the business level, the only way for the market to ultimately embrace cloud computing can be no other than services of true value. If the network foundation is not solid, without the essential improvements on network capacity, and especially the capacity of wireless transmission networks, the cloud computing development is to be severely limited to simple messaging services. Thus a revolutionary business development is impossible, and that is going to inevitably lead to a downturn in the industry. On the other hand, we must first build a solid network infrastructure, in order to nurture network applications that can live up to the human imagination. This is the only way leading up to further economic development.

On the political level, information are not only closely associated with the region's politics and economics, but are also directly integrated into the daily lives of the ordinary people. Developments in IT are going to have significant impact over people's psychology, will and behavior. A network is the information bearer, that it directly determines the transfer and sharing of information, which imposes direct constraints over the IT reality space. The communication network has become an important part of the national strategy for many nations on earth, that it embodies the fourth territorial dimension in addition to territories, territorial waters and airspace.

Network World-View and the Black Hole Effect

The so-called network world-view, is an exploration of the future goal of network development in accordance to the laws of science. Without the development and evolution of a world view, the future of the network is tantamount to illusions of a mirage, or strutting about like that of walking dead without a Soul.

One network world-view states: the future network is to essentially converge to a real-time video communication network, or more precisely, the ultimate network made for global communication is a completely transparent pipe, suitable for the transmission of video communication and information exchange. Cloud computing is based on "the triple network integration." The three networks refer to the mobile communication network, radio and TV broadcasting networks, and the computer based internet. The final converged network is to be seen as a combination of data, voice, video and a variety of communication protocols, but in essence it is still a video network. In terms of traffic capacity, the amount of information processing and quality requirements, video business is to be in the dominant position.

Specifically, from a service perspective, video communications pose the highest requirements for network capacity, quality and real-time functions. In providing video communications, the network can easily accommodate other contents and services. The same is true for a mobile phone to support the capabilities of a pager. From the flow-capacity perspective, the most important aspect of the broadband world is no other than video communications - as long as there is a small number of users that require video communications, video data is to occupy more than 99% of the network traffic. From a technical point of view, in providing video communication services, the question is not how much of such services can be provided, but if one can provide such services at all; there is no middle of the road approach possible. A network that cannot provide video communications is not considered a complete network.

The present online world map can be represented by four territories and four kingdoms. The so-called "four kingdoms" include mobile communications (2G/3G/LTE/4G, WiFi / WiMAX), Internet (NGI, IPv6, P2P), cable TV (NGB, DTV,

DVB, DOCSIS), fixed-line and cable telephone (NGN, IMS, IPTV). The so-called "four territories" are based on industry or geographical locations, i.e. the four international standardizations: the International Telecommunications Union (ITU), the European Telecommunications Standards (ETSI), the Internet Engineering Task Force (IETF) and the wireless camp (3GPP). Although the above forces are fragmented, they are highly competitive. They all have one thing in common: a foundation of strong existing business, and based on this foundation they try to direct the future industry developments by the attempt to build an all-embracing "intelligent multimedia network platform", that can adjust the transmission quality depending on business needs. The goal of which is to integrate all business services in a "perfect" way.

Going directly against the above world map, the world view that emphasizes the real-time video communications network states, that although on the surface it seems the future network services are multi-varied, but the purpose of the network traffic in essence is dominated only by real-time video communications. Therefore, the network must be communication-oriented, that non-communication oriented TV media and Download Play, being only a subset of video communications, can be disregarded. Video quality sets the standards for communication, and once the standard is set, details can be worked out. Non-video communication traffic, which accounts for less than a few percent of the total network traffic, is almost negligible. As long as the problem of real-time video interoperability is solved, the low entropy transparent network can accommodate any "smart" service of the future, thus achieving the separation of network and terminal, and the separation of transmission and content.

So far, the four major networks are unable to provide high-quality real-time video communication services. The reason being: on the wired side, due to the popularity of fiber optics, bandwidth are in excess, but the problem lies in the lack of bandwidth management (Gilder, 2002); in the wireless front, the main limitation is the lack of capacity resources due to insufficient bandwidth; wired (Internet) and wireless (mobile telecom) are two systems that have taken independent development paths. Another pressing problem is the seamless fusion between these two different systems. The above three problems have been plaguing the communications industry for a long time. An industry-wide consensus for realistic solutions is far from taking shape.

Once the problem of high-quality real-time video communication is resolved, the network's core target of the conversion from "intellectual content" to "emotional content" can be then achieved. Given the networks' convergent "winner takes all" and "clean sweep" nature, the huge-traffic business of video communications is like a black hole, devouring all related small-flow businesses. This is the so-called "network black-hole effect": wherever high-quality video communications goes, forming separate networks for any other small traffic network business may be deemed quite impossible, at least from the business standpoint. According to the network black-hole effect, a video communication network is going to impact and replace alternative network businesses established in the past few decades, including voice telephony, multimedia, one-way play and content downloading. This confirms the network world-view from a different angle, that the future network is essentially a real-time video communications network.

The Internet: Improvement or Revolution

The Internet is a computer network formed according to the network communication protocols between the WAN, LAN and PCs. Although the internet concept have been proposed for over forty years, but due to a lack of development in areas such as technology, business models and consumer awareness, it has not been put into widely

accepted civilian use until the early 90s of the last century. The birth of the Internet has revolutionized people's lifestyles and productive behaviors, and promoted global productivity growth and civilization development. People have been ushering in social and technological advancements one after another on the "information super-highway."

First, the Internet has opened up a new frontier for exchanges of data and information services. In a relatively fair, free and open virtual world of information, the concept of a global village has thus been realized. E-commerce, digital media, the Internet of Things, industrial and logistics management, with the introduction of many Internet-based information technology, have greatly improved productive efficiency and changed the way people live. At this stage, information as a new means of production and subsistence has become an essential element for the "third industrial revolution," pushing the society forward with rapid changes. Since the advent of the Internet, people can see farther, wider and deeper, and unprecedented progress has been made in the exploration of natural and social sciences.

Secondly, the Internet has rewritten the history of human communication. Internet-based communication services have broken up the monopoly of traditional telecommunications, so that people can access local, long distance and international communications at very low costs. Also the exchange of information has become increasingly diverse: real-time audio, video and multimedia communications are becoming more common. With the development of cloud computing and mobile Internet, Internet communication services, that integrate features for business and entertainment, are becoming a major carrier for social value creation.

However, since the Internet has been made available to the public, three main issues have been exposed: network security, quality assurance and business modeling. The fundamental causes of these difficulties are precisely the three core technology concepts, which are the reason why the Internet exists today, and they have helped to promote the very success of the Internet: the so-called "best-effort", "store forwarding" and "always online".

In March 2009, an influential popular science magazine in Europe "*New Discoveries,*" published an article titled "*The Internet's Collapse*"- it was a big hit. This article describes three facts: the hardship that the internet is suffering is more serious than anticipated; counter-measures currently employed are more ineffective than anticipated; any possibility of making adjustments for the Internet are more difficult than anticipated. In fact, the debate on whether or not the Internet has collapsed has been going on for the last 20 years. Interestingly, experts on both sides of the argument can agree for 20 years, that the Internet faces serious drawbacks and an uncertain future, but the Internet has since become irreplaceable.

Few years have passed, we are moving toward the cloud era. Two new characteristics of the times have become increasingly evident: first, the maturing fiber-optic technology has brought in a bandwidth-rich era. In fact, bandwidth resources have become forever abundant. Secondly, the living room and beyond consumer market, including handheld terminals, are entering the era of entertainment and experience economy. At this point, the above unresolved problems of the internet have become fatal, hindering further developments in the industry! This is mainly reflected in the following aspects: first, the Internet's transmission quality cannot meet the requirements for providing a great viewing experience; secondly, the Internet's download mode cannot meet the requirements for a synchronous exchange experience; thirdly, the Internet's security and management cannot meet the requirements for the business environment and billing models, of the video content consumption industry.

Faced with this reality, whether to build a future by modifying the original Internet, or start anew with a revolutionary design, is a choice to be debated among key industry decision makers.

Internet reformists believe: just like the engines of an in-flight airplane that cannot be replaced, Internet, being ubiquitous and irreplaceable, is going to continue to be the basis of future network. Internet problems are to be gradually eased with improvements made on high-performance routers, IP address upgrade, unicast and multicast technologies, a series of improvements and enhancement on congestion control, service quality controls and network security.

Internet revolutionaries believe that: a lofty structure cannot be constructed on the foundation of sand; crops cannot be sown in the Gobi desert; palliative therapies cannot cure diseases of genetic defects; numerous localized improvements cannot resolve fundamental defects of the system. The Future Network is going to be essentially different from that of today. Unless new functional network architectures are conceptualized, today's network thinking is poles apart from what we want for our future network, and we are never going to reach that future goal, without a drastic overhaul of what is exiting today.

One theory believes that for over 100 years, the theoretical system of communication networks has been highly complex, but from the perspective of technical principles, regardless the extent of development for these theories, they have all originated from one of the following two ancient network structures: the invention of the telegraph system in 1844, and another invention of the telephone system in 1876. The former can be classified as a discrete model, suitable for the transmission of data packets (intellectual content). The second can be classified as a continuous model transmitting streaming media (perceptual content). This is the "dualism" of the communication network, and it tells us that any communication network must have originated from one of these two basic structures: the telegraph system and the telephone system. The two basic types of content, on the implementation level, are files (intellectual content) and streaming data (emotional content).

The internet is essentially an improved telegraph system, with telegraph and computer files being the same type of content, where the "best effort" network technology is most suitable. If the network of the future is really a video-based network, with voice and video belonging to the same type of continuous streaming content, the "current connection" streaming network technology becomes more suitable. The future network is going to be very likely an improved telephone system, in order to meet the real-time video communication requirements. According to this theory, the history of the communication network development is going through the path of change from a telegraph network, to a telephone network, to an improved telegraph network (the internet), and finally an improved telephone network (the future internet). Negation of negation is inevitably the course of history.

The Ultimate Goal of Wireless Communications and Two Routes

The ultimate goal of wireless communications is the homogenization of wireless communications and the wired communication services. This goal implies that the wireless network service capabilities need to be raised to the level of the wired networks, rather than the wired network application relegating to the existing wireless levels.

The current two network systems in the wireless field are the mobile telecom and wireless LAN. They respectively correspond to the two technical directions of the macro and micro base-stations, which determine the two fundamentally different development routes for the future of wireless communications.

Based on the macro-base-station technologies, the second-generation mobile telecom (2G) has been a great success. The main business of the 2G wireless network has been voice transmission,

while its success is built on the fact that its voice quality is comparable to that of the fixed-line. Unfortunately, the next 3G technology is far inferior to 2G. The 3GPP Long Term Evolution (LTE) plan hopes to open up new frontiers for mobile communications, but when the communication bandwidth is overwhelmed by its intended use, most mobile operators are forced to abandon earlier commitments to quality, and accept lower service qualities.

Another wireless communication system, originated from the micro-base-station, is the wireless LAN. Led by the WiFi Alliance, the goal of the wireless LAN is to provide mobile communication within a small area. In order to expand the coverage area, the WiMAX Forum has been established in 2001, and directly competes with mobile telecom. However, WiFi and WiMAX are faced with the "five no's" predicament, namely: insufficient bandwidths, inconvenient roaming, lack of powerful network management, insufficient system security and no killer applications. Moreover, due to the irreconcilable bandwidth usage in between multiple WiFi networks and network equipment, WiFi networks can easily exceed its limit with the increasing number of wireless networks and devices.

Following 2G's success, wireless network's continued success depends on large-scale high-return applications. This directly implies a mobile multimedia network with video capabilities. Presently, the wireless camp is focused on wireless multimedia. However, the video data-flow requirements are much higher than voice. With one trigger for video applications, endless headaches of quality, cost, the number of users, and the level of satisfaction are to inevitably follow. This terrible Pandora's Box once opened, would repeat the same nightmare of the internet today, caused by the introduction of video services. The internet has been fortunate, that these issues can still be resolved with simple expansions based on the old structures, but the wireless evolution path (LTE), already limited by the macro-base-station architecture, is difficult to expand. The present wireless camp is limiting the market of wireless communications to the so-called time "fragmentation", requiring applications made for wired networks to relegate back to the wireless level, severely limiting development of the network economy.

In essence, the crux of the problem lies not in novel applications, but rather wireless bandwidth resources. This is the most fundamental problem of the wireless communication! In order to fundamentally resolve these technical issues, one must track down the source.

Shannon's theory defines a framework for the development of communication networks. It provides a channel capacity limit for a fundamentally noisy environment (Shannon, 1949). C represents the upper limit of the channel capacity, W denotes the spectral width, and S / N represents the signal-to-noise ratio (SNR). The relationship between the three is:

$$C = W \, Log \, (S \, / \, N)$$

By re-interpreting Shannon's limit theory, we can see that at first, the wireless bandwidth chip's computing capabilities do not follow the exponential growth of the Moore's Law. Namely it is infeasible to follow the "Long Term Evolution" route of numerous incremental improvements of that of the PC. Secondly, the Shannon limit is a logarithmic (Log) function, the higher the input, the lower the gain. In terms of bandwidth spectrum (in Bits/Hz), the wireless industry has nearly used up all its potential in the past 15 years. Thirdly, an important parameter in the Shannon's limit function is the spectrum width (W), but according to the essential characteristics of the electromagnetic wave propagation, low-frequency spectrums require a large antenna, while high-frequency spectrums are severely constrained by the surrounding environment. Also wireless spectrums are scarce public resources, and therefore the possibility of enhancing the communication channel capacity

by upgrading the spectrum is actually very low. Finally, another key parameter of the Shannon's limit function is the SNR (S / N). Assuming a constant noise (N) level, electromagnetic theory tells us that the signal strength (S) is inversely proportional to the square of distance to the antenna, which signifies a rapid rate of decay as we move away from the signal source. In other words, wireless communication's ideal operating areas are limited to the vicinity of the signal source (the antenna).

Digging to the root, we can see that in order to enhance wireless bandwidths there can be no more than three approaches: to improve the spectral efficiency, to use more spectrums, or to improve on the spectrum reuse rate. If the first two are infeasible, then we can only improve on the spectrum reuse rate in order to bring us an unlimited amount of potential wireless bandwidth. If this analysis stands, a re-examination of the Shannon theory in the cloud era gives the fundamental conclusion: In order to improve the wireless networks' level of quality and capacity, so that they can reach comparable levels of that of the wired networks, micro-base-station network is the only way to go. One cannot take the route of gradually improving on the macro-base-stations or the so called Long Term Evolution.

However, the future micro-base-station system is anything but today's micro-base-station system. The fundamental problem facing today's WiFi wireless LAN system is: how to synchronize the connected micro-base-stations that are thousands times the number, and at the same time realizing seamless switching and accurate billing. In addition, how to significantly reduce the cost of micro-base-stations is another important topic.

From an overall point of view, as long as the coverage radius is reduced, the effective spectrum resources are to grow at the rate of radius squared; by shrinking the coverage radius, this is to eventually lead to the degeneration of wireless communication to means of close access into wired networks! Thus, the transformation of the wired network and wireless networks must take each other into consideration on the top level design. Once such an understanding is reached, a viable structural design for a future of unified communication networks is ready to come into being.

Consequences of the Cloud Era Network Development

The true substance of communication tools can be found in higher efficiency, lower cost, and the possibility of synergy among more individuals spanning a wider range. Of tools by human invention, communication tools are ranked among the highest in terms of social value. Revolution in the field of communications is to have all pervasive social impacts on all aspects of life. The socio-economic contributions are highly prominent.

The communication network, in the cloud era, as a bridge connecting the cloud hub and terminals, determines the success or failure of the cloud computing industry model. Since most of the computing and information analysis are done in the cloud, the security and stability of the network transmission directly decide the future cloud service quality. This is the basis whether business users and consumers can eventually embrace the cloud computing industry.

Although the internet has experienced rapid developments in the past 20 years, its fundamental flaws have been well exposed, and are to become even more prominent in the cloud era. At the same time, the network black hole effect is driving the industry to widely accept the network worldview that is mainly based on the real-time video transmission services. The call for an internet revolution is loud and clear. Meanwhile, with the development of mobile Internet, the wireless communication network is becoming the basis for a cloud computing revolution. In the long run, facing revolutionary new markets and service applications, some fundamental issues cannot be solved by the long-term evolution of wireless communication technology and the WiFi wireless

LAN concept. The establishment of a new type of wireless communication network becomes inevitable.

The future "universal" communications network of the cloud era is going to be providing a whole new environment for the wired and wireless networks, so that the human society can enter into a new state of being. First, the great unified network is to integrate the four businesses of the media, entertainment, communications and information processing. Secondly, the great unified network is to integrate the three major networks: fixed-line networks, mobile communication networks and sensor networks. Conceivably that under the new pattern of all-fiber fixed-line and wireless networks, network bandwidth resources are no longer going to be a problem. The network architecture is to take the presence of development and growth into consideration, and become easily expandable. Operators and users transcend the physical limitations of the network. Human reliance on the network becomes like the air around us, inexhaustible, and ever present. Its existence can no longer be ignored by the human society. Under the solid backing of a great unified network, computing, information processing and network transmission are to gradually fade into the background, in its place, a variety of content service platforms are going to be presented in front of their respective users, the making of a brilliant cloud era!

INTELLIGENT TERMINALS OF THE CLOUD ERA

The intelligent terminal, also called the cloud terminal, is a general term for terminal equipment and terminal platform services based on cloud computing. In the cloud era, an intelligent terminal is a window of interaction between the information centers and the physical world, and it bears the mission of information gathering, human-computer interaction and information transfer. All kinds of cloud applications and services are provided through the terminal. Interactive user experiences are achieved directly from the terminal. Cloud computing represents not only a technical change, but also a business change and a social change, with the intelligent terminals being bound to play a crucial role in this transformation.

The Enormous Potential of Intelligent Terminals in Cloud Computing

Cloud computing has unleashed an enormous potential for intelligent terminals, and the development of intelligent terminals is to deepen the social impact of cloud computing. In the recent years, intelligent terminals are experiencing explosive growth. Applications of various industries and of the various scenarios are requiring the developing terminal to evolve and meet these new needs. In 2012 the total number of smart phone users has exceeded one billion. Taking into consideration personal computers, tablet PCs, smart appliances and other equipment, the user base has long exceeded billions. The intelligent terminal ushered in an unprecedented period of change. In the present, the industry's development model of "cloud + client" has been gradually gaining market acceptance. Comparing with the cloud movement, such as the vigorous building of data centers, the construction of cloud computing platforms, and the development of cloud computing applications, the development of intelligent terminals are right on track. The intense competition in this area is beyond industry expectations. The drama of survival and decline, involving the cloud era intelligent terminal's chip technology, operating systems, mobile applications and business models is being quietly staged.

In 2012, former IT industry giants such as Motorola, Nokia, BlackBerry and HP are faced with a turning point in fate: acquired by Google, Motorola continues with its downsizing; Nokia has placed all its bet on Windows Phones; Blackberry keeps delaying the release of its revolutionary product line, and HP trudges on with billions of dollars in quarterly losses. Although some analysts try to persuade the market to give them more time, one thing has become very clear: when the cloud computing opportunities are not seized, and the pace of technological change has not being kept up, the business empire is bound to collapse, no matter how big it has become in the past.

On the other hand, Apple, Google, Microsoft and a number of other computer companies are taking the leadership role in the cloud era intelligent terminal market with its mobile phones, tablet PCs and PCs steadily gaining market share. Whoever that has the user-base in the cloud era is to have the final say in cloud services. The large user base is helping the Big Three to effectively promote their cloud products and services. Apple's iCloud has quickly taken over the market, due to the huge success of its iPhone. After re-packaging its cloud based on e-mail, documents, social networking and picture storage functions, Google's cloud services is beginning to take shape. Microsoft through its latest release of the Windows 8 operating system has achieved a true sense of cross-platform services, where the Windows end users enjoy seamless docking services between their desktops, laptops, tablet computers and mobile phones. Microsoft's software products have been optimized to run on the different intelligent terminals. The reason why the Big Three - Microsoft, Google and Apple, have such a huge lead ahead of the rest of industry, is not only because their large user base, but also their comprehensive and competitive background in the terminal technologies.

Meanwhile, striving to develop their own software and hardware products, and at the same time introducing its intelligent terminals based on the Android and Windows 8 OS, Samsung continues to suppress Apple. Intel, Qualcomm and ARM are actively developing small, high performance and low energy consumption chipsets. Lenovo, Asus, Dell and other veteran PC makers are actively aligned with Microsoft's Windows 8 to enter the mobile terminal market. Xbox, Apple TV, Google TV and other home entertainment products are bringing the intense competition into the home appliances market. The war on the cloud computing's intelligent terminals has begun.

The great charm of cloud computing is that no single corporation can monopolize such a huge market. Cloud computing requires the opening up of the future scientific and technological environment. Regardless of platforms and products, intelligent terminals are required to provide computing services on-demand. Mobility, intelligent interaction and cross-platform compatibility are must-have features for the next generation of intelligent terminals. Such changes are to bring in a broader market and greater development potential. Think about it: when Apple has achieved the great success of the iPhone through the perfect combination of its media player, communication and industrial design alone, the future function-rich intelligent terminals are to greatly change the way we live - infinitely rich functionalities are to cover intelligent data acquisition, real-time video interoperability, natural language recognition, business intelligence analysis and virtual reality. This is to bring in potential markets of unimaginable size and demand. The excitation energy of the intelligent terminals is to give birth to third-party services and information processing intermediaries that have wide spaces for development.

With in-depth integration of IT and communication technologies, highly optimized hardware and software technologies, the intelligent terminal ridding on the wave of cloud computing and mobile internet is standing at a historical junction! Every click from the hands of the users reveals the great charm of IT innovation. This is not the end of an era, or the end of a certain product, but a new Nirvana!

Intelligent Terminal Developments and Trends

The deep integration of computing and communications has brought the industry to a "post-PC era." With increased competition and technologi-

cal progress, the dividing line between personal computers, mobile phones, TVs and tablet PCs are blurring. Intelligent terminals have gradually acquired mainstream status with increasingly more unified features. It is expected that in 2016, at least 50% of the corporate e-mail users are going to mainly rely on the browser, tablet PCs or mobile clients. Various types of cloud services are to act as the "glue" connecting the terminal equipments. With attention to user experience, the "people-oriented" design concept is the cornerstone of the intelligent terminal's success. From there, the communication between different objects is going to be the main factor that drives information growth. The physical world and the virtual world are going to realize a deep fusion on all levels, because there is no limit on population, space and time. In the development process of the terminal, three trends have become increasingly significant, and they are: thin terminals, three-terminal fusion and a new type of intelligent terminals.

Thin Client

With the popularity of cloud computing, the "smart-cloud" thin client concept has been widely accepted. Cloud computing is essentially a redistribution of computing capabilities: computing, storage and resource management. Its main manifestations are the simplistic terminals, with the transfer of intensive computation and huge storage space into the cloud. With a sufficiently efficient information hub and a smooth communication network, the terminal's hardware and software systems can be "downsized." It is possible for a terminal with simple processing and storage capacities to provide intelligent services, which can be sufficient for all of the daily information needs.

For large enterprises, the thin client system has a number of advantages. First, from the perspective of the scale-of-costs, large companies through a thin client system can greatly reduce the need to purchase IT equipment, and also lower maintenance and operating costs. Secondly, the popularity of the thin client is more in line with enterprise software and information security requirements: because the thin client can be understood as a simple platform for sending and receiving data, where data and related files are actually stored on the server-side, which greatly reduces loss, contamination, damage and etc. In addition, enterprises can exercise better high-level management and control of data and information, and real-time tracking of the business processes, thus improving productivity. Finally, because of its simple hardware configuration, the thin client principle can save energy, lower power consumption and promote green operations, all of which have very positive impacts on today's society.

The generalized theory of the thin client is just a direction of change for the intelligent terminal. It is not to say that terminals are to be blindly "thinned" down. Due to the different needs of the different users and scenarios, and also due to the fact that cloud hubs and network communications are still subject to a number of serious bottlenecks, plus the increasing demand on terminal intelligence, human-computer interaction, user experience and interactive entertainment, a high-quality high-performance terminal market continues to stay strong.

In the future, some intelligent terminal's central processor (CPU) and network transmission chips are to become smarter and more human-like, in commanding network computing and information processing. The future development of the intelligent terminal is to bring in more interactive features, making possible the popularity of voice, video and multimedia interactions. Correspondingly the ever smaller CPUs may need to become even more powerful. The intelligent terminal is required to have more powerful multimedia processing capacities. The importance of the display chips are in the limelight. The reliability of the intelligent terminal is to be tested through movie and game playing, also other entertainment features and activities. The smart terminal's operating system is going to be more intelligent, and

even more in touch with the need for simplicity and mobility. People are going to be freed from the shackles of the keyboard and the mouse. The touch and intelligent human-computer interactions are becoming increasingly popular.

Of course, as long as the network is good enough and in theory, the realization of any features is expected to be better and more efficient in the cloud than in the terminal. The speed of light is 300,000 km/s, or 300 km/ms. Assuming that the network equipment delay is negligible, then the CPU on the terminal, or 150 km away in the cloud, two-way data delay is not to exceed 1 ms, which is insignificant relative to the human-reaction time of 150 milliseconds. Therefore, as long as the network performance (bandwidth and real-time operability) keeps on improving, plus the breakthrough in artificial intelligence, "intelligent" application services are to be more and more from the cloud, rather than from the terminal. This is a general trend of the cloud era.

The Three-Terminal Fusion

The triple-play of mobile telecom, radio and TV networks, and the Internet is an inevitable product of technology development, which has created a brand new one-trillion-dollar market. Correspondingly, the three-terminal fusion is referring to terminals of the three networks, which includes television, computers, mobile phones, set-top boxes, tablet PCs and etc. This is going to further blur conceptual distinctions, and comprehensively unify products and services. The three-terminal fusion is to cover not only the end products, but also the integration of network protocols, platforms and software.

The three-terminal fusion indicates to us one development direction of the intelligent terminals of the cloud era: a phone will have TV, computer and communication functionalities, and TVs will be able to browse the web, perform real-time communication, and even run software applications like a computer. Despite significant differences that exist on the physical level, the intelligent terminal fusion is expected to provide consistent user experience. The operating model of cloud computing is to cause this fusion to be more fully realized.

Cloud resources and applications can be called on demand and at any time. The intelligent terminals are to accept and send service requests cross-platform. All these seemingly simple activities in fact come from a large and complicated background. Chip and storage hardware development, cross-platform operating systems and open network protocols are the driving forces behind the three-terminal fusion, and all of these form the basis for the human factor of an intelligent terminal. It is believed that the growing human demand and reliance for technology products are the driving forces behind the intelligent terminal's development, in providing increasingly more perfect services.

The New Smart Terminal

The rich imagination and creativity of international film and television makers have produced a lot of sci-fi movies, laying out the possible scenarios of a future technological society: virtual space travel, intelligent robots acting as human-servants, smart auto-piloting cars that can follow human instructions, or even smart cities that can automatically adjust and meet the needs of human survival, and so on. These dreams are to be realized in the near future. The future intelligent terminals not only exist in the form of a phone or a computer, but all kinds of new terminals are expected to appear: smart pets, smart cars, intelligent robots and virtual space capsules.

In fact, humanity's pursuit in artificial intelligence products can be traced back to the dawn of human civilization. From the singing and dancing puppet "actors" of the Chinese Western Zhou Dynasty, to the world-famous "wooden-ox and running horse", although they are not intelligent machines, these are all human visions for a better society in the future, and human endeavors to use technology to improve lives. Today, artificial intelligence is entering into a stage of fast-paced development. For instance, in 2012 the Google driverless car has received on-road licenses in both Nevada and California, and it is equipped with a global positioning system, radar systems, electronic sensor systems, an on-board camera and a central processor. This means that new smart terminal products, such as the driverless car, are expected to enter the consumer markets very soon. Another example is the popular "self-quantification" movement in the recent years, where people can automatically record their life, work, exercise, rest, diet, entertainment, mood data and many other kinds of personalized information through smart phones, portable sensors and other equipment, and then gain a better understanding of themselves, through data mining, analysis and comparisons, thus improve on the quality of life.

The development of the Internet of Things, and the maturation of touch, taste and vision sensors, are going to give the future terminals truly significant "smartness." In the cloud era, new intelligent terminal products are to integrate multiple systems, and through data acquisition, data analysis and self-judgment functions, to provide personalized and customized intelligent services. Scientists may even give intelligent terminals a true sense of "perception" and "emotion". Currently, smart homes, smart cities, smart robots and etc., are taking shape from concept to reality.

Consequences

The intelligent terminal market is going through a reshuffle. In this market of rapid change, all players regardless of their past glory, must embrace change in order to survive. Innovations on chip technology, the operating system, industrial design and service applications are going to further push the intelligent terminal into every aspect of human life, business and production.

Looking ahead, from the bird-eye view, services passed by the cloud era's "cloud-pipe-terminal" architecture consist of two major categories: "intellectual" and "emotional." The "intellectual" business is focused on the information itself, such as air-ticket booking, hotel booking, funds transfer and etc. The "emotional" business is focused on the user experience of pleasant feelings, such as nature, novelty and fashion interfaces, which also includes video interaction, games, virtual reality and etc. As for whether to place the management and treatment of service capabilities in the cloud or at the terminal, it depends on the resource environment.

In the present case, the "thin client" is sufficient for intellectual information services and general use, however emotional functions still cannot be achieved in the cloud. With the future progress of network performance (bandwidth and real-time), and enhancements in artificial intelligence, the "smart" elements within the terminal are going to be gradually moving into the cloud. Although the users see only more and more intelligent terminals, and increasingly intelligent services, but in fact the "smartness" is coming more and more from the cloud itself.

Technologies are born to serve the people. In the advent of cloud computing, the huge potential of intelligent terminals has been released, which has created an unprecedented three-dimensional market structure and demand. As the first interactive interface with the user and the physical world, the intelligent terminal is to undergo many changes. Reaching across the field of communications, entertainment and computing, intelligent terminals are going to enter into millions of households very soon. New terminals continue to become smarter, more easy to use, which in turn are sure to create a large number of new business scenarios and service applications.

CLOUD COMPUTING AND THE INTERNET OF THINGS

The Internet of Things (IOT) is becoming one of the hottest topics in the Chinese domestic information technology (IT) sector. In fact, the origin of the IOT is quite recent. In 1995, Microsoft founder Bill Gates has alluded to the concept of the IOT in his book "The Road Ahead" by using a different term. During the Mobile Computing and International Network Conference held in the United States in 1999, the term Internet of Things (IOT) has been used for the first time by Kevin Ashton. In the same year, the term has been referenced frequently, in articles published by the MIT Auto-ID Lab and various market analysts, to gradually bring it into the spotlight. Now, some are referring to the emergence of the IOT, together with cloud computing, as a new wave of development for the global IT industry.

Internet of Things as the Internet's Extension

Speaking of the IOT, we must first find out exactly what it means. There are many different definitions, but the most common one states: The IOT is a combination of information sensing devices, such as radio frequency identification (RFID) devices, infrared sensors, global positioning systems, laser scanners and so on, together with the Internet to form a huge network. From this definition, we can see that the IOT consists of two major parts, i.e., the sensing devices and the Internet. The nature of the IOT, that it is made up of the "Internet + sensors", expands the boundaries of the Internet, that it helps the internet to extend its reaches into the physical world. The popular acceptance of the IOT is to enable network coverage to go from "everyone connected" to "everything connected."

The internet and the IOT are closely related, but are also different from each other. The internet, since inception, has deep roots in our daily lives.

Each moment, there are hundreds of millions of people making contacts to the outside world and obtaining information through the Internet. It is no longer an exaggeration to say that without the Internet, the human society is not able to function. The IOT relies on the internet to play its role. Without the internet at the height of its development today, the IOT does not have the germinating soil to take root and grow, and its popular use quite impossible. Simply put, the Internet is at the center of the IOT. The Internet must be relied on for data transmissions, and it is the basis of information exchange for the IOT.

However, the Internet and the IOT have some clear distinctions. The main difference is the "objects" in the IOT that are connected to the Internet. Terminals connecting to the Internet are mostly computers and mobile phones. However, those connecting to the IOT are more diverse. They are not only computers and mobile phones, but also watches, televisions and cars, which may even extend to housing and aircrafts, plants and animals, all things relating to all aspects our lives. It can be said that all things relating to our lives, that have data being collected through sensors, and transmitted through the internet, can be terminals to the IOT. The overall intelligence of the IOT can far exceed that of the Internet. Information collected can be synthesized, summarized and analyzed, so as to provide better services to the human society.

To achieve diversity in the terminals connected to the IOT, the role of the sensors cannot be overlooked. Without those sensors, the IOT loses its information source. Sensors define the boundaries of the IOT, and together with smart phones and laptops, they all belong to the terminal side, the new terminals of the cloud era. Sensors are made for the tasks of data acquisition, data pre-processing and data transfer. With the above mentioned terminal diversity of the IOT, there are a variety of sensors being deployed, and each is suitable for a corresponding terminal. Also, because of the huge number terminals, the number of sensors being connected can also be massive. Sensor data are being obtained in real-time, so as to ensure the timeliness and reliability of information being obtained.

To summarize, by the IOT's smart computing, analysis and management functions, people can go from a passive exposure and use of the world's massive amounts of daily information, to the active acquisition of hidden knowledge from data, and thus reaching the goal of working and living more intelligently. The Internet of Things is certainly going to greatly improve people's qualities of life.

The Core of the Internet of Things (IOT) is Cloud Computing

Before cloud computing, it is impossible to achieve the IOT's objectives. Without the support of cloud computing platforms, there cannot be a true IOT, instead there can only be many disconnected islands of information.

Due to the enormous task of storage, management and analysis of the vast amounts of data being collected by terminals, without the support of cloud computing platforms, these tasks must be divided and conquered by a variety of terminals, which can inevitably lead to enormous pressure on those terminals. It is hard to imagine some terminals as small as a watch or a key to complete these tasks. Although some terminals can be equipped with a huge amount of computing power, but are inevitably going to require very expensive hardware. A lot of data are being collected by those terminals, but they cannot be stored in the terminals alone. IDC estimates: in 2015, there will be at least 150 million devices connected to the Internet globally. According to IBM's estimates: in the 5 to 10 years from 2010, the world is expected to have about 100 billion devices connected to the Internet. This exponential growth makes a strong central data

Figure 1. The Internet of Things (IOT) extending the boundaries of the Internet

processing system all the more important. This very central data processing system is what we call cloud computing.

With cloud computing, everything becomes easy. Cloud computing can mobilize all the computing devices within the network to handle the tasks at hand, while the huge data streams can be stored in the cloud, and thus easily resolving large-scale data processing and storage problems. Therefore, the future of the IOT can only rely on cloud computing to realize its ultimate goals. With cloud computing, the vast amounts of data collected by the IOT can be centrally processed within the cloud. The relationship between the IOT and cloud computing can be seen as the relationship between data collection and central processing. Cloud computing is the only economically viable

plan for the implementation of a connected, traceable and managed IOT, where all data processing are moved into the cloud.

In short, the emergence of cloud computing makes the IOT possible: It is the acquisition of data from all walks of life, with all kinds of formats, and the integration, management, storage and mining of the same massive amounts of data within the cloud, that makes the IOT's massive data computation and storage possible. At the same time, the super central processing capacity of cloud computing releases the pressure on the terminal side, which creates a large number of sensor-based simple terminals as value junctions. The IOT, though not created due to the cloud computing era, but its existence depends on cloud computing. Being one of the applications of cloud computing, it can be said that cloud computing is the core for the IOT to realizing its value, and that which gives the IOT wings to fly.

In this regard, then Microsoft China CTO Xianghui Zhang noted on the 2010 China International Internet of Things (sensor network) General Assembly, that cloud computing as information resources in support of the IOT is an optimal structure of capacity. Xianghui Zhang further summarized the three-level development path of the IOT: The first is the physical layer of perception. The second is some data acquisition as a single application. For example, in the healthcare sector, civic health data are collected in order to provide advice and suggestions for citizens, where some basic data on blood pressure and glucose levels are collected, reminding individuals to pay attention in some specific areas of health. Thirdly, and on the basis of the second level, when the amounts of data become massive, data mining technologies can be used for even deeper analysis. For instance, within a particular region, or within a hospital, a large number of the same disease can likely signify some deep underlying problems. This way, a single application can be further developed into field applications of deeper and wider coverage and analysis.

Cloud computing also enables the IOT to be truly intelligent, to help people make better decisions. With the emergence and growth of cloud computing, the IOT has become more clear and realistic. We have no choice but continue to promote the development of cloud computing. In the initial stage, the IOT can take advantage of the private cloud service model, in the deployment of the organization's private cloud. But with the IOT's further development, private clouds cannot meet those demands, and the use public clouds becomes inevitable. Platforms such as Microsoft's public cloud can be used to provide services.

In the recent years, Microsoft is using its technical and commercial strengths to vigorously develop its cloud computing technologies. Microsoft is the only application product developer in the industry, able to provide a complete terminal-to-terminal cloud computing architecture, and it is also the only product developer that has a relatively complete solution framework on the operating model. Microsoft's cloud computing operations in China has been in full operation, with some realistic applications, such as the "Pork Quality and Safety Traceability Regulatory System" for the City of Chengdu. For the IOT, Microsoft is not only able to provide services on the platform layer, but also services on the equipment terminal side. Microsoft's cloud solution services for the IOT are on the platform services layer, while its embedded programs are focused mainly on the device terminals.

Internet of Things' Technical Content is Not Difficult

The technical content of the IOT is not that difficult to realize. The foundation and core of the IOT technology is still the internet technology. The IOT is an expansion and extension of the next generation Internet, built on the cloud computing platform. Although its sensors have different requirements for different objects, but are mostly just ordinary instruments with an added network interface onto the sensors, which do not have a lot of technical content. The IOT's application technology requires far less technological innovations than that of the cloud computing and next-generation networks.

In 2005, the International Telecommunication Union (ITU) has reported that the IOT has four key technologies: radio frequency identification technology, sensor technology, intelligent technology and nanotechnology. The most discussed are the first three technologies. The nanotechnology is often classified into the sensor miniaturization design.

The RFID technology (Radio Frequency Identification) is also known as electronic tags. It is an automatic identification technology that rose to prominence in the 90s of the past century. The RFID technology is non-contact transmission of information using radio frequency signals through space coupling, and the information transmitted are used for identification purposes. Currently, the RFID technology is increasingly sophisticated, such as the single-chip electronic label, multi-electronic tag readers, wireless readable and writable, remote identification of passive electronic tags, and those adapted to the identification of high-speed moving objects. RFID technology and products are becoming a reality, moving toward real applications, and playing important roles in the field of intelligent transportation, retail and electronic identity.

Applications of the IOT are not possible without sensors. Sensors are the nerve endings of the IOT. A sensor itself is an independent technology. As early as 100 years ago, a simple physical sensor has been invented. More complex biological sensors are still in the early stages of development. In a sense, the development of the sensor technology determines the IOT's stage of development. Sensor networking can be done in countless ways: the first generation sensor networks use point-to-point transmission. The second generation sensor networks have gradually acquired some information synthesis and processing capabilities. The new generation of sensor networks is a wireless sensor network. With the breakthrough in technology, as well as the decrease in cost, wireless sensor networks are to become increasingly popular. Finally the design of sensor networks must take into consideration some localized conditions.

Smart technology originally comes from control theory. The original concept of the IOT does not include smart technology. However, with in-depth research and application development, smart technology is gradually being added to its concept, and becoming the core of its applications. In the future of the IOT, more artificial intelligence technologies are to be applied, such as multi-agent systems (MAS) and virtual reality. Actually, smart technology and the IOT complement each other: Intelligent technologies help to

achieve a powerful IOT, which has become the core of IOT applications, and at the same time, the rise of IOT also promotes the continued development of intelligent technologies. Microsoft has always been committed to the research and development of smart technologies, and continues to develop powerful intelligent tools, for instance, the development of business intelligence tools based on data analysis to help companies to have better storage, management and analysis of data. In 2012, Microsoft introduced SQL Server 2012. Recently, Microsoft's global chief strategy officer Craig Mundie, has presented the future functions of Microsoft's intelligent tool Power View, to the students of the Northwestern University, such as, the use of machine learning to find patterns in large data and identify mutual relationships, and the application of which being used in the analysis of data in the field of meteorology and healthcare. MIT Professor Sanchez commented: "The IOT has a fascinating future, but it also requires faster decision making to be based on massive amounts of data. To find and identify real useful information from massive data is indeed a huge challenge. In this regard, there are few companies like Microsoft, who can provide us with more complete answers in many different aspects. "

In order to truly realize all-object connectivity in the IOT, we cannot do without nanotechnology. The application of nanotechnology in the IOT is to miniaturize the design of a variety of sensing devices. It can guarantee, that sensing devices mounted on a variety of objects do not affect the normal operation of the object. For example, the sensors in the human body, not only should not affect the health of the person, nor should they generate any inconvenience and discomfort during our daily activities. The use of nanotechnology means, that the IOT can be applied among objects of increasingly smaller sizes. Nanotechnology is one of the core technologies of the future micro-sensors, which is a type of sensor being most widely used in the IOT. Research in this area has made great progress. For example, a Canadian company located in Waterloo, Terepac, recently released a product called TereTag, that allows almost all objects to be connected to the IOT.

IOT's Real Significance Lies in Its Applications

Since the technologies of the IOT are not difficult to realize, and therefore the applications of the IOT come into high prominence! As the IOT truly realizes the link between the Internet's virtual world and physical world, its applications can reach all walks of human society, touching on every aspect, every corner and every moment of our daily lives.

Intelligent transportation systems based on the IOT, for example, can monitor traffic information of various intersections in real time, and correspondingly regulate changes of traffic lights to ease traffic, and at the same time, useful traffic information can be provided to individuals. Suppose one day one driving to attend an important meeting, and the usual route has a severe traffic jam, the intelligent transportation system based on current traffic conditions can tell the time it is to take with the current route, and provide alternative routes for selection, or recommend the best route.

One example is the food safety system based on the IOT. Food safety concerns are on the high-priority list of people's daily lives. The IOT can play an important role in this regard. Through the establishment of the information security and traceability system on business participants, such as food processing, logistics and sales, we can ensure food safety. If the food being sold does not come from a certified and reliable vendor, when its barcode is scanned by the food safety system, problems are discovered immediately, and consumers are put on alert. If unhealthy additives are being added in the milk processing plant, sensors can immediately detect and alarm the food safety system, and notify the police or the food testing department. Then, intractable food problems in China such as sewage oils being used

for cooking, and poisonous Sanlu milk powders, are going to have no place to hide. Microsoft is bringing visions such as these into the lives of the ordinary people, bringing heaven on earth, to truly serve the public. The cloud computing center in Chengdu has realized "Pork Quality and Safety Traceability Regulatory System," with Microsoft's cloud computing technology, to achieve effective data tracking and real-time regulatory enforcement, in order to quality the quality and safety of pork. By providing their ticket information, people can easily trace to the origin, the handling route and examine its inspection certifications. With Microsoft's cloud computing, the people of Chengdu are beginning to enjoy the benefits of this technological improvement. It not only helps to convince the local governments to promote the development of the IT industry, and stimulates the local economy, and more importantly, it can also help to improve people's livelihood, making possible better government supervision, and improve the local food safety systems, so the public can eat pork three meals a day without any worries.

Another example is the personal safety system based on the IOT. Now more parents are worried about the safety of their children, with the fear of children being abducted by traffickers. A personal security system based on the IOT can help these parents. Tiny sensors placed in the body of a child can transmit the child's vital data to the parents in real-time, such as location, body temperature, current state (sleeping or doing sports). If the child has a fever, happens to be in an abnormal state, or a non-secure location, the system can immediately alert the parents or the police. The police can act in a timely manner based on these important information provided about the child.

The most classic case of an IOT application is the collision of U.S. Airways Flight 1549 with birds on January 15, 2009:

After the incident, the 57-year-old captain remained calm, and directed the aircraft to make a forced landing on the Hudson River in New York City. With all its 146 passengers and the five-member crew safe, this was the famous Hudson River miracle. In fact, it was more interesting to examine the way the U.S. government dealt with this incident behind the scenes. Six minutes after takeoff, there were bird strikes, and two engines failed. The flight crew immediately reported to the control tower; the control tower immediately briefed the EANS (emergency notification system), the Emergency Management Office of the United States and police centers and other departments, all at once. In Washington, U.S. Aviation Joint Management Committee also immediately received this information, and immediately made contacts with the military through another network, the DEM (Homeland sudden information communication network). At the same time, IOOS (Integrated Coastal concept sensing system), being used to monitor the hydrological conditions on the nation's waters, immediately transferred water information to the U.S. Coast Guard and maritime command center. Police and rescue workers with a large number of emergency supplies rushed to the scene. Because the aircraft had a full load of fuel, it was necessary to prepare for fuel leaks polluting the river. At this point, a large number of sensors being long since installed on the Hudson River began to showcase their power. In fact, information collection devices had been installed even in fish. With all these information being brought together, the emergency personnel in the command center, through the analysis of large amounts of data, had produced a visual model for decision making. This entire process lasted only a fraction of the hour.

From this, we must thank the crew for staying calm, but more so the powerful IOT and data analysis systems, that through multi-sectorial and multi-system synergy, to ensure the most important information, also the timely and accurate instructions, being delivered to the aircraft, and thus co-creating the "Hudson River miracle."

From exciting pictures such as these, it is not difficult to imagine the emergence of the IOT has brought about great changes to our lives! Some applications of the IOT can be classified into smart cities, smart homes, intelligent agriculture, intelligent judiciary systems, smart campuses, and smart logistics. In fact, applications of the IOT are far from being limited to these areas. It is to touch every aspect of our lives, such as healthcare, education, economy, military, entertainment and etc. It can be said, as long as there are "things" in existence, the tentacles of the IOT can be extended to get it connected with the human information system at large. The IOT is to become an indispensable partner to humans, and become the cornerstone of a harmonious society.

The Biggest Problem of the IOT is Security

Although we depicted a bright future of the IOT, it is still facing a number of problems and challenges. Basically, all the problems facing the IOT now have also been faced by the Internet in the past and present, but for the IOT these problems are to have more serious consequences.

Security is the biggest problem facing the IOT (Wang, 2009). Microsoft's senior vice president Yaqin Zhang has pointed out that the Internet's problems are the loss of information, the most serious being the loss and theft of important information. Therefore many public safety problems may occur, and we can alleviate these problems by data encryption and information backup, in order to reduce or even avoid loss. The IOT deals with the physical world, whether it is intelligent transportation, smart grid, smart medical or bridge inspection and disaster monitoring. The IOT must be connected with a variety of infrastructures, which brings the present security threats in the information world to the physical world. These problems may cause loss of life and property. Some IOT applications not only have perception functions, but also control functions. When control functions are present, in the event of an accident, the danger can be even greater. In some ways, this is somewhat similar to the relationship between nuclear power and the human society: nuclear power has brought a lot of convenience to our lives, security pitfalls and negligence in the event of failure can lead to disastrous consequences. One example would be the flood and spillway control intelligent system based on the IOT: the system can adjust water levels according to specific intelligence, but such a system in the event of failure or terrorist control, can endanger people's lives, property and even cause a great deal of national security threats. Another example is the intelligent transportation system based on the IOT, in the event of accidents, it may not only cause severe traffic congestions, but can also cause some serious or even life-threatening scenarios.

Wherever data exist, it is necessary to consider privacy issues. From the very first days of the Internet, we have been debating about its privacy issues. The IOT is also facing the same problems relating to privacy. It can be said that in terms of personal privacy, the IOT is facing a broader and more specific range of similar issues as that of the Internet. It is mainly because of the IOT is in contact to all aspects of our lives, anything we may come to touch. This aspect of the IOT brings a lot of convenience, but on the other hand, means that there is the risk of personal information leakage. In smart homes, for example, valuable personal possessions are connected to the IOT, and can be stolen by hackers. In addition, we can use data mining to extract useful information from the IOT's massive data, but users involved may not realize, or even have consented to the fact that their personal information are being used for data mining and analysis purposes. These questions in regard to privacy are not caused by the IOT alone, webcams being deployed all over cities similar to that being used by Google Street View, are also arousing great controversy on privacy issues. The development of the IOT must face up and resolve these problems.

There are two ways to solve the IOT's security and privacy issues: the first is the use of technology, such as strengthening the safety and security within the IOT, by building a firewall to prevent hacker attacks and the theft of public and private information. Another is through legal means, by establishing and perfecting the IOT's safety and privacy laws. By the simultaneous application of these two solutions, we can then ensure that the IOT is only for facilitating people's lives, at the same time effectively protect people's safety and privacy, so as to truly benefit the mankind.

The IOT is still in the preliminary stage of development. Any new products of the developmental process are expected to encounter some initial difficulties, twists and turns in fortune, which should not cause it to be given up for dead. Of course, we also must not ignore the problems being encountered. To further develop the IOT, we must address these upcoming problems head on. For the IOT projects that are closely related to the people's lives and property, decisions making must be done with much gravity and care, and only mature technologies and products should be put into full operation. In the development of the IOT, we must be realistic in terms of expectations, pay attention to the problems faced, until reliable solutions are found.

Consequences

Every wave of the information industry development brings tremendous changes to people's lives, gives birth to new industries, and leads the development of a large number of related industries. New technological revolution not only brings us improved living standards and economic prosperity, but also greatly liberates people's thinking, so that they can enjoy unprecedented freedom and convenience. Such is the case for the emergence of computers and the Internet. There is no doubt that the development of cloud computing and the Internet of Things are going to bring such changes and much opportunity.

CONCLUSIONS AND LOOKING TO THE FUTURE

Looking to the future, because the information industry has provided the basic tools to serve the human social life and various sectors of the national economy, cloud computing is going to bring about great changes to the national economies and the general society as a whole, including people's lifestyles, and even bring about new productivity and thinking paradigms.

The cloud era IT services can be categorized into three themes, information centers, communication networks and intelligent terminals. With the information hub in the center, its fundamental task is to construct the cloud storage and computing systems, and to complete the cloud-era tasks of ultra-large-scale and ultra-high complexity. Communication networks, on the other hand, are the pipelines that directly connect cloud services to their users, which are going to determine the depth and breadth of the cloud-era services. Intelligent terminals, the window of interaction between information centers and the physical world, are to bear the mission of information gathering, human-computer interaction and information transfer.

The main development paths of the IT industry have been dominated by two modes of thinking, the market-oriented and the goal-oriented thinking. Based on the technology and business scenarios at hand, and at the same time observing the surrounding details, we can predict the possible near-future direction of business, this is the so-called market-orientation, or incremental-orientation. Market orientation can help us improving the existing systems and polishing up a rough product, but this thinking mode cannot break the shackles of the traditional framework. In the era of change, market-orientation is often blinded by tradition, when applied in the general direction. If we can let go of the traditional bondage, free ourselves to embrace the imaginations of the future, lock-on to the next targets and then stepping back to find paths and methods to realizing that future, we call this goal-oriented approach with future goals to guide today's practice. Like sailing on the ocean with the Big Dipper and the compass, goal-oriented changes are often cradles for revolutionary ideas and innovations.

Throughout the history of computer and network development, its essence is the game of balance between computing, storage and network. If we string together the key advancements in this developmental process, then the evolutionary trajectory of the modern IT industry becomes clearly visible. Great many choices of the past have been reasonable due to the relative lack of resources. However, today's and the future's resource environments are experiencing tremendous changes. In this new environment, if we go back to those critical nodes of history to re-examine the original decisions, and make appropriate adjustments in line with the direction of the new era, we are to gain new spaces for creativity and development in leaps and bounds. In fact, some short-sighted choices that we have made in the resource-poor era, although expedient at the time, are going to result in long-term developmental bottlenecks. A series of superficial palliatives responses and remedial actions, which we have been doing at the moment, are only going to lead to paralysis of innovation in the near future. The courage to unfetter ourselves from this reality, and focus on the future, then stepping back, remake some important choices, thus creating new space for development, this is the essence for revolutionary innovation, and the original philosophy for leap forward development!

Cloud computing is a revolution; revolution represents qualitative leaps, rather than quantitative additions and subtractions. The future cloud-era information technology is not going to be a simple extension of the existing information technology. In order to win the key technologies of the future, one must have a thorough understanding of the existing global industries, overcome some of the mentality of the existing IT and technical ideas, and use epoch-making theory to guide epoch-making practices.

REFERENCES

Chandler, A. D. (1977). *The visible hand: The managerial revolution in America business*. Boston: Harvard University Press.

Chandler, A. D., & Cortada, J. (2000). *A nation transformed by information: How information has shaped the United States from colonial times to the present*. Oxford, UK: Oxford University Press.

China Ministry of Industry and Information. (2012). *Internet of things – 12th five-year development plan*. Retrieved from http://www.gov.cn/zwgk/2012-02/14/content_2065999.htm

Gao, H., & Shen, Y. (n.d.). *The cloud era information technology – A new world of computers and networks under resource rich conditions*. Peking, China: Peking University Press.

Gilder, G. (2002). *Telecosm: The world after bandwidth abundance*. New York: Touchstone.

Haykin, S. (1999). *Neural network: A comprehensive foundation* (2nd ed.). Upper Saddle River, NJ: Prentice Hall.

Miller, M. (2009). *Cloud computing: Web-based applications that change the way you work and collaborate online*. New York: Que Publishing.

Shannon, C. (1949). *A mathematical theory of communication*. Urbana-Champaign, IL: University of Illinois Press.

von Neumann, J. (1958). *The computer and the brain* (2nd ed.). New Haven, CT: Yale University Press.

Yang, J. (2011). *From the Turing machine to von Neumann machines*. New York: Academic Press.

Yu-Gang, W. (2009). *Enjoy the blessings of the internet of things, but we do have privacy?* Retrieved from http://news.xinhuanet.com/mrdx/2009-06/21/content_11575947.html

Chapter 3
Cloud Infrastructure:
Virtualization

Yushi Shen
Microsoft Corporation, USA

Ling Wu
EMC² Corporation, USA

Yale Li
Microsoft Corporation, USA

Shaofeng Liu
Microsoft Corporation, USA

Qian Wen
Endronic Corp, USA

ABSTRACT

This chapter focuses on the different aspects of cloud computing virtualization. It introduces the fundamental concepts of computer virtualization, storage virtualization, network virtualization, and application virtualization. Virtualization techniques, infrastructure, components, and implementation are described in detail.

VIRTUALIZATION OVERVIEW

What is virtualization? According to Wikipedia, virtualization is the creation of a virtual version of something, such as a hardware platform, operation system, storage devices or network resources. (Wikipedia – Virtualization)

A virtual computer is a logical representation of a computer in software. By decoupling the physical hardware from the operating system, virtualization provides more operational flexibility, and increases the utilization rate of the underlying physical hardware.

Virtualization overcomes the limitations of physical resources, and enables a single physical resource such as server, desktop, storage array or network switch to function as multiple resources, or multiple resources to function as a single resource. It uses the abstraction layer to hide the physical nature of the resources from the users.

When people talk about virtualization, they usually imply system virtualization, one computer appearing to be multiple computers (virtual machine). Each virtual machine has its own CPU, memory, network interface, storage disk and operating system. To the user, it looks like these virtual

DOI: 10.4018/978-1-4666-4801-2.ch003

machines are separate computers with their own network identity, applications, and user security. Therefore, virtualization is a technique for hiding the physical characteristics of the computing resources, in a way other systems, applications or end users can interact with those resources.

VIRTUALIZATION PROCESSES

Virtualization is achieved through three key processes: Encapsulation, Isolation and Partitioning.

- Encapsulation is to take a virtual machine, and turn it into a set of VDM files that can easily be copied, moved and backed up. Virtualized servers are encapsulated in storage, allowing the servers and applications to be moved, migrated or deployed.
- Isolation is to hide one virtual machine from another, running on the same hardware platform. So that when one virtual machine crashes, the other virtual machines on the same host remains unaffected.
- Partitioning is to divide the physical resources on a server, so that each virtual machine can access the resources it needs. This can increase server utilization and lower the operation costs.

Virtualization Types

Virtualization allows the sharing of resources between applications, clients and systems. The concept of virtualization includes virtualizations at different hardware resource levels:

- **Server Virtualization:** Enables a single physical server to operate as multiple servers, and in the multiple virtual environments. (Rouse, 2009)
- **Network Virtualization:** Combines the network resources and functionalities, of both hardware and software, into a single and centrally administered virtual network. Network virtualization allows the segmentation and isolation of network entities. (Lippis III, 2007)
- **Storage Virtualization:** Groups multiple network storage devices into a single virtual storage device, by virtual provisioning, block storage virtualization, file virtualization, virtual storage area networks and logical storage area networks (Rouse, 2006):
- **Virtual Provisioning:** Allocates storage capacity from a centralized pool of disks, according to application requirements. Virtual provisioning improves storage utilization by enabling storage capacities to be allocated on demand;
- **Block storage Virtualization:** Enables the user to move data while keeping applications online. Block storage virtualization optimizes storage resources and enhances performance, availability and data protection;
- **File Virtualization:** Enables the movement of unstructured data without disrupting the application;
- **Virtual Storage Network (VSAN) or Logical Storage Area Network (LSAN):** SAN is used to attach storage devices to servers. VSAN is a virtual SAN, and LSAN is a logical SAN. VSANs are a collection of ports from the switch, while LSANs can span multiple physical fabrics, and allow specific devices on the networks to get connected, and start communicating.

(EMC[2] Corporation, Virtualized data center and cloud infrastructure)

Advantages of Virtualization

Virtualization can help businesses improve on performance and profitability, while reducing costs. Through hardware consolidation and network resource sharing, virtualization can optimize the IT infrastructure, reduce costs of hardware, software, data center space and power consumption. Virtualization also enables fast resource provisioning, dynamic workload balancing, and provides a flexible and efficient infrastructure, that can increase the scalability and flexibility of a business.

Additionally, virtualization facilitates and enables Disaster Recovery (DR). When server data is encapsulated into a single virtual machine file, replication is much easier. DR costs can be greatly reduced or eliminated. Without virtualization, dozens of idle servers at the DR sites would be necessary to ensure the same level of DR protection. By improving on the DR solution, virtualization can reduce downtime, ensure business availability and continuity.

Virtualization provides a miraculous shield to application vulnerabilities, and improves on information security. Virtualized servers make it easier to isolate applications, and therefore provide faster disaster recovery solutions. Virtualized networks can offer enhanced security protection for sensitive data, by restricting access to specific VLAN.

SERVER VIRTUALIZATION

Overview

Server virtualization is the masking or abstraction of physical computing hardware resources from the server users: this includes the network identity of the physical server, processors, and operating systems, thus enabling multiple operating systems to run concurrently on a single physical machine. Instead of a single operating system running on a single piece of hardware, the physical server hardware can be masked and abstracted, such that multiple operating systems can run on top of the resulting abstracted hardware. Most of the time, neither the virtual machine nor the computer users need to know that the physical server has been virtualized; all appearances indicate that they are running on a physical server platform.

The virtualization layer, sitting in between the physical hardware and the operating system, is called the hypervisor. The hypervisor provides standard resources such as CPU, memory and network to all virtual machines. The hypervisor runs on a scalable set of hardware, and is portable.

The total utilization of the physical machine, over the course of its service life, tends to be fairly low. A data center is composed of many standard servers. Large servers can have 256GB RAM, 4 cores, each running at 3 GHz. Over the life span, its resource utilization rate might be only 15% or 20% of the full use cycle. There may be peak times, at 80% or 90% utilization of CPU or memory. But most of the time, the overall utilization is very limited. By virtualization, we are able to make better use of the physical hardware, by running multiple operating systems on the hypervisor, thus balancing the load. If one virtual machine needs more memory, and the other virtual machine only needs more CPU power, resources can be allocated accordingly.

Server virtualization ensures more flexible and less downtime in a data center. Without server virtualization, a physical machine is non-portable, nor can the operating system be moved, imaged and laid out among different pieces of hardware. Without its help, one cannot make an image of a physical Dell server, and install this image on an HP server and reboot. But all that can be done on the virtual machine. Since the virtual machines are highly scalable, they can be moved from hypervisor to hypervisor. A virtual machine on the Dell server can be copied and moved to an HP server, giving us a lot of added flexibility. Running on a physical server in a traditional data center, a single application failure could take down the entire operating system, and cause all other applications to fail as well. However with virtualization, individual applications can be isolated, by having each application running on a single virtual machine. If one application fails, it only affects the virtual server that runs this application, and no other application is to be impacted. A cluster, configured with auto failover, can be set up on the physical machine, that even if the physical machine that runs multiple virtual machines has failed all together, the virtual machines can be failed over to other physical machines immediately. (EMC[2] Corporation, Cloud computing foundations)

Hypervisor

The hypervisor is a software that does server virtualization. It enables multiple operating systems to run concurrently on a physical host computer, and to interact directly with the physical resources of the host computer. Hypervisor provides the attributes for the physical server that lies underneath the virtualized machines, running different operating systems. Hypervisor is the primary component of virtualization that enables computer system to partition hardware resources, such as CPU and memory, into virtualized resources.

Hypervisor has two components: the kernel and the virtual machine manager. The kernel works as the operating system, handling such tasks as process creation, file system management,

resources scheduling, IO stack etc. The virtual machine monitor (VMM), which resides below the operating system layer, is responsible for handling and sending the virtual machines' requests, also executing commands. When a virtual machine is created, resources such CPU, memory and I/O devices are assigned to the virtual machine. To execute processes, these resources need to be managed according to a time schedule on the physical machine. The VMM handles these requests and communications from the virtual level down to the physical level. The VMM's job also includes allocating and managing the system processor, memory, IO devices and other hardware resources that correspond to each individual virtual machine. When a virtual machine starts running, the controls are transferred to the VMM.

There are chiefly two kinds of Hypervisor: the bare-metal hypervisor and the hosted hypervisor.

- For the bare-Metal hypervisor, the hypervisor runs directly on the hardware. The Hypervisor itself functions as an operat-

Figure 1. Bare-Metal Hypervisor
(EMC[2] Corporation - Virtualized data center and cloud infrastructure)

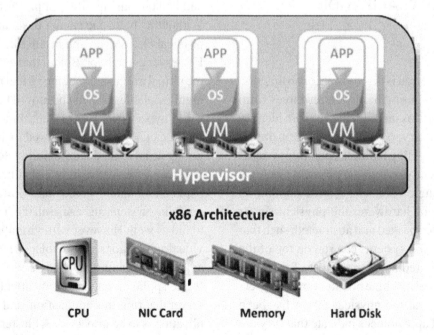

ing system, resides on ring0 processor, and executes commands against the hardware. This type of hypervisor requires certified hardware, so that appropriate drivers are available to communicate with the hardware. Since the bare-metal hypervisor is directly installed on the X86 based hardware, it could access the hardware resources more efficiently, and is scalable. When databases or ERP applications are being deployed in a production environment, the bare-metal hypervisor is most likely to be used, because it has much less overhead, and more hardware resources can be delicate to the application that runs on the virtual machine. The bare-metal hypervisor is the most predominant hypervisor, being used in the virtualized data centers. It is also the direction of the cloud virtualization.

- The hosted hypervisor is a hypervisor that runs inside the operating system. It is installed and run as an application on top of an operating system. Since it is running on top of an operating system, it supports a broader range of hardware configurations. One may have the Windows OS or Linux installed on the host machine, then VMware workstation or Microsoft Hyper-V can be installed and run as an application within the operating system environment. Instead of the hypervisor being at the operating system level, it is another application, and other applications can be running within the hypervisor application.

The hosted hypervisor focuses on the development process. For a developer using a windows OS machine, but needs to have the Linux environment to develop an application, Linux can be installed in the virtual machine and development done on the same laptop, while other applications continue to run in the Windows environment.

Types of Computer Virtualization

The X86 CPU architecture offers four levels of privilege known as ring0, 1, 2 and 3. In the traditional X86 architecture, operating system kernels expect direct CPU access running in Ring 0, which is the most privileged level. With virtualization, the virtual machine monitor can sit on Ring 0, and the guest operating systems sit on top of the VMM, so that the VMM can interact with physical resources and the guest operating systems.

In Brief, virtualization acts as an operating system. The operating system sits on the highest CPU level, which is ring0. Applications typically do not interact with hardware directly; they usually interact with the operating system for recourse and command executions. The user applications typically run in ring 3 with less privilege. So the challenge for virtualization is that the hypervisor needs to control the lower levels of privilege. The virtualization technique enables the hypervisor to sit on the lowest level of the processor, in order to interact with the physical hardware, and mask the operating system from having to see itself.

In full virtualization, the VMM sits below the operating system in Ring 0, emulates the underlying physical resources, and presents them to the guest operating system. The guest operating system is expected to sit in ring 0, the virtualization technique makes it believe that it is actually sitting in the higher ring with less privileges to the processor architecture. The guest operating system on the virtual machine is unaware that it is being virtualized. The host operating system might think that it is sitting on the lowest Ring 0 level of the processor architecture, but in reality it is actually sitting on the top of the hypervisor. The hypervisor can completely decouple the guest operating system from the underlying hardware.

All the commands are executed at the hypervisor level. The kernel is doing the interaction with the physical hardware, while the VMM is passing

Figure 2. Hosted Hypervisor
(EMC² Corporation - Virtualized data center and cloud infrastructure)

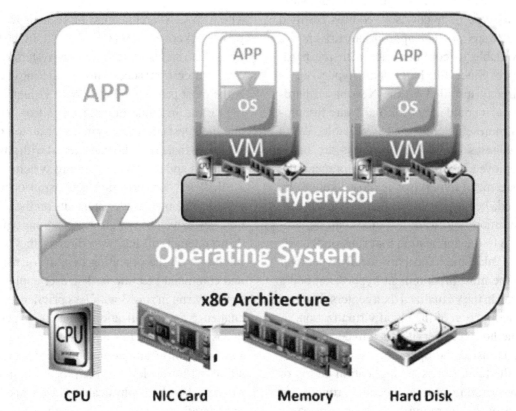

the guest operating system, doing the binary translation of the commands through hypervisor down to the physical hardware that lies underneath. All the commands, such as handling, timer controls, IOs, are executed at the hypervisor level, and the virtual machine is communicating through the virtual machine manager.

In full virtualization, if the console is opened up before powering up the virtual machine, the virtual machine BIOS setting is to come up. VMware ESX, ESXI and Microsoft Hyper-V that runs in the server core environment are some examples. Please be aware that the Microsoft Hyper-V can be run as an application within the windows environment. In a special Windows Server Core installation, which installs the most basic components, the Hyper-V server role can be installed, which distinguishes the operating system to be a

virtual machine itself, and layers the hypervisor underneath it. This installation makes Windows Hyper-V similar to the infrastructure layer as ESX in VMware. VMware and Microsoft are market leaders in the full virtualization technologies.

Para-virtualization is also called the OS assisted virtualization. In Para-virtualization, the operating system is aware of itself being virtualized. The guest operating system sits in Ring 0 with the Hypervisor beneath it. Rather than the hypervisor sitting on that level and doing all the translation for the virtual machine monitor, the Para-virtualization guest operating system sits there and interact directly with the hypervisor. Para-virtualization product examples are the open source Xen hypervisor and VMware Linux.

Hardware assisted virtualization introduces virtualization in the X86 processor architecture, and uses hypervisor-aware CPU to provide assistance to the hypervisor. With hardware assisted virtualization, the operating system could directly access the physical resources. It allows a fully virtual operating system to run in Ring 0, which gives the operating system direct access to the system resources without the control from the Virtual Machine Monitor. In 2006, Intel and AMD have released the first generation hardware assisted features, and have announced future development roadmaps, which includes hardware support for memory virtualization, as well as for I/O devices. The Intel Virtualization Technology (VT) and AMD virtualization (AMD V) both target privileged instructions with a new CPU execution mode feature, allowing the Virtual Machine Monitor to run in a new root mode below ring 0. They are building the chip set that increases CPU overhead, and allows the virtualization of the X86 instruction sets, while decreasing the hypervisor overhead. (EMC² Corporation - Cloud infrastructure and services.)

The graph below describes the Ring level for all three types of virtualizations:

Virtual Machine

Virtual Machine Files

A virtual machine is made of a set of files that reside in the underlying hypervisor file system. A virtual machine could be looked at from two different perspectives. From the user's perspective, a virtual machine is a generic set of hardware that runs an operating system and user applications. Like a physical machine, it has the same component as the physical machine, such as the CPU, memory, hard disk, network interface cards and other IO devices. From a hypervisor perspective, which manages and runs a virtual machine, a virtual machine is a set of files that include configuration files, virtual disk files, virtual BIOS files, virtual machine swap file and a log file.

The virtual machine configuration file stores the details of virtual machine configuration information, such as the virtual machine name, guest operating system, the number and types of virtual disks, the number of CPUs and the size of memory, the type of network adaptors and the associated MAC addresses, SCSI controller types and disk types.

The virtual disk file stores the contents in the disk drive belonging the virtual machine, and sits on the hypervisor file system. To the virtual machine, the virtual disk file appears and works as a physical disk drive. A virtual machine could have multiple virtual disk files, each representing a single disk.

Virtual BIOS files store the virtual machine's BIOS information. The virtual machine swap file is the paging file for the virtual machine, which backs up the virtual machine's RAM contents. This file is present only when the virtual machine is running. If we have allocated certain amount of memory and reserved the memory, the swap file is to show this difference.

The log file records virtual machine activities, such as the time the virtual machine got started, its activities and etc. It helps in troubleshooting when there is an application failure or some server problems.

File Systems in the Virtual Environment

The hypervisor has a file system. The virtual machine file system (VMFS) is a clustered file system that stores virtual machine files. Cluster SANS, internal direct attached storage, and external storage are presented to the hypervisor as virtual disks, formatted and attached to the server. The virtual disks are stored as files on a VMFS. VMFS allows multiple virtual machines to concurrently read and write data from the same storage device. The virtual machine file system is deployed on the FC and iSCSI storage, apart from local storages. Because we have the underlining cluster

Figure 3. Three type of server virtualization
(VMWare, Inc., 2007)

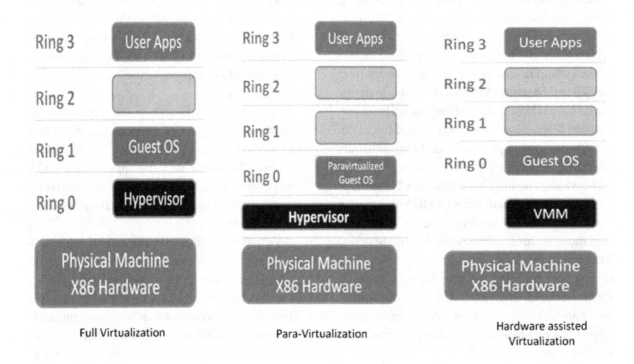

file system, when one virtual machine crashes, we can quickly deploy another VM.

The Network File System (NFS) is the data store for enabling virtual machine file storage on remote file servers (NAS device). These files could be accessed through an IP network. The network file system client is built into the hypervisor, and uses the Network File System protocol to communicate with the NAS device.

Virtual Machine Hardware

A virtual machine has the following virtual components:

- **Virtual CPU (vCPU):** A virtual machine can be assigned one or more vCPUs when it is created. And the number of vCPUs can be changed based on requirements;

- **Virtual RAM (vRAM):** Virtual RAM is the amount of memory allocated to the virtual machine. The size of the memory can be changed based on requirements;

- **Virtual Disk:** A virtual disk stores the virtual machine operating system, user applications and other program data;

- **Virtual NIC (vNIC):** It provides connectivity between virtual machines on the same computer system, virtual machines on different computer systems, and in between the virtual and physical machines;

- **Virtual SCSI Controller:** A virtual machine uses virtual SCSI controller to access virtual disks;

- **Virtual DVD/CD Rom:** Enables the mapping of the virtual machine drive onto either the physical drive, or onto the image iso file in the disk storage;

- **Virtual USB Controllers:** Enables a virtual machine to connect to the physical USB controller, and to access the USB devices being connected.

Virtual Machine Console

A virtual machine console provides the mouse, keyboard and screen functionalities. A virtual machine console is used to install an operating system, allow access to the BIOs of the virtual machine, offer the ability to power on/off the virtual machine, or reset it. It is typically used for virtual hardware configuration and troubleshooting issues.

Converting the Physical Machine to Virtual Machines

Physical to virtual machine (P2V) conversion is a process, where physical machines are converted into virtual machines (VMs). During the physical to virtual machine conversion, the converter clones data on the hard disk of the source machine, and transfers that data to the targeted virtual disk. The clone disk is an exact copy of the physical disk at the source. After cloning, system reconfiguration is performed on the destination virtual machine. The IP address and computer name need to be changed, device drivers installed, and then the VM is boot enabled.

The P2V converter includes three key components:

- The converter server is an application that is loaded on a separate physical machine. It is responsible for controlling conversion processes when the source machine is running its OS, i.e., a hot mode. During the conversion, the converter server pushes and installs a converter agent onto the source physical machine;

- The converter agent is installed on the physical machine. It is responsible for performing the physical machine to virtual machine transition, and is used in hot mode only;
- The converter boot CD is a bootable CD containing its operating system and the converter application. It is used to perform conversion when the source machine is not running its operating system, i.e., a cold mode.

Hot conversion and cold conversion can be used to migrate physical machines to virtual machines. Hot conversion is to convert the source physical machine to a virtual machine, while it is running its operating system, so the virtual machine is not an exact copy of the source physical machine. After the conversion, the destination virtual machine is synchronized with the source machine. The IP address and the destination virtual machine's name need to be changed, if both machines exist on the same network.

The process of the hot conversion is that the converter server installs the converter agent on the source machine, and the agent takes a snapshot of the source volume. The converter server creates a virtual machine on the destination machine. The agent uses the snapshot to clone the physical disk of the source machine to the virtual disk of the destination virtual machine. After cloning, the agent synchronizes the data and installs the required drivers, lets the operating system boot from a virtual machine, and customizes the virtual machine by changing the IP address and machine name.

Cold conversion is to convert the source physical machine to virtual machine, while it is not running the operating system, or when it is offline. During the cold conversion, the source machine is rebooted using a converter boot CD that has its own operating system and converter applications. The virtual machine is exactly the same as the source machine, because no changes have occurred during the conversion.

The cold conversion of a physical machine to virtual machine is to boot the source machine from the converter boot CD, and use the converter software to define conversion parameters. The converter application creates a new virtual machine, and on the destination physical machine, copies volumes from source machine to the destination machine, installs device drivers and customizes the virtual machine, by changing the IP address and machine name etc.

The P2V conversion enables the user to quickly set up a new virtual machine, and migrate legacy machines to a new hardware, without reinstalling the operating system, application or device drivers, and can also perform migrations across heterogeneous hardware. The P2V conversion does have some limitations. During the conversion, some hardware-dependent drivers and the mapped drive letters may not be preserved.

Since the target and source virtual machines have the same identities, if the configuration is not changed, running both machines on the same network might result in conflict. Even if the application functions correctly on the virtual machine after conversion, it might still have issues if they depend on specific characteristics of the underlying hardware, such as the serial number or the device manufacturer.

Computer Virtualization Benefits

Server virtualization benefits include:

- On the virtualization layer, the hypervisor takes care of the translation of the physical hardware. This hardware independence allows mobility of the profile between servers. The virtualized hardware enables decoupling of physical attributes, such as network identity, worldwide name, UID, firmware and etc., from the physical machine. This gives the freedom to move a virtual machine from one physical machine to another, without making any changes to the configurations, device drivers, operating system or applications;

- A virtual machine is a set of files that contain a complete configuration of virtual hardware resources, an operating system and applications. Encapsulation makes it portable and easy to manage. If you need to move one virtual machine from one location to another, you can simply copy and move the set of files to the new host server and then restart, and you can have exactly the same virtual machine running on the new location. Be able to take the virtual machine and move it, without relying on the hardware underneath. We can have two completely different sets of hardware, as long as they are running the same hypervisor, and we can move virtual machines between them;

- It improves performance and reduces application downtime. Server virtualization enables multipathing for effective and dynamic load balancing, which helps to better utilize available paths, automatic path failover, and reduce traffic overhead. An individual application could be isolated from crashing the other applications, because they are separated on the individual virtual machines. Although virtual machines that run on the same host server shares the physical resources of a physical machine, they remain completely isolated from others. When one virtual machine crashes, it would not affect the other virtual machines running on the same host server, and the applications running on the other virtual machines remain unaffected. When a server failure occurs, the server's physical attributes can be moved to a standby server, then the VM can be restarted, and data access continues;

- It increases resource utilization and reduces operations costs:
  - **Server Consolidation:** Since server virtualization allows running multiple virtual machines on a single physical piece of hardware, the requirements for physical servers can be reduced to save cost;
  - **Simple Provisioning:** Server virtualization allows more automation and simpler LUN provisioning to reduce operational costs;
  - **Reduced Direct Costs:** With server virtualization, many direct costs can be reduced. Office or data center space, whether leased or owned for physical machines, power and cooling costs, hardware including servers, switches, HBA cards and Fiber Channel cables, and annual maintenance costs can all be greatly reduced. CPU slicing, memory management techniques, or even the over-commitment of the amount of physical resources can all be assigned to the virtual environment.

STORAGE VIRTUALIZATION

Overview

Storage virtualization is the process of presenting a logical view of the physical storage elements to the host computer system. The logical storage appears as physical storage, directly connected to the host computer system. From a central console, the storage administrator can consolidate a whole pool of physical storage devices from multiple network storage devices, into what seems to be a single storage device. Storage virtualization techniques can be applied to different levels of a storage area network. Storage virtualization enables great flexibility in the utilization of the data center storage resources. (De Luca, 2010)

It is very common to see larger and more complex storage implementations in the classic data center. The heterogeneous nature of storage infrastructures adds complexity to the effective management and utilization of storage resources. Storage virtualization performs logical to physical storage mapping, which abstracts the physical storage devices ID, and creates a storage pool with virtual volumes, and which is then assigned to the computer system. Storage components such as disks, controllers and storage networks are pooled in a logical way, which can remove the physical barriers and maximize the full potential of these resources, and while the complexity of managing all these devices is being hidden from the user. To the host, they are actual storage devices, where the virtual machine does not distinguish the differences between the physical and virtual storage devices. The process of accessing the virtual volumes are the same as to the physical storage devices. The virtualized storage simplifies the infrastructure, and accommodates the increasing business and technology changes, pooling and sharing resources could maximize the utilization of IT resources and capacities, without any regard to physical limits.

Storage virtualization can be implemented at three infrastructure layers: server layer, network layer, and storage layers. The implementation involves everything from the operating system device file, to host bus adapter, storage network and storage arrays. At the host level, storage virtualization can be the volume management. Block-level or file-level virtualization happens at the network layer. Virtual provisioning and array HBA occur at the storage level.

Types of Storage Virtualization

Network Based Virtualization

What is network based virtualization? Network based storage virtualization is virtualized storage resources at the network layer. It provides a logical view of physical storage resources to the

Figure 4. Virtualized storage infrastructure in a virtual data center
(EMC² Corporation - Virtualized Data Center and Cloud Infrastructure.)

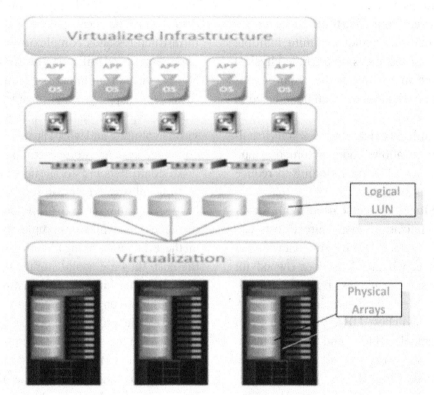

computer system. When an IO request is sent from the computer system, it is redirected through the virtualization layer, and at the network layer, to the mapped physical storage. Network based virtualization enables the user to pool storage arrays from different vendors, and manage this pool from a single management interface, which greatly simplifies the multi-vendor storage system management. It can also perform non-disruptive data migration, between different arrays from the pool.

For the block level storage virtualization, it creates an abstraction layer between the physical arrays and the virtual LUN. Instead of being directed to the LUNs on each individual storage arrays, the computer systems are directed to the virtual volumes on the virtual machine at the network. The virtual machine performs mapping between the virtual volumes and the LUNs on the arrays. Several LUNs from one or more arrays can be combined into a single virtual volume, which is then presented to the server as one LUN. A large LUN from an array can be sliced into smaller virtual volumes, and presented to the server. The block level storage virtualization supports storage dynamic increases, and consolidates heterogeneous storage arrays and transparent storage volume access.

Arrays may be virtualized on the block level or file level. Once an array is virtualized, it is presented as a logical unit to the host that comprises of slices of physical disks. Block level storage and file level storage are virtualized at the network layer, and provides an abstract view of physical storage resources. When an IO request is sent from the host server, it is directed through the network virtualization layer to the mapped physical storage. Block level virtualization is implemented at the SAN environment, while file level virtualization is at the NAS environment.

- **Block Level Storage Virtualization:** In a SAN environment, block level storage virtualization provides a translation layer between the host servers and the storage arrays. In a traditional SAN environment, the physical drive must be translated into a logical unit (LUN) for the operating system to read or write files. The storage network also needs to partition the physical disc into logical entities for host servers to access. A LUN is a logical unit that converts raw physical disc space into logical entities for the host to access. LUNs are often referred as logical volumes on each individual storage arrays, and are mapped to the host server. In the virtual storage configuration, multiple independent storage arrays are tied together and presented to the host as a single storage device. Instead of being directed to the LUNs on each individual storage arrays, the hosts are directed to the virtualized LUNs on the visualization device. The virtualization device translates between the virtual LUNs and the physical LUNs, on each individual array, regardless of the arrays' different vendors. Block level storage virtualization includes two types (Tate, 2003):
  - **Out-of-Band:** data traffic is separated from the control management flow, since data and metadata are separated into different places. Data traffic is first directed to the virtual devices, then physical devices, while the control and management traffic are sent along a different path to the management node. The out of band solution requires the host-based agent for splitting the out-of-band information from the data and send it to the management node. The virtualization layer does not impact I/O traffic, since the redirection of I/O's from file system requests to physical storage is happening somewhere outside the data path, either on the host or the storage array. In this solution, the host is to focus on the transfer of data to and from storage, while metadata and control information are processed separately. This type of solution can provide high performance and good scalability.
  - **In-Band:** both data traffic and control flow over the same path to the virtualization engine, without any splitting. Levels of abstraction exists in the data path, and storage could be pooled under the control of a domain manager. This type of solution does not require host-based agents, can work with almost any operating systems or server platforms. Since in-band solution is more about traffic redirection, it does add latency to all I/Os, thus might experience performance degradation in a busy SAN if it is not sized correctly. In band solutions are simple to deploy, easy to use and less complicated, and are the most common form of virtualization used today.

- File level storage virtualization is used in the Network Attached Storage (NAS) environment. It provides an abstraction in the file server, and eliminates the dependencies between data accessed at the file level and the location where the files are physically stored. It enables the files to move between NAS systems without impacting client access. In the traditional NAS environment, every NAS device is physically and logically an independent entity. The storage device handles the files and folders on the device. Each host knows where its file level resource is located. Files are stored in the specific file server, and when the file server fills up, files have to be moved from one server to another. Moving files across servers requires system downtime, where host and applications have to be reconfigured with the new path, which is complex and difficult for the system administrator, application administrator or storage administrators. File level virtualization simplifies the process. It creates a logical pool of storage, where users can use a logical path instead of a physical path to access files. An application is independent from the location where the files are physically stored. File virtualization eliminates the need to know exactly where a file is physically located; a global namespace can be used to map the logical path of a file to the physical path names. The user can simply look to a mount point or a logical path that shows all their files. In a virtualized file level storage environment, the user can implement a tiered storage. Data can be moved from a tier-one NAS to other tiers NAS, or network file servers automatically. Files that are less frequently accessed can be moved to a lower cost tier, while current production data can be stored in the high performance tier.

Server Layer Storage Virtualization

In the traditional computer environment, storage hardware devices connect to the servers directly. The magnetic disk presented to the servers and the operating systems as LUNs. Then the operating system translates LUNs into a "file system" for applications to store and process information. Storage virtualization at the server layer also happen through "files." The hypervisor allocates storage space to virtual machines, in the format of virtual disk files, regardless of the complexity of the physical storage. The virtual disk appears as a local physical disk drive to the virtual machine. The VM does not know whether the disk is a virtual one or physical one, and does not even know where the storage is.

A virtual machine is stored as a set of "files," on the storage devices assigned to the hypervisor. The hypervisor uses two file systems to manage the VM files: the virtual machine file system (VMFS), or the network file system (NFS). The VMFS is the native file system, which allows multiple computer systems to read and write to the same storage simultaneously. The on-disk locking ensures the same virtual machine is not powered on by multiple computer systems at the same time. When a computer system fails, the on-disk lock for each virtual machine, running on the failed computer system, can be released, and the virtual machines can be restarted on other computer systems. The VMFS can be expanded dynamically non-disrupted. The capacity of VMFS volume can be expanded, by adding LUNs to the source VMFS volume, or dynamically on the volume partition where it is located. The VMFS is used in the SAN environment, while the NFS is used in the NAS system, and both file systems are used to provide storage space for the VMS.

Virtual Provisioning and Storage Tiering

Storage virtualization consolidates multiple heterogeneous storage resources. Instead of managing storage resources from different vendors, allocated to different servers for different applications, storage virtualization masks the complexity of the underlying physical storage arrays, and enables storage technologies such as virtual provisioning, storage pools, automated storage tiering, which are widely used in storage virtualization, and provide simplicity for storage management.

Virtual Provisioning

Virtual provisioning is also called thin provisioning. It is the strategy of allocating physical storage space on an "as needed" basis. Storage space is allocated on demand to the devices. Virtual provisioning presents a higher storage capacity LUN to a server with more capacity than it is actually allocated.

In the traditional IT environment, the storage administrator is swamped by increasing requests from various applications. In order to meet the growing need for application data, a storage administrator usually allocates more space to applications based on anticipated storage growth, so that the application downtime can be reduced when new storage is required later on, and also management overhead can be reduced. But this results in lower storage capacity utilization. Virtual provisioning present a virtual pool of shared capacity, larger than the actual amount of physical storage to the host. The storage administrator can allocate capacity on demand from the shared storage pool. For instance, if a SQL server requires 200GB but is projected to grow to 2 terabytes within 12 months, traditional provisioning is to require the full 2TB to be allocated on day one, to avoid the SQL server downtime for volume expansion as the data grows. So, all full 2TB sit in the SQL server host with only 10% physical volume actually being used. Virtual provisioning allows a 2TB volume be presented to the SQL server with only 200GB of physical disks being reserved. The rest of free capacity is available and assigned to other hosts. When the storage usage for SQL server approaches 200GB, additional physical capacity can be added online non-disruptively. From the perspective of the host server, it does not know whether the LUN is the standard LUN or thin LUN, or if only a fraction of the physical storage is actually allocated. It sees the LUN with the full 2TB capacity; the storage array is to automatically allocate additional space as needed.

Virtual provisioning simplifies the storage management, and reduces the system downtime for adding storage capacity or migrating data between LUNs. It also improves the storage capacity utilization, by only allocating the "needed" space, and eliminates additional investment on high end storage arrays. By reducing the storage usage, fewer disks consume less power, cooling and office space, and therefore operational costs are also reduced.

Storage Tiering

Storage tiering is data leveraged on various types of media, to achieve the performance service levels and cost requirement. Storage resources are created as a hierarchy, and data is identified to relocate to the appropriate storage types, to meet the operation requirement at a minimal cost.

We all know that data is growing at a tremendous speed in today's world. Storage requirement is increasing with the cost of storage devices. Organizations require the capacity of storing the right data, at the right cost, with the right access. So, the storage tiering technology locate data to appropriate storage types, by identifying active or inactive data. For instance, high performance solid-state drives (SSD) or FC drives can be configured as tier 1 storage, and used to store frequently accessed data, to improve application performance. Low cost, high volume disks such as SATA can be used as tier 2 storage, to store less frequently accessed data, in order to reduce storage costs. The active or inactive data movement is based on a defined tiering policy, which is configured according to the frequency of data access, performance, application type and etc. The tiering policy is set up based on the statistical results from monitoring data access statistics and date profile.

Automated storage tiering proactively monitors application workload, and automatically moves the active data to the higher performing SSD or FC tier, and inactive data to the higher capacity, lower performance SATA drives tier. Automated storage tiering consists of three major building blocks:

- The storage type is a shared storage resource, with a combination of (SSD, FC or

SATA) drives and a RAID protection type (RAID 1, Raid 5 and Raid 6);

- The storage groups are a logical grouping of LUNs for common management. The tiering policy manages data placement and movement across storage types, to achieve service levels for one or more storage groups. For example, the Platinum policy indicates that up to 25% of the storage group's capacity is allowed to stay on SSD, up to 50% on Fibre Channel, and up to 25% on SATA.

The EMC Symmetrix VMAX arrays are famous for its fully automatic storage tiering (FAST) features. Not only does it use inter-array storage tiering, to automate the process of identifying devices that could benefit from higher performance flash drives or high capacity SATA drives, and also automates the movement of devices between tiers, that it features sub-LUN tiering and cache tiering to improve performance.

Benefits of the Storage Virtualization

- **Increase Application Availability:** Storage can be easily added or removed, without bringing down a running application, thus not affecting an application's availability;
- **Increase Storage Utilization:** Storage utilization can be increased, and thus reduce the cost of ownership. When the storage virtualization is implemented properly, storage can be brought from different heterogeneous array, multi-window array, and the workload can be spread out more appropriately. From the computer's perspective, it sees a logical storage, which can be optimized and provided to the virtual machine. The storage admin can migrate historic data to cheaper storage, or use thin provisioning to allocate less space than the operating system actually sees. Storage

virtualization allows storage to dynamically grow, to meet the business needs;

- **Non-Disruptive Data Migration:** Data are moved from one array to the other with virtualization, the machine does not even know that something has changes on the backend. Files can be accessed while migrations are in progress. Once data has been migrated, from the computer's perspective, it still sees the storage pointing to the same device. This leads to non-disruptive data migration between the storage arrays. For example, an application have access to the storage, and the response time is too high, the slower SATA drive can be simply replaced with the SSD drive. With the virtualized storage, data migration can be seamless and even automated;
- **Centralized Management:** A storage admin can manage many existing storage arrays through one central interface;
- **Enable Flexibility and Utilization in the VDC:** Virtualization in the middle takes care of mapping. The storage LUN can come from any vendor, be of any heterogeneity, yet the storage management can still be greatly simplified.

NETWORK VIRTUALIZATION

Network Virtualization Overview

We normally see the network as a composition of network cables, routers, switches physically connected to support network communications. How are we able to virtualize these components? What is the benefit of network virtualization? What is the key attribute of network virtualization?

Network virtualization is a process of logically segmenting, or grouping physical networks, and making them operate as a single or multiple independent networks, the so called "virtual networks." Network virtualization enables the best use of resources, where an IT organization can purchase and allocate hardware equipment on an as-needed bases. In a data center with more than one network, routers, routing tables, multiple switches, and other devices are needed, to allow networks to communicate together, which can be done through segmentation. All these devices are put together and applied on the virtual side, into a virtualized network in the virtual data center (VDC). All the virtual devices are grouped, and functional groups are created that work well together to ensure network communication.

In the traditional data center, bridges, hubs, switches, routers and network adapters create a physical network layer, providing nodes of connectivity among servers, servers and clients, servers and storage arrays for node to node communications.

When we install the hypervisor in the physical server, and run virtual servers on it, terminologies are adjusted to the virtual side as well. A NIC card (network interface card) is now called VNIC (virtual NIC), same for a switch now called a virtual switch, and a HBA as a virtual HBA. Within the hypervisor environment, a logical switch called the "virtual switch" is created, that connects through the hypervisor environment, and functions the same as the physical switch, by providing node to node communications among VMs. The VMs not only takes advantage of the virtual network within the hypervisor environment, but also have additional benefits. For instance, a web application can be loaded in one VM, and have the application database in another VM, and firewalls can be installed without allocating extra ports. VNIC can be assigned down to the hypervisor level, and allocate them to individual VMs.

We usually have many issues with network broadcasting, which causes a decrease of network performance in the traditional network. By creating the virtual network, traffic is segmented, restricted or allowed based on business justifications. Performance issue can be monitored, controlled and justified.

Network virtualization isolates and segregates network traffic and services. Network virtualization is done through virtual local networks (VLANS), or the virtual storage area network fabric (VSAN). The management for virtual network is performed on logical networks, instead of the physical network.

Network virtualization segregates networks into small segments, which reduces fabric needs, provides granularity to larger fabrics, consolidates equipment sprawl, reduces servers, networks and storage, and shrinks everything into smaller footprints, to reduce complexity and simplify management. It also enables tightened security, align specific services and network traffic types to particular network areas, zones, VSANs or VLANs. Traffic and workloads can also be comingled on converged networks, allowing multiple services and protocols on a single interface.

Both 1GB and 10GB Ethernets are implemented in the virtual network environment. The 1GB Ethernet is widely used in the data center environment, although the bandwidth per port is limited. Since higher bandwidth is required to support multiple applications, the 10GB Ethernet is then introduced in the data centers. Moving to the 10GB Ethernet provides large amounts of bandwidth per port, and reduces the amount of cabling. With faster bandwidth, servers and switches can be consolidated, and thus decreasing management overhead. The 10GB Ethernet is usually used for core networking, or in some devices where data speed is higher than required. For example, the EMC Greenplum appliance data are stored across many nodes in the system and processed in parallel. The appliance needs its own dedicated 10 GB Ethernet connectivity to achieve fast and parallel data processing as its computing requirement. The 10GB Ethernet of course is more expensive, and it also requires additional wiring infrastructure, or additional switches which have lower port density. The 10GB Ethernet are implemented for new data center implementations, which also are called the Greenfield implementation. If it is Brownfield implementation, which means working with the existing traditional data center environment, the existing hardware, cooling, switches, hot spots, all server overloads etc., need to be considered, in order to customize appropriate Ethernet types.

Virtual Network Components

Like the physical network infrastructure, a virtual network is made up of the same hardware as physical network, but are virtualized. The virtual network needs key components to connect each other to enable network traffic flow. It consists of not only virtual devices such as the virtual switch, virtual NIC, virtual HBA, but also includes physical hardware equipment such as physical adapters, switches and routers. Physical switches and routers provide connections among physical servers, clients and physical storage arrays. Physical switches directly connect to Ethernet, Fiber Channel, iSCSI or FCoE, and support the network protocol. Physical adapters such as Network Interface Cards (NIC), Host Bus Adapters (HBA) and Converged Network Adapters (CAN) provide the interface between the physical server and physical network, allowing network data communication between physical servers and the physical network.

The Virtual Switch

The core to the virtual network is the virtual switch. The virtual switch is a software-based layer 2 network switch that enables one virtual machine (VM) to communicate with another, and with the physical networks. The virtual switch enables traffic management for VMs and the hypervisor kernel, and provides enhanced networking and security capacity. Virtual switch includes three key elements:

- The forwarding engine is the core layer of the virtual switch. It knows how to route traffic, and forward the data packets to the relevant uplinks, and processes the Ethernet headers.
- VLAN Tagging, stripping and filtering units. VLAN tagging sends static tags to the Ethernet frame that includes a VLAN id. A VLAN id tells the switch that the data packet should go to which VLAN.
- The Layer 2 security, checksum and segmentation offload units. The data link layer, layer 2 of the OSI model transfers data between network entities, with interoperability and interconnectivity to other layers.

Figure 5. Virtual switches in the network
(EMC² Corporation - Virtualized Data center and cloud infrastructure)

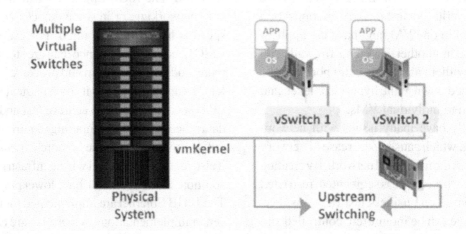

The security for layer 2 usually is a weak link, since it is limited by the physical boundaries. The virtual switch has a key unit to improve layer 2 security.

Switches are responsible for routing the network traffic intelligently to the appropriate destination. A virtual switch works similarly as a physical Ethernet switch, which controls how virtual machines communicate with one another. The virtual switch uses the physical network interface card (NIC), which is installed on the host server to connect the virtual network to the physical network. It maintains a MAC port forwarding table. When a frame arrives, it looks up each frame's destination and forwards it to one or more ports for transmission, and avoids unnecessary deliveries. Virtual network could be tightly integrated into hypervisor, and no additional hardware equipment is needed, so the performance is bound by the hypervisor. If the hypervisor encounters performance issues, sending packet across the port can be quite busy as well. The virtual switch cannot be powered off unless the hypervisor is shut down.

Virtual switches allow for isolation, since no interlink is available to communicate with each other. They just know which VM connects to them, what packet they need to send, and thus can maintain segregation and security. A virtual switch also prevents the Ethernet adapters from looping back, and each virtual switch has its own table being managed separately.

The Virtual HBA

The host bus adapter (HBA) is a device that provides IO processing, and the physical connection between the physical server and the network. I/O virtualization enables the physical HBA to appear as virtual HBAs. The virtual HBA enables a VM to access the Fiber Channel RDM disk or the LUN assigned to the VM, and ensures that each virtual machine only accesses its assigned virtual storage. The virtual HBA are configured using the N_Port ID virtualization (NPIV) technology, which enables a single physical HBA to function as multiple virtual ports, with each virtual port having a unique WWN identity in the FC SAN.

The Virtual NIC

A virtual network Interface card (NIC) is a software driver that provides network connection between VMs and the virtual switch. A virtual NIC works the same way as the physical NIC. When the virtual NIC receives the network I/O from the guest OS, it forwards the I/O in the form of an Ethernet frame to a virtual switch, then the virtual switch transfers it to its destination. Each

Figure 6. Virtual HBA in the network
(EMC² Corporation - Virtualized Data center and cloud infrastructure.)

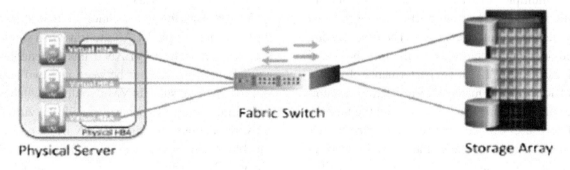

virtual NIC has a unique MAC and IP address; the hypervisor generates these MAC addresses, and allocates a MAC address to a virtual NIC at the time of VM creation, to provide a secure network environment.

The Virtual Router

The virtual router is a layered software that handles the routing framework on the virtual network and provides redundancy, failover and load balancing. Each virtual router is identified with a unique virtual router identifier. A virtual router consists of a virtual router identifier and a set of associated IP addresses, and is managed by the virtual router redundancy protocol (VRRP). Routers connect to the subnet or remote sites across the wide area links, and provide communication between VLANs and the VLAN access to shared resources.

VLAN and VSAN

Virtual LAN (VLAN) is a switched logical network created on a LAN, or across multiple LANS that consist of virtual and physical switches. VLAN takes a physical network and logically segments it into smaller divisions, by functions or applications, regardless of user's physical location. VLAN allows the network administrator to re-segment their network without physically rearranging the devices. Each VLAN can have their one and isolated segment run its own class, services and activities. With VLANs, a switch can be divided into multiple VLANS for better port density utilization. Broadcasting traffic can be reduced by staying within one VLAN. The broadcasting activities can be controlled by limiting the size of the associated VLAN. The performance of VLAN traffic can also be managed by restricting the number of switch ports in a VLAN, and the number of ports users. Since sensitive data in one VLAN can be isolated from any other VLANs, security is enhanced by using VLAN. It is easy, flexible and scalable to manage network, by implement-

ing the VLAN management software. Instead of configuring separate physical LANS for various communication groups, an administrator can easily move or group nodes, and change VLAN configuration with a single management interface.

A VLAN is created on the switches. If a VLAN is not known to a switch, the switch cannot transfer traffic across any of its ports for the VLAN. A network administrator defines VLAN IDs from the hypervisors' built-in VLAN ID pools, and assign a VLAN ID to a switch port or port group, which is to include the port to the VLAN. This is called a "port-based VLAN". There are other techniques such as "MAC-based VLAN," "protocol-based VLAN," or "policy-based VLAN" to configure the VLAN ID. Nodes become VLAN members when they are connected to the VLAN switch ports and filter, which can then communicate to other switches and routers within the network. The router connects to subnets, and routes information to the appropriate destination. Information are exchanged between interconnected switches and routers on the corporate backbone.

With VLAN, switching among multiple VLANS can be divided, which is to enable better port density utilization, and reduce the overall cost of deploying a network infrastructure.

When the VLAN traffic spans multiple switches, VLAN tagging is required. VLAN Tagging is a process that inserts or removes a tag, includes the VLAN ID into the Ethernet frame, so that VLAN ID tells the switch which port or interface it should go. A trunk port sends and receives tagged Ethernet frames.

VLAN trunking is a technology that allows traffic from multiple VLANs to traverse a single network connection. VLAN trunking enables a single network adapter between any two networked devices, such as VMs, routers, switches and storage arrays, to behave as multiple virtual network adapters. A single VLAN trunk port is capable of sending or receiving multiple VLAN traffic. VLAN trunking reduces the number of virtual NICs, storage ports and switch ports, and eliminates the need for dedicated network links for each VLAN, minimizing the complexity of managing network links. VLAN trunking is achieved by VLAN tagging.

Virtual Storage Area Network (VSAN)

VSAN is a logical partition in a FC storage area network (SAN). VSAN allows communication among a group of nodes regardless of their physical location in the fabric. By using multiple VSAN, a system is easier to configure and scale out. Network devices can be added or relocated without the need of changing the physical layout. When an issue occurs in one VSAN, it can be handled with a minimum disruption to the rest of the network, since VSAN allows traffic to be isolated within specific portions of the network.

Each VSAN has its own name server, zoning and dedicated fabric services, and needs to be configured separately. Since each VSAN acts independently, change configuration or traffic overhead in one VSAN does not affect the other VSAN. The general flow for managing a VSAN is to create the VSAN, populate it with ports, and then zone the members in the VSAN.

VSAN allows more efficient SAN utilization and flexibility, since the resources can be allocated to and shared among more users, while keeping secure segregation of traffic and retaining independent control of resources based on the individual VSAN.

Benefits of Network Virtualization

The benefits of network virtualization include:

- Reduces complexity and enables easier network management: With network virtualization in the data center, one deals with fewer hardware equipment, which reduces the risk associated with the complexity of managing whole bunch of servers, switch-

es, routers and cables. Since the network virtualization allows virtual machines to operate independent of network topology, deployment, migration or reconfiguration of the virtual machine can be achieved by management software from a centralized management workstation. Network virtualization allows the grouping of nodes. Regrouping nodes does not require physical equipment movement or re-cabling, which also greatly simplifies the network management.

- Enhances security and protects sensitive data: Network virtualization allows restricting access to nodes through the VLAN interfaces. By creating smaller, more manageable VLAN, we have more control and better ability to enhance the network security. Sensitive data such as financial information or personal confidential data can be limited to that specific VLAN only, and are isolated from other virtual networks. Network virtualization allows one to create only the ports needed, which closes any backdoor for hacker attack, ensure tighter security with virtual network segmentation.

- Enhances performance: Network virtualization segments traffic to smaller VLANs, which divides the broadcasting domains to service many applications. More bandwidth are dedicated to preferred applications, and network traffic performance is improved. Because we are dealing with smaller subsets and ports, we can also put in any parameter needed for that subset only. The flexibility and scalability can improve the virtual network performance.

- Improves utilization and reduces operation costs: Network virtualization facilitates physical resource consolidation - fewer servers, switches, cables and storages can be shared among multiple virtual networks, which reduces overall the management overhead and resource consumption, and reduces capital and operational expenses.

DESKTOP VIRTUALIZATION

Desktop Virtualization Overview

In the traditional environment, the desktop runs the OS, with the applications installed on top, the users have user state data and profile, where all these are tightly coupled. When the desktop or laptop is broken or lost, the operating system, the applications and the user's data are also lost, thus business productivity is affected. The virtualized desktop decouples the hardware from the operating system, application and user data. Instead of tying the operating system and applications to the hardware, the OS is separated from the hardware, running through virtualization a virtualized infrastructure.

With the desktop virtualization, the users have the ability to access the user desktop environment from anywhere. A client can work from their computer at home, a laptop from the coffee shop, tablet PCs or mobile phones. They can access all their user data with the same desktop environment through all the different end-point devices.

By separating these elements, computer management can be greatly benefited. It is a lot easier for the IT staff to support all desktops from a centralized location: the user data sits at the central location, rather than at an end-point device. This is to also provide better security.

There are many business drivers for desktop virtualization. The main driver is the manageability: One of the major tasks for the IT department in an organization is to manage its desktop infrastructure. From an administrator's point of view, one might have hundreds of thousands desktops with different brands, different models, running on different versions of operating systems and applications. Managing all these hardware and software is a big challenge. One has to deal with a variety of hardware models, face complicated PC refresh cycles, handle different versions of the operating system, and perform different regression tests for each application, with different protocols and support requirements. This requires the IT staff to spend most of the time supporting the existing environment, instead of deploying new technologies. By virtualizing the desktop on the server, one has generic hardware at the desktop level, requiring lower level of support.

Security is another important driver for the desktop virtualization. A virtual desktop resides in the cloud, in a virtualized data center somewhere in the world. If one's physical laptop is lost or stolen, all the work, user data and sensitivity information that sits in the machine are lost all at once. Damages due to data loss can lead to significant negative impact on businesses. From the user point of view, when the laptop is lost, even if it is replaced by a new one, it takes time to get the replacement, have the computer reimaged with proper operating system and applications, and can be difficult to get the user data backup. In a virtualized desktop environment, data resides in the virtual data center. One can quickly re-provision another desktop if needed, not mentioning one does not need to worry about the desktop security at all.

The cost of supporting virtualized desktop environment depends on the technology one uses in the VDC, RDS or VDI. All present a sizeable cost saving to organizations.

Desktop Virtualization Techniques

Desktop virtualization is to centralize the desktop operating system at the virtual data center. It allows the users to access centrally located data from any number of endpoint devices. Desktops hosted at the data center run as virtual machines, data storage and application execution are also done through data center. The end user accesses these desktops remotely over LAN or WAN from any kind of endpoint devices.

Desktop virtualization techniques provide the ability to host and manage the desktop environment in the data center, which are delivered remotely to end user's endpoint devices.

RDS and VDI are the two major desktop virtualization technologies.

Remote Desktop Services (RDS)

Remote Desktop Services (RDS) are also called Terminal Services. They are a session running on a windows server within the corporate environment. RDS typically are windows remote desktop sessions. A terminal server normally has an operating system with mostly windows being installed on it, and applications are installed into that environment, which are then shared out to the user on the basis as they connect in. It runs on top of the windows system, and maintains individual sessions to the client system.

In the RDS, a terminal service runs on top of a windows operating system and provides individual sessions to the client systems. The end user can remotely access the desktop environment via a terminal service client. Although the end users receive the visual image of the session, all resource consumption and data execution happen on the server.

The benefits for RDS is application delivery are in term of terminal services, where applications are installed at the server level, instead of installed at each individual terminal. If an organization wants to deploy Microsoft Office suites, once it is installed in the terminal server, all the users that have profile in the terminal server can use it, significantly simplifying the delivery of the application.

With virtualized desktops centrally located at the terminal server, data loss is no longer of concern, and security is greatly enhanced. Endpoint devices are used as access points and do not store data.

RDS can rapidly deliver applications, because applications are installed on the server, and accessed by the user from terminal client services, without requiring the applications to be installed locally. And since the applications and execution data are stored centrally, security is greatly improved. Plus, since the OS environment, applications, data setting and configurations all resides on the data center servers, managing one centralized user environment is easier than dealing with different distributed desktop environments. Software patches, application releases can all be completed on those servers, instead of on the different end user's machines.

A typical RDS solution can support 250 or more users per server, and is less expensive to implement in terms of the initial acquisition costs and supporting infrastructure.

The Virtual Desktop Infrastructure (VDI)

The Virtual Desktop Infrastructure (VDI) is favored in VDC as a method for virtualizing desktop computing resources. Just like virtualizing server and server applications, the VDI virtualizes the desktop. Instead of being a terminal desktop session within an application server, the entire operating system runs on that hypervisor. It can be accessed either through remote desktop sessions directly to the OS, or through the hypervisor client.

The hypervisor based client provides connection brokering, in order to facilitate the concurrency within the environment. The operating system is running within the virtual machine, on top of the hypervisor, in the VDC.

The VDI hosts the desktop operating system, running in a virtual machine, on a server, in the virtual data center. Each desktop has its own OS and applications installed. A user has full access to the resources of the virtual desktop. It can be a dedicated virtual machine or a pool of virtual machines, where user data are kept in share drives, in order to maintain that data, and provision virtual machines more dynamically at the same time.

The VDI architecture consists of Endpoint devices, the connection broker and VM hosting servers. Endpoint devices are what the user interfaces with in order to access the remote desktop. It can be a thin client, a desktop, a netbook, a tablet PC or even a smartphone. The connection broker provides the connection between the endpoint device and the desktop virtual machine, running on the VM-hosting server. If the VM is not dedicating to each individual user, the connection broker is needed to search the VMs in the servers, and then connect the user to an available VM. The connection broker needs to be compatible and supports the hypervisor that runs on the VM hosting server. VM hosting servers host the desktop VMS, and remotely deliver to the endpoint devices. The number of VMS, that a single server can support, depends on the hardware, software

configurations and user workloads of the desktop VMs. The desktop VM can run any desktop OS on top of the hypervisor.

The hosting server is the hypervisor, typically a bare-metal hypervisor. All the VM can be dedicated, which means that each user can have their own virtual machine, or depends on the level of concurrency, one can set up a pool of VMS to be used by many users at different times. For instance, a user can be using the VM desktop, saving all the data on the profile drive, and enabling some settings to be consistent. If an IT organization has thousands of users geographically distributed worldwide, but only hundreds of users need to access the VM concurrently, then one only needs to license couple

Figure 7. VDI components
(EMC² Corporation - Virtualized Data center and cloud infrastructure)

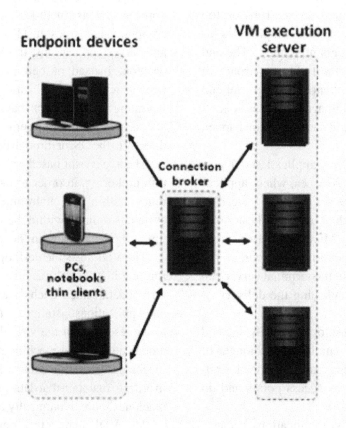

hundreds of VMs depending on the concurrency. The VM pool can help to save a lot of costs.

The VDI allows rapid deployment of the desktop. The desktop environment can be pre-provisioned and preconfigured, such that creating a new desktop can be a click of the template. Then the new VM can be deployed to the hypervisor.

Since the virtual desktop is centrally located and managed. All the VMS are stored into a file, and kept in the storage array, which can be replicated locally or remotely. It also facilitates local failover or remote back up.

Desktop Virtualization Benefits

Instead of purchasing desktops and laptops equipped with the necessary horsepower processor to run applications, we can move to thin clients. Users can choose their preference of end point devices, type of operating systems (Windows, Linux or Apple), and the IT organization can still be able to standardize the desktop environment, and ensure the corporate level security.

Data resides centrally at the VDC, not in any of the endpoint devices. There is no more security concerns, and no worry about equipment loss or sensitive data leakage.

In the traditional IT environment, when corporate IT does the data backup on the desktop, backup client requires network connectivity, requires user cooperation by login to the network and making the backup. Now with the data located centrally at the VDC, back up is simplified, that it can happened at the user state level, within a user session in the remote desktop environment, or the virtual machine in the VDI environment.

Patching, provisioning and creating the new user desktop, all these tasks are simplified due to the central VDC. With special provisioning, a new user desktop with a pre-defined template can be quickly rolled out on the hypervisor within a couple minutes.

Desktop virtualization provides flexibility of access. A corporate PC sitting on the desk in the office is no longer the norm, and there are many ways, with many type of endpoint devices, to access the desktop.

REFERENCES

Answers.com. (2013). *How do you create VLAN step-by-step?* Retrieved from http://wiki.answers.com/Q/How_do_you_create_VLAN_step-by-step

CISCO. (2013). *Network virtualization solutions.* Retrieved from http://www.cisco.com/en/US/netsol/ns658/index.html

Crump, G. (2009). *What is file virtualization?* Retrieved from http://www.storage-switzerland.com/Articles/Entries/2009/12/3_What_is_File_Virtualization.html

De Luca, A., & Bhide, M. (2010). *Storage virtualization for dummies.* Hoboken, NJ: Wiley Publishing, Inc. Retrieved from http://www.hds.com/at/go/virtualisierung/download/hds_storage_virtualization_for_dummies.pdf

Fehling, M. (2011). *IBM storage virtualization – Guildeline for SAP landscapes and SAP private clouds, version 3.* Retrieved from http://www-03.ibm.com/support/techdocs/atsmastr.nsf/5cb5ed706d254a8186256c71006d2e0a/3dfdbe503bafd370862577f80064e64a/$FILE/IBM%20Storage%20Virtualization%20Concepts%20for%20SAP%20landscape%20V3.pdf

IBM Global Education. (2007). *Virtualization in education* (White Paper). Retrieved from http://www-07.ibm.com/solutions/in/education/download/Virtualization%20in%20Education.pdf

I/O Virtualization. (n.d.). *Wikipedia.* Retrieved from http://en.wikipedia.org/wiki/I/O_virtualization

Lippis, N. J., III. (2007). *Network virtualization: The new building blocks of network design* (White Paper). Lippis Consulting. Retrieved from http://www.cisco.com/en/US/solutions/collateral/ns340/ns517/ns431/ns725/net_implementation_white_paper0900aecd80707cb6.pdf

Lowe, S. (2011). *Block level storage vs. file level storage: A comparison.* Retrieved from http://www.techrepublic.com/blog/datacenter/block-level-storage-vs-file-level-storage-a-comparison/3766

Ou, G. (2003). *An introduction to VLAN trunking: Technology for mortals.* Retrieved from http://www.formortals.com/an-introduction-to-vlan-trunking/

Rouse, M. (2006). *Storage virtualization.* Retrieved from http://searchstorage.techtarget.com/definition/storage-virtualization

Rouse, M. (2009). *Server virtualization.* Retrieved from http://searchservervirtualization.techtarget.com/definition/server-virtualization

Rouse, M. (2010). *Virtual switch.* Retrieved from http://searchservervirtualization.techtarget.com/definition/virtual-switch

Rouse, M. (2011). *Virtual storage area network (VSAN).* Retrieved from http://searchstorage.techtarget.com/definition/virtual-storage-area-network

Storage Magazine. (n.d.). *HBAs go virtual.* Retrieved from http://www.bitpipe.com/detail/RES/1163403108_503.html

Storage Virtualization. (n.d.). *Wikipedia.* Retrieved from http://en.wikipedia.org/wiki/Storage_virtualization

Tate, J. (2003). Virtualization: In-band and out-of-band - What is the difference? *IBM Redbooks.* Retrieved from http://www.redbooks.ibm.com/abstracts/tips0203.html

Virtualization. (n.d.). *Wikipedia.* Retrieved from http://en.wikipedia.org/wiki/Virtualization

VMware, Inc. (2007a). *Information guide: VMware virtual networking concepts.* Retrieved from http://www.vmware.com/files/pdf/virtual_networking_concepts.pdf

VMware, Inc. (2007b). *Understand full virtualization, paravirtualization, and hardware assist* (White Paper). Retrieved from http://www.vmware.com/files/pdf/VMware_paravirtualization.pdf

VMware, Inc. (2012). *VMware network virtualization paves the way for next generation cloud services at iland.* Retrieved from http://www.vmware.com/company/news/releases/vmw-iland-network-121712.html

Section 2
Data Management and Data Security

Chapter 4
Trusted Cloud Initiative Reference Architecture

Yushi Shen
Microsoft Corporation, USA

Ling Wu
EMC² Corporation, USA

Yale Li
Microsoft Corporation, USA

Shaofeng Liu
Microsoft Corporation, USA

Qian Wen
Endronic Corp, USA

ABSTRACT

The Trusted Cloud Initiative helps cloud providers develop industry-recommended, secure, and interoperable identity, access, and compliance management configurations and practices. The Trusted Cloud Initiative is to develop reference models and provide education in a vendor-neutral manner, inclusive of all CSA members and affiliates who wish to participate. The Trusted Cloud Initiative Reference Architecture is both a methodology and a set of tools, enabling security architects, enterprise architects, and risk management professionals to leverage a common set of solutions to fulfill their common needs. It enables them to assess their internal IT service and that of their cloud providers in terms of security capabilities, and to plan a roadmap to meet the security needs of their business. The purpose of this quick guide is to take a user through the Trusted Cloud architecture much like an owner's manual walks a consumer through a product.

OVERVIEW OF THE REFERENCE ARCHITECTURE

Out of the common needs, there come the common solutions. The Trusted Cloud Initiative Reference Architecture is both a methodology and a set of tools that enable security architects, enterprise architects and risk management professionals to leverage a common set of solutions. These solutions fulfill a set of common requirements, which risk managers must assess regarding the operational status of internal IT security and cloud provider controls. These controls are expressed in terms of security capabilities, and

DOI: 10.4018/978-1-4666-4801-2.ch004

designed to create a common roadmap to meet the security needs of their business.

Architecture must be guided by business requirements. In the case of the Trusted Cloud Initiative, these requirements come from a controls matrix guided by regulations such as Sarbanes-Oxley and Gramm-Leach-Bliley, standard frameworks such as ISO-27002, the Payment Card Industry Data Security Standards, and the IT Audit Frameworks, such as COBIT, all in the context of cloud delivery models, such as Software as a Service (SaaS), Platform as a Service (PaaS) and Infrastructure as a Services (IaaS).

From these requirements, a set of security capabilities have been defined and organized according to best practice architecture frameworks. The Sherwood Business Security Architecture (SABSA) defines security capabilities from a business perspective. The Information Technology Infrastructure Library (ITIL) defines the capabilities needed to manage the IT services of the company, which includes the security capabilities necessary to securely manage those services. The Jericho Forum defines technical security capabilities, which arises from the reality of the traditional in-the-datacenter technology

environments shifting to one where solutions span the internet across multiple datacenters, some owned by the business and some purely used as outsourced services. Lastly, The Open Group Architecture Framework (TOGAF) provides an enterprise architecture framework and methodology for planning, designing and governing information architectures, and thus a common framework to integrate the work of the security architect with the enterprise architecture of an organization.

You can interact with and learn more about the TCI Reference Architecture online at https://research.cloudsecurityalliance.org/tci/.

HOW TO USE THE TCI REFERENCE ARCHITECTURE

The TCI Reference Architecture can be used in multiple enterprise security design phases, from assessing opportunities for improvement and creating road maps for technology adoption, to defining reusable security patterns and assessing various cloud providers and security technology vendors against a common set of capabilities.

Figure 1. TCI reference architecture

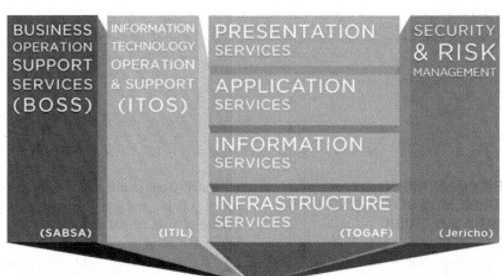

Figure 2. How to use the TCI reference architecture

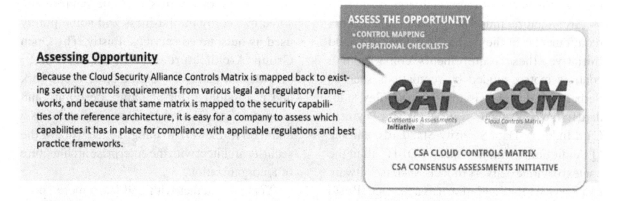

Assessing Opportunity

Because the Cloud Security Alliance Controls Matrix is mapped back to existing security controls requirements from various legal and regulatory frameworks, and because that same matrix is mapped to the security capabilities of the reference architecture, it is easy for a company to assess which capabilities it has in place for compliance with applicable regulations and best practice frameworks.

Road Mapping

After assessing the current capabilities of the organization, the reference architecture can be used to guide those capabilities which need investment based on the business needs of the company as either a cloud consumer or a cloud provider. For instance, in a cloud-based solution, the physical security controls and capabilities are less important to the cloud consumer and more important to the cloud provider. Furthermore, the capabilities of the reference architecture can be used to organize the technology standards portfolio of an organization to identify areas where multiple technologies exist for the same capability, demonstrating that those technology functions can be consolidated. Conversely, it can show capabilities for which a company does not yet have a standard technology in place.

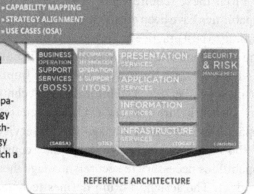

Reuse

As security patterns and best practices are built around the reference architecture, sharing of these patterns within and between companies will be enhanced due to the common capabilities models that tie them together. Vendors can certify their solutions against the set of capabilities and controls in the reference architecture, thus giving consumers of their solutions more assurance in, and understanding of, the vendors' solutions.

SECURITY AND RISK MANAGEMENT: PROTECTING DATA AND MANAGING RISK

Security and Risk Management includes the passwords, firewalls and encryption that protect computer systems and data. It is the processes that define policies, and audit systems against those policies. It uses ethical hackers and tools to test for weak spots in the systems. These services are what come up in the minds of most people, when they think of cyber security.

Description

The Security and Risk Management domain provides the core components of an organization's Information Security.

Programs are set in place to safeguard assets, detect, assess and monitor risks inherent in operating activities. Capabilities include Identity and Access Management, GRC (Governance, Risk Management and Compliance), Policies and Standards, Threat and Vulnerability Management, Infrastructure and Data Protection.

Example

An employee working from home must log into the corporate VPN, using the one-time password token on his key fob. A new website being built is tested for compliance with corporate security policies. A thief cannot read data on a stolen laptop if its hard drive has been encrypted.

Services Provided

- **Governance Risk and Compliance:** The GRC encompasses, integrates and aligns activities such as corporate governance, enterprise risk management, and corporate compliance with applicable laws and regulations. Components include:
  - Compliance management assures compliance with all internal information security policies and standards;
  - Vendor management ensures that service providers and outsourcers adhere to the intended and contractual information security policies, by applying concepts of ownership and custody;
  - Audit management highlights areas for improvement;
  - IT risk management ensures that risks of all types are identified, understood, communicated, and either accepted, remediated, transferred or avoided;

  - Policy management maintains an organizational structure and process, that supports the creation, implementation, exception handling and management of policies that represent business requirements;
  - Technical awareness and training increases the ability to select and implement effective technical security mechanisms, products, process and tools.
- **Information Security Management:** The main objective of Information Security Management is to implement the appropriate measurements, in order to minimize or eliminate the impact that security-related threats and vulnerabilities might have on an organization. Measurements include:
  - Capability Maturity Models identify stages of development of an organization, from an immature state through several levels of maturity, as the organization gains experience and knowledge;
  - Capability Mapping Models describe what a business does to reach its objectives, and promote a strong relationship between the business model and the technical infrastructure, that supports the business requirements, resulting in a view that can be understood by both the business and IT;
  - Roadmaps in the form of security architectures provide a road map to be followed by individual projects, serving individual business initiatives;
  - Risk Portfolios are where identified risks are registered, monitored and reported.

Dashboards for security management and risk management are used to measure and report the level of effectiveness of decisions, and help the organization make new decisions that are to maintain and improve that effectiveness. Analysis and plans for remediating residual risks are also part of the overall risk management framework.

- **Privilege Management Infrastructure:** Privilege Management Infrastructure ensures that the users have the required access and privileges, to execute their duties and responsibilities, with Identity and Access Management (IAM) functions such as identity management, authentication services, authorization services and privilege usage management. This security discipline enables the right individuals to access the right resources, at the right times, and for the right reasons. It addresses the mission-critical need to ensure appropriate access to resources, across the increasingly heterogeneous technology environments, and meet the increasingly rigorous compliance requirements.

The technical controls of Privilege Management Infrastructure focus on identity provisioning, password, multi-factor authentication and policy management. This security practice is a crucial undertaking for any enterprise. It is also increasingly business-aligned, and it requires business skills, not just technical expertise.

- **Threat and Vulnerability Management:** This discipline deals with core security, such as vulnerability management, threat management, compliance testing and penetration testing. Vulnerability management is a complex endeavor, in which enterprises track their assets, monitor and scan for known vulnerabilities, and take action by patching the software, changing configurations, or deploying other controls, in an attempt to reduce the attacks from surfacing at the resource layer. Threat modeling and security testing are also part of activities, in order to effectively identify the vulnerabilities.

- **Infrastructure Protection Services:** Infrastructure Protection Services secure Server, End-Point, Network and Application layers. This discipline uses a traditional defense in-depth approach, to make sure containers and pipes of data are healthy. The controls of Infrastructure Protection Services are usually considered as preventive technical controls, such as IDS/IPS, Firewall, Anti-Malware, White/Black Listing and more. They are relatively cost-effective in defending against the majority of traditional or non-advanced attacks.

- **Data Protection:** In the information age, data is an asset. However, most data remains valuable only if it is protected. Data protection needs to cover all stages of the data lifecycle, data types and data states. Data stages include creation, storage, access, roaming, share and retirement. Data types include unstructured data such as word processing documents, structured data such as data within databases, and semi-structured data such as emails. Data states include data at rest (DAR), data in transit (DIT), also known as "data in motion" or "data in flight", and data in use (DIU). The controls of Data Protection are data lifecycle management, data leakage prevention, intellectual property protection with digital rights management, and cryptographic services such as key management and PKI/symmetric encryption.

- **Policies and Standards:** Security policies are part of a logical abstraction of Enterprise Security Architecture. They are derived from risk-based business requirements, and exist in a number of different levels, including Information Security Policy, Physical Security Policy, Business Continuity Policy, Infrastructure Security Policies and Application Security Policies, as well as the overarching Business Operational Risk Management Policy.

Security Policies are statements that capture requirements specifying the type of security, and how much should be applied to protect the business. Policies typically state what should be done, while avoiding reference to particular technical solutions. Security Standards are an abstraction at the component level, and are needed to ensure that the many different components can be integrated into systems.

Internationally recognized standards for various aspects of security, from the standards bodies, include ISO, IETF, IEEE, ISACA, OASIS and TCG. Direction can also be provided in the form of operational security baselines, job aid guidelines, best practices, correlation of regulatory requirements, and role-based awareness. One way to approach security policy and its implementation is to classify information, and associate policies with the resulting classes of data.

RELATIONSHIPS TO OTHER DOMAINS

SRM provides the security context for IT Operations and Support. Security aspects of ITOS capabilities and functions are critical to the delivery of IT services supporting a business. SRM is a key component of Operational Risk Management under Business Operation Support Services, as Security Risks are crucial data points of the organization's business intelligence, which supplies information necessary to make sound business decisions. Human Resources supports the SRM agenda through vigilant attention to the workforce. SRM provides Identity and Access Management services that are prerequisite to the presentation of data to users. Protection of data in transit, at rest and in use is a critical underpinning to the processing and manipulation of data by application services. SRM has a dependency

on the core components and capabilities provided by Infrastructure Services, including physical security of facilities and patch management.

Information Technology Operation and Support: Managing IT Processes

The ITOS is the IT Department. It is the help desk that takes the call when a problem is found. It is the team that coordinates changes and roll them out in the middle of the night. It is the planning and process that keep the systems going, even in the event of a disaster.

Description

The ITOS outlines all the necessary services an IT organization needs, in order to support its business needs. This domain provides alignment of industry standards and best practices (PM BOK, CMMi, ISO/IEC 27002, COBIT and ITIL v3), providing a reference from two main perspectives, that enable the organization to support its business needs.

However, relationships between technology components are not intended to be a one-on-one match to the process touch points described in PM BOK, ISO/IEC 27002, CMMi, COBIT and ITIL v3.

Example

An employee receives a suspicious email, which she thinks may contain a malware program. She notifies the help desk. The help desk opens a security incident, and a response team works to block the sender, identify other affected users, and restore any damage that may have been done.

Services Provided

- **IT Operation:** IT Operation defines the organizational structure, skill requirements of an IT organization, and standard operational management procedures and practices to allow the organization to manage an IT operation and the associated infrastructure.

IT Operation capabilities are oriented to align the business and IT strategies. The management of the project and technological portfolios ensure architecture governance throughout IT.

- **Service Delivery:** Service Delivery deals with technologies essential in maintaining uninterrupted technical services. Services in this category typically include those that are more appropriate to the technical staff, such as availability management, service level management, service continuity and capacity management.

Although those categories alone are enough to satisfy ITIL service management guidelines, a number of other IT disciplines are closely aligned with service support and delivery, such as project management, service provisioning and portfolio management.

Service Delivery is primarily concerned with the proactive and forward-looking services, the business requires from Information Technology, in order to provide adequate support to the business users. It is focused on the business as the customer of the IT services.

- **Service Support:** Service Support is focused on the users, and primarily concerned with ensuring that they have access to the appropriate services to support the business functions.

To the business customers and users, Service Support is the entry point for service request. Users become involved in service support by:

- Asking for changes;
- Needing communication and updates;
- Having difficulties and queries.

The service desk is the single contact point for customers to record their problems. The service desk tries to resolve problems if there is a direct solution, or it creates an incident. Incidents initiate a chain of processes: Incident Management, Problem Management, Change Management, Release Management and Configuration Management (see following sections for details). This chain of processes is tracked using the Configuration Management Database (CMDB), which records each process and creates output documents for traceability (Quality Management).

- **Incident Management:** Architectural patterns for incident management include services for trouble ticketing and incident classification. Incident Management interacts with other areas of the architecture, either directly as with the service desk, indirectly through manipulation of common data, or asynchronously as part of a business process for incident management. Incidents begin their lifecycle either as a phone-in incident from a human, a detected error in the environment usually as a result of event correlation from the Systems Management domain, or via incident messaging from another applications.

- **Problem Management:** Problem Management deals with the incident, after it has started to cycle through the remediation process. The problem management architecture interacts with the service desk. Problem Management offers advanced root cause analysis tools and technologies, and interfaces with the information repositories, to perform trending and prevention services within the environment.

- **Knowledge Management:** Usually, as incidents are resolved, and the root-cause analysis takes place, a significant amount of knowledge can be lost, causing delays as some of these incidents appear again throughout time.

The Knowledge Management Process accumulates root cause solutions, or information regarding how incidents are resolved. Once this knowledge is collected, it is transformed to Frequent Asked Questions or Self-Service Capabilities, which the user and technical support communities can reuse to resolve issues with the IT services.

- **Change Management:** Change Management is a major pattern that acts as an intermediary between request, release and configuration/provisioning. It allows for management of scope, impact analysis, as well as scheduling of change. Change Management provides one of the primary inputs into configuration management, from a data maintenance perspective, in keeping the application data up-to-date.
- **Release Management:** The Release Management architecture is the set of conceptual patterns that support the movement of pre-production technical resources into production. Pre-production includes all the activities that are necessary to prove that a particular resource is appropriate for the technical, business and operational environment, and does not exceed a risk profile for a particular task. Significant Release Management patterns include those for release scheduling, release acceptance, and audit. Release Management plays a vital role both as a process and as a set of technologies, and it provides a vital control point for request, change, and configuration management processes and architectures.

Relationships to Other Domains

The use of the ITOS analytic services such as data warehousing, data marts, and common operational data stores are key to enabling an effective business operation service.

ITOS supports the Business Operation Support Services, in order to maintain tactical and strategic alignment between the business and IT.

ITOS implements Presentation, Application, Information and Infrastructure services.

BUSINESS OPERATION SUPPORT SERVICES: PARTNERS WITH THE BUSINESS

The BOSS domain is all the corporate support functions such as Human Resources, Compliance and Legal that are critical to a security program. It is also where the operations of the company and its systems are monitored for any signs of abuse or fraud.

Description

BOSS is designed based on best practices and reference frameworks, with proven success of aligning the business, and transforming the information security practice across organizations into a business enabler.

Most of the security architectures focus only on technical capabilities, missing the opportunity to create a dynamic synergy with the business, transforming reactive practices into proactive areas, which eventually can enable business command centers to providing relevant information about the health of information assets and business processes.

A common concern, when organizations decide to integrate services with cloud providers, is the level of security the provider is to offer, as well as the amount of exposure, when data is hosted on a multi-tenant model. This domain outlines aspects that must be considered besides the technological solutions, such as legal guidance, compliance and auditing activities, human resources and monitoring capabilities with a focus on fraud prevention.

Example

The security monitoring tool alerts an analyst that a customer withdrawal transaction is initiated from a workstation in the IT department, instead of the customer contact center. A special investigation is held with the help of HR and Legal, to determine that a disgruntled system administrator has been stealing from the company.

Services Provided

- **Compliance:** The main focus for Compliance capabilities is to track internal, external, third parties such as customers, audit activities and related findings. For compliance, it is necessary to have a common repository, which allows the organization to track and remediate the technical or operational gaps outlined by these findings.

Audit activities should include the development of an annual plan, which can simplify the audit process throughout the year, in preventing redundant tasks.

The use of a regulatory mapping process is to help the organization to organize and simplify control evidence, that each capability or process generates, and store it on the risk registry (Information Services Domain).

- **Data Governance:** As the organization manages data between Applications, Services and Enterprise Information Integration activities, there is a need to

have a well-defined governance model, that outlines and looks for compliance on how data is massaged, transformed and stored throughout the IT infrastructure, including internal and external services (i.e. SaaS, PaaS, IaaS, ASP or others).

The included processes are part of Data Governance, such as data ownership, how data should be classified, and responsibilities that data/asset owners have for their applications and services, as well the necessary controls for data throughout the lifecycle.

- **Operational Risk Management:** Operational Risk Management provides a holistic perspective for risk evaluation from the business perspective. Using the Risk Management framework gives insight to risks and threats to the organization, and the framework is to provide means to assess, manage and control the different risks across the organization.

The use of an Operational Risk Committee (ORC) should be in place, to periodically discuss the threat and compliance landscape that the organization has throughout time. Usually, the participants for this committee are grouped by business (i.e. CEO, COO, CIO and CFO), compliance (CRO and Compliance Officers) and control personnel (Audit, Security and Risk Management).

The use of business impact assessment methodologies are to help the organization to identify which processes are critical for the organization, plan accordingly to protect them, ensure proper continuity plans, and measure the associated risk using Key Risk Indicators.

Key Risk Indicators can be monitored periodically through a risk scorecard, integrating information from security monitoring services or information consolidated on the Information Services Domain.

- **Human Resources Security:** Often, security incidents and breaches happen to organizations because there are no formal controls, awareness, and guidelines for the most important asset that organizations have — people.

This section is created to make sure that formal procedures, codes of conduct, personnel screening, and other best practices are in place for the organization, especially for third parties that supports the cloud services that an organization may have.

- **Security Monitoring Services:** The security and availability monitoring services are positioned in the Business Operations and Support Services Domain, to ensure that the business is the focus, not the events or hardware. It is a common mistake not to focus the security function on the business operations, the processes, and the human behavior behind those processes. Transforming typical infrastructure monitoring into a business operations center, focused on fraud prevention, alignment with the business strategy, business impacts, and operational needs, is the goal of a successful security monitoring service.

Organizations usually concentrate their monitoring activities only on the reactive mode, losing the opportunity to become a business partner. By using monitoring services, businesses are able to identify new opportunities for process improvement, as knowledge about employees' behavior is collected.

In many institutions there are employees that have more access than others to the most critical information, such as customer data, credit cards, etc. If the Security Monitoring Services focus on those users and their behavior, potential fraudulent activities can be prevented.

As the monitoring services start to be less reactive, and more proactive, the focus of Security Monitoring Services is to shift from internal to external threats. This architecture outlines several capabilities oriented on cyber intelligence, looking to prevent threats before they become security incidents.

- **Legal Services:** As security incidents occur, the need for legal counsel is critical for organizations. There are several capabilities included that may help legal counsels lead compliance activities, deal with lawsuits, and track preventive awareness across the organization.

Capabilities that can help increase, track and manage regulatory compliance are also included and detailed in this section.

- **Internal Investigation:** The role for Internal Investigations varies across organizations; some companies have their information security teams performing forensic activities, and more mature companies may have a dedicated team focused on internal and/or external fraud activities.

To better assist investigators, capabilities are oriented to better enable Security Incident Response, Cyber Intelligence, Legal, Security Monitoring, HR and Information Security teams.

Relationships to Other Domains

Business Operations Support Services defines the high-level policy requirements for IT Operation Support Services, Presentation Services, Application Services, Information Services, Infrastructure Services and Security & Risk Management. BOSS embodies the direction of the business, and the objectives of the cloud consumer. BOSS is embodied in the Compliance objectives, Legal objectives, Human Resource requirements, Operational Risk tolerance, and Security Monitoring services that are required to satisfy a client's service-level objectives and jurisdictional legislative mandates.

The BOSS domain works to align the ITOS and the SRM domains with the business' desired strategy, capabilities and risk portfolio.

TECHNOLOGY SOLUTION DOMAINS

Description

IT solutions can be thought of as a stack of technology: the computers and networks are the bottom layer, followed by the data that runs on them, the applications that manipulate the data, and the actual interactions that the users have with the stack. The four technology solution domains (Presentation Services, Application Services, Information Services and Infrastructure Services) are based on the standard multi-tier architecture that is used to build these solutions. The CSA Reference Architecture does not get into all the details of how that architecture works, but instead gets into the details of the security concerns and the required services for each tier in the solution.

Presentation Services: Interaction with the User

Presentation is the website you see when you go to the online bank. It is the voice on the phone when you call the airline reservation system.

Description

The Presentation Services domain is where the end-user interacts with an IT solution. The security requirements for the Presentation Domain vary based on the type of user and the type of service being provided. For instance, a Business-to-Consumer (B2C) website is to have different security concerns comparing to a social media website. The security requirements are also to vary based on the types of endpoints being used by the end-user.

Example

A mobile device provides the risk of locally-stored data being lost with the device, and a shared public kiosk provides the risk of subsequent end-users having access to prior users' data.

Services Provided

- **Presentation Modality:** The Presentation Modality Services focus on the security concerns that differ based on the type of user and type of service. The two major types are consumer service platforms like Social Media, Collaboration, Search, Email and e-Readers, also Enterprise Service Platforms like Business-to-Consumer (B2C), Business-to-Employee (B2E), Business-to-Business (B2B) and more.
- **Presentation Platform:** The Presentation Platform Services focus on the different types of end-points, which the end-users utilize to interact with a solution such as desktops, mobile devices such as smart phones and tablets, portable devices such as laptops, or special purposes devices such as medical devices or smart appliances. The presentation platform also includes the different interaction technologies, such as Speech Recognition or Handwriting Recognition, used to interact with a solution.

Relationships to Other Domains

Presentation Services utilizes the Security and Risk Management domain to authenticate and authorize the end user, to protect the data on the end-point device and in-transit to the Application

Services domain, and to protect the end-point device itself from tampering, theft and malware. The Information Technology Operation and Support domain supplies services to deploy and make changes to the end points, and to manage problems and incidences that the end users experience. The Business Operation Support Services provides security monitoring of the end-points, HR and Compliance policies for end-user usage of IT solutions.

Application Services: Development and Implementation of Business Logic

Think of application services as the processes that developers use to write code, as well as the code itself.

Description

Application services are the rules and processes behind the user interface, which manipulate the data and perform transactions for the user. In an online bank, this might be a bill payment transaction that deducts the payment amount from the users' account, and sends a check to the payee. In addition to the application services of an IT solution, the Application Services domain also represents the development processes that programmers go through when creating applications.

Example

A developer is writing an Application Program Interface (API) that allows a banking system to exchange transactions with other banks. He scans the code with a source code analyzer, and identifies a section of code that is not protected against invalid input, which can corrupt the system. The change is made immediately and the new API is now safe to use.

Services Provided

- **Development Process:** The Development Process must address security concerns, while the solution is being built, using tools like source code scanners that can locate common security flaws in the code, and web application vulnerability scanners, to test if a web application can be manipulated with common techniques used by hackers.

- **Security Knowledge Lifecycle:** In order to build secure applications, a development team must keep up-to-date with the latest threats and appropriate countermeasures to use in development processes. A security framework is often used to provide reusable components, when a development team is building multiple applications.

- **Programming Interfaces:** Programming Interfaces allow one application to talk to another or allow pieces of an application to talk to each other. Input validation is important for these interfaces to make sure that only the expected input is being provided. Lack of this validation can create vulnerabilities, by allowing attackers to inject malicious code into the application, or to retrieve more data than they are supposed to have access to.

- **Integration Middleware:** Integration Middleware are tools like service buses and message queues that allow applications to exchange information without talking directly to each other. Security concerns for these services include making sure the messages being exchanged are not read or tampered with during delivery, and that they are only being sent by reliable sources.

- **Connectivity & Delivery:** Connectivity & Delivery services are the underlying mechanisms that Integration Middleware uses to move the messages between applications. These services must also provide protection for the messages being delivered, such as encrypting the messages to hide their content.

- **Abstraction:** When multiple applications do the same thing, they often use the concept of abstraction so that they have a common language others will understand. While airlines may manage their flights differently from each other, they all may use the same abstraction so that online travel services can find the flights across multiple airlines. These abstractions must include the proper security mechanisms, to ensure that only authorized users are accessing them, and that one user cannot access the information of another without permission.

Relationships to Other Domains

Application Services rely on the Security and Risk Management domain to encrypt messages sent between applications, and to authenticate and authorize applications to talk to each other. The development process of the Application Services domain relies on the threat and vulnerability management services of SRM, to assess the security of the solution being developed. Application Services typically receives input from the Presentation Services domain, and manipulates data in the Information Services domain. Application Services also require servers and network services from the Infrastructure Services domain. The Information Technology Operations and Support domain is used to manage changes to the Application Services. The Business Operations Support Services domain provides security monitoring services, enabling administrators to monitor application activities for any statistically unusual behavior.

Information Services: Managing Data

Information Services refers to the storage of data, usually in databases, but sometimes just in files.

Description

One of the most common sore points across organizations is the amount of data generated across the company, sometimes including redundant data such as different perspectives for the same threat or gap. All this data needs to be transformed into useful information, that business asset owners can use to prioritize, strategize and manage the risk portfolio they own.

This section manages the extraction, transformation, cleansing and loading of information into a common data model either for analytical or operational goals.

Typical Extract, Transform and Load (ETL) data normalization, data mining, balance scorecard, among other capabilities are to reside here.

This domain simplifies all these sources of data by having a data management approach. All data containers are allocated in this domain, where eventually they can be extracted, transformed and loaded into the following:

- **Operational Data Store:** All day-to-day and transactional information are allocated here, using a 360 degrees perspective around information assets, i.e. application and infrastructure vulnerabilities, patching gaps, penetration test results, audit findings and controls per asset.
- **Data Warehouse:** All historical transactions are used to develop a data warehouse or data mart that can measure the success obtained with the risk management program. Also, this model can be used to identify behavior patterns, trends, tendencies and systemic gaps across the organization.

Example

When an administrator creates a user account, the ID and Password are stored in a user directory. When that user logs into the system, a log entry showing the date and time of that log-in is stored in the security-monitoring database.

Services Provided

- **User Directory Services:** All authentication and authorization repositories are allocated in this section, with the goal to simplify the technology footprint for user directories.
- **Security Monitoring Data Management:** All data related to Security Monitoring are allocated here, considering the following main groups:
  - **External Monitoring:** brand protection, honey-pots, web crawling prevention and cyber intelligence.
  - **Internal Monitoring:** SIEM related data, trends, behavior patterns and forensic information.
  - **Executive Reporting:** balance scorecard, executive dashboard and ODS (risk registry).

Threat and vulnerability management data — application compliance, patching, configuration health-checking, infrastructure, application and vulnerabilities.

- **Service Delivery Data Management:** The SDDM focuses on structured or unstructured data related to the management of IT services across the company. This includes service level management, availability management, disaster recovery and recipient of services. A cost-benefit analysis should be performed when considering associated costs to these services.
- **Service Support Data Management:** All data related to providing services to the

business across the company reside here. This includes information related to the service desk, incident management, configuration management, problem management and knowledge management.

- **Data Governance Data Management:** As applications and IT services are rolled and managed across the organization, this section stores evidence, and proper compliance data throughout the software development lifecycle.
- **Risk Management Data Management:** All information related to the information security technical capabilities are stored here, including data governance, application security and data loss prevention among other sources of information that help improve the risk profile gathered per information asset.
- **ITOS Data Management:** This section has data related to the strategy and typical operations for an IT organization, such as the quality management, PMO, enterprise architecture compliance, business and IT alignment, and how all these services are transformed into agreements as we support the business needs.
- **BOSS Data Management:** All sources of data related to the Business Operations Support Services domain are allocated here.
- **Reporting Services:** All tools used to generate operational reports, decision making, balance scorecards, dashboards, and other capabilities that transform the different data sources and data models into useful information for the business, and proper support (operational and strategic) for the risk management strategy reside here.

Relationships to Other Domains

The Information Services domain provides contextual support for Application and Presentation service domains. The Information Technology

Operations and Support domain governs the Application Service change and deployment process periodically implemented and required by other domains. The Business Operations Support Services domain governs security monitoring for information service applications. The BOSS domain then monitors the activities being performed by applications for any unusual behavior.

Infrastructure Services: Facilities, Hardware, Network and Virtual Environments

Infrastructure Services can be visualized as the rows of computers, network cables, power supplies, cooling vents and fire suppression pipes you see inside any standard data center.

Description

Infrastructure Services (IaaS) provide the basic core capabilities that support higher-level capabilities in other areas of the architecture. This is the service layer that supports cloud applications, which are visible to the majority of cloud users. This level is comprised of the virtual machines, applications and databases. Often, IaaS services are deployed centrally and run standard machine images, with all necessary services preconfigured to support ease of integration and reliable connectivity and access.

As they provide a foundation, Infrastructure Services are largely invisible to end users of the cloud service. For example, a customer is likely required, by due diligence, to assure that cloud facilities provide physical security to match the risk characteristics of the uses they make of cloud the services, but may otherwise ignore the operational details of how physical access controls are implemented.

Example

Even the cloud needs to live somewhere physically. These datacenters are physically secured with fences, cameras, security guards, man-traps and badge activated doors. Availability of the infrastructure is ensured with lines to multiple Internet service providers, power generators in the case of power failure, and multiple computers to do the same job in case one fails.

Internal Infrastructure Services

The Internal Infrastructure services are mainly concerned with the physical assets used by the cloud service provider, to support the virtualized services actually seen by cloud users. In many ways, these services are the lowest level and least visible to the end cloud user, although they are the foundation that underlies reliable and secure operation of the cloud service. For instance, without good facility security, there is no need for an adversary to mount a network attack on a cloud service, as it is easier to just walk into the facility and unplug a server or network connection.

- **Facility Security:** Concerned with the security controls applied at the cloud computing facility, that assure a safe and secure operational environment for the physical components of a cloud infrastructure. Examples include restrictions applied to physical access and environmental controls.
- **Servers:** Concerned with the software images that are installed on the physical servers, and the controls applied to assure secure builds of those software images, and how those images are managed.
- **Storage Services:** Concerned with the provisioning, migration and sanitization of physical storage in the infrastructure. Controls at this level assure that storage is available when required, and that its redundancy/reliability requirements match the service requirements.
- **Network Services:** Concerned with managing the security risks posed by the network environment. Controls at this level

include proper network segmentation (for example, assets used by organization A are not visible to organization B), and provision of basic network services, such as an accurate and traceable time standard.

- **Availability Services:** Concerned with assuring the availability of infrastructure components to match the service level objectives. Controls at this level include mirroring of data between geographically dispersed sites, redundant components and the processes for switching between them.
- **Patch Management:** Concerned with assuring that required software fixes are applied, in a controlled and timely fashion, within the infrastructure. This includes both inventorying the services (operating systems, applications, embedded software, and etc.) actually present in the infrastructure, to identify the applicability of a particular fix, and monitoring the infrastructure to assure that required fixes are actually present and installed.
- **Equipment Maintenance:** Concerned with assuring that physical infrastructure devices are appropriately maintained, to assure their continuous operations. Examples include periodic inspection, cleaning, replacement of air filters, and proactive replacement of components when degradation is detected.

Virtual Infrastructure Services

The Virtual Infrastructure inherits some of the same services, as are present in the physical infrastructure. For example, software images must be securely built and managed, for the virtual servers that are hosted on the virtualization platform, provided on the physical server. However, there are also unique requirements for the virtualized infrastructure itself.

- **Desktop "Client" Virtualization:** Concerned with how virtual instances of the traditional desktop are created, presented and managed.
- **Storage Virtualization:** Concerned with how virtualized storage is created, allocated and managed. This includes both "block-based" storage, such as a SAN (Storage Area Network) and "file-based" virtualization, such as NAS (Network Attached Storage), whether provided by a file server or appliance. Controls at this level assure that the storage is adequate according to requirements, properly segregated and secured, and that its performance matches the profile specified in the service level agreement.
- **Server Virtualization:** Concerned with creating, accessing and managing a virtual server. Controls at this level assure that a server is configured correctly and includes the proper software image and hypervisor.
- **Network Virtualization:** Concerned with providing appropriate virtual network services. Controls at this level assure that the virtual network implements proper isolation (see "segmentation" above), required connectivity and proper access controls.

Relationships to Other Domains

Infrastructure Services provides many of the core components and capabilities, which support capabilities provided in other parts of the architecture. For example, the higher levels of governance provided in the Security and Risk Management domain is largely meaningless, without good physical security at the base level of the infrastructure. Service Delivery and Support under the ITOS domain similarly depends on the performance and reliability assurances provided at the infrastructure level.

Chapter 5
Security Information and Event Management Implementation Guidance

Yushi Shen
Microsoft Corporation, USA

Ling Wu
EMC² Corporation, USA

Yale Li
Microsoft Corporation, USA

Shaofeng Liu
Microsoft Corporation, USA

Qian Wen
Endronic Corp, USA

ABSTRACT

This chapter is about guidance and implementation prepared by the Cloud Security Alliance (CSA) Security as a Service (SecaaS) workgroup, which is made up of users and practitioners in the field of information security. In preparing this implementation guide, input has been sought from experts throughout Europe, the Middle East, and the United States. A lot of professional judgment and experience are applied in the architecture, engineering, and implementation of a Security Information and Event Management (SIEM) guide to ensure that it logs the information necessary to successfully increase visibility and remove ambiguity, surrounding the security events and risks that an organization faces. By providing SIEM as a service under SecaaS, the provider has to be able to accept log and event information, customer information and event feeds, and conduct information security analysis, correlation, and support incident response. By providing flexible real-time access to SIEM information, it allows the party consuming the SIEM service to identify threats acting against their environment cloud. This identification then allows for the appropriate action and response to be taken to protect or mitigate the threat. The simple step of increasing visibility and removing ambiguity is a powerful tool to understanding the information security risks that an organization is facing.

DOI: 10.4018/978-1-4666-4801-2.ch005

OVERVIEW

Purpose

This chapter provides guidance on how to evaluate, architect and deploy cloud based services providing SIEM services to both enterprise and cloud based networks, infrastructure and applications. The guidance addresses the leveraging of cloud based SIEM services in support of cloud environments, both public and private, hybrid environments and traditional non-cloud environments. While this document addresses SIEM as a cloud service, it does not preclude a hybrid environment for enterprises that have traditional SIEM deployments where the SIEM cloud service supplements.

Intended Audience and Document Organization

The target audience is primarily IT security managers, technical architects and systems managers that are responsible for monitoring and auditing their organization's infrastructure and applications. SIEM data can be used for both general monitoring, as well as security monitoring and auditing (Laundrup & Schultz, 2011). In addition to technical staff, other staff such as IT generalists, auditors and compliance managers may benefit from the understanding of higher level contents. Finally, reasonable technically aware C-level board members such as CTOs, CISOs, and CIOs can find this a useful reference, in providing an overview of cloud based SIEM services, and the areas that need to be considered, if they are to implement and consume such a service.

This chapter is arranged in such a way that the content becomes more technical in nature as the sections progress. The subsequent sections are organized as follows:

- **Requirements:** This section is intended as a high level overview of SIEM functions and implementation options. It address-

es several key functionalities for which SIEM can be leveraged. The section is to also touch on less traditional deployments, which can be implemented in specific markets, where regulatory or other compliances require it. The intended audience includes executives and the senior leadership responsible for IT and security operations, compliance officers, and other decision makers within the enterprise. The material is written for executive level discussions, and indicates a baseline for best practices on the implementation and design of security services in the Cloud.

- **Architectural Implementation:** This section details the considerations and concerns that should be part of the decision-making conversation, whether by an architecture team, auditing team, or within the context of a purchase decision. The section is written for those who are implementing, integrating, or performing a technical evaluation of cloud based SIEM. This section is also well suited for auditors, to help them understand typical services and capabilities that may be implemented for cloud based SIEM deployments.

- **Technical Implementation:** This section discusses in high technical detail those items described in the previous two sections. This material is written for system architects, designers, implementers and developers, and includes guidance for the implementation of secure Cloud-based implementation of the subject.

- **References and Links:** This section contains links to trusted sources of information regarding SIEM and Security-as-a-Service, and references used in the creation of this document.

Scope

This guide covers generic (non-industry specific) implementations only at this time. While some applications discussed herein may apply only to a few vertical markets, the examples and illustrations are very likely going to refer to a specific industry. Despite this, the guide should be regarded as neutral in all aspects, and any inference to a specific vendor or industry is purely accidental. This guide also does not address specific requirements that individual SecaaS providers may have in order to establish the service.

REQUIREMENTS

SIEM Functionality

Security Information and Event Management (SIEM) systems accept log and event information (Kavanaugh, 2012). Information can come from a broad range of systems, including traditional security systems, management systems or any other systems which provide a log output. Traditional security systems include firewalls, intrusion detection/prevention systems, anti-malware systems and the like. Management systems include Active Directory (AD), Identity and Access Management (IAM) systems, Network Management Systems and etc. Less traditional sources of data can include access control systems, video monitoring systems, elevator control systems, HVAC systems, telephone switches (VOIP or otherwise), email, DLP and etc.

Applications and devices, designed to achieve objectives such as protecting the perimeter, managing access rights and securing against challenging end point vulnerabilities, are often mutually exclusive in terms of their effectiveness, and offer no centralized oversight to the critical threats that can pose the greatest risk to a cloud infrastructure. A SIEM can help gain centralized visibility, leverage the value of existing investments, and prepare for potential threats that could compromise their critical information assets for business. A SIEM establishes an early warning system to take helpful preventive actions. An effective early warning sys-

tem detects threats based on a global perspective, and provides in-depth information about them. It also recommends measures that can be taken to protect the cloud infrastructure.

The information collected by the SIEM is typically aggregated (put into a single stream), and normalized (translated into a standardized format), by the SIEM to reduce variations and speed up the subsequent analysis. It is then correlated between data sources, and analyzed against a set of rules or correlation algorithms, in providing real-time reporting and alerting on incidents/events that may require intervention. The logs are typically stored in a manner that prevents tampering to enable their use as evidence in any investigations.

The SIEM provides maintenance and authoring of correlation rules, and allows the system rules to cover a multitude of conditions (Park, 2011). In addition to condition action rules, a SIEM supports rules that can fire based on arbitrary conditions, as well as statistical anomalies. An example of one of these types of rules is a negative condition rule, where the absence of an event over a period of time fires the rule, such as a back-up process that misses a scheduled routine.

Traditional 'on premises' SIEM implementations often take considerably more effort and time to implement successfully than businesses envision. As such, SIEM projects, especially in SMBs or larger enterprises with limited IT expertise, often either do not happen at all, fail or are only partially successful. While the promise of SIEM provided from a cloud based service can provide a scalable, fully managed SIEM service that the customer can leverage and integrate with public cloud, private cloud, and on premise systems and infrastructures, it is important to note that many of the same requirements are to still exist, and the business needs to ensure that adequate resources are devoted to the initial set-up, and subsequent monitoring and maintenance of rules. SIEM in the cloud enables the customer to test the service, and gradually deploy and integrate it with their systems, while only paying for the amount they are using rather than having to purchase a full SIEM solution up front. Some clients may opt to leverage cloud based SIEM services to monitor their systems in the public cloud space, while using their 'on premises' SIEM implementation for their private cloud and traditional system implementations.

Business Drivers

SIEM capabilities are highly flexible and are capable of addressing multiple needs within organizations. These drivers can be more practical, as in reducing the efforts by an enterprise to gather network and system usage information for network architectural purposes, for risk management, security, also regulatory and compliance uses. While each of these may seem unique and unrelated, they all rely on the same organizational data.

Log Data Management

A SIEM provides log retention and retrieval capabilities through flexible querying and reporting options, providing auditors and other related stakeholders the information they need. It can be leveraged to manage the ever growing volumes of log data that are needed to show compliance with legal and industry rules, along with best practices. A properly configured SIEM can search for the proverbial needle in a haystack, and find the data necessary in short order. This can include searches through archived data that may not reside immediately within the SIEM system infrastructure, but located in a storage cloud. Most enterprise class SIEM are also able to automatically sort, segregate and dispose of data based on multiple retention schedules, in order to discard excess information after its retention period, while maintaining data and event summaries for longer time periods.

Risk Management

A SIEM produces executive, technical and audit-level reports that are highly effective at communi-

cating risk levels, and the security posture of the cloud infrastructure. SIEM technology is being used not just to analyze data after an incident, but also perform near real-time detection, quickly followed by meaningful event management and subsequent forensic examination. Where SIEM is a differentiator, it is in the capability to quickly sift through a sea of security and log data, to detect behaviors in the enterprise that indicate malfeasance is afoot. This includes not just traditional threats presented by "hackers" on the web, but can include Advanced Persistent Threats (APT), insider threats, and malware threats to the network. It can also be used to detect other forms of questionable behavior such as insider trading, monitoring identity and access activities, unauthorized personnel looking at health records in hospitals, fraud detection, privilege escalation and more (Laundrup, 2008).

Newer SIEM logic capabilities now include the ability to identify threats and vulnerabilities in the cloud infrastructures, and provide remediation steps to address those threats in as close to real time as possible. This helps the enterprise to mitigate the added threats and vulnerabilities that come with migration of systems into the cloud infrastructure.

Regulatory and Compliance Requirements

There are a host of regulatory requirements that can be addressed by SIEM. Regulatory needs include national/international rules and laws, that businesses must show compliance along with industry specific rules and best practices which enterprises either want or must comply, in order to retain membership in the industry, and in some enterprises, internal policies and requirements that the senior leadership wishes to ensure compliance. They can be privacy laws such as the European Protection Directive, or the Personal Information Protection Law in Japan, banking rules such as those put forth by the Financial Services Agency (Japan), Healthcare rules such as HIPAA (US), international rules such as PCI imposed by the Payment Card Industry, or simply enterprise policies on matters such as Acceptable Use Policies or data retention rules. In the past, the requirement has been to show annual or biennial compliance to such rules, but the trend is for businesses and agencies to demonstrate continuous compliance, which is only made possible by using complex dynamic systems such as SIEMs. Many businesses may also find that it is less costly to invest in a SIEM solution, cloud based, traditional or hybrid, than the cost of the higher audit frequencies by major auditing firms or a large team of internal auditors. Compliance remains the most common justification for new SIEM implementations.

Incidents and Events

Any event sequence can be traced by a SIEM, in order to help reduce risks within the enterprise. A SIEM generated incident creates a workflow to facilitate the containment, eradication and recovery process. It can include the initiation and tracking of checklists for individual incidents, to ensure all necessary actions are being taken to minimize and contain the incident, in a standardized and policy-driven manner. This workflow can also feed a third party ticketing help-desk solution, wherein a ticket or series of tickets can be created to be worked on, and traced back into the system. If these events require additional scrutiny by regulatory or law enforcement agencies, a SIEM can generate forensically sound data subsets with time stamps, that can be exported and analyzed independently by the SIEM or third party forensic tools.

Implementation Considerations

In considering a SIEM solution, it becomes important to consider the problem or problems being addressed from an enterprise perspective, to ensure

it does not morph into an undefined and costly project addressing nothing. This should include documenting in detail each of the problems that need to be addressed by the solution, and the beneficiary of the solution. It should also include the perspective of how this would benefit the corporate departments in terms of security, risk, compliance, fraud, Human Resources, Audit and etc., and also how responses to actions generated are to improve processes over current solutions. This should include specific use case requirements.

Other implementation items to consider include reviewing the offering, and making sure it fulfills all the business requirements. Most SecaaS SIEM providers limit their offering in several ways, so an evaluation period may be an important step. When evaluating SIEM as a service offering, customer should check the following:

- **Monitored Devices:** Most providers market their offer based on the number of monitored devices. There could be a difference between how their SIEM product counts devices. Try to list all the devices that should be included. Some SecaaS SIEM vendors count a log server as a single device, whereas others base their count on the number of devices that report into the log server.
- **Supported Device vs. Unsupported:** Some SecaaS SIEM providers charge extra for unsupported devices or devices that have unique log formats. Insist on viewing the support matrix and understand how it affects the overall cost.
- **Number of Reports / Rules / EPS (Event per Second):** Some SecaaS SIEM provider charge extra on additional reports and events. Make sure that you are covered.
- **Standard vs. Custom Rules:** Some SecaaS SIEM vendors charge a per-rule fee for each rule invoked. They may also

charge extra for custom rules or rules that the enterprise creates ad hoc to examine a problem. This can become very expensive.

- **Number of Dashboard or/and Users:** The number of dashboards and services, made available for self service and customer internal use of SIEM, should be clearly defined. There is typically a "Per Seat" charge for the dashboards, and often the internal use of the SIEM is discouraged by charging extra for that service.

- **Log Retention, Log Access and Log Storage:** Make sure the offering matches your regulatory requirements. Also make sure that once the logs reach the retention limit, that they are deleted. If the retention policies require active and then long term retention, make sure that the vendor provides an option to transfer the logs to the enterprise in a standard (non-proprietary) format for internal long term retention.

Cloud vs. Hybrid System

As with any solution, there are several ways that a SecaaS SIEM solution can be implemented. It can be a stand-alone solution in the cloud that monitors the enterprise's traditional data center assets, private/public/hybrid cloud assets, or both (see Figure 1).

Another option is to enlist the services of a SecaaS SIEM provider to monitor the enterprise external or cloud assets, while using a traditional SIEM to monitor the traditional and private cloud infrastructures (see Figure 2). These can then be linked, by forwarding the SIEM traffic from the SecaaS SIEM to the 'Master' SIEM, in the enterprise network for overall analysis and monitoring. The advantage is that the enterprise minimizes its exposure of information to the SecaaS SIEM provider, and if the enterprise connectivity to the internet is broken, they still have the enterprise SIEM to collect, analyze and

Figure 1. SecaaS SIEM only

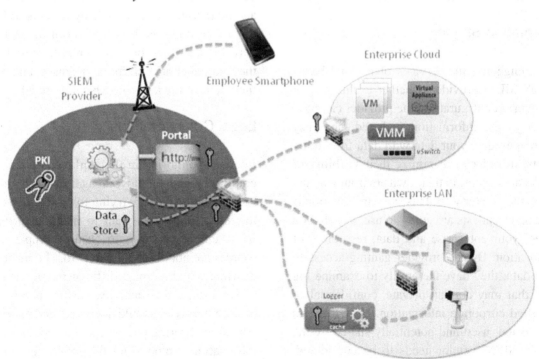

Figure 2. Hybrid SIEM Architecture

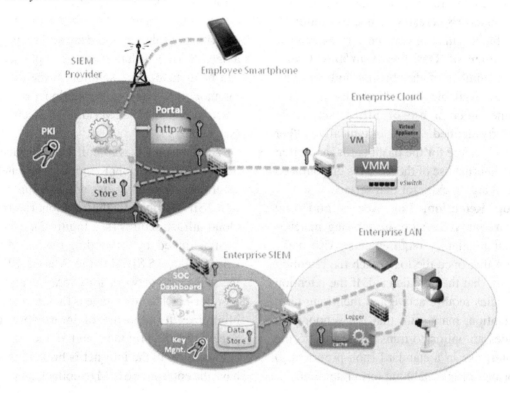

respond to an incident, while the SecaaS SIEM continues to monitor the enterprise cloud assets.

Information Sharing

When engaging the services of a cloud based SecaaS SIEM provider, whether exclusively or in a hybrid configuration, the provider can have access to the information gathered, and may opt to aggregate your data with data from other clients, in order to maximize their visibility of attacks and issues, in their own environment and within the greater web. This same information is what their analysts are going to use, to help you protect your enterprise and data, regardless of the location. By the provider gaining access to these data, they have the ability to examine log feeds that may contain private, confidential or classified corporate information. How the data is collected, used and potentially shared by the SecaaS SIEM vendor needs to be considered.

The data collected by the SIEM reveals a great deal about the weaknesses and vulnerabilities of an enterprise, it can be used by hackers to help them determine the best method of attacking a network, and it can be used in real-time to guide them to penetrate enterprise defenses, and alert them if such breaches have been detected.

Legal Considerations

Internet monitoring in the workplace often pits employers and employees against each other, because both sides are trying to protect personal interests. Employees want to maintain privacy while employers want to ensure company resources are not misused. Since SIEM collect log data that may show many different traffic streams, server logs, e-mail activity, surfing habits and more, enterprises should document and maintain ethical monitoring policies, and avoid the indiscrimination of monitoring the employees' online activities, whether it is inadvertent or otherwise. It could require changes to corporate policies, as well as employment and union contracts in some instances.

A secondary legal concern is that when data is collected, it may then create legal or political ramifications to having the data and failing to take action on it. Realizing that not every bit of data can be thoroughly analyzed, an enterprise must be ready to respond to questions as to why they had the data but did not act upon it. In some situations in some places, not having the data may be more desirable, than having the data, and then failing to take action.

Ethical Considerations

The security analysts and other personnel assigned to monitor the SIEM feeds may be able to view e-mail activity, social media, and more in the performance of their duties. While the legal issues must be addressed, there is a larger ethical consideration that must also be considered. The employees' privacy in these areas are to be compromised, as it becomes visible to the analysts. The analysts monitoring the information must be made aware of privacy and confidentiality expectations, as well as the employees being monitored should be able to expect some level of privacy and confidentiality, regardless of what the legal muster and enterprise policies may be.

Performance Requirements

When determining what level of security to contract out to a SecaaS vendor, the leadership needs to evaluate and consider the consequences to each decision. Considerations include but are not limited to questions such as:

- Who is responsible for monitoring alerts locally, and at the vendor level?

- What alert responses can the vendor perform? What does the enterprise IT staff do? A clear delineation of duties has to be spelled out, so that both the enterprise and the vendor have a clear understanding of what the expectations are, and how handoffs are to be accomplished.

- How does the vendor gain access in response to an alert? If the SecaaS SIEM vendor is expected to respond by actively protecting the enterprise cloud, they need to access and administrative right to it. Should they be expected to protect the enterprise network, they will need administrative access to the enterprise network.

- What actions are the vendors allowed to take? Granting administrative access to the vendor for the purposes of defending the network, with unfettered access to the network and its components.

- How much access does the vendor want/need? How much is the enterprise willing to give them?

- Graphical event overview (a map of the network and the issues) – This type of visual display enhances the abilities of analysts to respond to breaches and infections, by providing a quick look to determine where problems are, and how they are progressing and/or spreading. Is the vendor expected to provide analysts and network personnel for combating a breach or infection?

Service Level Agreements

The Service Level Agreements (SLAs) for cloud services are typically poorly written, and favor the SecaaS SIEM provider more-so than the user. This is because the providers wrote the SLA, so it is incumbent upon the enterprise senior leadership, and the legal staff to ensure the rights and needs of the enterprise is best served. Some areas requiring careful considerations are:

- Provisions for delegated and/or joint control must be described in detail in the SLA. This is particularly important, if the provider is tasked with monitoring and acting upon incidents, which are then worked by analysts of both parties;
- Requirements for availability, handling, storage and disposal of proprietary and personally identifiable information must be specifically stated;
- Any requirements for encryption of data at rest and/or in motion must be delineated in detail, including who holds and/or controls the key materials;
- Detailed requirements for incident response, business continuity and disaster recovery procedures and operations must be spelled out;
- Third-party audit arrangements must be made explicit. This is particularly important if law enforcement agencies require access to the data collected by the provider. If the data resides in a different continent, you may bear all the costs of the agency to travel to the location and collect it;
- Notification procedures, if the SecaaS SIEM provider is served with a legal dictate to provide access to data that may include your data;
- The requirements to ensure that the data collected by the SecaaS SIEM provider be collected and stored in a forensically sound manner, that meets the legal requirements of your particular country and regulatory rules;
- Availability requirements, to include the communications channels between the SecaaS SEIM provider and you;
- Privacy and security of the data;
- If and how access to the data is arranged in the event it is needed for forensic purposes.

Most providers grant you access to your own data only, but not to affiliated data that may reveal additional information that could be useful in an investigation;
- Ability to audit the SecaaS SIEM vendor and their facilities. This may be particularly important if your enterprise needs a SSAE 16 or SAS 70 audit, a PCI audit or other audit in order to demonstrate your ability to comply with a rule or regulatory requirement;
- Performance guarantees and warranties should a SecaaS SIEM provider acts negligently or even maliciously.

Ultimately, an organization's contracts and/or legal office is responsible for critically examining and approving terms of any SLAs, for the protection of the enterprise. It is incumbent upon the senior leadership to ensure that all potential issues are raised, addressed and understood up front. The signee must thoroughly understand the downside and worst cases in the cloud based SecaaS SIEM, to help ensure that appropriate provisions are included in the SLA. Ideally, the providers should include indemnity clauses, such that if they make mistakes that are costly to their customers (Net Forensics, 2008), the SecaaS SIEM providers have to provide monetary compensation to cover the harm done. Most providers do not want to do this, but it is in the best interests of the enterprise to ensure that all possible protections are in place, and that there are compensation clauses for mistakes and loss-of-service that results in costs to the enterprise. Any "hold harmless" clauses in a SecaaS SIEM contract or SLA should be automatically eliminated.

ARCHITECTURAL IMPLEMENTATION

The architectural integration of a Cloud based SIEM or hybrid SIEM should be carefully considered up front. The key to a successful architecture is understanding how the enterprise operates, what the key business patterns are, and what the key assets are. Other important knowledge is to understand what the identified business drivers for the SIEM system is, so that the architecture is optimized to support them. The approach documented herein is intended to address any SIEM system, and should be used every time a new problem that the SIEM system is designated to solve is identified. It does mean effort has to be applied, and with a clear objective. (NOTE: For the purpose of architectural (Section 3) and technical discussions (Section 4), the SIEM is referred generically as the SIEM or the SIEM system, in lieu of attempting to define it as a Cloud based SIEM, traditional SIEM or hybrid SIEM.)

Architectural Planning

In order to develop a successful plan, the architectural goals should ensure that the detection phase in the defended framework is made stronger, by increasing the breadth and accuracy of detection. It should also support other phases, by providing intelligence for decisions in protection, response and recovery, and ensure the best possible defense, by optimizing security management within and across enterprises, and into the cloud.

Figure 3. SIEM Reference Architecture

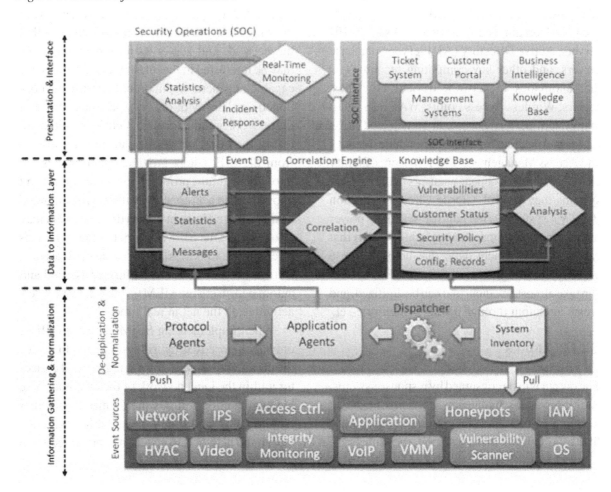

SIEM Inputs

The SIEM system gets input from other security solutions as sources, and provides output to response processes. SIEM is the core component to aggregate, normalize and monitor security events across a broad range of network, security, host, databases and application components. It also provides security information normalization, context, correlation and analytics.

In many SIEM solutions, Log Management is a built-in or add-on component. SIEM takes input from the network, host, database, application logs, and other security tools, such as Vulnerability Management systems, firewalls, anti-malware systems, Data Loss Prevention systems (DLP), honey-pot and honey-net systems and Intrusion Detection/Protection Systems (IDS/IPS). It may also gather data from network devices, servers such as Domain Name Servers (DNS), WEB servers, Active Directory (AD) servers, database servers, and other key computing resources so that anomalies in network devices (switches, routers, Wireless Access Points [WAPs] and etc.) and system performances can be detected. Less traditional sources of data can include Identity and Access Management (IAM) Systems, facility HVAC systems, occupancy sensors or the lighting systems they control, Closed Circuit Television (CCTV) systems, fire control systems, power management systems, and any other system that can provide pertinent data, that helps define a security event in the enterprise. A SIEM system can take almost any input that can be digitized, and create an output through a well written rule-set.

SIEM Outputs

The output is to be consumed by response systems, auditing systems, maintenance systems, helpdesk ticketing systems and other phases in the defense lifecycle. One of these systems, the Enterprise Security Intelligence (ESI) is a core analytics component, which extends the capabilities of a solid SIEM implementation. Security intelligence is an explicit deliverable, and aims at increased accuracy and breadth of security detection and protection, as well as optimal security management. Technically, ESI could be achieved by custom analysis, scripting or coding, as an extension of SIEM with strategic objectives for enterprises' IT security and risk management.

Other deliverables include system compliance reporting, to monitor real-time compliance with pertinent rules and regulations. These could be standardized reports created regularly or could include *ad hoc* reports in response to specific regulatory or leadership queries. Network and system performance data is often a security domain (availability) that many architects ignore. Since all the network and server systems feed their logs into the SIEM, it stands to reason that the network and server management functions may be interested in the infrastructure reports it is capable of generating, in order to ensure the continued availability of the enterprise network. For the network architecture and security architecture teams, the historical performance data available from the SIEM logs provide important insight into where future problem areas may arise, and allow them to act proactively to ensure continued availability and integrity. The HR department may also leverage the SIEM system to request reports on employee activities and potential malfeasance. Active investigations can be further assisted and automated, using the SIEM to track an employee's activities on the net in real time.

When implementing SIEM as SecaaS SIEM only (as opposed to a hybrid system), it is likely for the provider to install a log aggregator and collector within the local network of the customer. The log aggregator's abilities should match customer requirements, and should be suitably positioned within the network, to ensure it is protected from internal and external attacks. Here is a list of common requirement by customers to review with your SecaaS SIEM offering:

- The log aggregator should support all protocols used for logging within the enterprise;
- The log aggregator should have the ability to store logs for a specified amount of time, if the provider server is unavailable or somehow disconnected;
- Logs sent from aggregator to SecaaS SIEM provider should be encrypted, either by VPN, encrypting the logs at source, or using trunk encryption devices. Note that SSL VPNs typically add a 30% overhead to the data stream, which must be considered when planning for capacity;
- Some log aggregator can mask or filter out log items that contain confidential information. Internal compression of logs before sending SIEM provider can help handle risks such as network latency.

Operations

The SIEM system architecture should also reflect the security operation edicts set forth by the enterprise. This reflects how the alerts generated are monitored, and who is monitoring them. If the alerts are monitored locally, the infrastructure would be different than if monitored at the vendor. The subsequent response pattern should also be addressed, to include how communications are to occur between the monitoring center and the IT staff. If the monitoring is accomplished by the SIEM vendor, then a DOS attack would preclude the IT staff from receiving any email or SMS messaging alerting them. Conversely, if all alarms are monitored locally, a breach and subsequent DOS attack in the cloud can take hours to receive, eliminating the ability of the network and security personnel to respond.

The response to alerts is to dictate further security and architectural considerations, depending on how the incident response is directed. If the SecaaS vendor is accountable for the response to an alert, considerations must be given to how the vendor gains access to respond to the alert, and how the enterprise IT staff and management are kept appraised of their actions.

Considerations

Given all the possible advantages of a SIEM, there are significant considerations that must be given to ensure that all the functionality can occur without degrading the network. In developing the architecture, the architects must consider how the increased log data flows are to impact network performance. As this is a security system, it is important to also consider the network priorities. For normal operations, it is clear what systems take priority over others, but when the network is being compromised or suffering the effects of a Denial of Service (DOS) attack, the data priorities may change from an operational posture to a purely defensive posture. Whether the log data is to travel on the main network channels in existence, or if an alternate, back-channel infrastructure is created and installed to support contingencies, is a decision that must be made up front, and not when the Network Security Operations Center is in an all-out response mode.

Other considerations would be the network and external bandwidth requirements, data feed encryption, accessibility, and multipath architectures (a primary and a back-up path), so that security data can keep flowing regardless of how the network is being affected. One significant architectural decision, that must be made up front, is whether the SIEM should contain all log data, meaning whether a cloud SIEM needs a Big Data solution, or that the data should be filtered before going into SIEM, so data in SIEM is reduced to the bare minimum needed to support the business objectives. Another possibility is that the SecaaS SIEM becomes an intermediary SIEM, serving the enterprise Cloud infrastructure, which then reports directly to the traditional SIEM contained within the traditional data center.

Concerns

The major concern of a cloud based, SecaaS SIEM infrastructure is that when the infrastructure is under attack, a poorly architected solution means that the analysts and senior management lose the security provided by the SIEM infrastructure. An enterprise under a distributed DOS attack is most likely to lose connectivity, response and remediation data from the SIEM, if the SIEM systems share the enterprise network data flows. The response to the incident is only as good as the security information it is based upon. Therefore alternate routes for the security systems should be considered.

The deperimiterization of security controls, including the SecaaS SIEM, creates the most confusion in security today. With the integration of public cloud based services, private cloud services, traditional networks, and the mobile workforce, a well layered and segmented approach needs to be created in order to support a SIEM system. When the enterprise network is under attack or failing, the SIEM system infrastructure needs to be solid, so that the incident response teams can rely on the data to protect and remediate.

Disaster Recovery and Business Continuity (DR/BC) is another area of concern for network and security teams. Often, the data within the SIEM system holds the clues to what happened and what problem that needs to be addressed, before the enterprise can be returned to normal. Furthermore, consideration needs to be given, when the data feeds for the SIEM system fail, and what happens to the data at that time. Most

regulatory driven systems require that a back-up system exists to gather the information, so that when the security systems come back on line, a proper forensic examination can occur with backup log feeds.

Time standards and delays must be addressed in the architecture. Most SIEM systems require a standard time source and all data is time-stamped as it arrives. If the SIEM system includes both a SecaaS SIEM and a traditional SIEM, these timestamps must be synchronized to the same time standard, to ensure that the two logs (a local and a SecaaS SIEM vendor log) can be combined in a sound forensic manner for analysis. This is not an impossible task, since time delays between correlation at the vendor site and the return alert receipts along with timestamps in the network logs, can provide the information necessary to accomplish this.

Security of log data in transit and the security of log data at rest are also major concerns for the architects. Encrypted data is useless if the keys are somehow corrupted or lost. The security of logs at the vendor should not be protected by the same keys as those within the enterprise, and all the transactions between the vendor and the enterprise needs to be accomplished using keys that are regular.

TECHNICAL IMPLEMENTATION

While the legal and architectural details of a SIEM system implementation are crucial in ensuring the implementation of a successful SIEM system operation, it is the operational analysis and the rules that guarantee that it works.

The Operational Laws of SIEM

An effective enterprise security management system must encompass the six laws of SIEM systems:

Comprehensive Enterprise Coverage

All production layers (networks, hosts, applications, databases, identities) and environments (on-premise and cloud) must be considered as suspects of advanced attacks, and covered by SIEM system, even if they appear to be "healthy."

Information Interaction and Correlation

The SIEM system must have security data input sources from events and logs of all network devices, hosts, databases, applications and identity directories, in order to create a full threat knowledge base for the enterprise. It is vital to intelligently correlate information to derive meaningful information from a flood of data. Any systems not connected to the SIEM system is therefore a non-player, and its information cannot be used to detect and generate alerts, and any attacks on them are virtually undetectable.

Technology Interaction and Correlation

The SIEM system must be integrated with other security technologies, such as IDS/IPS, Firewall, DLP, IAM, Vulnerability Management, firewalls, and Anti-Malware systems. Those technologies are correlation sources, in order to lower false positive rates, increase accuracy and breadth of security detection.

Business Interaction and Correlation

The SIEM system must be aware of its business context. Advanced attacks are usually targeted with a great deal of business information. When interaction and correlation is extended with business information, ISRM is capable of thinking as the enemy, predict an attacker's priorities, reduce the noise, and derive more meaningful intelligence.

Cross-Boundary Intelligence for Better Decision Making

Security activities and the intelligence that results from SIEM output must not be in isolation. Organizational boundaries must be crossed by the SIEM system to achieve enterprise security intelligence and support decisions for protection, response and recovery.

Visualized Output for Dynamic and Real-Time Defense

The output of SIEM system must be visualized to help drive preventive and corrective controls, to stop advanced attacks or block data exfiltration attempts. Only easily consumable output can drastically reduce response time, minimize damage, and make possible quick responses to investigate and determine root cause of security issues and breaches.

Logging Configurations

The operational rules require specific log data from all the network systems being monitored. For example, merely by pointing the logs of a domain controller to the SIEM system does not guarantee that the logs related to employee login and log-off can be obtained. Unless the audit policy setting on a domain controller is properly configured, that data is not going to be sent out to the logging facility or SIEM system. Windows domain controllers offer 16 different options just for DNS logging. Similar logging criteria exists for nearly all other systems tied to the SIEM system. Thus it is incumbent upon the security analysts operating the SIEM system, to ensure that they receive the feeds necessary to make the proper analysis and alerts required by the business. In order to do this, the analysts should determine:

- What elements of the data provide us the necessary context;
- Which exact fields are relevant;
- If the data frequency supports the proposed solution;
- If the data resides in a centralized, easily accessed location;
- If the data is raw or has it already been aggregated, normalized or filtered in a way that could adversely affect our proposed solution.

Each of these factors should be analyzed, to ensure that they support the needs of any proposed rules. Logging configurations should be documented, with documentation as to why each data feed is needed. Finally, these data feeds should not be considered final in any way. As the needs of the business change, as vulnerabilities and operations change, the rules are to require different data feeds to accomplish the business objectives of the SIEM system.

Building Rule Scenarios

One significant stumbling block that most security teams have is selecting or building the rules provided by the vendor. Some are tempted to enable all the rules or a significant portion of rules provided, thinking that it can help secure the enterprise. It is most likely to bury the security staff in false positive alerts, and may more significantly allow situations that should have alerted go unnoticed (false negative). The simplest way to prevent chaos, and to start building the rule sets that support the business drivers, is to build individual scenarios to describe violations that should be detected and responded to. The scenarios should include the situation and the subsequent response, and are best when they contain active verbs. The following are a some examples of different scenarios:

Scenario 1: Enterprise Correlation and Sharing

Ed is a Security Analyst on the Security Investigation team. He uses a different SIEM system from the one used by IT and other organizations. Fortunately, all SIEM systems use a common information sharing format. Ed configures his SIEM as the hub to get aggregated information from all SIEM systems, both on-premise and in the cloud. He is able to correlate data companywide, share information with other IT organizations, and view the security posture of the entire enterprise from a single pane of glass.

Scenario 2: Incident Response Enablement

Georgia is a Security Analyst on the IT Ops Response team. Prior to the SIEM deployment, she spends most of her time collecting VI and triaging an event. Only a small percentage of her time has been spent dealing with real incidents, and working with the forensic team. After the SIEM deployment, her VI workload is taken over by SIEM in an automated VI feed. She can also quickly assess events during the triage time. The best part is that most events are correlated and classified as noise by SIEM automatically. When a real attack incident happens, Georgia is able to quickly contain the compromised system, and work with other teams to help with the recovery phase.

Scenario 3: Malware Protection

Matt is an Anti-Malware architect in the Security Ops team. Recently he feels that SCEP cannot cover 100% of his needs. Some modern malware do not have signatures. The enterprise malware reporting is provided by the Anti-Malware server, which is unable to correlate Malware events with other security events. Correlation rules are configured to link malware data with vulnerability data and asset data. The rule uses vulnerability data to qualify systems that has a chance for infection. The asset data helps to link infected systems to owners, business roles and other asset parameters.

Finally, alert rules have been set up, and for infected systems, alerts are sent to owners and the Ops team if the malware fails to be cleaned. Other alerts are also triggered for repeatedly failed signature updates or internal systems attempting to connect to systems/websites on the malware blacklist.

Scenario 4: Tracking User Actions across Disparate Systems

Kim is a security analyst on the Security Investigation team. One day, her manager calls her into an emergency meeting with people from the Security, Legal and HR teams. She learns that an anti-company article has been published on the Wall Street Journal. An anonymous author criticized her company for outsourcing jobs abroad that hurt employment in the US. A lot of detailed facts, such as contracts with India and Chinese outsourcing companies, are shown as examples. This article triggered several anti-corporate demonstrations. The team concluded that the author is an insider and asked Kim to help.

Kim then ran a SIEM user action report and specified a few disparate system logs including SAP system, contract management system, and IIS server logs used by outsourcing projects. Based on user access activities, the report generated a list of suspicious users. After further investigation of related activities, one of the users is identified as the top suspect, because he has tried to access related systems and servers more than others in this period of time. Additionally, he has downloaded related contract files that matches the content in the Wall Street Journal article.

Based on information from SIEM, the insider is caught. He cannot deny his activities, and is finally terminated based on company policy.

Scenario 5: Server User Activity Monitoring

Sam is a new hire on the Security Ops team. One day, he configures the newly deployed SIEM to collect login success/failure events, from all servers in both on-premise and cloud environments. In the next few days, he averages a daily baseline of failed logins in SIEM. Based on his analysis, he configures two additional rules on the SIEM.

- **A Correlation Rule:** The daily logon failure is ##% more than the baseline;
- **An Alerting Rule:** X number of login failures on any server in y number of minutes, followed by successful login within z number of minutes to the same server.

Finally, he tuned the numbers through testing, so SIEM can generate a reliable login anomaly report from the correlation rule and trigger alerts from the alerting rule, without producing "false positives".

After the rules are established, Sam's team is able to see the server login anomaly trends in the dashboard, add this data into the security health index for the CIOs scorecard, and receive alerts when a particular server is under a brute force password attack.

Scenario 6: Web Server Attack Detection

Wendy is a Security Engineer on the ACE team. She spends a lot of time performing Line of Business Web application security code reviews, static code scans and pen tests. However, she still cannot guarantee web applications are 100% security bug free. She knows that most of external attackers are exploiting website vulnerabilities, and this has led to a vast majority of security breaches.

Wendy is happy that the SIEM team has worked with her and her internal customers, to configure SIEM to detect attacks against Web Servers and Web Applications. They decide to feed Windows event logs, IIS logs and Web application logs into the SIEM.

Finally, she is able to use a rich set of reporting from the dashboard to monitor the websites:

- Report: Trends of errors by type over time
- Report: Injection attacks and patterns (*.exe or suspicious strings from visiting browsers)
- Report: Microsoft IIS – Top 10 page not found (error 404)
- Report: Microsoft IIS – Top 10 Script Errors (error 501)
- Report: Microsoft IIS – Top 10 Authentication Failure (error 401)

Rule Documentation

One of the most important items for a security team relying on rules is to carefully document all relevant information pertaining to the rule. The documentation should include the following information at a minimum:

- **Purpose:** What is the purpose behind the rule? What business need or vulnerability does it address?
- **Author**: Who do we go to if there is a problem?
- **Action**: Action(s) and/or Output(s) required from the system when the rule is triggered.
- **Actor**: Relative to a *(PERSON/TEAM)* who do we notify when the rule is triggered? If a significant corporate decision needs to be made as a response to the alert,

the actor should be empowered to make the decision by the senior leadership.

- **Event**: Specific scenario(s) to be evaluated. What action should we take when the rule is triggered? What do we go look for and where?
- **Context**: Relevant environmental conditions. How does our knowledge of this environment affect our response? How we can refine the analysis and output? Some examples of context that should be considered are:
  - Organizational Structure
  - Business Units
  - Application and/or Data Categorizations
  - Network Segmentation, System Configurations
  - Users
  - "Hot Lists"
  - Vulnerability Data
  - Data/System/User Criticality
  - other environment specific information
- **Timing**: Within, before, at, during and after. Receiving the exact time from your devices can be tricky, when working with a SecaaS SIEM, because the provider can monitor many devices from different time zones. Tests are required on each device to make sure the right offset is applied, and that the time stamps are clearly understood.
- **Logic:** Boolean Logic Statements (T/F) using AND, OR, IF, THEN and NOT as conditions.
- **Response:** These are the active statements that indicate what the response should be by all actors. "The system shall", "Security staff must page/notify Compliance". We have to" *(DO SOMETHING)*."

Without these above information, performing an analysis, or attempting to understand an alert can become a difficult and time consuming task. The documentation enables security analysts to quickly look-up pertinent information to the alert, and determine what actions to take. It also enables much quicker response times for newer personnel assigned to the Network Operations Center (NOC), Network Operations Security Center (NOSC) or Security Operations Center (SOC). It also ensures that any requirements to notify compliance officers, take actions or gather data for breach solution systems can be completed immediately. This is particularly important for healthcare, financial and banking industries, where breach notification requirements are legally required to be timely.

Correlation Rules

The most effective rules for correlation in a SIEM system rely on rules designed to address specific behaviors on compartmentalized segments of the network. While accessing financial management systems may be normal for systems in the financial department, accessing records in Engineering or Research and Development is not. Thus the rule set needs a baseline pattern and behavior, based on the business activities and systems they support.

SIEM tools also require a lot of tuning. Rules have to be built with great care and attention to details, in order to work as intended. Well written rule sets can minimize false negatives and false positives enabling the security staff to focus on meaningful alerts. The continued tuning of the rules, by the security staff, can ensure that progress is made in these areas, and that rules are updated to reflect changes in business practices, network behaviors and systems. By carefully documenting the logic and assumptions in each of the rules, when corrections need to be made, it can usually be pinpointed to a specific assumption or data point that needs to be corrected. Rules must be carefully tailored and tuned to address the specific event that they are attempting to detect.

Different SIEM systems leverage different rule constructions, as appropriate to address specific applications and events. These range from the simplest rules such as the audit rules, to the most intricate rules, the inference based rules. As always, complexity is the enemy of security, so rules should be developed using the simplest algorithms possible that can accomplish the task. Every rule could be written as an inference based rule, but it would consume excessive resources, and be more likely to fail when needed most.

For some SecaaS SIEM vendors, all rules are predefined, and an enterprise can choose to turn on or off any given rule based on their business drivers. While this may be effective for some situations, it does not allow for the tailoring or the development of rule sets to address typical network behaviors, and therefore may be of limited value to many enterprises. Some vendors provide standard rule sets, and then can create customized rules for individual customers to support specific business requirements, for a fee. The advantage is that an enterprise could simply express to the vendor how they want the rule to work, without having to have their own analysts know how to create or modify correlation rules. Then there are vendors who not only provide standard rules and rule writing for a fee, but also enable the enterprise analysts to tailor specific rules or author new rules to address specific business needs or vulnerabilities within the enterprise. While this is the most desirable for mid and large enterprises due to the flexibility it provides, it is often the more expensive option.

Audit Type Rules

The Audit rules are the simplest of the rules, as they are looking for a condition to exist or not. An example of an audit rule would be when there is a change in privileges for an account, when a password expires, or when there is a log-in failure for an administrator. The rule works as follows:

*Event***A** = *Alert***B**

It simply reports that an event has occurred. Due to its simplicity, very little processing overhead is spent on these, so these tend to be the most desirable of the rules, but because of its simplicity, it has a very limited use.

Signature-Based Rules

Most anti-malware systems rely on signature based rules to detect the infections of viruses, worms and attack tools. The signature is a list of patterns that when they occur, an alert is generated. An example of how the rule could work would be as follows:

Events (**A** OR **B** AND [**C** NOT **D**]) = *Alert***F**

These patterns are often used to detect specific malware or attack patterns in the enterprise, and react when a pattern is matched. The logic is typically very simple, and can generally be expressed in simple Boolean terms.

Heuristics-Based Rules

These rules leverage a collection of rules and patterns, based on prior structures, routines and behaviors. Where signatures detect events based on strict patterns, heuristics look at patterns and behaviors, and evaluate them by assigning each a risk factor. If the risk factor count exceeds a certain threshold, then the alert is triggered. These types of rules are commonly used to identify root-kits, because experiences have shown that root-kits can hide themselves from host based detection systems, but give indications of their presence on the network by the patterns they exhibit. It is often thought of as a means by which rules look

for similarities to known malware behavior. This is also what many systems refer to as zero-day-exploit detection, since the heuristic engine does not need to know the exact pattern, just the similarities between it and known malware patterns.

*Compare Patterns***A** AND **B** AND ....**F** *with Pattern***X**.

IF *similarity count exceeds***Y** *then Alert***Z**.

Inference-Based Rules

Rule sets that leverage Bayesian inference logic have become more popular, as the accuracy and understanding of Bayesian predictions grows. This type of logic has now been used for several years to help predict and combat spam. Using known patterns and changes in those patterns, a Bayesian inference based rule attempt to predict an event before it occurs. It relies on comparing a hypothesis that a given event may occur, given a series of prior events that may have shared some similarities. A Bayesian filter then takes a population of hypothesis, and compares it to the statistical similarities of the evidence presented, and estimates the probability that an event has occurred or is occurring. Like with the Heuristic based rules, if the probability exceeds a statistical level set by the organization, it triggers the alert.

This is particularly useful when attempting to detect criminal behavior (insider trading, IP theft, etc.), breaches, both internal and external, and other nefarious behavior. It is often used for behavioral anomaly detection. Certain behaviors on a network are extremely consistent over time. If the behavioral patterns of users and systems are recorded by the system, when the behaviors change more than a specified deviation, set by the analysts, an alert is triggered. While some behavioral patterns can be detected by heuristics, the more efficient rules rely on Bayesian inference to predict whether a deviation in the pattern is potentially nefarious or not. It is the most effective tool against zero-day attacks.

Rule Responses

Having the rules developed, it is also important to examine what reactions should take place as a result of a rule trigger. This should not be based on the rule type, but tied back to the business drivers to help determine the severity of an alert. Once the severity is understood, the response must also be examined to help determine the notification means. The documentation discussed in section 4.3 is to indicate who should be notified. Now depending on the severity of the alert, one also has to determine by what means the notification goes out. For high priority alerts, the most likely notification method can be a page, an SMS message, or a text message to a cell phone. For lower severity alerts, notification could be done via email or simply a data point that appears on a report. The following is an example of how an alert chart would look like:

This is only a short list of possible alerts and responses. A full list should be maintained and updated regularly by the security staff.

Operational Needs

When examining the operational needs of the response system, it is important to verify that all communications paths are redundant. VOIP phones should have a POTS line or cellular line as a back-up, and network connections for the SIEM connections to the SIEM vendor should have multiple independent paths identified. Other operational features that should be examined by the security staff include the placement of a graphical event overview (a map of the network and the issues), which enhances the abilities of analysts to respond to breaches and infections, by providing a quick look to determine where problems lie, and how they are progressing or spreading. Log Drill-down capabilities so that records can be examined by IP address (internal and/or external), Machine ID, User name and Protocols.

Quality Assurance

Quality Assurance is an ongoing activity. It ensures that rules can be properly tested in an operational environment, without the risks associated with testing them on the production system. A proper lab setup should mirror the production system,

Table 1. An example of an alert chart

Source	Name	Alert condition / Correlation	Severity	Alert type
Active directory	Changes Made to GPO	Change made to financial department OU	LOW	MAIL
Active directory	User created	Created in off hours	MEDIUM	SMS
Check Point	Failed login to CP console	Over 3 times in one hour	HIGH	SMS
Firewall + VPN device	Port scan and auth attempt	Detected port scan followed by authentication attempt from same IP in one hour	MEDIUM	MAIL
SAP R3	User access transaction SU01	Source terminal is not IT department	MEDIUM	MAIL
Active directory	No check-in for 30 days	A computer has not checked in to the network for 30 or more days	LOW	REPORT ONLY

in every way to ensure the outcomes on the production network systems are predictable. Using canned or irrelevant data/systems renders the tests meaningless. Knowing how the system is going to respond before implementation into production saves time, effort and a lot of headaches.

QA should include simulating all rules agreed between customer and provider, to make sure they are triggered correctly, tests including disconnecting the line to the provider to make sure logs are not lost, and the testing of response scenarios on a quarterly or semi-annual basis.

Finally, if a rule fails to function, the first place to look is to ensure that the system generating the log data needed for correlation, must be supplying it. The number one reason for support calls, with SIEM rules, are remedied by turning on the log data at the source, so the SIEM facility can see it.

REFERENCES

Kavanaugh, K., & Nicolett, M. (2012). *Magic quadrant for security information and event management*. Stamford, CT: Gartner Inc..

Kurtz, G., McClure, S., & Scambray, J. (2012). *Hacking exposed 7: Network security secrets & solutions* (7th ed.). New York: McGraw-Hill.

Laundrup, J. (2008). *Detecting insider trading using automated correlation*. Adelphi, MD: University of Maryland.

Laundrup, J. (2009). *Data security breaches: An unstoppable epidemic?* Sacramento, CA: The State of California Office of Information Security.

Laundrup, J. (2011). *Implementing SIEM in the enterprise: A plan for success*. San Carlos, CA: Emagined Security Inc..

Laundrup, J., & Schultz, E. (2011). *Cloud computing security and auditing*. Seattle, WA: ISACA.

Net Forensics. (2008). *10 mistakes to avoid in evaluating security information management solutions*. Edison, NJ: Net Forensics Inc..

Pack, D. (2011). *Using correlation rules to perform decentralized threat detection*. The DiaLog powered by LogRhythm. Retrieved from http://blog.logrhythm.com/security/using-correlation-rules-to-perform-decentralized-threat-detection/

Schultz, E. (2009). *The in's and out's of SIEM technology*. Paper presented at the IX National Computer and Information Security Conference. Bogota, Colombia.

Schultz, E. (2010). *Cloud computing security: A look into the future*. San Carlos, CA: Emagined Security Inc..

APPENDIX: USEFUL LINKS

The following is a list of places where additional information can be gathered about SIEM implementations:

- Book review, but provides some SIEM details and links to a potentially useful SIEM book for those who want to read further; https://365.rsaconference.com/blogs/securityreading/2011/02/24/security-information-and-event-management-siem-implementation
- Details some SIEM challenges; http://www.darkreading.com/security-monitoring/167901086/security/security-management/227500819/index.html
- SIEM dos and don'ts; http://www.csoonline.com/article/509553/siem-security-info-and-event-management-dos-and-don-ts
- Cloud creates SIEM blind spot; http://www.darkreading.com/security-monitoring/167901086/security/security-management/228000206/cloud-creates-siem-blind-spot.html
- Cloud vs SIEM challenges; http://securecloudreview.com/2010/08/service-provider-of-tomorrow-part-9-as-the-cloud-thrives-siem-will-suffer/

Chapter 6
Enterprise Security Monitoring with the Fusion Center Model

Yushi Shen
Microsoft Corporation, USA

Ling Wu
EMC² Corporation, USA

Yale Li
Microsoft Corporation, USA

Shaofeng Liu
Microsoft Corporation, USA

Qian Wen
Endronic Corp, USA

ABSTRACT

In the past few years, we have witnessed cyber-attacks of unprecedented sophistication and reach. These attacks demonstrate that malicious actors have the ability to compromise and control millions of computers that belong to governments, enterprises, and ordinary citizens. If we are to prevent motivated adversaries from attacking our systems, stealing our data, and harming our critical infrastructure, we have to first understand emerging threats to develop proactive security solutions to safeguard the information and the physical infrastructure that rely on it. This chapter discusses one possible approach to defending against malicious actors at the enterprise level.

EMERGING THREATS: ADVANCED ATTACKS

The academic research community categorizes emerging information security threats into 3 types (Kruegel): *cybercrime*, *targeted attacks* and *emerging cyber warfare*. The information security industry has widely adopted the term "advanced persistent threat" (APT) to describe what some see as an emerging form of cybercrime, advanced attack and in some cases, even cyber warfare. For the purposes of this chapter, we are to adhere to the industry categorization for information security threats, and acknowledge that any cyber-attack resulting from the three categories above can come in the form of either traditional threats or

DOI: 10.4018/978-1-4666-4801-2.ch006

advanced persistent threats. There are four major characteristics that signify an advanced threat versus a traditional threat (FireEye, 2013):

- **Stealthy:** APT attacks are usually launched quietly and generate minimal network anomalies;
- **Unknown & Zero Day:** APT attacks typically use custom malware, that is not detectable by signature-based anti-malware products;
- **Targeted:** APT attacks are typically highly targeted, and the result of significant reconnaissance;
- **Persistent:** APT attacks generally have an end goal, and the attackers are willing to endure until the end goal is achieved.

Figure 1 shows the new threat landscape from traditional threats escalating to advance threats.

Figure 1. The new threat landscape

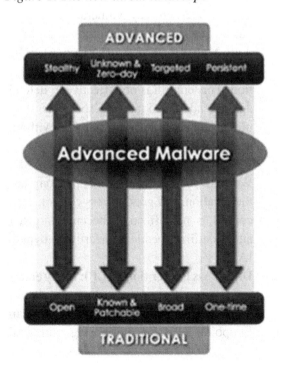

The following are some recent examples of publically acknowledged attacks from each category listed in Table 1:

- **Cyber Crime:** Sony (Play Station Network attack), attacked by the RBN (Russian Business Network);
- **Advanced Attacks:** 70+ Organizations in 14 Countries (Operation Shady RAT), Google (Operation Aurora attack), RSA (SecurID attack);
- **Cyber Warfare:** the Iranian Nuclear Power Plant (Stuxnet attack).

PROBLEMS IN DEFENSE: INADEQUATE ACTIONABLE INFORMATION AND ORGANIZATIONAL SILOS

The industry suffers from the same challenges experienced by the U.S. military services back in the late 1970's. Organizations, businesses and missions all contribute to isolating the operational security players in the enterprise itself. This isolation can allow attackers to move freely across boundaries, repeating attacks that have been successful in one silo to other silos. Unique business requirements in each of the silos can cause one group to overlook an attack that is significant in another group. Lastly, unequitable preventative controls can allow an attack that is thwarted in one silo, to be successful in another (Gartner).

Weak Detection

The defense for enterprise and national IT must take a 4-phase life-cycle approach (Microsoft Corporation), as shown in Figure 2. This cyber security model identifies the people, processes and technologies needed to protect systems, detect attacks, respond to security events and recover systems. In this chapter, we use four quadrants: *Protection*, *Detection*, *Contain* and *Recovery* for

Table 1. Categories of Cyber Attacks

Category	Goals	Funding/Resources	Impact	Frequency
Cyber Crime	Financial gain; Interruption of Service	Low; organized by criminal groups or ideological movements	High	High
Advanced Attacks	Intellectual Property Theft; Hacktivism	Medium; organized by nation-state or large adversaries	Very high	Medium
Cyber Warfare & Terrorism	Loss of life; degradation of societal norms	High; organized by cyber military force or terrorist organizations	Highest	Low

Figure 2. The 4-phase life-cycle approach

a complete defense. In each quadrant, certain security controls are utilized and together they achieve a "defense in depth" strategy. The types of controls are typically grouped as and primarily used for: preventive controls for protection quadrant, detective controls for detection quadrant, and corrective controls for response and recovery quadrants.

Arguably, we have done a good job in the Protection quadrant with preventive controls. However, to combat new threats, preventive controls are frequently found to be inadequate. The detective controls are equally important, but they are overlooked in most enterprises. In conjunction with containment, they are the last line of defense to stop the attackers from achieving their goals, when an enterprise is under advanced attacks. To

be successful at all in defenses, we must use detective controls to make new, creative and effective use of data that reveals the true nature of risk exposure, including emerging threats. As more and more organizations are penetrated by advanced attacks, the need for detection and response has never been greater.

Currently, the following major preventive controls are widely deployed to protect us:

1. **Vulnerability Management:** We patch OS and secure applications for known vulnerabilities. This control is not effective to defend against advanced attacks, because they utilize zero-day vulnerability which has no patch available during the attack;

2. **Anti-Malware (AM)/Anti-Virus (AV):** We have AM/AV products installed in production. This control is not effective to defend against advanced attacks, because they utilize unknown custom malware without signatures;

3. **Identity and Access Management (IAM):** We have identity management, strong authentication, and good access control. This control is not effective, because targeted attacks utilize social engineering to bypass IAM;

4. **Data Loss Prevention (DLP):** Many enterprises are in the process to deploy Endpoint DLP. The Network DLP has more value than Endpoint DLP for monitoring outbound

data-in-motion at network edge, but it is not deployed yet. However, DLP is kept separate from other monitoring logs. Because DLP systems capture the full text of the message or session, in which sensitive information are detected, it is inappropriate to pass the full information to a central repository, where the operators may not be authorized to see the sensitive data;

5. **Network Firewall:** The advanced attacks have moved up in the stack to exploit application and host vulnerabilities. Enterprise data is also going into the cloud. The corporate network is no longer a barrier to attackers;

6. **Encryption at Rest:** To minimize the risk of losing highly confidential information, the data stored in large repository is encrypted by cryptographic technology. However, current encryption solution is weak in addressing online attacks, if system or database administrator's credential is compromised.

Now, let's examine major detective controls that can be used to detect attacks to enterprise:

1. **Log Management:** This is a technology to enable, then transport and eventually store all logs from networks, hosts and applications into a central location,

2. **Vulnerability Management:** Security Information and Event Management (SIEM) is a combination of SIM and SEM (Gartner, SIEM Enables Enterprise Security Intelligence). The SIEM market is moving to converging solutions for event monitoring and log management. SEM deals with real-time monitoring, correlation of events, notifications and console views. SIM provides long-term storage, analysis and reporting of log data;

3. **Network IDS/IPS:** This control is not effective in detecting advanced attacks, because the attacks are usually stealthy with quiet network traffic, and without known signatures, and network load might a problem;

4. **Edge Content Inspection:** This technology inspects outbound/inbound traffic through tools such as Network DLP, Content Monitoring Appliance and Web/App Gateways. Even though transmitted data is encrypted, the data can be opened for inspection. This is an effective way to detect command & control traffic and leaked confidential information. However, the network load might a problem.

Currently, many security professionals have realized the importance of the detective control's role in enterprise defense. In a large enterprise, usually multiple security teams deploy their own SIEM solutions, and other detective controls from different vendors. However, cases of SIEM use differ between real-time event, log management and non-real-time investigations. Each security team is looking for the quickest solutions for their specific problem, but these quick solutions may fall short, while the enterprise matures in the use of SIEM technologies. This approach unveils another big problem in enterprise: organizational silos.

Organizational Silos

A large enterprise includes multiple distinct businesses, environments and technology layers managed by different divisions or properties. The security teams are organized for alignment accordingly. From the security perspective, most security teams and many properties work in silos. Except security policy, each silo has its own security controls and security information/event islands. The organizational silos also introduce other silos, such as technology silos and environment silos. Different technologies and environments are managed by different teams and systems. It is very inefficient for detective controls to correlate information and events, and share security intelligence across the boundaries of these silos.

The enterprise intelligence and defense as whole is broken into individual unrelated pieces (as shown in Figure 3). Therefore, the boundaries have confined the power of next generation detective control deployment to detect advanced attacks.

This segregation results in redundant and incomplete security efforts, and robs the enterprise its ability to recognize attacks that exhibit themselves across multiple technologies and organizational boundaries. The organizational boundaries not only reduce the effectiveness of detective controls at the enterprise level, but also enable advanced attacks to target an environment with weak protective and detective controls.

COUNTERMEASURE SOLUTIONS: CROSS-BOUNDARY ENTERPRISE MONITORING

To resolve these problems, we propose a companywide Enterprise Security Monitoring (ESM) solution. The goals of the ESM are:

Figure 3. Segmented organizational silos

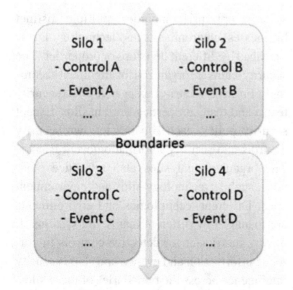

- Make the detection quadrant strong by increasing accuracy and breadth of detection.
- Support other quadrants by providing intelligence for decisions in protection, response and recovery.
- Achieve optimal defense by optimizing security management within and across enterprises.

ESM is the next generation detective solution, with SIEM as the foundation and the Enterprise Security Intelligence (SIEM) as enhancement (Gartner, Prepare for the Emergence of Enterprise Security Intelligence). ESM also gets input from other security solutions as sources, and provides output to response processes. SIEM is the core component to aggregate, normalize and monitor security events across a broad range of network, security, host, also database and application components. It also provides security information normalization, context, correlation and analytics. ESI is another core component to extend the capabilities on top of SIEM, to recognize security intelligence as an explicit deliverable, and aim at increased accuracy and breadth of security detection and protection, as well as optimal security management. ESM takes input from network, host, database and application logs, and other security tools such as Vulnerability Management, Anti-Malware, DLP, IAM, and IDS/IPS. The output of the ESM solution is to be consumed by the response phase, and other phases in the defense lifecycle.

Six Laws of the Next Generation Enterprise Security Monitoring

To successfully build an effective enterprise security monitoring system, 6 design principals must be applied. Here are the laws of the next generation ESM (Gartner, 2011):

1. **Comprehensive Enterprise Coverage:** All production layers (networks, hosts,

applications, databases and identities) and environments (on premise and in the cloud) must be considered as suspects of advanced attacks, and should be covered by the ESM solution, even if they appear to be "healthy";

2. **Information Interaction and Correlation:** The ESM solution must have security data input sources from events and logs of all network devices, hosts, databases, applications and identity directories, in order to create a full threat knowledge base for the enterprise. It is vital to intelligently correlate information to derive meaningful information from a flood of data;

3. **Technology Interaction and Correlation:** The ESM solution must gravitate toward security information and event management (SIEM) as a foundation, and integrate it with other security technologies, such as IDS/IPS, Firewall, DLP, IAM (Gartner, SIEM and IAM Technology Integration), vulnerability management and anti-malware. Those technologies are correlation sources to lower false positive rates, increase accuracy and breadth of security detection;

4. **Business Interaction and Correlation:** The ESM solution must be aware of its business context. The advanced attacks are usually targeting a great deal of business information. With the interaction and correlation extended with business information, ESM can think like the enemy, predict attacker's priorities, reduce the noise and derive more meaningful intelligence;

5. **Cross-Boundary Intelligence for Better Decision Making:** Security activities and the intelligence that results from ESM output must not be in isolation. The organizational boundaries must be crossed by the ESM solution, to achieve enterprise security intelligence, and support decisions for protection, response and recovery;

6. **Visualized Output for Dynamic and Real-time Defense:** The output of the ESM solution must be visualized to help preventive and corrective controls, to stop advanced attacks or block data exfiltration attempts. Only easily consumable output can drastically reduce response time, minimize damage, quickly investigate and determine root cause of security issues and breaches.

The Reference Architecture of Cross-Boundary Enterprise Security Monitoring

Based on our design principles, we have proposed Reference Architecture for ESM (as shown in Figure 4). The core component is the SIEM with its common capabilities and data sources. Log Management can be a separate component or an integral component within SIEM. Extended from Content-Aware SIEM (CA-SIEM), ESI further takes the technology and business context information, and provides intelligence for actions and decision making. For example, if the intrusion prevention system sees an attack on the network, which application events (if any) are related to that event, and what constitutes a good or bad event pattern? The Cross-Boundary ESM should be able to get all the dots connected, and all the patterns recognized.

The input data sources include but are not limited to:

- Events from network devices, hosts, applications, databases and directories;
- Technology Context Information from Vulnerability Management system, Anti-Malware system, DLP system, Firewalls and IDS/IPS;
- Security Information from internal/external threat intelligence sources, vulnerability intelligence sources, crowd intelligence sources, such as manual incident reporting

121

Figure 4. The enterprise security monitoring reference architecture

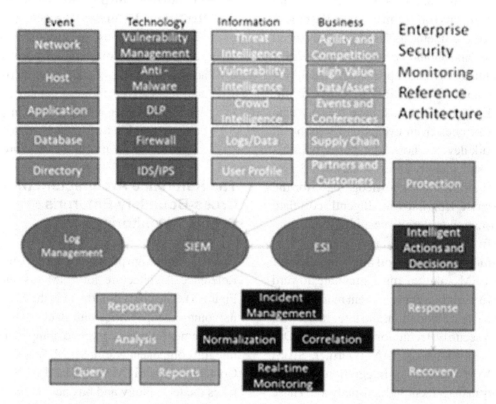

UI, logs and other data such as geospatial data, and user profiles such as HR employee background check records;

- Business Context Information from business units, and business intelligence systems Page Numbers, Headers and Footers.

The output alerting and reporting are to provide security intelligence, which is consumable by personnel responsible for protection, response and recovery. Security intelligence may parallel the world of Business Intelligence (BI) in the development of highly flexible ESM platforms and ESI analytic toolkits, that enable security data analysts to adapt analysis of advanced attack patterns.

Core Capabilities of Enterprise Security Monitoring Solution

The following is a common set of capabilities and requirements of the cross-boundary ESM solution. The list is not considered as complete or accurate feature specs. It is intended to serve as a high level template, and can be extended and modified for technology evaluation, selection and solution designs.

- **Correlation Capability:** This capability is to utilize rules to analyze patterns of a large number of events from different sources, to derive the full picture of an attack or a fraud;
- **Monitoring Capability:** This capability is to watch for anomaly activities and alert security operations in near real-time;

- **Incident Management Capability:** This capability is to automate incident management process through integration with incident ticketing, management systems and tools;
- **Reporting Capability:** This capability is to generate various reports and graphs, to help managers and analysts to understand the results and trends;
- **Capability:** This capability is to transform events with different format into a set, which the correlation engine can understand and consume;
- **Agent Capability:** This capability is to capture all security related events at endpoints, devices and sources, and pre-process them for performance, control enforcement or other purposes.

MONITORING INFORMATION SHARING

The Cross-Boundary ESM is an effective detection control, to defend against the advanced attacks and cyber terrorism. However, if its service is broken into pieces and deployed to organizational silos, its power would be confined by the boundaries again. To deploy cross-boundary ESM solution as a service, we recommend a "Fusion Center" approach.

The Fusion Center Model

The Fusion Center model has been initiated by the US government (US Government – Director of National Intelligence) (US Government – White House, 2010) (USE Government – ISE), for sharing data on terrorism and crime threats. Fusion centers serve as hubs for bringing together information from distributed sources, including the federal government, state, local, tribal and territorial governments, and the private sector. Fusion

centers gather this information for the purpose of collection, retention, analysis and dissemination. In 2004 and 2005, many states have begun creating fusion centers with various local, state and federal funds. At the time, the fusion centers are isolated. There have been no standards or guidelines in existence, to assist with interoperability and communication between fusion centers. As a result, fusion centers designed to share information are actually silos of information, incapable of information exchange. In 2006, the Fusion Center Guidelines have been developed collaboratively between DOJ and DHS (US Government – DHS/DOJ) (Microsoft Corporation, 2013). It provides guidance on the establishment and operation of fusion centers, at the federal, state, local and tribal levels. These efforts have also laid the foundation for the expansion to integrate the public safety and private sector entities.

A fusion center is defined by the guide as a "collaborative effort of two or more agencies that provide resources, expertise and information to the center, with the goal of maximizing their ability to detect, prevent, investigate and respond to criminal and terrorist activities." Among the primary focuses of fusion centers are the intelligence and fusion processes, through which information can be collected, integrated, evaluated, analyzed and disseminated. Nontraditional collectors of intelligence, such as public safety entities and private sector organizations, possess important information (e.g., risk assessments and suspicious activity reports) that can be "fused" with law enforcement data, to provide meaningful information and intelligence about threats and criminal activity.

Information fusion involves the exchange of information from different sources—including law enforcement, public safety and the private sector—and, with analysis, can result in meaningful and actionable intelligence and information (NIEM, 2011) (Westerman & Hunter, 2007). The fusion process turns this information and intelligence into actionable knowledge. Fusion also allows for relentless reevaluation of existing data, in context with new data, in order to provide constant updates. The public safety and private sector components are integral in the fusion process, because they provide fusion centers with crime-related information, including risk and threat assessments, and subject-matter experts, who can aid in the threat identification process.

Success Story: The Massachusetts Fusion Center

The Fusion Center Guideline describes the technology agnostic capabilities, standards and processes for the fusion centers. To implement technical solutions for the fusion centers, the US Government has adopted the Fusion Framework and the Fusion Core Solution from a vendor. The Fusion Framework develops a replicable mission-critical technology reference architecture, for a public safety collaboration platform that enhances information sharing and security with the following five objectives:

- Create a collaborative environment for intelligence and information sharing;
- Leverage existing databases and systems to maximize information sharing, both internally and externally;
- Create seamless information exchange, using NIEM (National Information Exchange Model) to integrate existing systems;
- Develop appropriate security measures to help ensure that access to information is controlled and monitored;
- Integrate technology, systems and people through a senior leader vision, and an IT architecture driven by operator analysts.

Based on the framework, a Fusion Core Solution has been developed, an easy-to-use, quick-to-configure solution that combines the robust capabilities of the ESRI ArcGIS Advanced

Enterprise server and SharePoint Server. Fusing dynamic data, such as real-time 911 incident data, weather, and sensor detections with foundational data, such as infrastructure and streets, into a geographic model helps to identify potential threats and assets at risk. This solution has been implemented at multiple fusion centers, e.g. the Massachusetts Commonwealth Fusion Center (http://www.esri.com/library/brochures/pdfs/data-fusion-centers.pdf).

With the Fusion Core Solution, government agencies can seamlessly move information from intake to analysis, to dissemination in a multiagency and multilevel environment. The solution incorporates existing assets and domain-specific applications, to offer clear information, within a familiar context, that helps agencies to work together, and mitigate possible risks, respond to events as they arise, and counter potential threats and criminal activities.

Proposed Capabilities for a Fusion Center in the Enterprise

By utilizing the fusion center model, we propose to start up an enterprise "Fusion Center", a service for cross-boundary ESM collaboratively funded, built, operated and used by multiple security teams and business units in the enterprise.

The Goals of the "Fusion Center" are:

- Provide people, processes, technologies, and funds to turn cross-boundary ESM into a service;
- Maximize design/development/deployment resources and streamline service operations;
- Provide finished security and intelligence service to all business units and security teams;
- Establish an enterprise-wide view of preventative, detective and corrective security controls;

- Create the ability to identify common trends and threats across security teams;
- Create the ability to track malicious activities across organizational boundaries;
- Provide artifacts in support of strategic program and funding decisions;
- In the future, share information externally as a private sector "fusion center".

In addition to those capabilities outlined above, the "Fusion Center" should also adhere to some of the baseline capabilities in the Fusion Center Guidance, in order to share information externally in the future. The areas for such capabilities are broad and beyond security:

- Planning and requirements development for information,
- Suspicious activity reporting,
- Risk assessment,
- Alerts and warnings,
- Data sources,
- Training exercises and coordination with the private sector,
- Information gathering strategies and mechanisms,
- Processing and analyzing information,
- Intelligence analysis and production,
- Information linking and open-source analysis capabilities,
- Managing the centers and protecting privacy rights, through privacy policies, protections, outreach and accountability,
- Ensuring information is secure, staffing and personnel training,
- IT/communications infrastructure, systems and equipment,
- Continuity-of-operations plans,
- Funding and investment strategy.

VISION: GLOBAL CORRELATION AND INTELLIGENCE

With the Cross-Boundary ESM solutions delivered as "Fusion Center" services for the short and medium terms, we take a look at solutions for the long term.

Crossing External Boundaries

In addition to the US Government, other companies and organizations also fear advanced attacks are to steal their intellectual property, secrets and customer information. However, the Cross-Boundary Enterprise Security Monitoring has limitations, because the information correlation and security intelligence is limited within one enterprise or organization. If the attack targets multiple enterprises in one industry, for example China Mobile and China Telecomm, and gets detected in one of them, the other ones and the rest of the industry would also benefit. To collectively defend themselves from advanced attacks, it is logical that companies and organizations should cooperate and learn from each other's experiences. The dots need to be connected across enterprises and national borders. Sharing the events and log data that lead to compromises, can help them recognize the symptoms of attack, traffic patterns of intrusion, and system/application events that, if correlated, would have raised alerts (Gartner, Understanding IT Controls and COBIT & Leveraging Event and Log Information: A Strong Case for Standards).

Beyond enterprise boundaries and national borders, ESM is to face more technical and legal challenges. To address the legal challenges, collaboration between governments is required, and the scope is beyond this paper. The technical challenges are mainly from security, interop and scalability concerns.

Companies are reluctant to share security data with their peers for many reasons, including fear

Figure 5. Global sharing and correlation

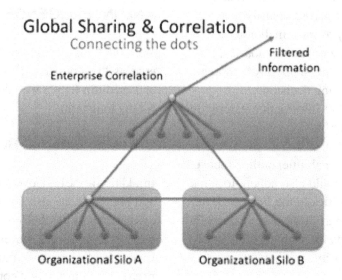

of embarrassment or further compromise of sensitive information. The solution is to filter and mask private data. If filtered and masked properly, e.g. the sensitive data either removed or replaced with dummy data, outgoing data would only contain vulnerability and threat information.

The interop issue is a big challenge. Every organization uses different security tools to keep the information and events. The taxonomy, format and metadata may look totally different in various organizations and systems. This makes it very difficult for event data normalization and for organizations to share information.

The amount of data from multiple organizations is many orders of magnitude more than data from one enterprise. The data for correlation at the global level is growing like an avalanche. Issues such as scalability, processing power and storage capacity have to be addressed.

Information Sharing Environment (ISE) and Standards

One of the effective ways to deal with the interop is to create a security ISE and the associated information exchange standards. Organizations agree to use a metadata dictionary to facilitate the data communication. In an information exchange model, with the metadata being agreed upon, each organization can continue to "speak" its own "language", leaving the existing security systems unchanged except for the tagging of information. But each organization can now also send and understand messages to and from others, because the ISE serves as the "translator". The ISE concept has been supported and promoted by Gartner and the US Government.

Recently, Gartner has defined ISEs as communities united by a common purpose and mutual trust, that willingly and intentionally share information, among those who have the information with those who need it. Gartner's unified information-sharing model links the process of enterprise information architecture with the discipline of enterprise information management.

In 2004, the US Government (the President and the Congress) established the ISE as an organization, "for the sharing of terrorism information in a manner consistent with national security, and with applicable legal standards relating to privacy and civil liberties". The ISE initially supports 5 communities (intelligence, law enforcement, defense, homeland security and foreign affairs), to ensure that those responsible for combating terrorism have access to timely and accurate information. An improved ISE is being constructed, on a foundation of trusted partnerships among federal, state and local governments, the private sector and foreign allies. Currently, ISE is leading the process for developing a new "National Information Sharing Environment Strategy," which is based on the 2007 "National Strategy for Information Sharing."

ISE endorses the XML-based information exchange model, to enable all participating entities to quickly translate and share data between their systems. In 2005, the US Government further created a standard for information sharing among fusion centers. The National Information Exchange Model (NIEM) is an XML-based information exchange framework. NIEM represents a collaborative partnership among agencies and organizations across all levels of the government (federal, state, tribal and local), and with the private industries. The purpose of this partnership is to effectively and efficiently share critical information at key decision points, throughout the whole of justice, public safety, emergency and disaster management, intelligence and homeland security. NIEM is designed to develop, disseminate and support enterprise-wide information exchange standards and processes, enabling jurisdictions to automate information sharing.

The NIEM exchange development methodology results, in a common semantic understood among participating organizations, and data are formatted in a semantically consistent manner. NIEM standardizes content (actual data exchange standards), provides tools and manages processes by:

- Bringing stakeholders and communities of interest together to identify information sharing requirements, in daily operational and emergency situations;
- Developing standards, a common lexicon and an on-line repository of information exchange package documents, to support information sharing;
- Providing technical tools to support development, discovery, dissemination and re-use of exchange documents;
- Provide training, technical assistance and implementation support services for enterprise-wide information exchange.

Standard Event Formats

Another way to overcome the interop hurdle is to standardize on a common event format for all organizations. Currently, there are three groups actively working to create a common event and log standard, that allows event logs and audit records to be shared and understood, across many products and systems. The good news is that they are talking to each other:

- Common Event Expression (CEE) language, led by Mitre Corporation;
- X/Open Distributed Audit Standard (XDAS), led by Open Group;
- Syslog Protocol, led by the Internet Engineering Task Force (IETF) Syslog Working Group (WG).

CEE has the U.S. federal government backing, SIEM vendor participation and a broad vision of standardization. XDAS plans to replace its older version with one that includes a new object model and syntax for auditable events. Syslog enables event messages to contain structured information, but lacks taxonomy and data dictionary elements. Additionally, there are other SIEM vendor efforts to standardize the event format, such as CEF (Common Event Format) by HP ArcSight, and CEI (Common Event Infrastructure) by IBM Tivoli.

The business benefits of creating a common event standard would be considerable:

- Reduced log management and SIEM system integration costs:
  - Reduced volume of event data and simplification of SIEM architecture,
  - Reduced need for (and increased effectiveness of) normalization;
- Reduced cost of integrating new solutions with security management infrastructures and frameworks;
- Lower cost of integrating event management, and audit into cross-enterprise applications (such as federated identity management);
- Faster and simpler data exchange between organizations, vendors and incident response services, supporting real time response to threats and attacks;
- Better forensics for a common defense;
- A common taxonomy for events to enable normalization, correlation and search.

Event and log standards could also enhance organizations' operational efficiency, compliance reporting, security response, investigations and other IT business objectives. The combined efforts of the Common Event Expression (CEE), the X/Open Distributed Audit Service (XDAS), and the Internet Engineering Task Force (IETF) offer some promise if coordinated, but success is not assured. We recommend that an enterprise starts standardizing internal event and log environments, and push 3rd party vendors to help develop and then comply with industry standards.

Cross-Enterprise Security Monitoring as a Service in the Cloud

A cloud based cross-enterprise ESM service is a natural solution to addressing Big Data and scalability issues. The infinite power of computing and storage in the cloud, combined with Big Data technology such as Hadoop, can be leveraged to process and store massive amounts of data. A cloud provider, either Huawei, Inspur or someone else, may provide security as a service for all enterprises and governments worldwide.

With a cloud ESM service, the dream of global correlation and intelligence could come true.

Return on Investment (ROI) Considerations

Making a business justification for investment in cross-boundary ESM is an exercise to help funding decisions by senior leaders in the company. Here we quote the rough estimate on return on investment for a well-known IT company that employs the cross-boundary ESM solution.

Benefits

The benefits of a cross-boundary ESM fusion center can be qualified by looking at cost break-even points, and cost avoided with this solution:

- Reducing risks and avoiding damages from advanced attacks;
- Removing inefficiencies through automation;
- Avoiding infrastructure expansion costs;
- Preventing expenditure for compliance penalties;
- Reducing loss through fraud;
- Adverting losses due to system outages.

If we had to come up with a hard financial figure, we can solely focus on advanced attacks, and use the data from RSA SecurID attack as the base for calculation. In July, 2011, the Washington Post reported, that the security breach, which

Figure 6. The global information correlation and intelligence sharing vision

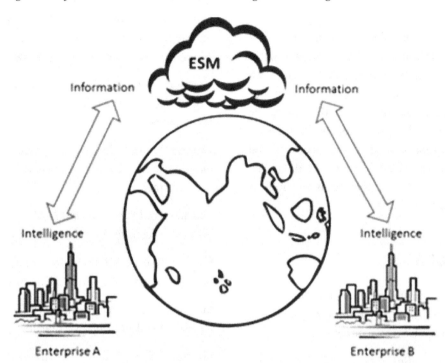

targets sensitive data relating to RSA's SecurID two-factor authentication product, costs parent company EMC $66m in the second quarter alone. As of August 2011, the market capital of the company is $211 billion, and that of EMC is $46 billion. Therefore, we use 60 x 211 / 46 = $303 million as a rough estimate for such damage if a similar advanced attack were to happen to the enterprise. This amount would be the minimum benefit the enterprise gains, if they could detect and avoid the attack. From the risk management perspective, we assume the control is very low, and the incident probability is medium and averages once per 5 years. The rough estimate of ROI is:

$303 M / $9.5 M = 32

Cost

Next, we calculate the capital expense and 5 year operational expense. In 2009, DHS supplied more than $250 million in startup money for 58 fusion centers in US. As of 2011, there are 72 fusion centers nationwide in the US. 250 / 58 = 4.3 million is the average capital expense for a state fusion center.

As we know, there are 30 people (most information analysts) employed at the Washington Fusion center. In the enterprise environment, more budgets should be allocated on tools for automation instead of manual labor. We assume our "fusion center" or ESM service can be supported by 10 fulltime employees. The capital and operational expense is calculated as follows:

- **Software:** 3rd party SIEM product license: 300,000 servers x $10 = $3 million;
- **Hardware:** server hosting fee: 30 VMs x 10,000/year x 5 year = $1.5 million;
- **Personnel:** 10 people x $200,000 annual salary x 5 year = $10 million;
- **The Total Cost of Ownership Is:** 3 + 1.5 + 10 = $14.5 million.

CONCLUSION

With emerging threats of advanced attacks, traditional isolated solutions become more and more inadequate for reliable cyber defense. Here we have discussed one possible approach to defending against malicious attacks at the enterprise level. The proposed approach is based on cross-boundary information security management, and the fusion of enterprise-wide security data. The cross-boundary ESM as a service in the cloud is also discussed as a vision.

REFERENCES

DHS/DOJ. (n.d.a). *Fusion center guidelines—Developing and sharing information in a new era.* Washington, DC: US Government.

DHS/DOJ. (n.d.b). *Baseline capabilities for state and major urban area fusion centers.* Washington, DC: US Government.

Director of National Intelligence. (n.d.). *The national intelligence strategy.* Washington, DC: US Government.

Federal Aviation Administration. (2009). *Review of web applications security and intrusion detection in air traffic control systems.* Retrieved from http://www.oig.dot.gov/sites/dot/files/pdfdocs/ATC_Web_Report.pdf

FireEye. (2013). *Next generation threats.* Retrieved from http://www.fireeye.com/threat-protection/

Gartner. (2011). *2011 planning guide: Security and risk management.* Washington, DC: Gartner.

Gartner. (n.d.a). *In defense of silos.* Washington, DC: Gartner.

Gartner. (n.d.b). *Leveraging event and log information: A strong case for standards.* Washington, DC: Gartner.

Gartner. (n.d.c). *Overcoming silos: Evolving from stand-alone information architectures to shared-information architectures for the emerging data economy.* Washington, DC: Gartner.

Gartner. (n.d.d). *Prepare for the emergence of enterprise security intelligence.* Washington, DC: Gartner.

Gartner. (n.d.e). *Security information and event management technology assessment.* Washington, DC: Gartner.

Gartner. (n.d.f). *SIEM and IAM technology integration.* Washington, DC: Gartner.

Gartner. (n.d.g). *SIEM enables enterprise security intelligence.* Washington, DC: Gartner.

Gartner. (n.d.h). *Understanding IT controls and COBIT.* Washington, DC: Gartner.

Gorman, S. (2009). *FAA's air-traffic networks breached by hackers.* Retrieved from http://online.wsj.com/article/SB124165272826193727.html

Gross, M. J. (2011). *Exclusive: Operation shady RAT – Unprecedented cyber-espionage campaign and intellectual-property bonanza.* Retrieved from http://www.vanityfair.com/culture/features/2011/09/operation-shady-rat-201109?printable=true&currentPage=2

Hall, S. (2011). *DOT issues vulnerability report on the FAA's ATC system.* Retrieved from http://avstop.com/april_2011/dot_issues_vulnerability_report_on_the_faa_s_atc_system.htm

Harwood, M. (2009). *Dept. of transportation: Air traffic control systems have been hacked.* Retrieved from http://www.securitymanagement.com/news/dept-transportation-air-traffic-control-systems-have-been-hacked-005617

ISE. (n.d.a). *National strategy for information sharing.* Washington, DC: US Government.

ISE. (n.d.b). *Information sharing environment profile and architecture implementation strategy, version 2.0*. Washington, DC: US Government.

Kruegel, C. (n.d.). *Automated malware analysis*. Santa Barbara, CA: UC Santa Barbara, Computer Security Group.

Microsoft Corporation (2013). *Microsoft fusion framework and fusion core solution*. Retrieved from http://www.microsoft.com/industry/government/solutions/Fusion_Framework/default.aspx

Microsoft Corporation (n.d.). *Managing cyber risk in the face of sophisticated adversaries* (White Paper). Microsoft Corp.

National Information Exchange Model (NIEM). (2011). *Business information exchange components*. Retrieved from http://reference.niem.gov/niem/guidance/business-information-exchange-components/1.0/

Servo, T. (2008). *Boeing's new dreamliner has serious security vulnerability*. Retrieved from http://www.freerepublic.com/focus/f-news/1949826/posts

STUXNET. (2012). *Wikipedia*. Retrieved from http://en.wikipedia.org/wiki/Stuxnet

Westerman, G., & Hunter, R. (2007). *IT risk: Turning business threats into competitive advantage*. Boston: Harvard Business School Press.

Whitehouse. (2010). *National security strategy*. US Government. Retrieved from http://www.whitehouse.gov/sites/default/files/rss_viewer/national_security_strategy.pdf

Chapter 7
Data Protection in the Cloud Era

Yushi Shen
Microsoft Corporation, USA

Ling Wu
EMC² Corporation, USA

Yale Li
Microsoft Corporation, USA

Shaofeng Liu
Microsoft Corporation, USA

Qian Wen
Endronic Corp, USA

ABSTRACT

In this chapter, the authors examine a potential enterprise customer's strategy and scenario to protect its data in the cloud computing era. CorpFort is the name of a hypothetical company. This chapter starts with the problem statement in the data protection space at CorpFort. Then, it describes a vision in the protection of data in the ideal state. Finally, it creates the strategy and solutions for realizing the vision.

INTRODUCTION

Information wants to be free (because of the new ease of copying and reshaping and casual distribution), AND information wants to be expensive (it's the prime economic event in an information age)... and technology is constantly making the tension worse. If you cling blindly to the expensive part of the paradox, you miss all the action going on in the free part. (Brand, 1987)

CorpFort perpetuates the Information Age by its very existence, while sharing the need to protect data with other enterprises. The CorpFort intellectual property is created on the fly by the minds of its workforce, and then moved through files and e-mails, and finally being converted into software and cloud services. CorpFort gathers, stores and transfers information about its workers and customers, as it manipulates that data for service and profit. In all its various forms,[1] enterprise

DOI: 10.4018/978-1-4666-4801-2.ch007

information now represents a significant percentage of the corporate wealth. Information assets represent real equity that affects CorpFort's stock value. In this Information Age, *data[2] is the asset*. However, most data have value only when proprietary, meaning it is information solely owned by CorpFort, and not available to any other. That is, *data is valuable only if it is protected*. Protection of proprietary data is a key criterion for ensuring CorpFort's legal rights to it.

Ironically, what makes data so valuable is, in large part, the very reason that protecting it is so much harder. Data is pushed and pulled, extracted and aggregated, and disseminated throughout the enterprise. The workforce is provided with mobile technologies, to squeeze more productivity from busy schedules and itineraries. Valued enterprise data ends up being readily available on cheap and inconspicuous devices, ostensibly intended for the consumer market. User and service demands accommodate the use of inadequately-protected laptops and other mobile devices, which are all too frequently lost or stolen. Incidents of lost or compromised data, and the resulting financial and reputational consequences have become commonplace. (Geer, 2008) Users who are generally unaware of the risks, succumb to the temptation to move valuable data to "the cloud," where there continues to be a lack of security controls, from which data can be accessed *anywhere* by any device, resulting in a global threat. Paper contracts between companies and their outsourcers, including cloud providers, are relied on to protect that data. Meanwhile, valued data is mined by underground professionals, which can be then sold on the black market. (Privacy Rights Clearing House, 2013)

Businesses that depend on vendor and partner relationships have become so numerous and complex, that their distinctions with the employees have blurred, making access decisions difficult. The huge number of principals, needing varied degrees of access to nearly incomprehensible amounts of information, creates a scaling challenge that is so formidable, that some believe it is impossible to be fully addressed.

Safeguarding information is a huge challenge, in today's businesses, where there is a fine line between employees, vendors, partners and cloud providers. The usefulness of data is directly proportional to its range of movement, and therefore a myriad of highly portable computing devices, with huge storage capacities, enable and entice users to widely distribute the corporation's valued data.

All of these characteristics lead to the observation that data is simultaneously expensive and free. (Brand, 1987). It is expensive because it is the asset upon which the enterprise depends for its livelihood. It is free because it now moves with frequency, volume and distance using a broad suite of devices, machines and media. The tension between the two – value and freedom – presents the problem. How can CorpFort keep so much information at play, and at the same time ensure its own data protection?

Out of necessity and purpose, the business focuses on profit. The competition for money and market share is fierce. Business strategies and tactics must be cunning, agile and aggressive. In the frenzy, focus is on function. Security is an afterthought, if thought of at all. When businesses outsource or move to the cloud, to reduce overhead and improve margins, they typically do not know the exact value of the information they are handing over to outside custodians.

However, the importance of information protection cannot be denied. *CorpFort employees are bound by non-disclosure agreement* to protect confidential information.[3] And when that data is Personal Identifiable Information (PII), *CorpFort has a published obligation as a good Corporate Citizen* to avoid causing any harm to people who have entrusted their personal information to CorpFort, by disclosing that data. If this isn't sufficiently compelling, there is an increasing tide of privacy and compliance legislation intended to catch the attention of enterprises such as CorpFort.

For data to be protected, a determination needs to be made as to who can access it and how those authorized can use it. Given the enormous volume of data involved, such assessment can only be achieved if the accountability and responsibility is clearly assigned and assumed, and with those who fully understand its value and purpose. A tipping point has been reached where producers, owners and delegates must now take an active and deliberate role in the protection of data. Today when data owners think of function, they must consider the security of their data as an intrinsic part of that function. This obligation cannot be ignored and is not going to be seamless, but must be fulfilled.

CorpFort needs to enable these data owners to protect their valued data, by providing services based on improved technologies that are targeting comprehensive data protection, regardless of the state of the data or its lifecycle.

UNDERSTANDING THE PROBLEM

One of the largest risks for CorpFort is compromising its data. Given that, a key problem CorpFort faces is unprotected valuable data.

This problem space is dissected into the following 5 areas:

- Lack of interoperability and data collaboration;
- Lack of data protection across data states and data lifecycle;
- Poor usability and too much complexity;
- Lack of responsible leadership and PII data stewardship;
- Lack of awareness of accountability and responsibility for data security.

Lack of Interoperability and Secure Data Collaboration

At CorpFort, effective internal and external collaboration is the key for business success. Collaboration requires data sharing in many different scenarios, for example asynchronous collaboration, i.e. e-mail, team workspace and discussions, real-time collaboration, i.e. presence, instant messaging and Web conferencing, and business process collaboration such as workflows. Security is even more challenging in external collaboration environments, where data is accessed by multiple users from different locations. A 2007 Ponemon study (survey from 15 market sectors) shows:

- Average Cost dealing with a breach: $6.3 million;
- Cost of data breach per record lost: $197 (up 8% from 2006);
- Cost of lost business per record lost: $128. (Information cited at Ponemon Institute, 2013)

Data must be protected by both trusted technologies and trusted users. This results in two main collaboration problem categories, interoperability and secure collaboration.

Interoperability: Problems Associated with Trusted Technology

International systems, networks and various other standards provide some common structure and order in today's digital world. At one time, operating systems all have their own network stack or functions, making interoperability an issue. Now, 20 years later, this same lack of interoperability exists for data. The challenge is how to create a data security standard, which would allow for uniformity across multiple platforms and applications. There are too many data security technologies, which have little in common, that use their own in-house proprietary code. An example is the RMS (Rights Management Server) being non-compatible with the other ERM (Enterprise Rights Management) products, though they are technical cognates.

As a result, there are no compatible technical mechanisms for employees and partners to securely exchange and transfer data, or collaborate in the cloud and across different enterprise environments.

- Users must apply different tools and processes to secure data across platforms and environments. For example, a CorpFort user may use one set of tools to encrypt files sent to partner A on a Windows machine, and a different set for partner B on a Linux machine.
- None standard protection mechanisms shared by CorpFort and its partners. For example, RMS does not work for partners running on open source platforms.

Secure Collaboration: Problems Associated with User Trust Levels

External users generally have a lower trust level than internal users, because external practices and policies are not aligned, or are in conflict with CorpFort's policies:

- External user's identity and authentication can be vague. For example, CorpFort has issued external partners non-corporate SmartCards, for two-factor authentication to allow access to source code. Some of these external partners have shared their credentials with others.
- Authorization and access control are more difficult to achieve for external users. For

example, partners may have changed their role, and no longer need access to CorpFort data, but their entitlements are not dynamically managed.

- The existence and extent of data protection is unknown for external locations. The secure data handling policy may not be enforced outside of CorpFort. For example, if a partner carries CorpFort's data from one country to another, the data can be inspected by that country's government.

Lacking Data Protection throughout the Data Lifecycle

Data is characterized by its complete lifecycle, from creation to end of life. In addition, data characteristics also include data states - at rest, in use and in transit, and data types - structured and unstructured. Protective mechanisms exist for some of these conditions, but not for all. In addition, multiple and dissimilar solutions exist for protecting data in transit and data at rest, leaving data unprotected during the transition between states, i.e. "gas to liquid"— as it changes states from structured to unstructured, or from at rest to in use. For example, currently CorpFort's Line of Business (LOB) application users can export data from a database to a spreadsheet. The control, that has once protected the data in the database, does not exist in the spreadsheet.

If CorpFort is to meet its acknowledged responsibilities to shareholders and customers, it must provide end-to-end data protection. When designing ways to protect data from unauthorized access, it is important to consider protection mechanisms and strategies for applying them, that are effective for both structured and unstructured data, in all three states, and while in transition from one condition or state to another. These lifecycle stages, types and states are described below.

Data Lifecycle

Information Lifecycle Management is the process of managing business information throughout its lifecycle from the time the data is conceived to the time it is destroyed, and in accordance to its value to the organization. This is sometimes referred to as Data Lifecycle Management, and has six stages as shown in Figure 1. While each phase of the lifecycle presents opportunities for strengthening data protection, the real challenge is consistent data management throughout the data lifecycle.

The authoring or acquisition of information is usually dedicated to current business objectives, with little regard for its future re-use. The problem is that today's information is generally digital,

and subject to rapid digital deterioration, starting in as little as three years. Information Lifecycle Management (ILM) addresses the identification of key information at the point of authoring or acquisition, and places this information on a predetermined path to preservation, and easy future location and re-use.

The data lifecycle has been defined by many system vendors, as an evolution of storage management. From this point of view, the data is managed based on its container, as opposed to its attributes. Certain data forms do have attributes, but the attributes seem to be underused for data management, and the attributes do not follow the data, as it transitions between various platforms or applications.

Figure 1. The Information Lifecycle

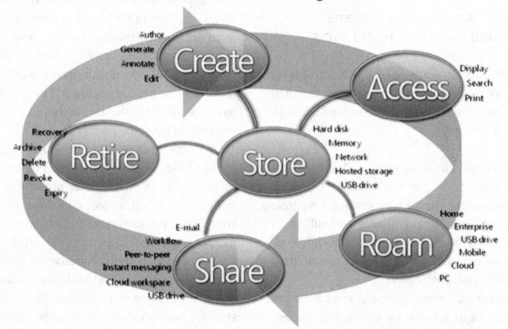

Data Types

Structured Data

Structured data is anything that has an enforced composition to the atomic data types. Structured data is managed by technology that allows for querying and reporting against predetermined data types and understood relationships. (Weglarz, 2004).

Unstructured Data

Unstructured data consists of two basic categories:

- **Bitmap (Binary) Objects:** Inherently non-language based, such as image, video or audio files.
- **Textual Objects:** Based on a written or printed language, such as Microsoft Word documents, e-mails or Microsoft Excel spreadsheets (Weglarz, 2004).

This includes data that started out as structured, and then are changed or converted into unstructured data.

Data Conversion

Protected data becomes vulnerable, as it goes through the transition between structured and unstructured conditions.

Data States

Data in Use

The "in-use" state is arguably the most difficult to address. In order for data to be considered in use, the data must be accessible and in a consumable format. Any encrypted data must be decrypted to make it usable. While various technologies exist to help restrict unauthorized or unintended access to data while in use, the simple fact of the matter is that none of the current mechanisms are truly effective. All the existing solutions rely upon the end user who is to consume the data. There are no technological mechanisms that can ensure compliance with polices and requirements. For example, RMS can restrict what users can do with documents and e-mail messages, including limiting such actions as forwarding, copying, printing or performing screen captures. However, users with malicious intent can easily circumvent these restrictions, simply by taking a digital photograph of the screen that is displaying the data, or manually writing the information down on paper, or into another digital document. They can then distribute the copied data as freely as desired. Data-in-use controls are designed to reduce the negligent release of data, but are not designed to prevent the malicious release of data.

Data-at-Rest and Data-in-Transit

Historically, data protection mechanisms have targeted one of these two states, but not both. Consider SSL and IPSec network encryption. Both can provide very effective protection for data in transit, by encrypting the network tunnels through which data travels. However, the encryption boundaries do not extend beyond the connection points, and do not extend protection to the data either before or after the transmission. An alternate example would be the use of Encrypted File System (EFS) or BitLocker for data encryption. Both are effective at providing protection through file and/or volume level encryption, but neither extends the encryption protection beyond the host, upon which the data currently exists. If the data needs to travel across any network boundary, it must be decrypted before it can be transmitted.

Poor Usability and Too Much Complexity

Today's data security is unnecessarily complex. Current security solutions overburden data handlers with different classifications and requirements, compelling them to make decisions about how to secure data. To comply, they must understand certificates, keys and rights management technologies. There are too many data protection technologies that users must embrace. Due to the inability of users to recognize and use the appropriate technologies to properly secure transactions and data, the data is either not protected or it is inadequately secured. Additionally, because the user experience of protecting e-mail with S/MIME is not simple, many users do not use the technology.

Because many existing security solutions lag behind business demands and industry trends, IT system administrators and data producers must exert additional effort and resources to make them work in today's environment. For example, LOB application owners must manually determine whether or not their applications contain confidential data, requiring more time and increasing the likelihood of errors and data compromise. IT administrators struggle to recover different encrypted customer data or legal requests. Existing data protection solutions lack the enterprise manageability, scalability and supportability needed to reduce this complexity.

Lack of PII Data Stewardship and Responsible Leadership

At one time, PII data has not caused the problems it faces today. Data has not been as easily linked as it is today, and thus not as likely to result in breaches of confidence. Many colleges and universities have used students' Social Security Numbers (SSNs) as student IDs. Much PII data

do not have value because it could not be combined into useful information to create profiles. Because it has been hard to combine the data into more comprehensive individual profiles, the consequences of breach to the PII owner have been much lower. The combination of the demand by financial and commercial entities for easier and more cost-effective ways to do business, and the growth of the Internet as a business channel, has fueled advances in PII data collection, leaving the data protection policies and technologies to catch up.

Individuals have been at risk for having their personal information stolen and used to commit identity-related crimes long before the emergence of the Internet. What the Information Age has changed, however, is the method by which identity thieves can access and exploit the personal information of others. (Peretti)

Companies gather all kinds of user data for various purposes, such as sales leads, marketing and research. The hope is that all these data are to result in competitive advantages. SOX, HIPAA, GLBA, PCI and other government and private regulations have been enacted for the purpose of keeping this data secure, through the use of audits and fines. However, industry that includes cloud customers and cloud providers must take responsibility for the impact of compromised PII data, that go far beyond lost corporate revenue or penalties, and that have the potential for serious negative effects on the individuals represented by that data.

The PII is far more than just some numbers and letters representing someone's records. It is a digital representation of someone's life stored in a database, shown on a screen or printed on paper. It can include SSNs, names, addresses, medical information and financial data. If that profile is compromised, a person's life can be seriously impacted. Financial loss and the inconvenience of repairing one's name, credit scores and the overall financial profile are just the tip of the iceberg. Physical or other threats related to a compromised identity are also possible once a personal profile makes into the wild.

The PII is now so valuable that it has become a profitable black market business. With the click of a button someone's digital life can be traded on the underground ID and credit card "stock market" (see Figure 2), complete with bids and asks for certain types of data. The PII owners would then have to deal with the resulting potential losses.

Cyber-crime has evolved significantly over the last two years, from dumpster diving and credit card skimming to full-fledged online bazaars full of stolen personal and financial information. (U.S. Secret Service, 2006)

But the more lucrative business model is to go after the custodians of massive repositories of the PII and financial data, such as online retailers, corporations and governments, with millions of records that can produce a big payout. A PII database might be secure enough to withstand various attacks,[4] but when broken business operating

Figure 2. Screenshot of price list for stolen credit card numbers and available balance amounts discovered on the web by McAfee Avert Labs (Mills, 2008)

Bank Name	Country	Balance	Price
Bank of America (BOA)	USA	...	Sold
Amsouth Bank	USA	$16,040	€700
Washington Mutual Bank(WAMU)	USA	$14,400	€600
Washington Mutual Bank(WAMU)	USA, Multi-currency acct.	$7,950 + £2,612	€500
Washington Mutual Bank(WAMU)	USA	...	Sold
MBNA America Bank	USA	$22,003	€1,500
BANCO BRADESCO S.A.	BRAZIL, Dollar Account	$13,451	€650
CITIBANK	UK, GBP Account	£10,044	€850
NatWest	UK, GBP Account	£12,000	€1000
BNP Paribas Bank	France, Euro Account	€30,792	€2200
Caja de Ahorros de Galicia	Spain, Euro Account	€23,200	€1200
Caja de Ahorros de Galicia	Spain, Euro Account	€7,846	€500
Banc Sabadell	Spain, Euro Account	€25,663	€1450

processes allow exceptions and careless handling of PII, the data makes its way into less secure containers such as laptop drives, USB storage device, mobile phones, network shares and Excel spreadsheets that are not designed to protect PII, and from there it is consumed by sales, marketing, billing and many other departments, even more pathways to compromise are to be opened up. For an in depth discussion of this threat, see Kimberly Kiefer Peretti's paper, "Data Breaches: What the Underground World of 'Carding' Reveals."

Fortunately, CorpFort has a good corporate privacy policy. Unfortunately, it has not implemented a robust and centralized system of accountability, necessary to both enforce adherence to the policy and drive the development of data protection tools.

Lack of Awareness for Accountability and Responsibility of Data Security

Recently, emphasis on security has pushed the development of information and network security technologies. Corporations such as CorpFort have built mega networks, server farms and walls of security in an attempt to protect its digital assets from outside intruders. That seems to work until the Internet has become a core business component for every enterprise. Businesses are now conducted on the Internet and in the cloud, and the "hiding behind the wall" practice no longer keeps the prowlers at bay. People have become complacent with data security. For instance, they feel that data is secure, because it is safely behind a firewall on a Corpnet or on the laptop.

Today's security practices have evolved from security on the network, to applying controls at the host and application levels, with an eye towards controls on the data itself. But less emphasis is put on one core element – people. Without people's active awareness and participation in protecting data, all the technology and massive security walls are useless. There would still be opportunities for insider threats, insecure copying of corporate's confidential information, removing or setting improper Access Control Lists (ACLs) and social engineering tactics. The effort to pursue security awareness is often undermined, due to the added cost for training, and concern for lost productivity due to change of business practices, processes and adaptation. Many corporate IT managers would rather spend money and resources on technology solutions, than on requiring business people and executives to increase security awareness and training. Information security starts with the people who create, change, collaborate and exchange data amongst themselves. Systems do not decide where and when the data should go; in most cases it's the person handling the information who makes these decisions. If data users do not understand the potential risks for a piece of valued data to be compromised, they would not know how to handle it or apply the appropriate security protections.

THE VISION: WHERE WE WANT TO BE

The vision for Data Protection in the Cloud Era can be viewed from four perspectives. Development of a successful strategy for achieving the vision must consider each of these perspectives.

Security Perspective

Data is protected regardless of its type, state or lifecycle stage. Data is also protected regardless of its environments, either on premise or in the cloud. All valuable data are to be accessed and used in accordance with the intent, defined by the owners accountable for its security, in policies which persist with the data elements themselves.

Data Owner Perspective

Valuable data are accessed and used only as intended by the owner, accountable for its security.

Data User Perspective

Valuable data are accessed and used by the users, when and how they need it.

Service Perspective

Security tools, consulting, compliance and auditing functions for protecting data are sought out as an IT-provided service or cloud service by data owners.

THE STRATEGY: HOW WE GET THERE

Reaching that vision for Data Protection, in the Cloud Era, requires a strategy that provides direction and perspective to guide the effort. Without a strategy, organizations tend to overlook trends and create solutions that are not future-proof, and could be conflicting or regressive. The strategy

of Data Protection in the Cloud Era consists of Strategic Stages and Strategic Goals (see Figure 3).

There are four Strategic Stages. The stages represent where we are today (Working in Today's World), the mechanisms we need to put in place that are to enable future solutions (Building for the Future), the solutions we expect to come to fruition within the next five years (Implementing the Future), and the end state where the vision is realized (Realizing the Vision).

There are five Strategic Goals. Each goal relates to one of the five problem areas described in the Problem Section above. The goals are intended to drive solutions that address the problem areas. The strategic goals permeate all strategy stages, and extend throughout the strategic timeline. In a sense, the goals can be utilized as quality measures, to gauge improvement as the environment moves through all stages, towards the realization of the vision.

Strategic Goals are discussed in detail below, followed by an explanation of the Strategy Stages.

Figure 3. Strategy for Data Protection in the Cloud Era

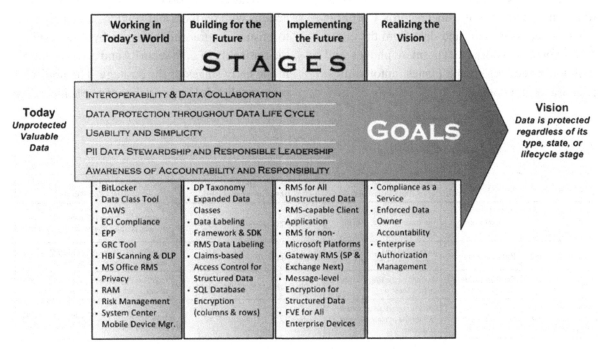

Strategic Goals

The five Strategic Goals are:

- Improved interoperability and secure data collaboration;
- Increased data protection throughout the data life cycle;
- Increased usability and reduced complexity;
- Enforced data stewardship and responsible leadership;
- Enhanced awareness of accountability and responsibility.

Each of the Strategic Goals is described in detail below, along with proposed action items.

Goal: Improved Data Collaboration and Interoperability

There are few places from which CorpFort data cannot be accessed, actively downloaded, viewed or edited. CorpFort data are distributed across well over one-million endpoints at CorpFort alone, any of which can contain valuable data, such as intellectual property, company confidential information, source code and customer records. CorpFort workers access e-mails and data from the cloud or corporate network, using smart phones and mobile devices, on trains, planes, automobiles, restaurants and hotels.

In many collaboration scenarios, data can also be accessed and used by non-CorpFort workers from multi-vendor, platforms, in a non-CorpFort environments. Partners want to download, upload and print CorpFort data at public places, in countries throughout the world.

Four major collaboration scenarios that need to be considered are described in Table 1.

Interoperability is crucial for effective data collaboration. The environment needs to extend the use of existing CorpFort and third party solutions, for collaborative use by CorpFort, partners and other businesses.

A critical aspect of data collaboration is the data protection effort, which enables CorpFort to securely collaborate with businesses and share data whether in transit, the cloud, corporate environment or home office. This effort needs to include authentication using trustworthy identities, and consider federation issues and technologies. This crucial step is primarily dependent upon CorpFort to build services and tools, that facilitate data protection interoperability, with CorpFort partners and vendors. Without taking this step, CorpFort would not be able to progress with data protection.

Because CorpFort data is at risk during interactions with partners and vendors, it is important to ensure secure collaboration by emphasizing the criticality of data security and access control, in the early stages of the strategy. The ability to protect valuable CorpFort data can be achieved by

Table 1. Data Collaboration Scenarios

Scenarios	Users	DAR (Data Repository)	DIT (Data Communication)	DIU (Data End-Points)
B2E	CorpFort workers	Located on the CorpFort site, outsource vendor site, in the cloud	within corpnet, extranet, the Internet	CorpFort PC, home PC, public PC, mobile devices, peripheral, media, human brain
B2B	Partner workers	Located on the CorpFort site, partner site, in the cloud	within corpnet, extranet, the Internet	CorpFort PC, home PC, public PC, mobile devices, peripheral, media, human brain
B2C	CorpFort business customer workers	Located on the CorpFort site, in the cloud	within corpnet, extranet, the Internet	CorpFort PC, home PC, public PC, mobile devices, peripheral, media, human brain
Outsource Vendors & Cloud Providers	CorpFort workers	Data stored on the outsource vendor site or cloud provider's datacenter	the Internet	CorpFort PC, home PC, public PC, mobile devices, peripheral, media, human brain

providing a set of industry-standard tools and software that other businesses use, along with system vendor's and cloud service provider's products and services. For longer term, it is imperative that their products and services provide an open platform for data protection. System vendors and cloud service providers must improve compatibility with other software and operating systems and applications, and enhance usability of data protection products. For example, a cloud service provider could support the software ecosystem by providing rights management software development kits for Apple iOS, Google Android and Microsoft Windows Phone OS. Doing so would provide a level playing field for data protection within the ecosystem. Another effort could take on the cloud service providers to expand the interoperability goal in order to lead and support open standards adoption. As an example, Microsoft as a cloud service provider has reached a significant breakthrough milestone with the support and adoption OOXML.[5] By acknowledging open standards, Microsoft is becoming a more valuable and important participant in the software ecosystem and the cloud.

The industry needs an open standard similar to OOXML, which is a step in the right direction for the rest of the cloud community. Similar data security open standards need to be sponsored and agreed upon by all major OS vendors and cloud service providers, so a data protection framework can be added to Linux, Android, MacOS, iOS, UNIX and Windows. Rights management needs to become a cross platform technology, and be part of each and every popular operating system with unified APIs and SDKs. The industry can no longer wait for the technology battles to end. The industry needs a Rights Management unified technology framework, sooner rather than later.

To reach the data protection vision, cloud providers need to become an integral part of a data protection ecosystem, and even take the lead in developing software and online services, to support open as well as proprietary data security and access control standards. It is important for ERM technologies to work with each other, for the common benefit of data security, regardless of the data's location or format.

Extending ERM and end point protection to RMS and beyond is the key to protecting unstructured data. RMS could serve as a foundation for these services. RMS efforts need to expand beyond the Windows and Office platforms and concentrate on increasing functionality and support for other operating systems and applications. Ideally, a "Data Security Standard" could be integrated as an additional layer in the OSI or another cloud computing models.

See Table 2 for action items and proposed approaches for improving interoperability and data collection.

Goal: Increased Data Protection throughout the Data Lifecycle

Data Lifecycle

CorpFort should create a data lifecycle management process, and ensure that it includes the data taxonomy as a subset of the data lifecycle. Data should be managed from its inception, to its archival or deletion, and should be managed based on its attributes or metadata. Metadata or data attributes should be standardized, and used with data as it moves throughout its lifecycle. The metadata should change based on location, but location should not be its only defining attribute. Data should have lifecycle attributes, or metadata that describe its current state, and where it is within its complete lifecycle. The lifecycle data should follow the data between media, platforms and applications. The security attributes can be used to apply security controls, and manage the data all the way through its end of life.

Table 2. Action Items for Improved Interoperability and Data Collaboration

Description	Proposed Approach
Message-level encryption for structured data[6]	• Develop Reference Architecture (RA) and Standards that implement industry-standard message-level encryption, with technologies such as WCF, WSE 3.0
Open data security standards	• Work with Standards Team to ensure that enterprise rights management standards are developed and applied industry-wide • Evangelize the standards throughout the industry
Software Runtime SDK for data labeling and handling	• Create and deploy standardized data protection framework for use by developers
Enterprise device full volume encryption	• BitLocker on Windows and Mac laptops • Encryption for mobile phones (iPhone, Android, Windows Phone) and PDAs except OS • Encryption for other enterprise devices requiring encryption (printers, USB drives, etc.)
Structured data access control	• Develop credible identity, strong authentication, and authorization policies, and audit log • Provide Enterprise key recovery capabilities for SQL Server, Oracle, DB2
Expansion of RMS to include other operating systems and applications	• Put RMS functionality in other products such as database and web servers • Make use of rights management technology as the default setting in e-mails • Work toward expansion of rights management technology and towards pervasive data self-protection • Improve RMS so that it works with third-party products • Improve RMS so that it works in all ERM systems • Provide Enterprise key recovery capabilities for SQL, Oracle, DB2 • Create RMS clients for non-Windows OS platforms, such as MacOS, Linux, iOS, Android
Secure collaboration with unstructured data between partners in the cloud	• Integrate RMS and federated authentication in the cloud to support multiple Identity Providers

Data at Rest and Data in Transit

One obvious solution is to simply employ multiple types of protection mechanisms that protect the data both at rest as well as during transit. This can be effective, however one of the goals of any successful strategy is that it should be as simple and easy to deploy as possible. In achieving this goal, it would be undesirable to have to rely on multiple mechanisms, rather than a single mechanism that could accomplish the same goals.

Data in Use

Any data protection strategy needs to consider that true protection of DIU is effectively unattainable. This does not mean that all such efforts should be abandoned. On the contrary, mechanisms such as those employed by RMS do provide value by helping to prevent unintended and non-malicious data compromise. Such mechanisms should continue to be developed and implemented, along with user education on how to employ such mechanisms and properly handle data.

Data-centric Protection

The goal is to move towards a model in which the core of data protection persists with the data itself. That is to say that the primary protection mechanism is applied directly on the data, but that the protection itself remains in effect, regardless of the host upon which the data resides, and whether or not the data is in transit or at rest.

The goal is to move towards a model in which the core of data protection persists with the data itself.

With such a mechanism in place, protection would be pervasive and could be counted on to provide its intended protection regardless of host, platform, hypervisor, virtual machine or data state. An example of such a mechanism would be the current implementation of RMS. With RMS protection applied on an Office document or e-mail message, the contents of the file or message are encrypted, providing protection against unauthorized access. This encryption exists regardless of whether the data is at rest or in transit. Additionally, it also applies controls on how the data can be used by authorized users, by implementing restrictions on the ability to forward, copy, print and etc. Protection is provided to the data through encryption, and access to the keys needed to decrypt the data is provided only to authenticated and authorized individuals.

Ideally, such mechanisms can be developed and implemented, as a single solution for addressing the majority of data protection scenarios, and are effective and simple to deploy and use. Additionally, an ideal solution would be scalable, such that it can be applied to all types of files, not just Office documents. It should also be a solution that can potentially be used on multiple platforms, and not limited to Windows clients.

Data has unique characteristics depending upon whether it is structured or unstructured, and also its state (see Table 3). The data protection strategy must take these differences into consideration, and select the appropriate solution depending on the nature of data.

When *structured data is at rest* (that is, in a data repository or archival area), it is usually under IT management and has better controls. Encryption plus Access Control are to provide adequate protection for data, without incurring the operational performance penalty of ERM in structured data query.

When *structured data is in transit* (that is, on the wire or a removable medium), malicious users can access it with tools such as a network sniffer. Therefore, access control does not apply, and instead the data must be properly encrypted at the right level, so only the receiving party can decrypt it.

When *structured data is in use* (decrypted at end point), negligent users and unhealthy end points cause a greater risk for data than data in the other states. ERM may help to a certain degree, but it is not enough. Endpoint protection mechanisms, such as full volume encryption, awareness, accountability and data loss prevention (DLP), are necessary complementary protections for data in use.

For *unstructured data*, operational performance is not as significant a concern, as it is for structured data. Thus, enterprise rights management (ERM) is the standard solution for securing unstructured data in all its states. For unstructured data in use, the risks are the same as for structured data in use, so we need to apply the same security measures and solutions.

Table 4 lists action items needed to accomplish the goal of protection of data, across data states and throughout the data lifecycle.

Goal: Increased Usability and Simplicity

Data security has to be simpler and more transparent to the user. Data should be automatically protected, and the only necessary user action should be authorization. The owner must be accountable for deciding who has access to the data, and how it can be handled. However the owner should not be faced with the burden of selecting between a myriad of technical and proprietary solutions such as PGP, EFS, RMS and DRM. In most cases these are tailored toward a specific

Table 3. Data security under various conditions

Data Security	At Rest (Both Negligence & Maliciousness)	In Transit (Both Negligence & Maliciousness)	In Use by User (More About Negligence than Maliciousness)
Structured Data (and some service-oriented data) Elements & attributes; rows and columns	Encryption *plus* Access Control	Transport Level *and/or* Message Level Encryption	Enterprise Rights Management and/or End Point Protection, *plus* Awareness and Accountability, *plus* data loss prevention (DLP)
Unstructured Data File content in unstructured format	Enterprise Rights Management	Enterprise Rights Management	Enterprise Rights Management and/or End-point Protection, *plus* Awareness and Accountability, *plus* DLP

Table 4. Action items for protection across data states and data lifecycle

Description	Proposed Approach
Data classification	• Define criteria for users to classify their unstructured data.
Develop a Data Lifecycle Framework	• Create a data lifecycle management framework. • Make the data protection taxonomy a component of the lifecycle management framework. • Create lifecycle attributes or metadata that describe its current state and location within its complete lifecycle. • Ensure that protection follows the data between media, platforms, and applications and persists throughout its lifecycle. • Promote adoption of the framework.
Protection of structured data in use with RMS	• Investigate data in use protection for structured data.

organization or business, and do not work with other platforms or systems. Access control and authorization mechanisms should be simplified, to make it more user-friendly and more intuitive for consumption. Data protection needs to move into the application, deep into the OS layer, and become an integral part of the everyday business and collaborative applications. Most importantly there should be a similar feel and functionality across applications, so that the most appropriate actions become intuitive for users. Data protection technologies should also be future-proof, and changes such as stronger encryption and key management should be left for backend and IT operations to improve. The user should not be burdened with such actions.

A good start is the RMS integration with Office applications today. The actual security mechanisms are more transparent to the user. However, usability should be simplified even further, and expanded to other applications or, even better, integrated into the OS as a fundamental standard layer, which would be available to application developers for incorporation of data security logic in their applications.

CorpFort implementers can enable, hinder, or stop the business. It all depends on the approach and ability of an IT organization to support the business mission, while protecting its assets. It is

within CorpFort's ability to reduce complexity. While CorpFort has been on the forefront of many initiatives aimed at supporting the business, there is much more that can be done. CorpFort needs to take data protection more seriously, provide more awareness, improve tools, secure collaboration and reduce complexity. CorpFort efforts should concentrate on providing easier ways for the users to protect the data they are working on, so they can share it with other parties securely, without changing or compromising its integrity due to the complexity of security and the lack of interoperability. Data security needs to be moved into the application space, so that security can be built into all of the major applications that are used both inside CorpFort and for external collaboration. The data owner should be held accountable, for who should have access to the data and how it can be used. Security should happen in the background. To achieve this goal, CorpFort needs to expand its influence over its system vendors and cloud service providers. CorpFort has to take the lead in solving this data protection crisis in partnership with all the impacted stakeholders.

Table 5 lists action items needed to accomplish the goal of improving usability and increasing simplicity of data protection.

Goal: Enforced PII Data Stewardship and Responsible Leadership

CorpFort needs to recognize the implications of PII risk beyond financial penalties and fees, and embrace its commitment to good citizenship:

Good citizenship is just good business. It's the right thing to do. It's who we are as a company. It's our commitment to communities around the world. It's really that simple.

CorpFort believes that it can make the greatest contribution to society, when its business operations and citizenship efforts are closely aligned.

Table 5. Action items for improved usability and increased simplicity

Description	Proposed Approach
Simplified user interfaces for data protection, to make RMS more consumable by end users	• Influence system vendors to make RMS more intuitive for users; • IT to create additional RMS template options, focused on document security; • Simplify the process for users to protect data.
LOB application developer support for RMS	• Integrate RMS into LOB applications.
Data management standards	• Develop a data protection taxonomy, • Expand data classification, • Create RMS data labelling, • Develop an enterprise-wide authorization management tool to manage access policy.
Access control for structured data	• Develop claim-based authentication, authorization and access controls for structured data.

Corporate citizenship is also core to the CorpFort business strategy, and the way that we interact with customers, partners, governments, and employees. It is a way of doing business that recognizes the effect that CorpFort has on society, and the effect that society has on our business.

The significance of this responsibility is especially relevant to Personally Identifiable Information (PII). Many corporations have corporate citizenship programs. However most are missing one very important component—the promise to users, shareholders and customers alike, that their PII are protected at all costs to reduce the negative affect that lost and compromised PII have on people's lives. Companies need to embrace the fact that there is a lot more at stake than a financial loss to the company, and therefore more emphasis needs to be put on accountability and responsibility for handling PII.

CorpFort needs to work with others in the corporate community, to ensure the safety of personal records and the lives they represent.

Just publishing privacy policies on the Web no longer makes users feel safe that their information is protected as promised. Corporations need

to show that they care about their users' PII, by handling it properly and not leaving it to the mercy of inadequate business processes and technologies, improperly trained staff or budget cuts. Protecting PII should become one of the most important Corporate Citizenship programs. A top priority for business leaders should be to recognize and drive awareness of the importance of PII, and its protection throughout their organizations.

Devaluation of PII

A PII profile is most valuable when it is complete. That is not to say that pieces of a PII profile are not valuable. They are; it just takes time to collect the whole profile, piece by piece. PII has insinuated itself as a replacement for authentication on the Internet. Web sites can barter a username and a password for a user's partial or complete PII profile, through the sign-up process for their services. To devalue PII, it must be kept as fragmented as possible, and it must not be used as authentication credentials. With the push of technologies such as CardSpace, PII can remain in the background and not be used for direct authentication; instead a digital card representation is used, and the PII is safely stored at either the user's computer or the identity service provider. This is one way to devalue the use of PII, and therefore its importance for Internet commerce and transactions.

In the back end, devaluing of PII might mean to scrub or "censor" PII data extracted, from databases used for marketing or sales purposes. The majority of the data extracted are not usually needed in its original state. For example, a sales database export for finding leads would not need a complete PII, including SSN, CC and other information. It could be limited to name, address, an e-mail address or phone number. It is still important for PII, but the most important components remain in one or few centralized databases. Taking this a step further would mean automating it in the back end, through a brokerage service between the PII database and the sales department. Sales can just key in the queries, and the system would take care of the rest without exposing the data or making it available to them. An automated, mass e-mail or other action can occur as controlled by the sales or marketing department, but the data remains secure. Microsoft has created some similar solutions, but has not been able to scale them without negatively impacting performance. Consider a centrally managed, but distributed storage data protection model, using the data access program and incorporating Web services to provide more centralized controls for PII, firm accountability, compliance and etc.

Although failure to prevent the breach of PII is not criminal, CorpFort has an ethical obligation to prevent breaches that could result in financial, time, reputation and other burdens on the PII owner.

More needs to be done. PII data handlers, from clerks to customer support, database administrators, application developers, business managers, sales and marketing need to exercise much more caution, when collecting and handling this type of information. A change in the direction regarding PII needs to occur that goes beyond current regulations. Government regulations should be viewed by the industry as the minimum bar for protecting PII and financial data, and solutions should extend beyond those bare minimum requirements. Meeting those regulations, without exceeding is no longer enough. That's where Responsible Corporate Citizenship starts. It is everyone's job to ensure that PII remains protected, much the same way as precious metals are, because in today's world, PII profiles are often worth more. Exhibiting desire and effort to protect PII for social benefit, can also serve as a clear sign that enterprises can act in the interest of citizens, without waiting for government regulation.

Table 6 lists the action items necessary for ensuring improved PII data stewardship, and responsible data protection leadership.

Table 6. Actions for PII stewardship and responsible leadership

Description	Proposed Approach
Set a single point of ultimate ownership and accountability for PII, throughout the company:	• Make Chief Privacy Officer accountable for protection of all PII, PCI, and PHI throughout the company, • Maintain close ties between InfoSec and the Corporate Privacy Group.
Provide mechanisms for identifying data as PII, and limiting how it is handled:	• Develop data classification tools, • Develop PII data handling processes.
Ensure PII controls and usage are monitored and enforced:	• Develop tracking tools for monitoring PII data labelling and handling, • Determine policies for enforcing PII data labelling and usage, • Ensure that all PII is in the form of structured data.

Goal: Enhanced Awareness of Accountability and Responsibility for Data Security

Awareness is the prerequisite for promoting accountability and responsibility.

Before people can accept accountability and responsibility for protecting valued data, they must understand the reasons why protections are important and their specific roles in the data lifecycle. Until they understand their impact on data security and the consequences to themselves of how they handle data, users are more likely to mishandle data. Proper data handling starts with people's understanding of the data classification and their desire to protect the data.

Everyone connected to the data—Owners, Delegates, Producers, Custodians and Users—must take an active role in the protection of the data. To do this, they must understand their roles in the protection of CorpFort digital assets. In the case of PII, no CorpFort entity, function or team should be allowed to waive security controls or accept the risk of doing so. While no risk-taking is allowed for PII, risk-taking is allowed for all other types of data; that is, the data owner can make the classic risk decision, regarding whether the cost and burden of security controls are

Table 7. Data protection roles

Data Protection Roles[7]				
Personally Identifiable Information[8]			**All Other Types of Data**	
Owner	Individual identified, characterized, and described by the PII.	Owner	Is ACCOUNTABLE for the assessment and assignment of the value of the data, classification of the data, and definition of access and usage intent, making risk decisions regarding security controls for that data, and understanding and accepting the impact of those risk decisions. Reports directly to the business division leader.	
Delegate	The Chief Privacy Officer (CPO) or a delegate assigned by the CPO. The CPO or delegate is ACCOUNTABLE for defining the value of the data, the requirements for data access and data usage, for making risk decisions regarding security controls for that data, for accepting the impact of those risk decisions and for ensuring the security of the digital assets.	Delegate	Is given by the Owner the RESPONSIBILITY for assessing and assigning the value of the data, classifying the data, defining access and usage intent, making risk decisions regarding security controls for that data, and understanding the impact of those risk decisions. The Delegate may name sub-delegates to provide the level of granularity needed.	
Producer	Not applicable.	Producer	Is RESPONSIBLE for understanding the value (either realized or potential) of the data produced, and assuming all of the ACCOUNTABILITY of an Owner or transferring the data to an Owner, who then becomes accountable. In an e-mail, the User is often also the Producer.	
Custodian	Is RESPONSIBLE for protecting the data usage and data access policy, as specified by the Privacy Owner or Delegate. IT often serves in the role of Custodian for PII.	Custodian	Is RESPONSIBLE for protecting the data usage and data access as specified by the Owner and/or Delegate. IT or Cloud Service Provider often serves in the role of the Custodian.	
User	Same responsibilities as the Custodian.	User	Same responsibilities as the Custodian. In e-mail, the User is often also the Producer.	

worth the penalty or financial loss, that could result in the absence or reduction of those security controls.

Table 7 summarizes these roles.

While the vision, from the perspective of the user, is that the protection of data should be automatic and transparent, the reality is that even users must take responsibility for ensuring that CorpFort assets, coming into their possession, are protected to the degree intended by the asset owner. Technology alone simply cannot be relied upon. The willing cooperation of the user is critical. For users to be willing to accept the inconveniences this entails, they need to understand the importance to the company and to themselves, and the consequences to them if not cooperating. For example, if users refuse to cooperate, one alternative is simply to lock down everything, and make users responsible for reducing the security level on a case-by-case basis.

CorpFort must focus on the awareness and the infrastructure to support controls that result in role changes, that foster greater accountability and responsibility.

Table 8 lists the actions and approaches needed to improve awareness for protecting data.

Table 8. Actions for improved awareness of accountability and responsibility for data security

Description	Proposed Approach
Move the culture of the entire company to value protection of data	• Get leadership support from all C level executives, and in ongoing data security messaging throughout the company.
Enforce privacy and data protection training for all employees	• Ensure that existing data protection training addresses the vision (Data Protection 101); • Create modules as necessary to meet differing data handling needs for PII and for all other data.
Educate users in how to protect data	• Educate users about the risks to them of losing control of their own data; (Talk to Awareness group.) • Make data protection awareness training required for CorpFort workers, partners, independent software vendors (ISVs), cloud service providers, and business customers to gain authorization for data access.

Strategic Stages

There are four Strategy Stages:

- Working in Today's World,
- Building for the Future,
- Implementing the Future,
- Realizing the Vision.

These stages are not crisp chronological demarcations. Nor are they rigorously serialized. Many of the activities at one stage are not dependent upon completion of activities in a previous stages; they can take place in parallel. For example it is expected that work on Building for the Future is to begin now. Just as it is unwise to merely focus on the present, it is not prudent to build for the future without providing near term solutions to present-day problems. Therefore while preparing for the future, it is also necessary to apply due diligence to security problems, by providing security controls such as those that are currently deployed or planned. When simultaneously considering both the present and the future, it is possible to consider today's controls in light of the Vision and strategic goals, in order to:

- Determine whether or not today's solutions are strategic,
- Avoid overinvestment on solutions that are not strategic, lest they become entrenched, and detract from the ability to evolve to better strategic controls.

Working in Today's World

An excellent example of a current tool that represents the best effort dealing with today's security problem, but which can also be improved, is Data Classification. It is widely held throughout the industry that a Data Classification scheme is an expected information security control. Absence of such a scheme would indicate that a company fails to demonstrate due diligence. As a result most mature, and even many immature Information Security Programs, have a data classification scheme in place. As shown in Figure 4, CorpFort currently uses a 3-tier classification system, where designation is based on value, that is, High Business Impact (HBI), Medium Business Impact (MBI), and Low Business Impact (LBI). In addition, each classification is mapped to Data Handling Standards.

Though well-intentioned, CorpFort's published Data Classification Scheme meets expectations for due diligence, and though it is assumed to provide significant value as a security control, it does not. The value criteria are vague. For example, in order to classify a piece of data as HBI, the owner needs to know if and how much mate-

Figure 4. The existing CorpFort Data Classification Scheme

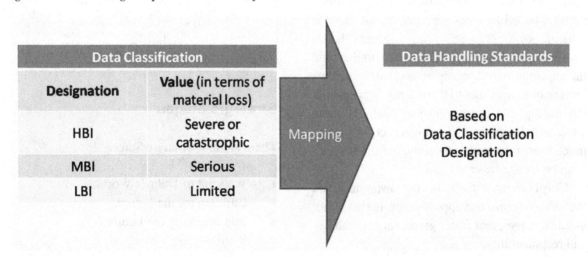

rial damage to CorpFort would result from compromise, and then guess as to what the adjectives "severe," "serious" and "limited" translates in terms of dollar value.

Once the value has been selected, a designation (HBI, MBI or LBI) based on this ambiguous value ranking is assigned which, in turn, is then mapped to prescribed data handling standards. Perhaps worse, there is no relationship between the data classification scheme and data handling standards, with usage or access control. The only guidance given is that HBI and MBI data should be accessed only by those with a "need to know."

However suboptimal the current Data Classification scheme is, it has had a very positive awareness impact on workers. Many workers now think about the value of data and how they should handle it.

Data Classification is only one of the many security solutions that are either in place or are being deployed - refer to bullets in "Working in Today's World" stage depicted in Figure 3.

Building for the Future

Before optimal controls can be implemented, preparation is necessary. At this stage, a strategic foundation is laid, that facilitates and steers effort towards solutions that are to ultimately realize the vision.

Returning to the example of Data Classification, we believe that a better approach than the one currently in place is necessary, to reflect the true intention of the business in terms of what the data is, who should access it, and how it should be handled. Work should be started to create improved Data Classification and Data Handling Standards. In this new model (see Figure 5 below), CorpFort would create Data Classifications and Data Handling specifications, based on important characteristics of the data rather than value. These

Figure 5. Proposed CorpFort Data Classification Scheme

Data Classification						Data Handling												
Designation	Answers					Answers												
	Where did the data originate?	Who owns the data?	Who controls the data?	Who or what holds the data?	What type of data is it?	Who or what can use the data?	For what purpose?	Can it be shared?	Where will the data be kept?	How long is the data retained?	Does it need to be safeguarded?	At rest?	When backed up?	During use?	How can the data be disclosed?	What subset can be disclosed?	What protection must be implemented?	Does the data need to be watermarked?
Class 1																		
Class 2																		
Class ...																		
Class n																		

characteristics can be defined by answering a set of prescribed questions. (Bilger, 2006)

As an example, consider a class of data that has the following characteristics, based on answers to the data classification questions shown in the figure:

- The data originated from consumer account enrollment;
- The data is owned by the consumer;
- The data is controlled by CorpFort Marketing;
- The data is stored in the "consumer account" database;
- The data is structured.

This class could be called "Structured Consumer" data. Knowing these characteristics, data handling standards can be defined for all data thus classified. For example, when considering the class of data called "Structured Consumer" data, answers to the Data Handling questions shown in the figure would yield the data access and data usage policy:

- The data can only be used by database administrators;
- The data can only be used for the purpose of authentication;
- The data can be shared only under the condition that the consumer has agreed to the sharing;
- The data is only to reside in the "consumer account" database;
- The data must be safeguarded at rest and when backed up;
- The data is to be kept until the consumer indicates that the account is to be closed or if there is evidence that the account has been compromised;
- CorpFort is not responsible for safeguarding it when in use;
- The data can only be disclosed if the consumer has agreed to the sharing;

- Name, address, and e-mail address is the only subset of data that can be disclosed;
- The data must be encrypted;
- The data does not need to be watermarked.

At this point the data has been classified using meaningful criteria, and has been assigned data handling requirements that provide descriptive intent. With this information, it is now possible for data access and data usage policies to be created, that are strongly tied to business intent.

To build a better data classification standard for the future, work should also be done to create a taxonomy that provides a granular description of the data type, thereby providing a more descriptive answer to the question, "What type of data is it?", and to build data labeling framework and SDKs. This and other solutions that build for the future are found in bullets under the "Building for the Future" stage depicted in Figure 3.

Implementing the Future

At this stage, strategic security controls for Data Protection can be implemented using foundations built in the previous stages. For example, assume that an expanded data classification scheme that uses a granular taxonomy, as well as data structures that can hold that information as metadata, are available. Enhancements to data-centric technologies, such as RMS, could be implemented, that preserve the intent of the data owner and ensure the data is handled as intended. If the goal of interoperability were also considered in the building stage, it should be possible to implement RMS on non-Windows platforms, so that federated scenarios could be supported, that would allow CorpFort to exchange protected data with its partners and vendors. These and other strategic security solutions are listed in bullets in the "Implementing the Future" stage depicted in Figure 3.

Realizing the Vision

Once the optimal strategic controls are built, and have replaced legacy sub-optimal controls, the CorpFort Enterprise is to have a comprehensive data protection solution suite. Meeting the Vision however requires more than a collection of solutions. In a fully mature data protection environment:

- CorpFort internal IT provides data protection as a service that the business seeks out, rather than a tax burden they eschew;
- Data owners willingly take accountability for their data, because they realize that protecting it benefits them and their business;
- Users get access to the data they need, but they clearly understand how owners of that data intend it to be handled and by whom;
- High-value data, including PII, is protected regardless of its state (at rest, in transit or in use);
- Security controls exist at the data level, and also at the network and host levels as necessary;
- The combination of encryption and granular access control metadata that persists with the data in the form of metadata exists for both data at rest and in transit;
- Data owner's intention persists beyond the delivery of the data to the authorized recipient;
- Major security risks to data are mitigated.

NEXT STEPS: CONSIDERATIONS FOR REFERENCE ARCHITECTURE

The following guidelines are meant to provide a starting point for teams developing the Reference Architectures and Solutions derived from this strategy:

- Once CorpFort puts accountability and responsibility in place, users are going to request better tools, justifying the solutions needed to create better data protection mechanisms;
- Determine whether the various data protection tools currently available (for example, RSA Datacenter DLP solution) are strategic or simply short-term/partial solutions, so CorpFort does not over-invest in them;
- Develop data classification/labeling/handling tool necessary for requiring personal accountability and responsibility for both structured and unstructured data;
- Create centralized authority for managing regulated data, including data that resides on distributed storage media;
- Encrypt regulated data (HSPII and PCI and HIPAA, etc.) at rest and in transit;
- Protect unstructured data with RMS or similar tools;
- Determine how to define data classification when data is aggregated from disparate sources;
- Protect browser with RMS, if possible;
- Provide message-level encryption for structured data in collaboration with Applications team;
- Create business requirements for each solution.

REFERENCES

Bilger, M., et al. (2006). *Data-centric security*. IBM Corporation. Retrieved from http://www-935.ibm.com/services/us/cio/risk/gov_wp_data_centric.pdf

Brand, S. (1987). *The media lab: Inventing the future at MIT*. New York: Academic Press.

Geer, D. E. (2008). Beware the IDs of March. *IEEE Security and Privacy, 6*(2).

Mills, E. (2008). *What is your stolen data worth? McAfee Avert Labs finds price list for stolen bank account and credit card data.* Retrieved from http://www.news.com/8301-10784_3-9939862-7. html?part=rss&subj=news&tag=2547-1_3-0-5

Peretti, K. K. (n.d.). Data breaches: What the underground world of carding reveals. *Santa Clara Computer and High Technology Journal, 25.*

Ponemon Institute. (2013). *Ponemon institute research findings.* Retrieved from http://www. ponemon.org/

Privacy Rights Clearing House. (2013). *Chronology of data breaches.* Retrieved from https://www. privacyrights.org/data-breach-header-top

U.S. Secret Service. (2006). *U.S. secret service press release: United States secret service's operation rolling stone nets multiple arrests.* Retrieved from http://www.secretservice.gov/ press/pub0906.pdf

Weglarz, G. (2004, September). Two worlds of data – Unstructured and structured. *DM Review Magazine.*

ENDNOTES

[1] This includes but is not limited to source code, pre-release builds, technical know-how, product plans, specifications, milestones, usability surveys, test results, bug data, sales and marketing information, competitive intelligence and business or legal strategies.

[2] While authors recognize that information represents data that has been analyzed and interpreted, the terms "data" and "information" are used interchangeably unless otherwise noted, per IT convention.

[3] CorpFort Information Policy.

[4] Attacks may come via Web pages, SQL injection, etc.

[5] Open Office XML. See http://www.openxmlcommunity.org/

[6] Message level security is at the application layer, for example XML encryption or S/MIME encryption.

[7] All data must have an identified owner. The owner is responsible for assessing and assigning value, defining access and usage policy, and making risk decisions regarding security controls for that data. The owner is accountable for all risk taking for that data, that is, the owner assumes any and all penalties that arise from breaches that result from waived security controls. As owners of their own data, they have responsibility for understanding and characterizing the appropriate classification for their data, make decisions on who can have access, what usage is acceptable for those granted access, and they must understand and assume the risk of improper handling of that data.

[8] PII is owned by the person identified and characterized by the PII. No CorpFort entity, function, or team should be allowed to waive security controls or accept the risk of doing so.

Section 3
Data Storage and Big Data

Chapter 8
Big Data Overview

Yushi Shen
Microsoft Corporation, USA

Ling Wu
EMC² Corporation, USA

Yale Li
Microsoft Corporation, USA

Shaofeng Liu
Microsoft Corporation, USA

Qian Wen
Endronic Corp, USA

ABSTRACT

This chapter provides an overview of big data and its environment and opportunities. It starts with a definition of big data and describes the unique characteristics, structure, and value of big data, and the business drivers for big data analytics. It defines the role of the data scientist and describes the new ecosystem for big data processing and analysis.

INTRODUCTION

Today we have heard a lot about Big Data. What is Big Data? (Press, 2013) Is there a definite size over which data becomes Big Data? Is it the number of rows or the number of columns? Is a spreadsheet that contains a million rows Big Data? Is a database that has a billion records Big Data? How big is Big Data?

Wikipedia defines big data as "a collection of data sets so large and complex that it becomes difficult to process using the available database management tools. The challenges include how to capture, curate, store, search, share, analyze and visualize big data. The trend to larger data sets is due to the additional information derivable from the analysis of a single large set of related data, as compared to separate smaller sets with the same

DOI: 10.4018/978-1-4666-4801-2.ch008

total amount of data, allowing such correlations to be found to spot business trends, determine the quality of research, prevent diseases, link legal citations, combat crimes and determine real-time roadway traffic conditions. " (Wikipedia, 2012)

In today's environment, we have access to more types of data. These data sources include online transactions, social networking activities, mobile device services, internet gaming and etc. While the public open data is growing, increasingly powerful ERPs also bring corporate data to a new level. Big data is changing the world. Data sources are expanding, data from Facebook, twitter, YouTube, Google and etc., are to grow 50X in the next 10 years.

An IDC study shows that in 2010, there have been 1.2 zettabytes (1,200,000,000,000,000,000,000) of information, a trillion billion bytes of information to be managed and analyzed. It is estimated that by 2020, there is going to be 35 zeta bytes of information. Data deluge is to grow 44X in this decade. About 90% of this information being created is unstructured, like website clicks, mobile phone calls, Facebook posts, call center conversations, tweets, videos and emails. (Gens, 2013) Where are all these big data going? It is going to be run in the cloud. When we talk about cloud computing, we cannot miss big data.

BIG DATA DEFINITION

Big data is defined in Wikipedia that as the "data sets that are too large for storage, management, processing and analysis, it present challenges beyond traditional IT techniques." (Wikipedia, 2012) BIG is a term that is relative to the size of the data, and the scope of the IT infrastructure that is in place. Transforming big data could benefit scientific discovery, environmental and biomedical research, and national security. In order to do that, big data requires the use of new technical architectures and analytics tools, to

generate business value from the huge volume of data, in order to create insights.

Big Data comes in all kinds of forms: from highly structured ERP (Enterprise Resource Planning) data, or CRM (Customer Relation Management) data, to multi-million rows of text file, to video files and machine generated sensor data. The common feature is the high data volume and data complexity. Most of big data is unstructured or semi-structured, and require new techniques and tools to analyze.

Big Data examples are everywhere in our lives. With the popularity of mobile computing and the self-expression tolls, everyone has the ability to share their thoughts and ideas worldwide. Smart phones carry sensors like GPS, accelerometer, microphone, camera and Bluetooth which can collect huge amounts of data, and allow research on behavioral and social science, with the large scale mobile data to characterize and understand real-life phenomena. In 2011, there have been 6 billion mobile phone subscribers, growing 45 percent annually for the past four years. (ITU, 2011) A quarter of them use smartphones. By 2014, mobile internet use should overtake desktop internet use.

There are more than 845 million active Facebook users by the end of 2011, 50 percent log onto Facebook every day; 30 billion pieces of content are shared every month. Every 60 seconds, there are 510,000 posted comments, 293,000 status updates and 135,000 uploaded photos. 20 million Facebook applications are installed per day. In just 20 minutes, over 1 million links are shared. (Protalinski, 2012)

Twitter has 100 million active users around the world; more than half of them log in to twitter each day to follow their interest. The average user has 115 followers. An average of 190,000,000 tweets are sent per day. Tweeter handles 1.6 billion queries per day. 34% of marketers have generated leads using Twitter and 20% have closed deals. (Twitter, 2011)

YouTube has over 800 million unique visitors per month, which generates 92 billion page views. 72 hours of videos are uploaded every minute and over 4 billion hours of video are watched each month. More videos are uploaded to YouTube in 60 days, than the three major US TV network programs created in 60 years. (YouTube.com Statistics)

Google has 4.7 billion searches per day in 2011. Google Plus reaches out to 10 million users in 16 days, it is been reported that it has 400 million users in just one month. (Statistic Brain, 2012)

LinkedIn has 135,000,000 users; Wikipedia hosts over 17 million articles; Foursquare sees 2,000,000 check-ins a week; Instagram reaches out to 13 million users in 13 months after its launch, and have 150,000,000 photos uploaded; Flickr hosts over 5 billion images. (Decision Stats, 2011) (Pring, 2012)

BIG DATA CHARACTERISTICS

Aside from the ability to managing more data than ever before, we have access to more types of data. These data sources include Internet transactions, social networking activity, automated sensors, mobile devices, scientific instrumentation and many others. In addition to static data points, transactions can create a certain "velocity" to this data growth. As an example, the extraordinary growth of social media is generating new transactions and records on the fly.

Big Data characteristics include 3 V's: Volume, Velocity and Variety. (Baunach, 2012)

- Huge Data Volume refers to the size of big data, which is definitely huge. Big data is a relative term. For some organizations, 10 terabytes of data is unmanageable, other organizations may find 50 petabytes overwhelming. For instance, Twitter alone generates more than 7 Terabytes of data every day, Facebook generate 10 TB. From 2010 to 2020, data is to increase 44X from 1.2 Zettabytes (ZB) to 35.2 ZB. Enterprises are facing massive volumes of data.

- As a ZE.net article reports: According to Oracle president Mark Hurd, the number of devices supplying data back to businesses and enterprises are booming to 50 billion by the end of the decade. He also mentions that "data is growing by 35 to 40 percent a year" and that the world is "drowning" in vast amounts of data, which has grown eightfold in the past seven years, and companies are running out of storage space. With more than nine billion existing devices connected to the Internet, businesses are struggling to cope with the storage of the vast amounts of data they collect. (Whittaker, 2012) (Oracle, 2013)

- Velocity is the speed of data input and output. This becomes increasingly more important as more and more machine-generated data explode by the millisecond. For example, click stream data from web sites, sensors that monitor movements, and cellphone providers that generate GPS data. New and modified data must often be immediately available upon creation. Search and analysis of data on the move are required as they happen. There might be hundreds of thousands of data events per second. When a data event occurs, the handling speed becomes increasingly more of a challenge.

- Velocity is all about the rate of change in the data, and how quickly it could be used to generate value. The velocity of large data streams power the ability to parse text, detect sentiments and identify new patterns. Big Data systems need to be designed to handle large amount of new and updated data flowing into the system, by providing real-time metadata analysis, 1st minute updates to existing data, real-time activity streams delivered in context to users' applications, and the immediate incorporation of the users' activity data and feedbacks. Real time offers require that promotions be aligned with geo-location data, and customer purchase history. (Oracle, 2013)

- Variety refers to the various types of data that cannot easily be captured and managed in a traditional database. It also reflects various degrees of the data structure that includes structured, semi-structured and unstructured data, as well as rich media and transactional data with various data types: such as content, geo-spatial, machine, mobile, streaming, audio, video, text, weblogs and social media data. (Halfon, 2012) (Clegg, 2012)

Big data implementations require processing, managing and analyzing the variety of data formats and types. The big data platform should be able to analyze and ingest all of these various data types and fuse them in search results and analytics to produce insights.

The challenges of dealing with the three V's of big data have been taken to a new level, by a growth of unstructured data sources. Social networks and mobile devices generate more data, but the big data solutions require the support of a wide variety of unstructured data, and vast volumes of data, real-time analytics, diverse data models and application platforms. (Lopez, 2012)

BIG DATA VALUE

As a core business asset, the value of data lies within a company's strategy. The value of big data is reflected on leveraging big data solutions, which can actually solve real world business problems, such as the complexity of product proliferation, and help companies better align their product offerings and supply-chains based on the consumer buying patterns.

Big data presents big challenges, but it also presents new opportunities, for businesses to achieving unprecedented competitive advantages. From enterprises to merchants, every organization can use big data such as consumer information, transaction details, product inventory, as well as web logs, Facebook contents, and Youtube videos to improve their strategy by using the insights from Big Data, which has been previously discarded or could not be processed due to technology limitations.

Big data analytics examine large amounts of big data, uncover the hidden patterns, unknown correlations and other information, to reveal insights which can provide competitive advantages over rival organizations, or help better business decisions for more effective marketing and customized services of increased revenue.

Big data analytics can be achieved through data mining and predictive data analytics. Due to the size or the level of the data structure, it cannot be efficiently analyzed using the traditional database and the related tools. New big data technologies such as NOSQL database, Hadoop, MapReduce and MPP have emerged, which support the big data analytics.

With the Big Data analytics technology, by combining a large number of signals from user activities and those of their friends, organizations can offer better products, develop deeper customer relationships, and more predictive business strategies. Vendors are able to craft highly personalized user experiences, and create new kinds of advertising business, products and services.

Being empowered by Big Data, and in turning Big Data into valuable business assets, organizations become more efficient. They enjoy improved responsiveness, such as faster time to market, better business strategies and timely execution of operations to gain competitive advantages.

A report issued by The Mckinsey Global Institute (MGI) "Big data: the next frontier for innovation, competition and productivity," shows that data are becoming a factor of production, like physical or human capital. Companies that can harness big data can trample data-incompetents. Data equity, a newly coined phrase, is to become as important as brand equity. MGI believes that big data has already been widely adopted by businesses, and are creating value.

Companies have realized the value of big data and use them to generate more detailed pictures of their customers. A British retailer named Tesco collects 1.5 billion pieces of data every month, and uses them to adjust its prices and promotions. An American retailer named Williams-Sonoma, uses information such as income, expense habits and house value of its 60 million customers, to produce different iterations of its catalogue. Online retailer Amazon claims that 30% of its sales are generated by its recommendation engine. When we purchase items from Amazon, we always get recommended products through "you may also like xxxx", which tempt us to buy more. The mobile revolution adds a new dimension to consumer-targeting. Companies such as America's Place Cast are developing technologies, which allow them to track potential consumers, and send them enticing offers when they are within a few yards of Starbucks.

The big data revolution is also changing the established industries and business models. Can you imagine IT firms involving themselves in the healthcare markets? Google Health and Microsoft HealthVault allow consumers to track their health, and record their treatments. Manufacturers are transforming into service companies: IBM has changed itself from a hardware manufacture to a service (solutions) provider; BMW uses sensor-data to tell its customers when their cars need to be serviced. Insurance firms monitor the driving style of their customers, and offer them rates based on that data, instead of their age and gender.

Even government agencies are changing their model of operations. Government agencies use big data to generate statistics, to help them understand local and global patterns and trends, in order to improve their services. Tax authorities depend on the big data analytics to identify and predict fraudulent activities, estimate the tax gap, and simulate the effectiveness of policy changes on the tax behavior, and model financial risk. For example, German Federal Labor Agency managed to cut its annual spending by $14 billion over the three years, while reducing the length of time people spend out of work, by a detailed study on its clients.

MGI believes that big data cold create a new wave of productivity growth. With proper use, big data can enable retailers to increase their operating margins by 60%.

Some retailers are using data modeling to optimize their marketing expenditures. Retailers also use the big data technologies to analyze in-store camera video, and create mapping for consumer foot traffic throughout the stores. These combined with the sales data, help to optimize store layout planning and product placement to attract consumers. Big data is also used to better utilize the distribution networks, and delight customers with improved on-time deliveries of their web orders.

Recently, The University of Pittsburgh Medical Center (UPMC) announced a five year, $100 million investment, to create a comprehensive data warehouse, which is to bring together clinical, financial, administrative, genomic and other information from more than 200 sources, across UPMC, UPMC Health Plan and other affiliated entities. UPMC believes that by enhancing the collection of big data, and translating it into actionable insights, can drive greater efficiency, and help the personalization of healthcare, and better define patient populations with a greater level of granularity. The analysis of unstructured patient data and the mining of claims data for insights can improve wellness and patient compliance, advanced medical research, also can help government and insurance agencies better detect fraud, identify best care delivery practices and improve on bio-surveillance. (Lewis, 2012)

Big data is already starting to have an impact on patient care. In the paper "Supercomputer Speeds up Cancer Analysis," (Lewis, 2012) oncologists are taking advantage of a supercomputer, that reduces the time it takes to do a genomic analysis of a cancer tumor from eight weeks down to 47 seconds per patient. This allows the oncologists to prescribe treatment based on the molecular pathways of the tumor, rather than on its anatomical location, reducing the chances for wrong treatments.

The Centre for Economics and Business Research (CEBR) has an independent economic study on 'Big Data". (CEBR, 2012) In the study, they investigated how United Kingdom organizations could unlock the economic value of big data through big data analytics. Based on the fact that with high performance analytic solutions, organizations could analyze huge amounts of data quickly to reveal previously unseen patterns, and make better and faster business decisions.

CEBR estimates that data equity has a worth of 25.1 billion pounds to UK private and public sectors in 2011. The increasing adoption of big data analytics technologies is to expand this number to 40.7 billion pounds on an annual basis by 2012. According to their research, enhanced customer intelligence informed by big data is able to meet consumer demands, and evaluate customer behavior more effectively, thus to produce 73.8 billion pounds in benefits over the years 2012—2017. They forecast that the supply chain is to gain 45.9 billion pounds by predictive analytics forecasting demand, anticipating replenishment points, optimizing stock and resource allocations to greatly reduce costs. They also anticipate the public sector is to save 2 billion pounds in fraud detection, and generate 4 billion pounds through better performance management. They estimate that big data innovation can lead to 24.1 billion pounds in contributions, by assisting in the evolution of new products, services and the creation of new business markets. Especially, the utilization of advanced analytics can lead to new product development benefits of 8.1 billion pounds over the next 5-year period.

BIG DATA STRUCTURE

What does Big Data look like? What kind of data is Big Data? Big data has some common characteristics: millions if not billions of rows, data that is too large to be stored on a single storage array, too large to be processed by a single machine, and growing at a high rate. The most important feature of big data is its structure. Big data can be divided by two data types: structured and unstructured data. Unstructured data can be subdivided as semi-structured, quasi-structured and completely unstructured data.

Structured data is data that contains a defined structure, type and format. Unstructured data is data that has no inherent structure and no data type definition. Semi-structured data and quasi-structured data are in-between: Semi-Structured data includes textual data files with a discernable pattern, while quasi-structured data is textual data with erratic data formats, can be formatted with effort, tools and time.

Although the above data types are different, they can be in reality mixed in many cases. For example, a CRM application that records customer support information for a call center. The backend database is Microsoft SQL server, which stores call logs for a customer support call center. The SQL database can store structured data such as date time, ticket number, customer name, account number, problem type, and tier 1 support's name, which could be entered by the support help desk person from a GUI. The application is to also store unstructured data, such as call log information from an email ticket, or an actual phone call description. Around 80-90% of the future data growth comes from unstructured data types. (Oracle, 2012)

Structured Data

Structured data (Figure 1) refers to a set of data that is identifiable and organized in a structure. Spreadsheet and database are typical structured data, because they are organized with rows and columns. Structured data is usually used for creating, storing and retrieving data. It is accessible through applications, and managed by technology that allows for query and reporting against some predetermined data types and relationships.

The real benefit of the structured data has been the separation of content from format. Since structured data is easily understood and queried by search engines, the benefit has been extended to improved metadata and data management.

Structured data examples include database, data warehouse, spreadsheet, emails, reports, metadata, enterprise ERP or CRM systems.

Semi-Structured Data

Semi-structure data are intermediate between "Structure Data "and "Unstructured Data". It

Figure 1. Structured Data
(Google search – Structured Data)

Structured Data

			Employment (In thousands, Seasonally Adjusted)				
			Using New OMB* Definitions for Metropolitan Statistical Areas (MSAs) Please se				
A	B	C	NONAG EMPLOYEES (Establishment Basis)		D	E	CIVILIAN EMPl (Household E
		Feb-2007	Feb-2006	PCT CHG	Feb-2007	Feb-200	
UNITED STATES							
National Estimate	137,442	135,410	1.5%	145,919	143,31		
Sum of State Estimates	136,969	135,204	1.3%	146,084	143,60		
NORTHEAST	**25,563**	**25,336**	**0.9%**	**26,785**	**26,58**		
NEW ENGLAND	**7,017**	**6,955**	**0.9%**	**7,318**	**7,25**		
CONNECTICUT	1,691	1,673	1.1%	1,777	1,75		
Bridgeport-Stamford-Norwalk CT	439	435	0.9%	451	44		
Hartford-West Hartford-East Hartford CT	625	620	0.7%	600	59		
New Haven-Milford CT	381	379	0.4%	423	41		
MAINE	616	613	0.4%	682	67		
Portland-South Portland-Biddeford ME	266	264	0.8%	284	28		
MASSACHUSETTS	3,265	3,232	1.0%	3,237	3,22		
Barnstable Town MA	96	96	0.2%	115	11		
Boston-Cambridge-Quincy MA-NH	2,434	2,407	1.1%	2,280	2,26		
Springfield MA	296	292	1.2%	334	33		
Worcester MA	333	327	1.9%	378	37		
NEW HAMPSHIRE	642	639	0.5%	716	70		
Manchester-Nashua NH	208	206	0.6%	221	21		
RHODE ISLAND	496	491	1.0%	554	54		
Providence-New Bedford-Fall River RI-MA	723	717	0.9%	824	81		
VERMONT	308	307	0.2%	348	34		

represents data that do not conform to a strict schema, due to frequent changes in the structure of data. It is also called schema-less data or self-describing data.

In semi-structured data, similar entities are grouped together, but entities that belong to the same class may have different attributes. Not all attributes are required, the size and the type of the same attributes in a group may be different as well. The order of attributes are not necessarily important.

Semi-structured data (Figure 2) needs to be provided electronically from file systems, or databases or via data exchange formats such as EDI and XML. It includes textual data files with discernable patterns, such as XML data files that are self-describing, and defined by an XML schema.

As the amount of on-line data grows, we can find more and more semi-structured data.

"Quasi" Structured Data

The term "Quasi" comes from Latin, which means "as if" or "almost". "Quasi" structured data are data not exactly structured. "Quasi" structured data consists of textual data with erratic data formats, and can be formatted with special technology.

Figure 2. Semi-Structured Data
(Google Search on Semi-Structure Data)

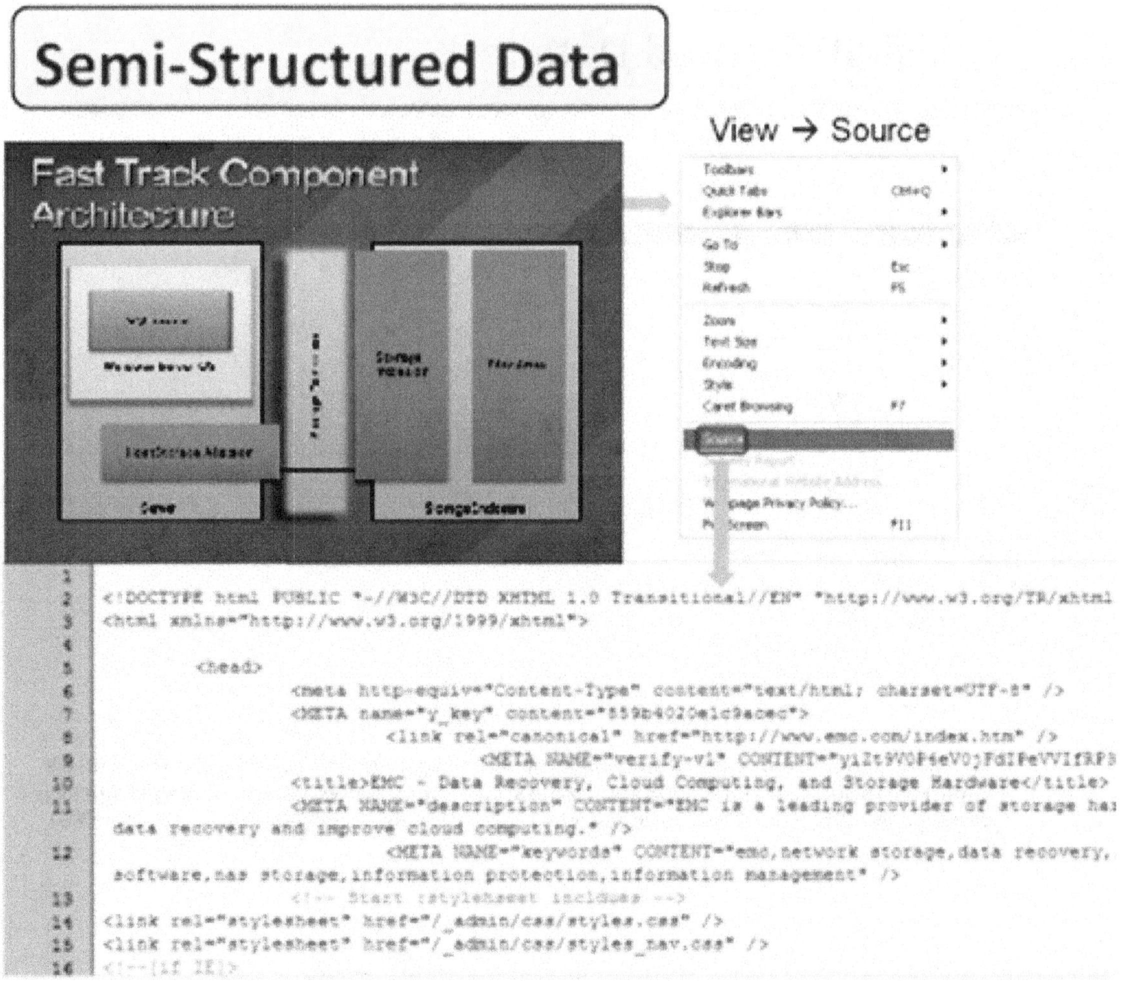

An example of Quasi-structured data (Figure 3) is the web clickstream data, which may contain some inconsistencies in data values and formats.

Unstructured Data

Comparing to the structured data, unstructured data has no identifiable structures. Unstructured data consists of any data stored in unstructured format, without any conceptual definition and data type definition.

Unstructured data falls into two basic categories:

- Media objects, which are not language based, such as image and audio/video files,
- Textual objects, which are language based, such as Microsoft word documents, Excel spreadsheets or Outlook emails.

Unstructured data examples include images, video /audio files, the contents of a word document, the body of email messages and data in each cell of a spreadsheet.

Figure 3. Quasi-Structured Data
(Google Search on Quasi-Structured Data)

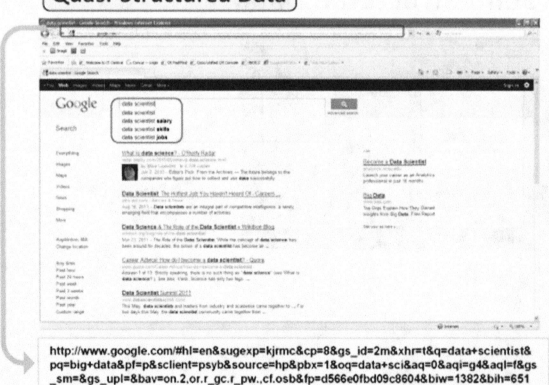

BIG DATA ANALYTICS

Businesses have tried all the ways to deliver relevant information and promotional offers, to targeted consumer marketing channels, such as televisions, direct mailings and online advertisements. All these methods are aimed at consumer interest, because for businesses, the #1 rule of marketing is: Know your customer. How do you know your customer? Do you know your customer's name, age, income, hobbies, tastes, interests and buying behaviors? Do you know what your customers watch, read and hear? What are their likes and dislikes? Who is your potential customer?

If companies can know their customers deep enough to answer all the above questions, and use the info for marketing purposes and business insights, they can be wildly successful. On the other hand, companies that lack customer information often fail, but getting to know your customers is not easy. Especially with big data exploding, organizations have become more analytical and data driven. How do you retrieve useful data, analyze the consumer behavior patterns from a vast amounts of data? Traditional data analytic technologies are not competent to handle the volume and complexity of big data. As a result, new big data technologies are being developed, which include NOSQL databases, Hadoop and MapReduce.

Business Intelligence vs. Data Science

Companies, organizations and manufacturers combine and compare data, in an effort to optimize business operations, lower cost, improve quality, increase productivity and create new products. Businesses are becoming more data driven, and analytics are playing an increasingly more important role. When it comes to business intelligence and data mining, both technologies are based on Enterprise Data Warehouse.

Data warehouse has been widely used in the industry. It integrates corporate data from different sources, uses business intelligence to analyze data and streamline day to day business operations, with insight into how to optimize business operations. Simple reporting, spreadsheets and some sophisticated drill-down analysis, have become commonplace usage for business intelligence, using a consistent set of metrics to measure past performance, and inform business planning.

Data are managed by Database Administrators (DBA), where a data analyst must depend on the DBA for access and changes to the data schema. Tight security also means longer lead times for the data analyst to get data, and more complex process for schema changes. Another implication is that the security for data warehouse restricts data analysts from building data sets, or modifying data properties, which can cause shadow systems to emerge within organizations, that contain critical data for creating analytic data sets.

"Business Intelligence (BI)" refers to the use of company data, to understand the business operation and facilitate decision making. In traditional data warehousing, business data are gathered, stored and analyzed in data warehouse to develop business reporting. The traditional business intelligence combines the tools and systems that are used for enterprise data storage and analysis. IT provides a single data source through which a company's critical data can be stored and analyzed, and then allows users to execute queries and generate reports. Typical BI tools include features such as data accessibility, decision support and end user guidance. The Microsoft Business Intelligence Studio and Oracle Business Intelligence Studio are some common BI tools that are used for relational databases.

Data science refers to the tools and methods that are being used to analyze large amounts of data, to make sense of big data, to find out what the data can tell about how to do business better. By querying millions or billions of rows, and analyzing terabytes or even zetta-bytes of information, businesses are enabled to predict prices, and design future products that are more people oriented. The use of data science varies from detecting risks to catching criminals, and it has the potential to impact every industry. "The future belongs to the companies and the people that can use data science to turn data into products." (Lohr, 2012)

In the traditional business intelligence, business users determine what questions to ask, such as monthly sales reports, customer surveys and product profitability analysis. IT departments capture structured data from the source system, analyze data to answer users' questions. With the new data science approach, IT delivers a platform to store, refine and analyze various data sources that enable creative discovery; business users then explores what questions can be asked: such as how can we have preventative health care? How to maximize asset utilization? What is the best product strategy? Rich data allow users to tackle questions that are impossible to answer by the traditional BI systems.

The traditional business intelligence tools allow users to retrieve insights from historical data. Data science gathers data, massages it into a tractable form, then tells the story, and predicts future trends.

Data science is not just about the data, or finding out about what the data might mean. It is about testing some hypotheses, and making sure that the conclusions retrieved from the data are accurate. Data science is not about just processing vast amount of big data either. It is more about connecting the information that seem isolated, analyzing the patterns behind the data mess, creating models or patterns for business productivity. It connects the seemingly isolate dots, and retrieve meaningful information quickly.

For example, an employee's daily activities could be totally irrelevant: passes a security camera to enter the building, replies email in the office, calls his boss or customers, browses the internet, and maybe reserves a business trip online. These activities are totally disjointed if taken alone. But for a company such as Cataphora, it can process this information, determine patterns and predict everything from a person's mood to their skill.

We publish posts, review other's blog and tweet on tweeter. Have we thought of analyzing the blogs, posts or tweets, and find out: "What is the best day of the week to publish your post? What time of day can you get your content the most page views and tweets? Are shorter posts better than longer ones?" These challenging questions are being asked by the data scientists. (Feinleib, 2012) Obviously, it is very important for marketers and blog owners to know who visits their website on a regular basis, and what the best time is to publish a post online. The answer can help these online authors make strategic plans to figure out how to move their business forward. But it seems impossible to answer these questions, with hundreds and thousands of public articles online. A big data analytics company named Datameer took this challenge. Datameer collects 30 days of big data articles on Feobes.com, from July 9th 2012 to August 8th 2012, by gathering the information about the publication date, time, page views, tweet, headline and full text of all these articles, the company has come up with some compelling insights:

- Wednesdays and Thursdays are the most popular days to publish, but contents published on Mondays and Saturdays get more views and tweets;
- The most popular words for headlines don't lead to the most popular post;
- Just after lunch on the East Coast is the best time to publish the post.

Interesting? If a company thrives on the number of its daily website visitors, this information is extremely critical for their survival. It could help them manage their data in a way that leads to increased number of hits. Data science becomes the vital tool in defining business strategies.

Google is a pioneer in data science. Google's PageRank algorithm has been among the first to use data outside of the page itself. Tracking links has made Google searches much more useful and the PageRank is a key ingredient to Google's success. Google search can detect spelling errors in a search and suggest correction to the misspelled search. Google has made huge stride by using voice data, that they have collected and integrated voice search into the search engine, and provides speech recognitions. (Loukides, 2010)

Facebook uses patterns of the friendship relation to suggest other people you might know; LinkedIn finds jobs or groups that a user might like to know about; biotech companies can analyze gene sequences in billions of combinations to design and test new drugs; Amazon saves your search, correlates with what other users search for, and uses it to provide appropriate recommendations. All these companies track the consumer's data trail, analyze it, mine it and create "data product" suggestions and recommendations to take advantage of big data. It is very common to be able to collect vast amounts of data in today's information exploration era, but how to use data effectively, not just data owned by the private companies, but all data that is available and relevant. The core value of data science is to take the data collected from users, and provide added value. Data is only useful when something can be done with it.

Data Analytical Architecture

Let's first review the typical data analytical architecture for structured data.

Figure 4 shows a typical data warehouse operation. Data from various sources go through the significant pre-processing and checkpoints, then enters into secured controlled data warehouse environment, for data exploration and analytics.

- **Data Extraction and Loading:** Data from the transaction or other operational databases use integration techniques to transfer data into a data warehouse. Data needs to be well understood, structured, and normalized with appropriate data type definitions. The ETL process extracts data from all data sources, brings it into the data warehouse, then transforms the data into the database structures and internal formats, of the staging area of data warehouse.

- **Data Staging:** Data is cleansed in the staging area. Duplications are removed to ensure data integrity and data quality. Another process then loads the cleansed data into the data warehouse database.

- **Data Aggregation:** Data is pre-calculated with totals, averages, medians, grouping and etc., for statistical analysis. Data aggregation is a key part of the data warehouse, which provides a cost effective means of query performance improvement.

- **Data Reporting:** Analysts get data provisioned for the downstream analytics, which includes: dashboards, reporting, BI applications, summary and statistical query, and visualization tools for high density data. Data warehouse provide complete views of customers for successful sales and services. For example, a BI dashboard or report provides the business manager with the sales and inventory information.

Growing volumes of unstructured data lead to new challenges for data analytics. New capacities to access and analyze all available data, that enable faster insight through self-service and collaboration, are in demand. It is challenging for traditional data warehouse and business intelligent technology to meet the requirement of volume, velocity and variety. Advanced analytical techniques, especially distributed parallel processing

Figure 4. Typical data analytical architecture
(source: EMC Big Data Overview)

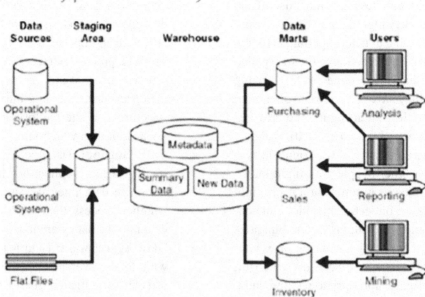

technologies, have been developed to provide real time and scaled processing capability for big data (See Figure 5).

The graph above describes the capacity map that bridges the traditional BI architecture and the big data architecture. Various data, that include master data, reference data, transaction data, machine generated data, social media data and images, video/audio data are captured, then stored and processed in traditional DBMS, simple files or NoSQL and HDFS distributed file systems. The integration layer handles the ever-growing volumes of structured and unstructured data, and bridges the gap between the traditional and big data processing framework. After the data management and processing phase, output are inserted into data warehouse or data mart for further analysis. The BI layer is also the decision making layer, it is equipped with BI applications, advanced analytics, statistical analysis and visualization analysis for reporting, dashboard or interactive discovery.

The big data techniques complement the business intelligence tools to unlock the value from business information, help businesses anticipate consumer behavior, form advertising and marketing strategies, increase sales, improve market pricing, optimize business process with efficiency, help businesses grow with profitability and derive more business values. It also helps businesses to reduce risk, customer churn rates, avoid fraud and predict new business opportunities.

Big Data Analytics

Big data analytics are the process of analyzing various types of huge data volume to uncover hidden patterns, unknown correlations and other useful information, to provide better business prediction and decision making. Big data can unlock hidden values by analyzing the vast volume of information, allow narrower segmentation of customers and much more precisely customized products and services, develop innovative next

Figure 5. Big data architecture (Oracle, 2012)

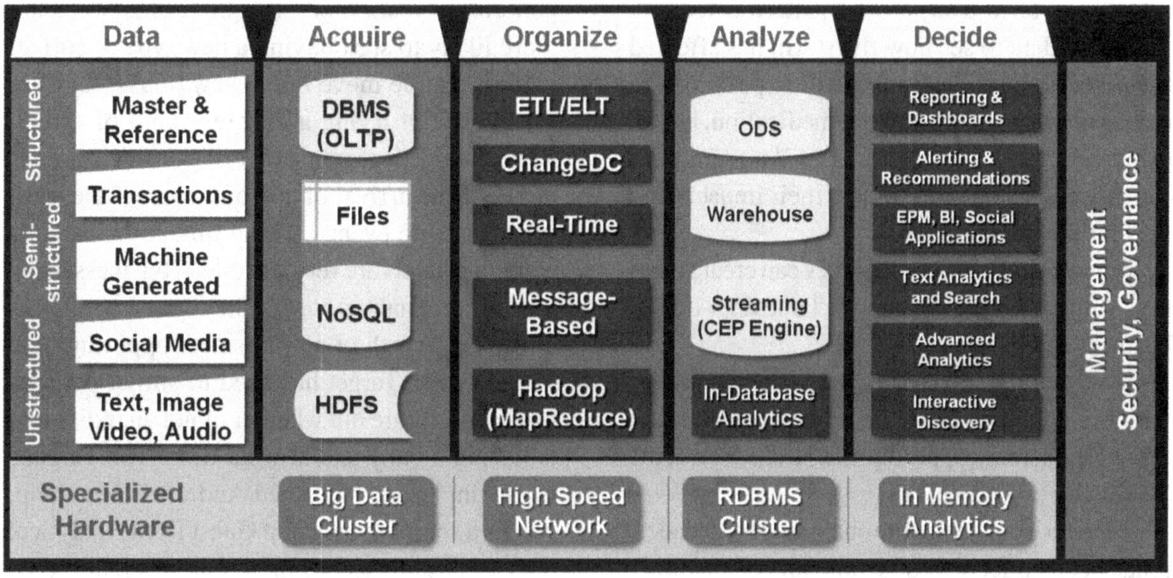

generation products, minimize risks and improve decision making. In a word, big data analytics is a solution for getting the most advantages out of big data. The big data analytic tools are developed for faster and more scalable processes, in order to extract value from the vast amounts of unstructured data produced daily. Predictive analytics and data mining are the two main categories in the big data analytics.

Big data analytics can be used in many area including: the analysis of customer segmentation and behaviors, optimized marketing campaigns, identification of data driven products, defining marketing strategies and risk management, the analysis of social networks and relationships, detection and prevention of fraud, attrition prediction. Big data analytic tools have the ability to converge data from multiple data sources, with both structure and unstructured data types; databases are scaled-out and distributed, with fast and scalable processing capabilities.

Big data analytics have quickly spread from retail and finance to every business field. It provides a way to understand the market, analyze consumer interests and spending habits, mine

product profitability and predict future sales and investments. Data driven analysis can help to make better decisions in just about anything.

A Forbes article, "Is Big Data Right for Your Business? President Obama Thinks So!" (Sabhlok, 2012) describes that president Obama's re-election victory has been propelled by a talented team of data scientists. Huge amounts of data have been mined and analyzed to raise over one billion dollars in campaign funds, an amount far exceeding any other election in history. Sophisticated analysis have been used to perfect fundraising e-mail campaigns and messaging that would yield the best results. Polling data has been gathered in real time, to understand where the campaign was losing ground, and to allocate resources surgically. Television ads have been data driven as well, enabling the campaign to specifically target persuadable voters and run ads during programming that appealed to a particular demographic profile. History is to look at the 2012 election as the "Big Data" election. (Sabhlok, 2012)

Even for the recovery efforts of the recent Hurricane Sandy on the East Coast, big data analytics play important roles. Direct relief, an emergency response organization, uses big data analytics tools to perform analysis and pattern detection. They pull data to see how the storm has affected the districts, and determine which parts of the region might need equipment, medication, health resources, food and shelter. Big data analytics can also forecast events, assess their impacts and prevent further damages.

Businesses can succeed if they can create business value from big data, in the large data-driven business revolution.

How can the advanced analytical techniques with big data produce more effective analysis to fuse new business opportunities? Let's look at the Target story. (Hill, 2012)

Target is a big retail store chain, and for decades, it has been collecting large amounts of customer data. Target's IT system gives each customer profile an ID number, and tons information that are relevant: such as credit card number, when does the customer use coupons, fill out the questionnaire survey, mail returns, call customer service, place order on the Target website and etc. With this ID, the customer's demographic information such as age, marital status, have children or not, home address, salary, distance from home to Target stores and etc., are also recorded. In addition, Target purchases other information from data collectors, such as the customer's race, employment history, credit score, credit history, purchase record, reading habits and so on. When worked by a data scientist, the wonders hidden within these data are to be readily uncovered.

By a study of the customer's everyday purchases, like soap, toothpaste, trash bags and toilet paper, it is found that the customers pay almost no attention on product promotions or coupons. Their purchasing habits are hard to change, regardless of any marketing campaigns. However, when they are going through a major life event, like getting a new job or moving to a new place, their shopping habits become more flexible. It is best during this time, for the retail merchants to predict and explore potential business opportunities. A precisely timed advertisement can change someone's shopping pattern for years. For example: newly-weds are more likely to start buying a new type of coffee; when a couple move into a new house, they are likely to start trying a different kind of cereal; when divorced, people start trying different brands of beer. The arrival of a baby is one of the most important life events. At the time, new parent's shopping habits are very flexible. If businesses can identify pregnant shoppers, they can earn millions of dollars' worth of new business opportunities.

Likewise, Target has tried to attract parents-to-be, and figure out whether or not an individual is having a baby and at what time. The Target's marketing group has asked Andrew Pole to help, who is a senior manager at Guest Data Analytical Service Team. According to Target's request, he is to set up a model to identify pregnant women, before they are in their second trimesters. Target does not want to wait until the baby is born to find out about the pregnancy, because as soon as the birth record comes out, the newborn mother is going to be flooded with product promotions. If Target can identify the women that are pregnant in advance, the marketing department can send them tailored advertising earlier on, and lock valuable sales opportunities, ahead of competition.

However, pregnancy is very private and personal information, how can Target determine which customer is pregnant? Andrew Pole starts with data modeling, based on the Target customer data on baby shower registrations. He discovers a lot of useful information with the data model. For instance, the model suggests that many pregnant women start buying large packages of unscented hand cream, and large amounts of Centrum supplemental such as Calcium, Magnesium and Zinc etc., in the first twenty weeks of pregnancy. Andrew Pole then selects twenty five typical commodity consumer data, and builds a pregnancy prediction index. With this index, Target can forecast customer pregnancy within a small error range, and then send out coupons timed to very specific stages of the customer's pregnancy.

According to Andrew Pole's big data model, Target has developed a completely new marketing campaign, and results in explosive growth in the sales of pregnancy supplies. The big data analysis technique has also expanded from targeting pregnant women, to all other customer groups by ages, income, gender and education level etc. Target's revenue has grown from $44 billion in 2002 to $67 billion in 2010. They have continued to create and focus on items and categories that appeal to specific customer segments.

With the pregnancy prediction index, Target has figured out a teenage girl's pregnancy before even her father having the slightest knowledge. One day, an angry father comes into a Target store at Minneapolis, to complain about his high school daughter receiving coupons for baby clothes, cribs and maternity items from Target. In a fury, he wants to know why the company is sending his teenage daughter such promotions. The store manager apologizes after verifying that the student is indeed receiving baby related offers. A few days later, however, the father calls in to make an apology to Target. On the phone, the father is somewhat abashed: "I had a talk with my daughter," he says, "It turns out there's been some activities in my house I haven't been completely aware of. She's due in August. I owe you an apology."

It can be really shocking for some, when businesses find out about their private and personal information, such pregnancies in advance. Big data analytics make it possible, through the collection of a vast volume of information, sorted and analyzed for patterns and trends. When the personal nature of pregnancy hit the mark, Target is able to identify and predict the trend, and therefore can benefit from highly tailored marketing campaigns.

Big data is the driving force behind a commercial revolution. The massive consumer data has already gone beyond the scope of the traditional function of data storage and database management, and from which, one can dig up tremendous commercial value. Businesses need to face the big data challenge: they must decide if they want to rise up in this revolution, or get buried and perish in it.

THE BIG DATA ECOSYSTEM

Big data is becoming mainstream. With the explosive growth on the types of data sources: applications, digital media, mobiles, sensors, emails, blogs and videos, data can be complex and have varied formats. Massive data storage, scalable infrastructure, analytical applications, robust visualization tools and increasing bandwidth availability are all needed for the distributed and parallel processing of big Data. Enterprises have realized that the data they collect is very valuable, and they need a marketplace for tools, skills and services to take advantage of big data. A new big data ecosystem is being created. It comprises of technology vendors, resellers and service providers, to enable the development and adoption of business applications for big data technology.

Companies use technologies such as Hadoop to conduct natural language processing, and analysis on unstructured data from all different data sources.

Some pioneers in the industry have already been using big data tools in their businesses (Rainmakers, 2012):

- Facebook uses Hadoop to store copies of internal logs and dimensional data sources, and as a source for reporting/analytics and machine learning. There are two clusters, a 1100-machine cluster with 8800 cores and about 12 PB in raw storage, and a 300-machine cluster with 2400 cores and about 3 PB in raw storage;

- Yahoo deploys more than 100,000 CPUs in > 40,000 computers running Hadoop. The biggest cluster has 4500 nodes (2*4cpu boxes with 4*1TB disk & 16GB RAM). This is used to support research for Ad Systems and Web Search, and do scaling tests to support the development of Hadoop on larger clusters;
- EBay uses a 532 node cluster (8*532 cores, 5.3PB), Java MapReduce, Pig, Hive and HBase;
- Twitter uses Hadoop to store and process tweets, log files and other data generated across Twitter. They use both Java and Scala to access MapReduce APIs, as well as Pig, Avro, Hive and Cassandra;
- LinkedIn uses daily batch processing with Hadoop. For example, they pre-calculate data for the "People you may know" product by scoring 120 billion relationships per day, in a MapReduce pipeline of 82 Hadoop jobs that require 16TB of intermediate data. LinkedIn also builds an index structure in the Hadoop pipeline, which creates a multi-terabyte lookup structure that uses perfect hashing. This process trades off cluster computing resources for faster server responses, which takes LinkedIn about 90 minutes to build a 900GB data store on a 45 node development cluster. (Bodkin, 2010)

The Data Ecosystem Overview

With huge volumes of data, how are you going to treat your data? With the help of some data analytic tools, some companies see Big Data as trunks of petabytes, which can generate meaningful business insights. But the Big data ecosystem is more than just that, it is comprised of a lot more complex layers. To dig out more value, the huge amount of raw data needs to be processed and refined, by trained and skilled IT professionals. Raw data can come from videos, images, texts, websites, PDF files, and also emails or cameras. Before generating all these data, some most important questions need to be answered: what do you want to do with these data? What value are you going to retrieve from these data? Enterprises demand tools, skills and services to take advantage of big data.

The foundation of the big data ecosystem is data, which includes ERP data and transactional data (See Figure 6).

ERP stands for Enterprise resource planning. According to Wikipedia, "Enterprise resource planning (ERP) systems integrate internal and external management information across an entire organization. ERP systems automate this activity with an integrated software application. Their purpose is to facilitate the flow of information between all business functions, inside the boundaries of the organization and manage the connections to outside stakeholders." An ERP system is a shared database, which supports multiple functions, used by different business units. Typical ERP system examples include: Oracle and SAP, who are sharing 50% of the market share. ERP data are mostly operations management and planning data, which cover the areas of Finance, Accounting, HR, CRM, inventory management or supply chain, etc.

Transactional data is the data for point-of-sale, and some other data sources. Data comes from OLTP (online transaction processing), which is characterized by a large number of on-line transactions, fast query processing, and effectiveness measured by number of transactions per second. In last decades, transaction data has gone big, applications, having once held megabytes of data, now have expanded to petabytes and zetabytes. The increasing volumes of transaction data is degrading enterprise application performance, and demanding scalable storage hardware and network resources.

Data from ERP or OLTP are to be transferred through ETL (extraction, transformation and Loading) into departmental warehouses or local

Figure 6. Typical business intelligence work flow (EMC Big Data Overview)

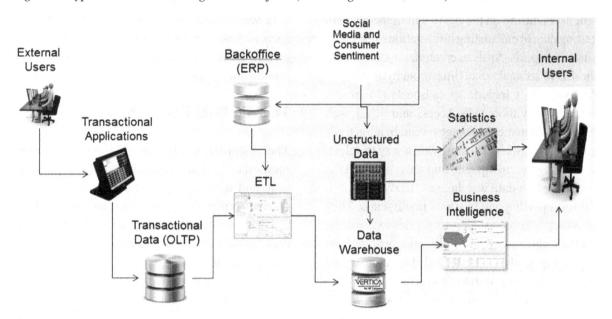

data marts, before finally loading into enterprise data warehouse. In order for the source data to be loaded correctly, data needs to be well understood, structured and normalized with appropriate data types. Data needs to go through staging area, become pre-processed and massaged before the loading process starts. Some factors need to take into consideration: what is the data source quality and the data integrity? How long does it take the database to handle the ETL batch-processing? What is the right tool for the ETL? Is it Microsoft SQL Server Integration services, Informatica, or any third party software?

Departmental data warehouses and local data marts have less security and structure constraints, and give business users more flexibility for departmental business analysis. The next step of data workflow is the Enterprise Data Warehouse (EDW), which is the central storage container for the company's most critical data. Online analytical processing (OLAP) technologies are used in EDW, where data are consolidated into multi-dimensional views of various kinds of business,

and OLAP enabled users to analyze multidimensional data from multiple perspectives.

OLAP data is typically stored in a star schema or snowflake schema. Dimension tables and Fact tables are the main components in the OLAP data. Dimension tables describe the hierarchical business entities of an enterprise, such as time, region, departments, customer and product, and can be looked up as reference tables. Fact tables describe the transaction details, and usually store the data sets. OLAP cube provides a means to understand the business performance. A cube aggregates the facts at each level of each dimension, and contains all the data in an aggregated form. OLAP calculation engines turn massive volumes of raw data into actionable business information, summarized, derived and projected information from the source data in the data warehouse. The analytic component needs to support sophisticated and autonomous end-user queries, quick calculations of key business metrics, planning and forecasting functions of large data volumes, which include historical data. Data warehouse's core activities are mostly read, so the analytic solution must support a large number of concurrent users hitting on the EDW simultaneously, in getting data or calculating information to generate business reports. Analysts create data extracts from the EDW to analyze offline in analytical tools. Analysis tools include spreadsheets (Microsoft Excel), query tools (MS Access and SQL), web browsers, statistical packages, visualization tools and report writers. They provide a way to select, view, analyze, manipulate and navigate the data.

Enterprise data warehouses (EDW) are critical for reporting and business intelligence. They provide performance reporting, sales forecasting, product inventory, customer relationships and marketing analysis. Historical data is analyzed by transforming it into projected data. With unstructured data coming, social media, blobs, clickstream or call center data flow into the EDW, massive volumes of information can quickly grow

beyond the performance capacity of traditional data warehouse. Businesses encounter challenges such as how can they adopt new analytics and architectures to manage big data, and turn such into business value?

The Big Data Ecosystem

The typical data architecture is designed for storing mission critical data, support enterprise applications and enabling business intelligent reporting. Big data is generating enormous amounts of data, requiring advanced analytics technology. The big data ecosystem (Figure 7) becomes a new approach for these analytics.

Big data ecosystem consists of data devices, data collectors, data aggregators and data users. Data devices collect data from multiple locations.

Figure 7. Big data ecosystem (EMC Big Data Overview)

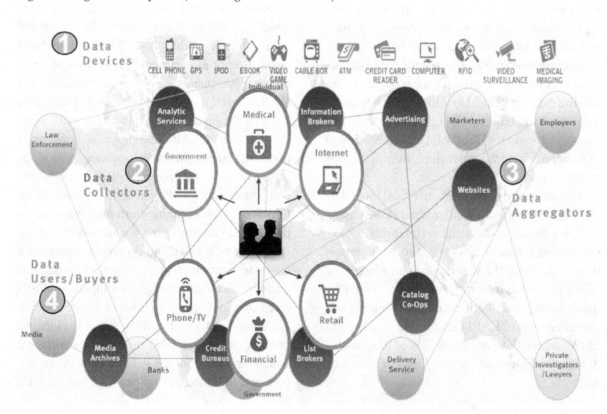

For each gigabyte of new data, a petabyte of data is created about that data.

For example, someone plays video games through TV or PC at home. Data is captured about the levels and skills attained by the player. Additional data are logged, such as the dates and times, when the player plays certain games, the skill level of the players, and the new levels of games are unlocked based on player's proficiency. The users can also purchase new games or additional features, to enhance the games which are offered via recommendation engines. All these information are stored in the local consoles, and also are shared back with the manufacturers, who analyze the gaming habits and opportunities for up-sell and cross-sell, and identify the user's profile.

Smart phones are another rich source of data. A smart phone stores and transmits basic phone usage and text message, as well as data about users' internet usages, SMS usage and real-time location. Many grocery stores issue store loyalty cards to the customers. Customers scan the card when shopping to get promotion price or collect point for events. The loyalty cards not only store the amount the customer spends, but also the store locations this customer frequently visits, types of products the customer tends to buy. Through the data analysis tool, it shows the customer shopping habits, and the likelihood of being targeted for certain types of retail promotions.

Data collectors include organizations that collect data from the device and users. Data are being captured through web surfing logs, HTML text of web browsing history, web registration, questionnaires, interview etc., by various companies. This can range from the phone company tracking internet usage, the cable TV provider tracking the shows being watched, the prices one is willing to pay for premium TV content, retail stores tracking the path a customer takes for daily grocery shopping, the IRS analyzing the bank reported information to track tax returns, to the insurance company capturing a customer's health

records and diet habits to decide on a health and life insurance premium.

Facebook is the biggest social network that collects the people's personal information. Users fill out profiles with their name, age, gender, email address, or even more detail information such as address, phone number and relationship status. Their new profile pages even invite people to add historical information, such as places they have lived and worked. What can Facebook do with these data? Besides data mining for their own business, Facebook sells the data to marketers who are looking for consumer information and trends. Marketers can then use the data to customized ad-campaigns, which can target on consumer's interests. User data collected through phone companies can be used to analyze traffic patterns, by scanning the density of smart phone in certain locations, also can track the speed of cars of the relative traffic congestion on the busy roads. Collecting the customer's driving behavior through a smartphone, can help one to obtain a better insurance premium, for being a safe driver. There are hundreds of companies specializing in collecting marketing data, and creating consumer profiles across the country.

Data aggregators are organizations that analyze the data collected from various sources. Acxiom and ChoicePoint are the two big companies that compile information from collected data on individuals, and selling that information to others. They originate data from public records, compile data from device usage patterns or from online activities, transform data into information, and package into aggregated reports, and then sell the data to brokers, who then want to market consumer lists as targets for specific ad campaigns, or cross-selling opportunities. They also compile personal data packages, which contain the customer's professional licenses, educational background, criminal history and length of residence, and sell these to employers for employee background checks, or to insurers to be used for insurance coverage and pricing, and so on.

Data users or data buyers are the direct beneficiaries of the information collected and aggregated, in the data value chain. Big companies purchase data, which includes customer's name, phone number, address, buying habits, interested merchants etc. According to McKinsey Global Institute, data is now a $300 billion a year industry, and employs 3 million people in the United States alone. (Morris & Lavandera, 2012) For instance, retail banks may want to know which customer has the highest likelihood applying for a new credit card, or a home equity loan. They are to purchase data from a data aggregator showing demographics of people living in specific locations, and those who seems to have been searching the web for relative information. Obtaining from these various sources, the retail bank can have more specific targeted marketing campaigns, which would not have been possible 10 years ago, due to the lack of information. Big companies trying to get information about their potential customers, and what they might be interested in buying, so that they can deliver more relevant offers, products and services to them. Detailed marketing information is definitely critical in the success of businesses.

Data Scientist in the Big Data Ecosystem

In the data driven era, the efficient operation of organizations relies on the effective use of big data. Enterprises are putting in a lot of money and efforts to make sure they have the infrastructure for managing big data, and the analytical tools to benefit from big data tools. But finding the people who have big data skills and understand data science is far more important in solving the big data puzzle.

In a May 2011 McKinsey report, some numbers are being put on the demand: "Now, the US government has earmarked $200 million to support research in big data. But the advancement and use of big data technology can be inhibited by a lack of deep analytical talent. By 2018, the United States alone can face a shortage of 140,000 to 190,000 people with deep analytical skills, as well as 1.5 million managers and analysts with sufficient knowledge, to use the analysis of big data to make effective decisions." (Manyika, 2011)

Data scientists are in big demand with the emergence of big data. A data scientist is a professional, who has deep technical background, can expertly manipulate data, and have massive scales of complex analytical skills. These professionals can be people with advanced training in quantitative area, such as statistics, mathematics, economist and data scientists. They need to have the combination of skills to handle raw data and unstructured data, strong technical knowledge, strong analytical skills and background. In a word, the ability to straddle both the business and technical sides of an organization is a must for a data scientist. But what makes a data scientist unique is the ability to use technical skillsets to solve actual real world problems.

A data scientist should have a combination of complex skills, advanced quantitative knowledge, business skills, technical experience and problem solving capacity. He should be analytical, curious and skeptical, can tell a story with the data in overcoming business challenges. A data scientist is the combination of following qualities:

- A variety of academic backgrounds providing a good foundation for a data scientist. Graduate students or PHD students from computer science, statistics, applied mathematics, physics or economist who have advanced proficiency with mathematics;
- Technical expertise is required. Software engineers, or software programmers/developers who have computer programming skills;
- Mathematicians or statisticians who have advanced quantitative skills;
- He needs to be passionate about data, and always seeking creative ways to solving

data problems, and mining information from data. Instead of asking "what happened", he is more interested in "what is going to happen?" and "what can we do about it?"

- He needs to have skeptical view of his work, and always exam his work critically. He needs to be willing to question old assumptions, reanalyze business problems and come up with the solutions;

- He needs to have an understanding and experience of business, knowing the value of analytics and how the analytics data fits in the organization.

A Data scientist needs to have business knowledge, that ensures the correct positioning of projects, by which actionable insights can be derived from data, and he knows how to make an impact on the business.

A Data scientist needs to be passionate in manipulating and analyzing any data, even the incomplete, disorganized, and huge volumes of unstructured data. He needs to have experience in a variety of domains, and in working with different issues, so that he can brainstorm a particular machine learning algorithm or a new statistical model.

A data scientist needs to know the programming and scripting languages, such as R, Python, Hadoop, HBase, Cassandra or SAS. He needs to be able to discuss the differences between graph databases, document stores and key value stores, where BigTable implementations are become more and more important.

Besides the essential skillsets to do a good job, a data scientist needs to be creative and innovative. Data scientists must be able to innovate the collection of data, analyze it and think of it in fantastic ways, so that the data can be put to the best advantageous use. A data scientist can create

the tools used to interpret and translate the streams of data into innovative new products.

At Facebook for instance, social analytics are becoming more important. When a data scientist looks at the Facebook's social behavior data, such as click-through rates, social media comment, family photos, conversations, life achievements, he needs to identify the differences in individual attributes and interpersonal interactions, mine the insights and create innovative and interactive features, to encourage users to get interested and stay with Facebook. One example is in helping Facebook provide products such as identifying users that one may know but haven't friended. Through the data, he needs to reveal patterns of information and clusters of affinity, patterns in communication balance and network change overtime, and help Facebook best utilize network resources. Data scientists must be able to demonstrate actionable innovation and creativity.

Facebook's Data Science Team, led by Cameron Marlow, has 12 researchers. They use math, statistics, computer programming skills and social science to mine the data for insights, which helps Facebook's business. One of their innovations is the "Like" button, which Facebook offers on both the Facebook site and general user's website. With the like button on Facebook site, one can click after looking at a friend's photo or comments or any content on Facebook. The Like button, out of the Facebook site, plays a very important role. Beyond Facebook's website, when a user visits a website with Like button on it, they can click on it to let their friends know that they like the site. After clicking on the button, they have a pop-up asking for login to Facebook. Once they have logged in, they can see the button on the right shows which of their friends like that page, along with their friend's profile picture. After clicking the like button, a story can be posted automatically to their Facebook page telling their friends that they like the site. For instance, if someone is looking at a webpage about their favorite songs, and they click the like button, the song can then be added to the like button, and that user can post the website they visited online, to also track activities on the internet, and invite people to hit the Like button. Within the first five months after this feature's launch, Facebook catalogued more than five billion instances of people listening to songs online.

Google has their data sciences team as well. By tracking consumer clicks or capturing information from Gmail, Google plus, they have assembled huge volumes of data, and analyzed web traffic to predict patterns being increasingly applied to other fields. This is a product driven role; the ideal candidate needs to be an expert with a full list of technical skills, and have strong communication skills. To qualify, you need:

- BA/BS Degrees in Statistics or Engineering, Applied mathematics, etc.;
- Experience working with large data sets with statistical software such as R, s-Plus and Matlab;
- Familiarity with large SQL databases;
- Excellent communicator who can collaborate with a multi-disciplinary team of engineers and analysts;
- Ability to draw conclusions from data, by using appropriate techniques and recommend actions;
- It is preferred that one is proficient at processing data set, with machine learning language such as Python and Java script.

The right candidate for this job is able to find new ways to make money from the online search data. The goal for the data scientist is to find patterns among the data, which can then be used by the product team. It is the data scientists who have built the Google self-driving car, designed Google glasses, or developed an algorithm to automatically translate Google's search site from English to Japanese.

Data science is the defining force that shapes the evolution of every industry. Organizations are using data science to shift the balance of power, and exploring how to optimize people and strategies to realize the full potential of data science. The data scientist job is considered as the "sexiest job of the 21st century."

REFERENCES

AI3. (2005). *Semi-structured data: Happy 10th birthday*. Retrieved from http://www.mkbergman.com/153/semi-structured-data-happy-10th-birthday/

Accelerated Analytics. (2010). *Making sense of retail link data*. Retrieved from http://www.acceleratedanalytics.com/blog/2010/10/1/making-sense-of-retail-link-data.html

Accenture. (2011). *How big data can fuel bigger growth*. Retrieved from http://www.accenture.com/us-en/outlook/Pages/outlook-journal-2011-how-big-data-fuels-bigger-growth.aspx

Autonomy. (n.d.). Retrieved from http://www.autonomy.com/content/Technology/what-is-big-data/index.en.html

Baunach, S. (2012). Three vs of big data: Volume, velocity, variety. *Data Center Knowledge*. Retrieved from http://www.datacenterknowledge.com/archives/2012/03/08/three-vs-of-big-data-volume-velocity-variety/

Biddick, M. (2012). Feds face 'big data' storage challenge. *Informationweek*. Retrieved from http://www.informationweek.com/government/information-management/feds-face-big-data-storage-challenge/240000958

Big Data. (2012). *Wikipedia*. Retrieved from http://en.wikipedia.org/wiki/Big_data

Bodkin, R. (2010). *LinkedIn's data infrastructure*. Retrieved from http://www.infoq.com/news/2010/08/linkedin-data-infrastructure

Brenner, M. (2012). What is big data? *Business Innovation from SAP*. Retrieved from http://blogs.sap.com/innovation/big-data/big-data-what-is-it-05326

BrightPlanet. (2012). *Structure data vs. unstructured data*. Retrieved from http://www.brightplanet.com/2012/06/structured-vs-unstructured-data/

CEBR. (2012). *Data equity: Unlocking the value of big data*. Retrieved from http://www.sas.com/offices/europe/uk/downloads/data-equity-cebr.pdf

Chang, F., Dean, J., Ghemawat, S., Hsieh, W. C., Wallach, D. A., & Murrows, M. ... Gruber, R. E. (2006). Bigtable: A distributed storage system for structure data. *OSDI*. Retrieved from http://static.googleusercontent.com/external_content/untrusted_dlcp/research.google.com/en/us/archive/bigtable-osdi06.pdf

Clegg, D. (2012). *Big data: The data variety discussion*. IBM The Big Data Hub. Retrieved from http://www.ibmbigdatahub.com/blog/big-data-data-variety-discussion

Condliffe, J. (2012). *How Facebook uses you as part of a giant sociological experiment*. Retrieved from http://gizmodo.com/5918319/how-facebook-uses-you-as-part-of-a-giant-sociological-experiment

Cosentino, T. (2012). *Gaining time to value from big data*. Retrieved from http://tonycosentino.ventanaresearch.com/2012/08/30/gaining-time-to-value-from-big-data/

Data Structure. (n.d.). *Wikipedia*. Retrieved from http://en.wikipedia.org/wiki/Data_structure

Davenport, T., & Patil, D. J. (2012). Data scientist: The sexiest job of the 21st century. *Harvard Business Review*. Retrieved from http://hbr.org/2012/10/data-scientist-the-sexiest-job-of-the-21st-century/ar/1

Davis, A. (2012). The government and big data: Use, problems and potential. *Computerworld*. Retrieved from http://blogs.computerworld.com/19919/the_government_and_big_data_use_problems_and_potential

Decision Stats. (2011). *Statistics on social media*. Retrieved from http://decisionstats.com/2011/11/17/statistics-on-social-media/

Dijcks, J.-Pi. (2012). *How to implement a big data system*. Oracle Technology Network. Retrieved from http://www.oracle.com/technetwork/articles/servers-storage-admin/implementing-bigdata-1502704.html

Duhigg, C. (2012). How companies learn your secret. *The New York Times*. Retrieved from http://www.nytimes.com/2012/02/19/magazine/shopping-habits.html?pagewanted=all

Evans, B. (2012). Big data set to explode as 40 billion new devices connect to Internet. *Forbes*. Retrieved from http://www.forbes.com/sites/oracle/2012/11/06/big-data-set-to-explode-as-40-billion-new-devices-connect-to-internet/

Exams, E. M. C. (n.d.). *Which data asset is an example of quasi-structured data?* Retrieved from http://www.aiotestking.com/emc/2013/01/04/which-data-asset-is-an-example-of-quasi-structured-data/

Farr, C. (2012). *These are the skills you need to be a data scientist at Facebook*. Retrieved from http://venturebeat.com/2012/08/27/these-are-the-skills-you-need-to-be-a-data-scientist-at-facebook/#G8PrucQJM7C8ORGg.99

Feinleib, D. (2012). The big data science behind today's most popular content. *Forbes*. Retrieved from http://www.forbes.com/sites/davefeinleib/2012/09/07/the-big-data-science-behind-todays-most-popular-content/

Fineberg, S. (2012). *Big data storage options for Hadoop*. HP Storage. Retrieved from http://snia.org/sites/default/files2/ABDS2012/Tutorials/SamFineberg_Big_Data_Storage_Options_Hadoop-v1-7.pdf

Flaster, M., Hillyer, B., & Ho, T. K. (n.d.). *Exploratory analysis system for semi-structured engineering logs*. Retrieved from http://ect.bell-labs.com/who/tkh/publications/papers/xlog.pdf

Forsyth, C. (2012). *For big data analytics there's no such thing as too big*. Retrieved from http://www.cisco.com/en/US/solutions/ns340/ns517/ns224/big_data_wp.pdf

Genovese, Y. (n.d.). *Getting value from big data*. Retrieved from http://www.gartner.com/technology/research/pattern-based-strategy/

Gens, F. (2013). *IDC PrEd.s 2013: Competing on the 3rd platform*. Retrieved from http://www.idc.com/research/Predictions13/downloadable/238044.pdf

Gentile, B. (2012). *Creating big value from big data*. Retrieved from http://slashdot.org/topic/bi/creating-big-value-from-big-data/Chapter 6

Goldman, D. (2010). *Rapleaf is selling your identity*. CNN. Retrieved from http://money.cnn.com/2010/10/21/technology/rapleaf/index.htm

Google. (n.d.). *Data scientist job description*. Retrieved from http://www.google.com/jobs.

Google Developers. (2012). *Providing structured data*. Retrieved from https://developers.google.com/custom-search/docs/structured_data

Google Webmaster Central. (2012). *Introducing the structured data dashboard*. Retrieved from http://googlewebmastercentral.blogspot.com/2012/07/introducing-structured-data-dashboard.html

Gottlieb, I. (1986). *Structured data flow: A quasi-synchronous Interpretation of data driven computations*. New York: City University of New York.

Gray, J., Chaudhuri, S., Bosworth, A., Layman, A., Reichart, D., & Venkatrao, M. (1996). Data cube: A relational aggregation operator generalizing group-by, cross-tab, and sub-totals. *Data Mining and Knowledge Discovery*, *1*, 29–53. doi:10.1023/A:1009726021843.

Graziano, D. (2012). *Google+ now home to 400 million total users*. Retrieved from http://bgr.com/2012/09/17/google-plus-stats-2012-400-million-members/

Hadoop Wiki. (n.d.). Retrieved from http://wiki.apache.org/hadoop/PoweredBy

Halfon, A. (2012). *Handling big data variety*. Retrieved from http://www.finextra.com/community/fullblog.aspx?blogid=6129

Hall, A. (2012). To succeed as an entrepreneur, know your customer. *Forbes*. Retrieved from http://www.forbes.com/sites/alanhall/2012/06/14/to-succeed-as-an-entrepreneur-know-your-customer/

Hammer, J., McHugh, J., & Garcia-Molina, H. (n.d.). *Semistructured data: The TSIMMIS experience*. Retrieved from http://www.cise.ufl.edu/~jhammer/publications/ADBIS1997/adbis97.pdf

Hardy, Q. (2012a). Google ventures' big data bet. *The New York Times*. Retrieved from http://bits.blogs.nytimes.com/2012/04/11/google-ventures-big-data-bet/

Hardy, Q. (2012b). How big data gets real. *The New York Times*. Retrieved from http://bits.blogs. nytimes.com/2012/06/04/how-big-data-gets-real/

Hardy, Q. (2012c). *Rethinking privacy in an era of big data*. Retrieved from http://bits.blogs. nytimes.com/2012/06/04/rethinking-privacy-in-an-era-of-big-data/

Hill, K. (2012). How target figured out a teen girl was pregnant before her father did. *Forbes*. Retrieved from http://www.forbes.com/sites/ kashmirhill/2012/02/16/how-target-figured-out-a-teen-girl-was-pregnant-before-her-father-did/

Horowitz, B. T. (2012). Big data analytics, HIE could aid hurricane sandy recovery efforts. *eWeek*. Retrieved from http://www.eweek.com/ enterprise-apps/big-data-analytics-hie-could-aid-hurricane-sandy-recovery-efforts/

Horton, C. (2012). *My smartphone told me to buy it: Big data hits mobile*. B2C. Retrieved from http://www.business2community.com/online-marketing/my-smartphone-told-me-to-buy-it-big-data-hits-mobile-0280565

IBM. (n.d.). *Vivisimo is now part of IBM*. Retrieved from http://vivisimo.com/solutions/bigdata.html

Inmon, W. H. (2005). *Building the data warehouse*. New Delhi: Wiley India Pvt.

Internet Marketing Solution (IMS). (n.d.). *How to use the Facebook like button*. Retrieved from http://www.adsforfacebook.com/the-facebook-like-button.php

Johnson, M. E. (2012). Hurricane Sandy: Big data predicted big power outages. *Information Week*. Retrieved from http://www.informationweek.com/ big-data/commentary/big-data-analytics/bog-data-helped-to-track-hurricane-sandy/240115312

Kelly, J. (2012). *Big data: Hadoop, business analytics and beyond*. Retrieved from http:// wikibon.org/wiki/v/Big_Data:_Hadoop,_Business_Analytics_and_Beyond

Keylock, M. (2012). *The unstructured data challenge by AdExchanger*. Retrieved from http:// www.adexchanger.com/data-driven-thinking/ the-unstructured-data-challenge/

Kimball, R., Ross, M., Thornthwaite, W., Mundy, J., & Becker, B. (2008). *The data warehouse lifecycle toolkit*. Hoboken, NJ: Wiley Publishers.

Lewis, N. (2012). Pittsburgh healthcare systems invests $100M in big data. *Information Week*. Retrieved from http://www.informationweek. com/healthcare/clinical-systems/pittsburgh-healthcare-system-invests-100/240008989

Lewis, N. (2012). Supercomputer speeds up cancer analysis. *Information Week*. Retrieved from http://www.informationweek.com/healthcare/ clinical-systems/supercomputer-speeds-up-cancer-analysis/240008817

Lohr, S. (2012). The age of big data: Big data's impact in the world. *The New York Times*. Retrieved from http://www.nytimes.com/2012/02/12/ sunday-review/big-datas-impact-in-the-world. html?pagewanted=all

Lopez, M. (2012). The 4 phases of big data. *Forbes*. Retrieved from http://www.forbes.com/ sites/maribellopez/2012/10/31/the-four-phases-of-big-data/

Loukides, M. (2010). *What is data science?* Retrieved from http://radar.oreilly.com/2010/06/ what-is-data-science.html

Manyika, J., Chui, M., Brown, B., Bughin, J., Dobbs, R., Roxburgh, C., & Byers, A. H. (2011). *Big data: The next frontier for innovation, competition, and productivity*. McKinsey & Company. Retrieved from http://www.mckinsey.com/insights/ business_technology/big_data_the_next_frontier_for_innovation

Martinek, L. (2012). *Big data analytics*. Retrieved from http://searchbusinessanalytics.techtarget. com/definition/big-data-analytics

McDonnell, S. (2011). Big data challenges and opportunities. *Spotfire Blogging Team*. Retrieved from http://spotfire.tibco.com/blog/?p=6793

McGuire, T., Manyika, J., & Chui, M. (2012). Why big data is the new competitive advantage. *Ivey Business Journal*. Retrieved from http://www.iveybusinessjournal.com/topics/strategy/why-big-data-is-the-new-competitive-advantage

Morris, J., & Lavandera, E. (2012). Why big companies buy, sell your data. *CNN*. Retrieved from http://www.cnn.com/2012/08/23/tech/web/big-data-acxiom

Neal, H. (2011). *Business intelligence 101 – A beginner's guide to BI software*. Retrieved from http://plotting-success.softwareadvice.com/beginners-guide-to-bi-software-1113011/

NetSuite. (n.d.). *What is ERP*. Retrieved from http://www.netsuite.com/portal/resource/articles/erp/what-is-erp.shtml

Nimmons, S. (2012). *CIO agenda: Big data ecosystem*. Retrieved from http://stevenimmons.org/2012/02/cio-agenda-big-data-ecosystems/

Noguchi, Y. (2011). *Following digital breadcrumbs to 'big data' gold*. Retrieved from http://www.npr.org/2011/11/29/142521910/the-digital-breadcrumbs-that-lead-to-big-data

NOKIA. (2012). *Mobile data challenge: Big data for mobile computing research*. Nokia Corp. Retrieved from http://research.nokia.com/files/public/MDC2012_WorkshopFrontmatter.pdf

Nusca, A. (2012). Big data: Brainstorming the possibilities. *ZDNet*. Retrieved from http://www.zdnet.com/big-data-brainstorming-the-possibilities-7000007278/

Open Data Center Alliance. (2012). *Big data consumer guide*. Retrieved from http://www.opendatacenteralliance.org/docs/Big_Data_Consumer_Guide_Rev1.0.pdf

Oracle. (2012). *Oracle information architecture: An architect's guide to big data*. Retrieved from http://www.oracle.com/technetwork/topics/entarch/articles/oea-big-data-guide-1522052.pdf

Oracle. (2013). *Oracle: Big data for the enterprice* (An Oracle White Paper). Retrieved from http://www.oracle.com/us/products/database/big-data-for-enterprise-519135.pdf

Pant, P. (2009). *Business intelligence (BI), how to build successful BI strategy*. Deloitte Consulting LLP. Retrieved from http://www.deloitte.com/assets/Dcom-SouthAfrica/Local%20Assets/Documents/Business%20intelligence%20that%20aligns%20with%20enterprise%20goals.pdf

PCMag.com. (n.d.). *Definition of structured data*. Retrieved from http://www.pcmag.com/encyclopedia_term/0,2542,t=structured+data&i=52162,00.asp

Press, G. (2013). *What's the big data*. Retrieved from http://whatsthebigdata.com

Pring, C. (2012). 216 social media and internet statistics. *The Social Skinny*. Retrieved from http://thesocialskinny.com/216-social-media-and-internet-statistics-september-2012

Protalinski, E. (2012). Facebook has over 845 million users. *ZdNet*. Retrieved from http://www.zdnet.com/blog/facebook/facebook-has-over-845-million-users/8332

Provoost, L. (2010). *The structured vs. unstructured data dilemma*. Retrieved from http://www.dachisgroup.com/2010/01/the-structured-vs-unstructured-data-dilemma/

PwC's Financial Services Institute (FSI). (2011). *Getting to know you: Building a customer-centric business model for retail banks*. Retrieved from http://www.pwc.com/us/en/financial-services/publications/viewpoints/assets/viewpoint-retail-bank-customer-centric-business-model.pdf

Rainmakers. (2012). *Hadoop on massive clusters drive social business.* Retrieved from http://rainmakerfiles.com/2012/07/hadoop

Roe, C. (2012). *So you want to be a data scientist?* Retrieved from http://www.dataversity.net/so-you-want-to-be-a-data-scientist/

Sabhlok, R. (2012). Is big data right for your business? President Obama thinks so. *Forbes.* Retrieved from http://www.forbes.com/sites/rajsabhlok/2012/11/15/is-big-data-right-for-your-business-president-obama-thinks-so/

SAP. (2012). *Big data for retail is flying off the shelves.* Retrieved from http://www.forbes.com/sites/sap/2012/05/11/big-data-for-retail-is-flying-off-the-shelves/

SAS. (2012). *Big data meets big data analytics: Three key technologies for extracting real-time business value from the big data that threatens to overwhelm traditional computing architectures* (White Paper). Retrieved from http://www.sas.com/resources/whitepaper/wp_46345.pdf

Savitz, E. (2012). The big value in big data. *Forbes.* Retrieved from http://www.forbes.com/sites/ciocentral/2012/09/25/the-big-value-in-big-data-seeing-customer-buying-patterns/

Scherer, M. (2012). *Inside the secret world of the data crunchers who helped Obama win.* Retrieved from http://swampland.time.com/2012/11/07/inside-the-secret-world-of-quants-and-data-crunchers-who-helped-obama-win/#ixzz2JbhjDs88

Schumpeter. (2011, May 26). Building with big data. *The Economist.* Retrieved from http://www.economist.com/node/18741392

SearchStorage FAQ. (2007). *What is unstructured data and how it is different from structured data in the enterprise?* Retrieved from http://searchstorage.techtarget.com/feature/What-is-unstructured-data-and-how-is-it-different-from-structured-data-in-the-enterprise

Semi-Structured Data. (n.d.). Retrieved from http://www.dcs.bbk.ac.uk/~ptw/teaching/ssd/notes.html

Shaw, R. (2011). What is business intelligence? *Database Trends and Applications.* Retrieved from http://www.dbta.com/Articles/Editorial/Trends-and-Applications/What-is-Business-Intelligence-73502.aspx

Simonite, T. (2012). *What Facebook knows?* Retrieved from http://www.technologyreview.com/featured-story/428150/what-facebook-knows/

Spakes, G. (2012). Turning big data into value. *SAS Voices.* Retrieved from http://blogs.sas.com/content/sascom/2012/04/12/turning-big-data-volume-variety-and-velocity-into-value/

Statistic Brain. (2012). *Google annual search statistics.* Retrieved from http://www.statisticbrain.com/google-searches/

Structure Data. (n.d.). *Wikipedia.* Retrieved from http://www.webopedia.com/TERM/S/structured_data.html

Subbaraman, N. (2012). *A nosy smartphone app. wants your data.* Retrieved from http://www.technologyreview.com/view/429421/a-nosy-smartphone-app-wants-your-data/

Telecom World, I. T. U. (2011). *The world in 2011: ICT facts and figures.* Retrieved from http://www.itu.int/en/ITU-D/Statistics/Documents/facts/ICTFactsFigures2011.pdf

Terry, K. (2012). Health IT execs urged to promote big data. *Information Week.* Retrieved from http://www.informationweek.com/healthcare/clinical-systems/health-it-execs-urged-to-promote-big-dat/240009034

Twitter. (2011). *One hundred million voices.* Retrieved from https://blog.twitter.com/2011/one-hundred-million-voices

University of Minnesota Extension. (2011). *Market analysis: Consumer survey*. Retrieved from http://fyi.uwex.edu/downtown-market-analysis/understanding-the-market/consumer-survey/

Unstructured Data. (n.d.). *Wikipedia*. Retrieved from http://en.wikipedia.org/wiki/Unstructured_data

Utz, S., & Krammer, N. C. (2009). The privacy paradox on social network sites revisited: The role of individual characteristics and group norms. *Cyberpsychology (Brno)*, *3*(2).

Vergano, D. (2012). *Big data disguises digital doubts*. Retrieved from http://usatoday30.usatoday.com/tech/science/columnist/vergano/story/2012-06-16/big-data/55628002/1

Walker, M. (2012). *Traditional BI vs. data analytics approach*. Retrieved from http://www.datasciencecentral.com/profiles/blogs/traditional-bi-vs-data-analytics-approach

Wallace, J. (2012). *How big data is changing retail marketing analytics*. Retrieved from http://www.revolutionanalytics.com/news-events/free-webinars/2012/how-big-data-is-changing-retail-marketing-analytics/

Wang, R. (2012). *Monday's musings: Beyond the three v's of big data – Viscosity and virality*. Retrieved from http://blog.softwareinsider.org/2012/02/27/mondays-musings-beyond-the-three-vs-of-big-data-viscosity-and-virality/

Whittaker, Z. (2012). Oracle's hurd: World is drowning in data, wars of overload. *ZDNet*. Retrieved from http://www.zdnet.com/oracles-hurd-world-is-drowning-in-data-warns-of-overload-7000006141

Woods, D. (2012). What is a data scientist? *Forbes*. Retrieved from http://www.forbes.com/sites/danwoods/2012/07/23/what-is-a-data-scientist-tom-wheeler-of-clickfox

Wuorio, J. (n.d.). *7 ways to use customer data*. Retrieved from http://www.microsoft.com/business/en-us/resources/management/customer-relations/using-customer-data.aspx?fbid=FSaxUpiCGfC

YouTube.com. (n.d.). *Statistics*. Retrieved from http://www.youtube.com/t/press_statistics

Chapter 9
Big Data Techniques, Tools, and Applications

Yushi Shen
Microsoft Corporation, USA

Ling Wu
EMC² Corporation, USA

Yale Li
Microsoft Corporation, USA

Shaofeng Liu
Microsoft Corporation, USA

Qian Wen
Endronic Corp, USA

ABSTRACT

This chapter covers big data technologies and tools, including the NoSQL database, HDFS, MapReduce, SMAQ stack, and the Hadoop Ecosystem. It also introduces the appliance products that help the customer for their big data analytics.

INTRODUCTION

In the era of big data, data are counted by GB-TB-PB. Data must be distributed among many machines. Building a useful big data database is an extremely complex process. How do you select only data that is appropriate from available data sources? How can you remove duplicated, corrupted or meaningless data, and convert the remainder to useful information for business insights? How do you store the lot, so that the user can handle the volume and variety with limited resources?

New approaches to processing and analyzing big data have some common characteristics. They take advantage of commodity hardware, to enable scaled-out and parallel-processing techniques, use non-relational data storage capacity to process

DOI: 10.4018/978-1-4666-4801-2.ch009

unstructured data, and apply advanced analytics and data visualization technologies, to convey insights to businesses.

BIG DATA TECHNOLOGIES

Hadoop is an open source framework for processing, storing and analyzing huge amounts of unstructured data. The fundamental concept is to break Big Data into multiple smaller data sets, so each data set can be processed and analyzed in parallel. Hadoop is best for large, but relatively simple database filtering, sorting, converting and analysis. (Wikipedia on Apache Hadoop)

The Hadoop ecosystem is made up of a number of complimentary sub-projects. Here is a list of Hadoop components (Apache Software Foundation, 2013):

- Hadoop Distributed Filesystem (HDFS), which creates replicas of data blocks, and distributes data on computer nodes over the cluster (Borthakur, 2013);
- MapReduce - MapReduce divides jobs into two parts. The "Map" function divides a query into multiple jobs, and the "Reduce" function combines the results to form the output (Hadoop – MapReduce Tutorial, 2013);
- HBase is a Hadoop database that provides random, real-time read and write access to HDFS;
- Hive is an analysis tool: it uses a SQL like syntax to rapidly develop queries. Mostly used for offline batch processing, ad-hoc querying and statistical analysis of large data warehouse systems;
- Mahout is a framework for deploying many machine learning algorithms on large data-sets, mostly used in clustering, classification and text mining.
- Pig is the platform that analyzes large data sets. The Pig structure is amenable to sub-

stantial parallelization, so as to effectively handle very large volumes of data sets. Pig uses a language called Pig Latin, and has the characteristics of easy programming, auto optimization and extensibility;

- OOzie is an open source workflow scheduler system to manage Apache Hadoop data processing jobs. Oozie workflow consists of actions and dependencies. Users create Directed Acyclical Graphs (DAG) to model workflow. Oozie manages the dependencies at runtime, and executes the actions when the dependencies identified in the DAG are satisfied. Yahoo!'s workflow engine uses OoZie to manage jobs running on Hadoop (Yahoo!, 2010);
- ZooKeeper is a centralized service, which enables highly reliable distributed coordination. It maintains configuration information, provides distributed synchronization and group services for distributed applications;
- Flume is a distributed system that brings data into HDFS. The Apache Flume website describes Flume as "a distributed, reliable and available service for efficiently collecting, aggregating and moving large amounts of log data. It enables applications to collect data from its origin and send it to the HDFS;"
- HCatalog provides table management and storage management for data created using Hadoop. HCatalog provides a shared schema and data type mechanism, can interoperate across data processing tools such as Pig, Hive and MapReduce.
- BigTop is a project for packaging and testing the Hadoop ecosystem. It puts 100% open source apache Hadoop big data stack together, including Hadoop, Hbase, Hive, Mahout, flume and etc. This full stack of components provide the user a complete data collection and analytics pipeline (Apache Incubator PMC).

NoSQL Database

NoSQL is a general term, meaning that the database is not a RDBMs that supports Structured Query Language (SQL) as primary access language. It is a new type of database management systems, also called the non-relational, or "cloud" database (Wikipedia – NoSQL). NoSQL databases are not built on tables, and usually do not use structured query language for data manipulation. It uses cluster server to manage the exploding data, and the huge transaction volumes. The most important characteristic of NoSQL is the ability to store and retrieve large quantities of data. NoSQL uses the distributed and fault tolerant architecture, with the data held in a redundant manner on the cluster servers. So the system can easily scale out by adding more servers, and failover when one server node crashes.

NoSQL databases that are currently available:

Hbase

HBase is an open source, non-relational, distributed database written in Java, and runs on top of HDFS, providing the ability to store very large quantities of data for Hadoop. It is well suited for sparse big data sets, with billions of rows and millions of columns. Since it is not a relational database, it does not support a structured query language like SQL (Baranau & Gospodnetic).

Since it is a NoSQL database, features for an RDBMS are not available, such as typed columns, triggers, secondary indexes and etc. The Hbase system comprises a set of tables. Each table contains rows and columns. Each table must have an element defined as a Primary key. A column in HBase represents an attribute of an object. In HBase, many attributes can be grouped together into column families. A data row has a sortable key and an arbitrary number of columns. HBase is largely used in the application that has a variable schema, where each row is slightly different.

Hbase is good for processing hundreds of millions or billions of rows. It can provide strongly consistent reads/writes, automatic handling, automatic failover, Hadoop/HDFS integration, and massive parallelized processing via MapReduce.

Cassandra

Cassandra is an open source distributed database management system, designed to handle very large amounts of data, spread out across thousands of commodity servers, while providing a highly available service without single point of failure. It is initially developed by Facebook, and powered their inbox search feature until the late 2000s.

Cassandra is a hybrid between key value and row orientation. Each key maps to multiple values, which are grouped into column families, and column families can be grouped into super column families, which can be considered as tables. A table in Cassandra is a distributed multi-dimensional map indexed by a key. (Melli, 2012)

Casandra's main features include:

- **Decentralization:** It means every node in the cluster plays the same role; data is distributed across the cluster without a master, as every node can service any request;
- **Scalability:** Read and write throughputs can be increased, by adding new machines with no downtime or interruption to application;
- **Fault Rolerant:** Data is automatically replicated to multiple nodes for fault tolerance. Failed nodes can be replaced by any other machines, in the cluster, without downtime;
- **Redundancy and Disaster Recovery:** The distributed architecture enables deployment for redundancy, failover or disaster recovery, across multiple data centers.

MongoDB

MongoDB is a member of the NoSQL family. It is an open source document-oriented database system. It stores structured data as JSON-like documents with dynamic schemas. MongoDB does not support joint nor transactions. It emphasizes on performance and features, such as master-slave replication with automated failover, and built-in horizontal scaling via automated range-based partitioning. (Wikipedia – MongoDB)

Data models for MongoDB:

- A Mogo system holds a set of databases;
- A database holds a set of collections;
- A collection holds a set of documents;
- A document is a set of fields;
- A field is a key-value pair;
- A key is a string;
- A value is a document, an array of values, a basic type such as string, integer, float, binary and etc.

Main features for MongoDB include:

- **File Storage:** MongoDB can be used as a file system, since it is a document-oriented database system. In a multi-machine MongoDB, file can be distributed and copied multiple times between machines, to create load balancing and data replication for fault tolerance;
- **High Availability:** MongoDB supports master-slave replications. A master can read and write data, and a slave copies data from the master, which can only be used for reads or backup. A server can be replicated with automatic master failover;
- **Load Balancing:** MongoDB uses sharding to scale horizontally. A shard key is chosen to determine how the data in a collection is distributed. Then the data is split into ranges and distributed across multiple shards.

- **Indexing:** This document-oriented feature for MongoDB enables any field in the document to be indexed;
- **Ad Hoc Queries:** MongoDB supports search by field, range queries and regular expression searches.

MongoDB can be used for content management system, mobile applications, gaming, e-commerce, analytics, archiving and logging. (MongoDB. org, 2013)

CouchDB

Like MongoDB, CouchDB is a NoSQL database that uses JSON to store data, use JavaScript as query language to define map and reduce phases, use MapReduce and HTTP for an API. Because CouchDB supports HTTP and JSON natively, and can run JavaScript procedures on the server, applications can be developed without a middleware, which means the browsers communicate directly with the database. (Wikipedia – CouchDB)

The primary data unit in a CouchDB are documents. Documents can be edited by client applications. CouchDB does not store data and relationships in tables. Instead, each database is a collection of individual documents. Each document has its own schema and maintains its own data.

CouchDB is fault–tolerant, that it only appends to the database file on disk. It allows master-master replication. CouchDB has browser-based GUI that it is very easy to replicate - a simple POST request can replicate the Couch database. CouchDB can replicate to devices, such as smartphone to go offline, and handle data sync when the device is back online. With the replication and synchronization capacity, CouchDB works well with web and mobile applications.

CouchDB's main features include (Apache Software Foundation, 2012):

- **Document Storage:** Data are stored as "documents" in CouchDB and has a unique id;
- **Map/Reduce Views and Indexes:** The stored data is structured using views. Views are consisted with JavaScript functions. A function takes a document and transforms it into a single value during the Map/reduce operation. A view can be indexed and updated when a document is added, removed or updated;
- **Built Offline:** CouchDB can replicate to devices for offline processes. Data can be sync'ed when the devices are back online;
- **REST API:** CouchDB use REST API, which uses the HTTP methods POST, GET, PUT and DELETE for the four basic CRUD (Create, Read, Update and Delete) actions;
- **Distributed Architecture with Replication:** CouchDB is featured with bi-directional replication and off-line operation. So multiple replicas can have their own copies of the same data, which can be modified offline, and changes sync at the later time when back online.

DynamoDB

DynamoDB is a NOSQL database service offered by Amazon, as part of the Amazon Web Services portfolio. It is a distributed database in the cloud. In DynamoDB, data are stored on SSD (Solid State Drive), which offers predictable performance and greatly reduces latency. Developers can purchase a service based on throughput, instead of storage, and can request more read and write throughput capacities based on their need. (Wikipedia – DynamoDB)

The key feature for DynamoDB is that it is a managed service. When the customer needs more database capacities or better throughput performance, they don't need to worry about configuring new hardware, scaling or partition-ing databases, or patching software, Amazon Web services can do all for them. Customer can go through the AWS management console, and tell DynamoDB how many requests it is going to need per second, then AWS spreads the database table across its server farms to provide it. If traffic grows unexpectedly, customer may dial up more request capacity at the console. DynamoDB replicates data synchronously across multiple AWS zones to provide high availability. (Amazon Web Services, 2013)

DynamoDB offers the following features:

- **Sorted Range Keys:** Keys can be single values or based on a key-attribute combination, and allow users to store sorted data more effectively;
- **Automated Storage Scaling:** An unlimited amount of data can be stored in DynamoDB; the service can automatically allocate more storage;
- Fully distributed, shared nothing architecture;
- **Built-In Fault Tolerance:** To automatically and synchronously replicate data for high availability and disaster recovery;
- **DynamoDB is Flexible:** It does not have a fixed schema. Each data item may have a different number of attributes.

BigTable

BigTable is a large scale distributed storage system for managing structured data, designed to scale to petabytes size. It is built on top of the Google file system, and can handle millions of reads/writes per second. Many projects at Google store data in Bigtable, including web indexing, Google Earth, Google maps, and Google Finances etc. (Chang & et. al., 2006)

BigTable is designed to scale into the petabyte of data, across thousands of cluster machines. BigTables are split into multiple tablets in the Google File Systems. Each table has multiple dimensions. BigTable scales to store billions of URLs, hundreds of terabytes of images and maps, and preferences for hundreds of millions of Google users.

BigTable uses the distributed Google File System to store log and data files. A BigTable cluster typically operates in a shared pool of servers that runs other distributed applications.

Big Table distribute multi-dimensional sorted map, which is indexed by two arbitrary string values (row key and column key) and timestamp, each value in the map is an un-interpreted array of bytes.

The BigTable API provides functions for creating and deleting tables, and column families. IT can also change cluster, tables and columns metadata.

BigTable involves two types of servers: One master server and many tablet servers.

- The master servers track where tablets are located, assign tablets to tablet servers, balance tablet server load and handle schema changes;
- The Tablet servers manage a set of tablets and process read/write requests for tablets. Tablet servers can be added or removed from a cluster to accommodate workload changes.

BigTable can be used with MapReduce to process large scale parallel computing tasks.

HyperTable

HyperTable is an open source database system written in C++. (Wikipedia – HyperTable) Similar to Google BigTable, HyperTable is good for storing and processing very large sets of data. It stores data in a table that are sorted by a primary key. There is no typing for data in the cell - all data are stored as un-interpreted byte strings. Data is stored as value pairs in Hypertable. A typical key for a single cell is:

```
<row>
<column- family>
<column-qualifier>
<timestamp>
```

HyperTable is designed to manage the storage and processing of information, on a large cluster of commodity servers, and power high traffic websites. Users can start with small architecture, and add new machines as traffic increase. User can control how column data is physically stored through the Access Group.

Scalability is the most important characteristic for HyperTable. Many NoSQL database are based on a hash table design, through which the data is not kept physically ordered by any meaningful key, which make them difficult to become well suited with applications, that required fast access to ranges of data. Since HyperTable stores data with a primary key and data is physically sorted by that key, it is a good fit for a wide range of applications. (HyperTable, Inc., 2012)

Accumulo

Accumulo is a distributed, sorted data storage and retrieval system. Based on Google's BigTable design, Accumulo is built on top of Hadoop, Zookeeper and Thrift. Accumulo features cell based access control and server-side programming mechanism, that can modify key/value pairs at various points in the data management process. (Apache Software Foundation, 2013)

Accumulo has been originally developed at the National Security Agency. It provides high levels of consistency with scales to thousands of nodes and petabytes of data, and processes data in near real-time. The cell-level security allows administrators to extend the access and functionality to the maximum number of users, while still maintaining applicable privacy and security regulations. Users are allowed access to the database with specified, regulated and encrypted cells, otherwise they are blocked out of the database due to compliance and regulation limitations.

Hadoop

The name Hadoop comes from Doug Cutting (Apache Lucene) after his son's toy elephant.

What is Hadoop? Hadoop can mean different things to different people. For some it represents a parallel programming paradigm, and massive unstructured data storage using commodity hardware. For others, Hadoop refers to HDFS that implements the unstructured data storage, or the set of Java classes by which a Java programmer can access HDFS data, or write Java code that provides the map and reduce functions. To simplify the above, we consider the following four definitions of Hadoop:

- Hadoop can be referring to the Map/Reduce parallel programming paradigm;
- Hadoop can mean massive unstructured data storage on commodity hardwares;
- Hadoop can simply refer to HDFS (Hadoop distributed file system);
- Hadoop can represent Java classes for HDFS types and Map/Reduce job management.

Hadoop has two main subprojects: MapReduce that understands and assigns work to the nodes in a cluster and HDFS, and a file system that spans all the nodes in a Hadoop cluster for data storage. Meanwhile, it is supplemented by other extended projects such as Pig, Hive, Hbase, Cascading, Mahout, HCatalog, Flume and Zookeeper, etc.

Hadoop is an open source distributed computing framework built on Java. It stores and processes large amounts (Petabytes) of data. It is used to solve big data complex algorithm problems. When there is huge file that cannot fit into RDBMs, Hadoop is used to process huge datasets on large clusters of computers. Hadoop has become the predominant tools with Big Data processing and analysis. Since it is open source, the total cost of ownership is low, and any form of data can be combined, without defining data types or schemas. With the power of MapReduce, it can get the fast result with massive parallel processing power.

Hadoop can interact with existing systems. Hadoop has native support for extracting data over JDBC. It is not hard to dump the entire existing database to Hadoop on a regular basis, or just incrementally export the updates since the last data load. For the semi-structured log files that do not fit in relational databases, Hadoop can extract these log files into a central repository, and easily run analysis over any time-frames worth of logs. Hadoop can break any type of data into manageable chunks, replicate them and distribute multiple copies across all the nodes in the cluster, so that users can later process data easily and reliably. The aggregations, summaries and reports can be exported to any type of BI systems.

Hadoop's impacts are specified by the following four characteristics:

- **Scalable:** Hadoop scales in storage capacity and in computer capacity. New nodes can be added as needed, and without changing data format, the way that the data is loaded, and how the application on top runs;
- **Cost Effective:** Hadoop is open source, which make it very cost effective. The cost of ownership is low. Hadoop brings massively parallel computing to commodity servers;
- **Flexible:** Hadoop is schemaless. It can absorb any type of data, structured or unstructured, and from any type of data sources.

Data from multiple sources can be joined and aggregated in arbitrary ways to enable deeper analysis.

- **Fault Tolerant:** Hadoop is fault tolerant in the face of hardware failures. When you lose a node, the system redirects the work to another location in the cluster, and continues the process without missing a beat.

Besides the two main subprojects: i.e., MapReduce and HDFS, Hadoop is supplemented by an ecosystem of other Apache subprojects as follows:

- **Pigs:** A high-level data flow language for data analysis and an execution framework for parallel computing;
- **Hbase:** Column based storage for semi-structured data, scalable, and distributed database, which supports structured and semi-structured data storage for large tables;
- **Zookeeper:** High performance coordinating services for distributed applications;
- **Hive:** SQL-like query language and metastore, a data warehouse infrastructure that provides data summarization and ad hoc querying;
- **Madout:** Machine learning and data mining library;
- **Cassandra:** A scalable multi-master database with no single points of failure;
- **Chukwa:** A data collection system for managing large distributed systems;
- **Avro:** Data serialization system.

HDFS (Hadoop Distributed File System)

The Hadoop Distributed File System (HDFS) is a distributed file system designed to store very large files, with streaming data access running on a cluster of commodity hardware. It provides high throughput access to application data, and works best for very large data sets.

HDFS is based on Google's GFS whitepaper, logically separating the file system metadata, and the data itself. A block is a minimum amount of data, read or written on the disks. File system blocks are abstractions over disk blocks. In HDFS, file is split into blocks and stored across the cluster, a typical block size in the HDFS is 128MB. Blocks of the same file can reside on multiple machines in the cluster. Each block is stored as a file, in the local FS of the data node. Data stored on disk is not accessible via the local file system. Hadoop API is used to access data, manage replication, node failure and rebalancing.

The HDFS has a master/slave architecture. An HDFS cluster consists of a single NameNode, and a number of DataNodes. A Namenode is the master, data nodes are slaves. The NameNode is a master server that manages the file system, file metadata and determines the mapping of blocks to DataNodes, and also regulates client access to files. Any change to the file system namespace or its properties is recorded by the NameNode. DataNodes store named blocks, and communicate regularly with the NameNode. The DataNode lets clients read data stored in the node, or write new block data in response to the instructions from its NameNode. It also responds to the file system operation request from NameNode, to delete or copy blocks, to or from other DataNodes. There is usually one DataNode per node in the cluster, to manage storage attached to the node. The NameNode keeps track of available DataNodes and file locations across the cluster (See Figure 1).

The HDFS architecture diagram above describes the basic interactions among NameNodes, the DataNodes and clients. The client contacts the Namenode for a file metadata operation. The NameNode manages file system namespace, maps a file name to a set of blocks, and then maps a block to the DataNodes. The DataNodes process read and write requests, and performs block creation, deletion and replication upon instruction from the NameNode.

Figure 1. HDFS Architecture Diagram
(Apache Software Foundation - Hadoop 0.20 Documentation)

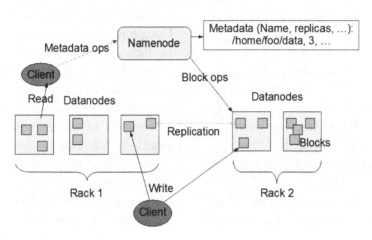

The Namenode and DataNodes maintain the HDFS namespace, file system tree and metadata, maintain the mapping from each file to the list of blockIDs, where the files are located. The NameNode metadata includes a list of files, blocks for each file, DataNodes for each block, and the file attributes such as creation time, replication and the transaction log that records file creation/deletions.

The secondary NameNode, also called checkpoint node reduces data loss when the NameNode fails. Persistent data is stored in two files in NameNode—the fsimage and the editlog. All changes in the file metadata go into the EditLog. The secondary NameNode periodically downloads the current NameNode fsimage and editlog files, merges them into a new image, and uploads the new image back to the current NameNode. When the NameNode fails, the Secondary NameNode has the latest image. The administrator can copy metadata files from the NFS to the Secondary NameNode and run it. Failover is not automatic.

A DataNode is the slave; it stores data in the local file system, the metadata of a block, and serves these data and metadata to clients. Each cluster has many DataNodes. Each file is replicated and divided into fixed sized data blocks, which are spread across the cluster data nodes. The DataNodes report all blocks to the NameNode upon startup, and sends a periodic "heartbeat" to the NameNode. It serves read/write requests, performs block creation, deletion and replication upon instruction from the NameNode. User data never flows through the NameNode. Clients access data directly from the DataNode.

DataNodes send heartbeats to the NameNode, and the NameNode uses heartbeats to detect DataNode failures. When a NameNode detects DataNode failures, it chooses new DataNodes for new replicas, and balances disk usage and communication traffic to the DataNodes.

The HDFS is a fault tolerant distributed file system. It is designed to store large files across the server in the cluster. Each file is stored as a sequence of blocks. The blocks of a file are replicated for fault tolerance. The NameNode receives a Heartbeat and a Blockreport from DataNodes periodically, implying that the DataNode is functioning properly. A block replication is detected and triggered by the NameNode. When the local file accumulates a full block of user data, the client retrieves a list of DataNodes from the NameNode. The list contains the DataNodes that host a replica of that block. The client then flushes the data block to the first DataNode. The DataNode starts receiving the data, writes to the local repository, and then transfers to the second DataNode on the list. The second DataNode then writes to its repository, and send that to the third DataNode. The third DataNode writes the data to its local repository. When the NameNode detects a DataNode failure, the file is recovered from its replica.

In the HDFS, there is one replica on the local node, a second replica on a remote rack, and a third replica on same remote rack, additional replicas are randomly placed. Clients read from the nearest replica.

Here is a list of some major HDFS users (Wikepedia – Apache Hadoop):

- Yahoo has launched what it claims to be the world's largest Hadoop production application in 2008: the Yahoo! Search web map that runs on more than 10,000 core Linux clusters, and produces data that is used by the Yahoo web search. By 2009, Yahoo has a HDFS system with 20,000 nodes in 10 clusters, with 100k plus CPUs, and 14 PB of raw storage; (Zawodny, 2008)
- Facebook claims that they have the largest Hadoop cluster in the world, with 21PB of storage in 2010. Then in July 2011, they have announced the data have grown to 30PB. In 2012, data have grown to 100PB; (Wikipedia – Apache Hadoop)
- Microsoft Powerset has up to 400 instances, and uses HDFS for the Powerset search index (wiki.apahce.com., PoweredBy);
- Other notable users include Amazon.com, Apple, eBay, Federal Reserve Board of Governors, American Airlines, AOL and etc. They all use HDFS to run large distributed computations.

MapReduce

Besides the HDFS, MapReduce is another feature of Hadoop. MapReduce has been created by Google, in order to meet the challenges of processing large data sets, and create web search indexes. The key innovation is the capacity to take a query over a large data set, split and run it in parallel over many nodes. This parallel processing distributed architecture solves the problem that the data is too large to fit into a single computer system.

Based on a whitepaper by Google, MapReduce is a framework for running tasks in parallel. Same as HDFS, MapReduce has a master/slave architecture as well. JobTracker is the master that schedules tasks on nodes, monitors tasks and retries failures. When Jobtracker receives a MapReduce job execution request from the client, it does sanity checks to see if the job is configured properly, then computes the input splits. After it loads the resources required for the job into HDFS, it assigns splits to Tasktrackers for the map and reduce phase. Tasktrackers are slaves; they create a new process for the task, and execute the individual map and reduce task on each cluster node. They send periodic heartbeats to the Jobtracker, along with other task information. Map/Reduce functions operate on smaller parts of the problem in parallel, and are distributed across multiple nodes.

MapReduce splits input data into distributed chunks, defines the steps to process these chunks, then runs the process in parallel on the chunks, to produce the final result set. During the process, the "Sharding" technique is introduced. Sharding partitions data so that IO operations can precede without concern or conflict with other users.

MapReduce, from the name, means that it consists of two parts: Map and Reduce. The map phase takes care of dividing input data into splits, small blocks or chunks. One map task per split, Hadoop is to run the user-defined map function on a node, where the data split resides. After the data is processed, it is sorted as the result, transformed into an intermediate data set, sent to the

Reduce nodes. Then the Reduce nodes reduce the intermediate results into a summarized data set, and produce the desired end results.

The diagrams shown in Figures 2 and 3 depict how the data is reduced from the Map phase to the Reduce phase.

The process of running a MapReduce job with Hadoop involves the following steps:

1. Defining the MapReduce stages in a Java program;
2. Loading the data into the file system;
3. Submitting the job for execution;
4. Retrieving the results from the file system.

Here are some more details about how MapReduce works:

- The input to MapReduce is a set of key/ value pairs;
- The map function is run on each key/ value pair, producing a bag of intermediate key/ value pairs: map (in_key, in_value), the input key/value pair is processed with a list of intermediate pairs;
- The MapReduce implementation groups the intermediate pairs by the intermediate key: list (out_key,intermediate_value). Despite the name, this grouping is very

Figure 2. The Hadoop Mapping function creates a new output list
(Yahoo!, Hadoop tutorial)

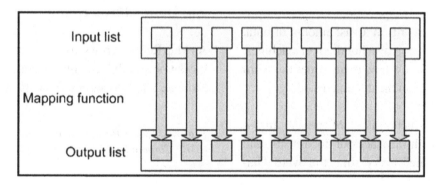

Figure 3. The Hadoop Reducing function produces an aggregate value as output
(Yahoo! Hadoop tutorial, 2013)

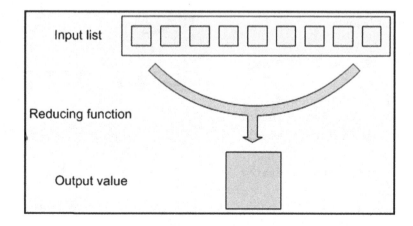

different from the grouping operator of the relational algebra, or the GROUP BY clause of SQL. Instead of producing only the grouping key and the aggregate values, if any, MapReduce grouping also outputs a bag containing all the values associated with each value of the grouping key. In addition, grouping is separated from aggregation computation, which goes in the reduce function;

- The reduce function is run on each distinct intermediate key, along with a bag of all the values associated with that key: reduce (out_key, list (intermediate_value)). MapReduce combines all intermediate values for a particular key, and produces a set of merged output values list (out_value).

Let's look at the MapReduce example for word count, counting words in a vast amount of data, millions of documents over hundreds of machines. If we wanted to know how many times the word "hadoop" appears in the documents.

- The Map function is word specific, that it runs through the stacks of documents, and counts "One" every time the word "hadoop" appears;
- The Reduce function collects all the input from the mapper, and aggregates the results to total the count for the word "hadoop".

Coding example as below:

```
map(String input_key, String input_
value):
    // input_key: document name
    // input_value: document contents
    for each word w in input_value:
        EmitIntermediate(w, "1");
reduce(String output_key, Iterator
intermediate_values):
    // output_key: a word
    // output_values: a list of
```

```
counts
    int result = 0;
    for each v in intermediate_val-
ues:
        result += ParseInt(v);
    Emit(AsString(result));
```

Figure 4 shows the input data provided to the map. The map splits the function and assigns a number of worker tasks to process in parallel. Then the mapped data is presented to the Reduce function with summarization. The Reduce function aggregates the values, and provide the final value as output data.

MapReduce is suitable for big data processing. It is mostly used for log processing, web search indexing and ad-hoc queries.

Big Data SMAQ Stack

As MapReduce grows in popularity, a stack for the big data system has emerged. It consists of layers of Storage, MapReduce and Query (SMAQ). SMAQ

Figure 4. Map/Reduce work flow
(EMC² Corporation Big Data Overview)

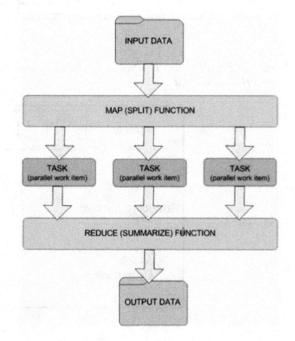

has been proposed by Edd Dumbill (Dumbill, 2010). SMAQ is a stack of big data technologies, and underpin a new era of innovative data driven products and services. The stack is characterized by distributed and unstructured contents. Storage is the foundation; MapReduce is the intermediate layer that enables the distribution of computation across server farms, and support batch processing for data retrieval. The top layer of the stack are Query functions, which are featured by the ability to define computational efficiently functions, and provide a platform for user friendly analytics (See Figure 5).

Storage is the foundation of SMAQ. Storage distribution and replication are handled automatically. The data in the storage can be structured and unstructured, so the design and features of the storage layer needs to fit the structure requirements, and also able to interact with MapReduce. The standard storage mechanism in the SMAQ is the HDFS, a core part of Hadoop. The HDFS provides a simple file system interface for database storage. HBase (Big Table) built on the top of HDFS, offsets the HDFS' missing indexing capacity, and makes the HDFS more usable. Hbase creates indexes so that user can have fast and random access to the data through simple queries. The SQL-Like interface allows the definition of sparsely populated database, with millions of rows and columns.

MapReduce is a framework for easily creating highly concurrent data flows. Map and Reduce are purely functions, which do not rely on process state. As we have described in the previous ses-

sion, MapReduce can be divided on two parts: Map applies a function to each value in the list, and returns a new list; while Reduce applies a function to a list of values, and returns a single value. MapReduce results then are fed back into the database for later querying. The key for the MapReduce is running the divided query in parallel over many data nodes. The distribution solves the problem of data set being too large to process by a single machine.

Query sits on the top of SMAQ stack, and is used to query the results from the intermediate MapReduce layer, to produce higher level and lower latency data accesses. The Query layer not only handles the computation, but also loads, saves and processes the data on the MapReduce cluster. The Hadoop Ecosystem includes many query languages, which can leverage the MapReduce frameworks and the HDFS. Pig and Hive can be written in java to implement the Map and Reduce function. Pig is a data flow language that breaks processing into separate steps, which can be translated into Map/Reduce tasks to extract data. Hive is a SQL like language built on the top of Hadoop by Facebook. It offers a web interface for simple query building functionality. Anyone who knows the SQL query language can easily use Hive.

MPP technology is the core characteristics in the Hadoop project. MPP databases have a distributed architecture, with independent nodes running in parallel. MPP is mainly used in data warehousing and analytics. (Kasibhotla, 2012) Some vendors have MPP database products with MapReduce functionality built in, such as EMC Greenplum and Teradata Aster nCluster. EMC Greenplum database is based on the PostreSQL database management system, and runs on clustered commodity hardware. It has MapReduce built in to enable fast, large scale analytics. Teradata Aster nCluster system has the MapReduce operations invoked using Aster Data's SQL-MapReduce technology, to enable the intermingling of SQL queries with MapReduce jobs. Other market ven-

Figure 5. SMAQ (Dumbill, 2010)

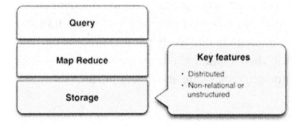

dor provide connectors with Hadoop, to support the MapReduce functionality.

BIG DATA APPLICATIONS

The ability to gather massive amounts of data gives organizations better control, and the ability to detect patterns that allow them to grow and beat their competitions. Big data can transform the way companies do business, and deliver better performance. In order to fully exploit data, companies need to have the following capabilities:

1. Organization must be able to identify, combine and manage data from various sources. Many organizations already have the data they need to tackle their business problems, but managers just do not know how to transfer the information into key decisions. Executives need to have broader thinking about the data, not only the internal data, but external data that are generated from social media, or unstructured data from photos, videos, sensors and monitoring processes. Managers need to find deliberate ways to identify usable data, define milestones and opportunities.
2. Organizations need to build the big data environment. Simple and efficient platforms are required for the Big Data environment. The Big Data infrastructure requires highly automated architecture, which can deliver processing capacity on the fly, without increasing operational costs. How to embrace big data, maximize its value and gain deeper insight?
   a. Build on a storage foundation that can scale quickly, expand storage capacity to petabytes or exabytes, and still provide linear performance, while keeping the operational cost within budget;
   b. Create a unified analytic platform, to quickly integrate and process both structured data and unstructured data, with real time feeds and queries; analyze and collaborate on all data and results with faster and deeper business insights;
   c. Incorporate the insights into execution to act on business decisions, and adjust marketing campaigns;
   d. Provide the platform for the customer to manage and deploy a widely distributed Big Data Environment;
   e. Have an architecture that is easy for managing cloud storage, provisioning with secure multi-tenancy, driving data lifecycle with automated policies and providing self-service access.
3. When building business models that predict and optimize business opportunities, data is essential. But using the advanced analytic models to predict business opportunity, and optimize business performance is more important. If business managers cannot effectively use the analytic results to enhance business performance, big data approach is to lead to a waste of data.

The Big Data Appliance

Since big data involve petabyte-scale staging, transformation, pre-processing and refinery for unstructured data, workload-optimized hardware and software nodes are some essential blocks for big data machines. The Big data appliance now becomes the dominant approach for enterprises to put Hadoop and other cloud ecosystem into production. The principal for the big data appliances is enterprise data warehousing solutions, to implement massively parallel processing. The Big data appliance is characterized by big data storage, processing and development.

Big data appliances provide scaled, efficient and high performance applications for key data consolidation, big data processing, and big data development. Big data appliance should support massive parallel execution of advanced data processing, manipulation and analysis. It should have all the metadata, models and other services needed to support query, calculation, data loading, data integration and data aggregation.

Current industry leaders have announced their big data appliances: EMC Greenplum DCA, Oracle Big Data Appliance, IBM Netezza High Capacity Appliance, Teradata Appliance, and Microsoft Parallel data warehouse appliance.

The EMC Greenplum Data Computing Appliance

After acquiring Greenplum in 2010, EMC has quickly launched the Greenplum Data Warehousing appliance –Greenplum Data Computing Appliance (DCA). Greenplum DCA integrates all the database software, servers and storages to perform big data analytics. Greenplum DCA is one box that supports multiple quarter-rack deployments, which can be mixed, matched and scaled. Greenplum appliances use industry standard commodity hardware instead of specialized hardware. The Greenplum DCA has also been developed around the EMC key technologies, such as Data Domain deduplication storage system that reduces the amount of disk storage needed to retain and protect data.

The Greenplum DCA runs on a Greenplum database, which is based on the shared nothing and MPP (massively parallel processing) architecture, and supports incremental growth of data warehouse through its ability to automatically redistribute existing data across newly added computing resources, and could load 10 terabytes per hour.

Greenplum DCA is built from modules that include GPDB, DIA and GPHD. Greenplum Database (GPDB) modules are blocks of servers that host the Greenplum database. Data Integration Accelerator(DIA) modules are high capacity loading servers, preconfigured with Greenplum software for the easy loading of data onto GPDB modules. Greenplum Hadoop (GPHD) modules are configured with Greenplum's Hadoop distribution, and are ready for high performance unstructured data queries (See Figure 6).

The Greenplum DCA consists of the following components: hosts, segments and switches.

Figure 6. EMC Greenplum DCA (Virtual Geek, 2011)

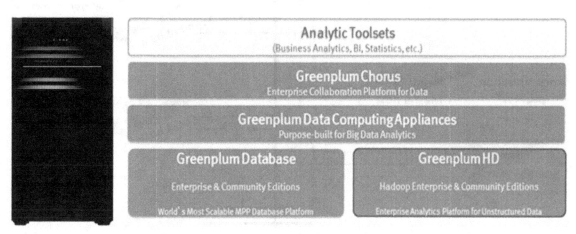

- The master host is the main server that accepts and distributes queries. Master host itself does not store data; it provides a single abstracted view to all the data across the segments;
- The standby master provides cluster function. It is activated when the master host is unavailable;
- The segment host or node runs database server processes (segment instance). It supports one or more segments depending on the processor cores in the node;
- The primary segment stores data, and is responsible for handling queries. Each time data is loaded into the database, a distribution algorithm is used to determine which segments are to store what data. When a query is sent to the master host, the master develops a query plan and sends it to the segments. Each segment is to execute the query on its set of data;
- The mirror segment is a standby segment, and has the same function as the standby master;
- Interconnect switches are responsible for the communications of the Greenplum DCA system. (EMC Education Services – Greenplum fundamental concepts.)

See Figure 7 for an example of Greenplum Physical Architecture.

EMC Greenplum has formed a data warehousing alliance with Cloudera, so the Greenplum Chorus platform and Greenplum database can integrate with the Cloudera's distribution of Hadoop, and support the Cloudera connector that bridges structured and unstructured data.

Figure 7. Greenplum Physical Architecture (EMC² Corporation Greenplum Architecture)

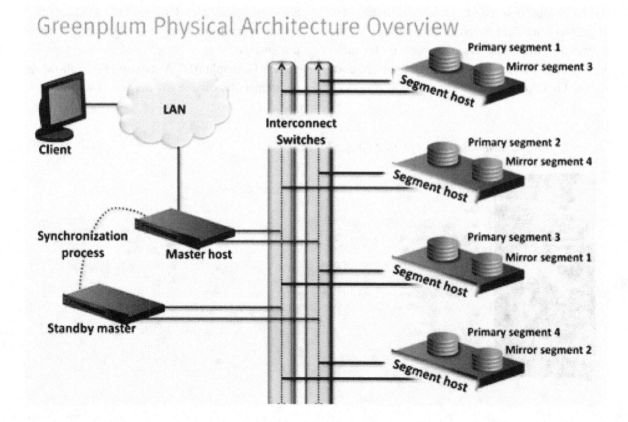

The Greenplum DCA starts out as a single Greenplum Database module, which can be configured with a maximum of 48 modules, up to 12 racks. The multi-rack-appliance configuration offering enable businesses to achieve the maximum flexibility and scalability.

The Oracle Big Data Appliance

Oracle has announced its Big Data Appliance in Oct 2011, partnering with Cloudera, the leading provider of Hadoop system management tool and support services.

The software bundle for the Oracle big data appliance includes Oracle NOSQL database, an open source distribution of R software and key software from Cloudera (Cloudera's distribution of Apache Hadoop, Cloudera manager, administration and management console for Hadoop). The Oracle NoSQL database is used for transactional and key value store database, without a predefined relationship schema, and R is used for predictive analytics and statistical modeling.

The Oracle Big Data Appliance (Figure 8) has been built on the Oracle Sun hardware. In a full-rack configuration, each rack of Oracle BDA offers 864 gigabytes of main memory, 216 CPU cores, 648 terabytes of raw disk storage, and 40 gigabit-per-second InifiniBand internal connectivity between nodes. (Oracle, Big Data Appliance)

IBM Netezza High Capacity Appliances

IBM has developed the Netezza 100 series appliances. The Netezza 1000 series appliance is for entry level and standard data warehouse for rapid and deep data analysis. The machine allows the customer to operate on the data directly inside the appliance, instead of having to offload it to a separate infrastructure, and deal with the associated data preprocessing, transformation and movement.

In 2011, IBM has announced the IBM Netezza high capacity Appliance, enabling users to store, query and analyze up to 10 petabytes of big data.

Figure 8. Oracle Big Data Appliance

 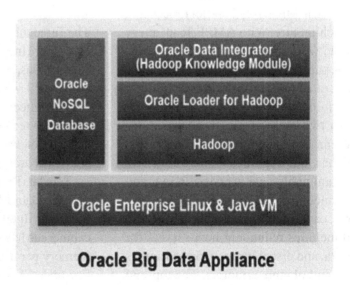

Figure 9. IBM Netezza High Capacity Appliance

**IBM Netezza
High Capacity Appliance**

Storage Subsystem
- 576 TB user data / rack
- High-speed streaming to S-Blades™
- Redundant storage
- Redundant disk controllers
- Spare drive pool

Redundant Host Servers
- Data loading & distribution
- Query planning & optimization
- Workload management
- Adminstration & security

Snippet Blades (S-Blades)
- Streaming disk I/O:
  - Decompression
  - Filtering
  - Projection
- Parallel database engines
  - SQL operations
  - Streaming joins
  - Aggregations
  - Sorts
  - Advanced analytical aAlgorithms

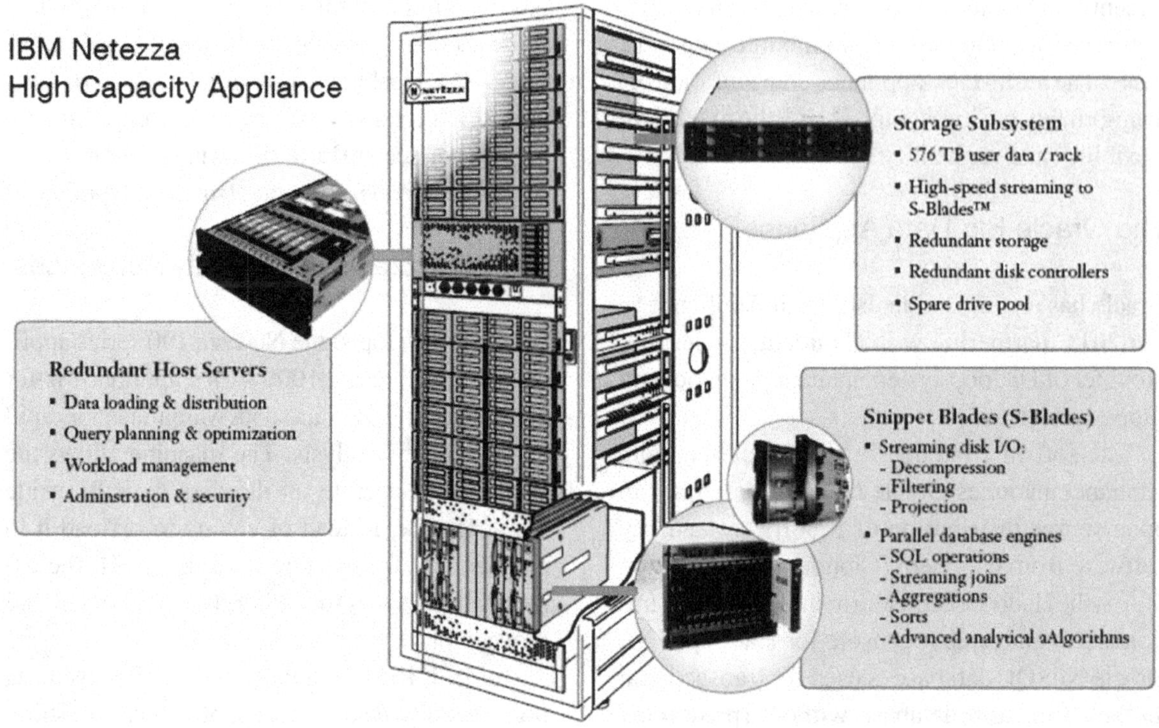

The Netezza High Capacity Appliance (Figure 9) is a workload optimized system, based on the IBM BladeCenter technology and Asymmetric Massively Parallel Processing (AMPP) architecture. With AMPP, load, query and analytic work are split into many pieces, and run in parallel to accelerate results. The IBM Netezza Analytic runs with the Hadoop Map, Combine and Reduce operations. It comes in a two-rack or four-rack configuration, and can scale up to six or eight racks. Each rack has four S-Blades with 32 cores, 32 field programmable gate arrays (FPGA), and 144TB of uncompressed data in a dozen disk enclosures, each with a dozen 2TB drives. The rack also includes redundant host servers for loading data, and distributing workload across the cluster and planning queries. The top-end model is to have 256 cores, FPGAs, 1.15PB of uncompressed data space and 4.4PB of compressed capacity. (IBM, 2011)

The Teradata Extreme Data Appliance and The Teradata Big Analytics Appliance

The Teradata Extreme Data Appliance is powered by six-core Intel Westmere Xeon processors in the server nodes, and large capacity disk drives (scales to 180+PB with 2 TB SAS drives), that use the MPP architecture, and is enabled by the Teradata optimizer technology of drive lineup, with the capacity of 180 PB, for deep-dive analytics and analytical archiving jobs.

Teradata Extreme Data appliance supplied with one Teradata Managed Server, in a full cabinet with dual Intel six core xeon processors, each cabinet can have up to two active nodes and 48GB memory per node. The appliance can scale up to five nodes. Six disk arrays per node line up with 1TB or 2TB SAS drive and up to 144 disks per cabinet. Its software bundle includes the functionality of administration, data loading, data management, connectivity and SQL generation. Teradata Viewpoint, Teradata Parallel Transporter, Teradata Meta Data services, Teradata analyst pack, data connectors and Teradata SQL assistant etc., are all equipped in the appliance, to provide deep strategic insights from massive amounts of data.

The Teradata Big Analytics Appliance (Figure 10) is a powerful system for demanding computation and analytics. It combines Teradata Aster and Apache Hadoop technology into a single, integrated and optimized appliance. The appliance comes with dual 8 core 2.6GHz new Intel Xeon E5 "SandyBridge" processors, with 256GB memory and 40 GB/s Infiniband connection. The ample memory and high bandwidth interconnection supports extreme analytics execution. Worker nodes use 900GB 2.5" disk drive, while back up and Hadoop nodes leverage larger 3TB drives. The larger cabinet enables higher density and better data center utilization. The system includes Teradata Aster SQL-MapReduce and Aster SQL-H, offers pre-packaged analytical functions, for the

customer to have transparent access to Hadoop data, and analyze machine-generated data quickly and efficiently. The appliance can gather data from social networks and other resources, and combine it with customer data for deeper analysis. (Conway, 2012)

Teradata Aster Big Analytics suite includes:

- Embedded SQL and MapReduce engines for massive parallel processing;
- Integration between standard SQL, business intelligence applications, visualization tools and Hadoop data;
- Advanced server management interface provides proactive monitoring with diagnostic tools to quickly detect and address any issue to minimize downtime;
- An intuitive graphical interface for configuration, management and monitoring the system, and enables easy monitoring with dashboards, views of query and process execution;

Figure 10. Aster Big Analytics Appliance
(Teradata Corp. – Aster Big Analytics Appliance)

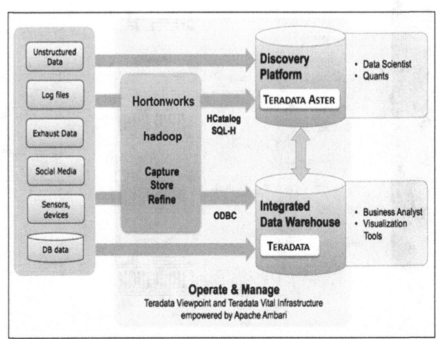

- A Web-based suite of management and monitoring applications that allows administrator access to vital system management information. (Teradata Corp. – Aster Big Analytics Appliance)

Microsoft Big Data

Microsoft has announced its SQL Server Parallel Data Warehouse appliance in SQL Pass 2011. The SQL Server Parallel Data Warehouse appliance is a massive parallel processing (MPP) product, that bundles with either HP or Dell hardware. MPP provides scalability and query performance, by running each server node in parallel, and can handle up to 600TB of data. The SQL Server PDW implements a shared nothing architecture, where each computer node has its own memory

and disk, and has the ability to add computer nodes as expansion when necessary. This method improves the scalability and performance. (Microsoft Corporation, Appliance: Parallel Data Warehouse (PDW))

Besides the SQL Server Parallel Data Warehouse appliance (Figure 11), Microsoft has added big data processing capabilities to SQL Server 2012 based on Apache Hadoop. Hadoop is to run as a service on Microsoft's Azure cloud platform, and on windows servers in the future. Data are to be passed between SQL and Hadoop, more likely from Hadoop into SQL, and the results of big data processing jobs on Hadoop can be analyzed with SQL analysis tools. Microsoft also adds a Hive ODBC driver, to enable customers to use Microsoft Business Intelligence (BI) tools to

Figure 11. Microsoft Parallel Data Warehouse (PDW)
(Microsoft Corporation, Appliance: Parallel Data Warehouse (PDW))

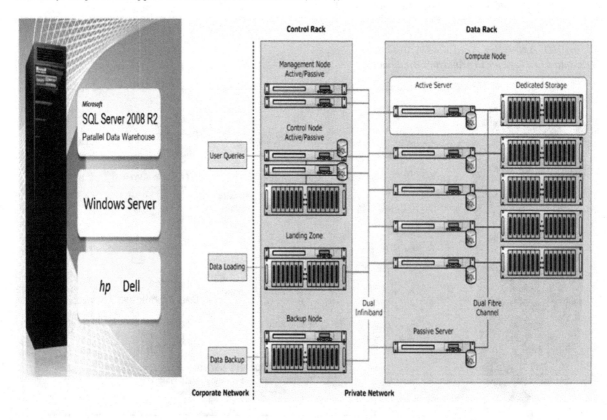

analyze data directly within Hadoop. (Microsoft Corporation – SQL Server)

Hadoop enables the big data appliance approach, and provides the customer quick and easy access to Hadoop analytics. It has become a core force in the business computing industry, with its capacity of storing and analyzing massive data volumes at an affordable price. Market Research Media predicts that the worldwide market for Hadoop MapReduce ecosystem is to expand at a compound annual growth rate of 58 percent over the next few years, to $2.2 billion by 2018 (Kolakowski, 2012). The Hadoop MapReduce system is going to grow with the data warehouse, business intelligence, predictive analytics and data visualization technologies.

BIG DATA SERVICES

IDC estimates the big data market value is to hit $6.8 billion in 2012, growing almost 40 percent every year to $17 billion by 2015. Big data business is to grow with the big data volume increase. Not only enterprises, governments and organizations make use of big data technologies, to mine social media and other data, to better understand their customers, lead innovation and to stay ahead of emerging trends, but small and medium businesses across all industries have to embrace the big data value. (Sterling, 2013)

According to the report, big data pure-play vendors account for $300 million in big data related revenue. Due to the fact that deploying and managing big data technologies is a challenge for many enterprises, there is the huge opportunities for vendors that can help organizations, enterprises or governments to fill the big data infrastructure and skillset gap, with technical and professional services.

There are many ways for service providers to address the big data market with data as-a-service offerings, such as:

IaaS

IaaS, infrastructure as service, provides infrastructure equipment for client's business operation. The infrastructure equipment includes servers, storage and networking components. Service providers own the hardware equipment, provision processing, storage, networks and other computing resources, and are responsible for hosting, backup and recovery. Clients can deploy and run arbitrary operating systems and applications, and pay on a per-use basis.

IaaS provides secure, scalable and flexible host IT infrastructure with on-demand access to the virtual computing resources. With IaaS, IT services can be delivered as a subscription service, eliminating the upfront facility and equipment renting or purchasing cost, and reducing the ongoing support cost. Lower IT cost is a major benefit for small to medium businesses (SMB) to shift to IaaS, and reallocate their operational expense to the service provider. At the same time, instant and easy deployment of IaaS enables companies to anticipate and evolve with rapid changing business requirements, flexibility and low-cost nimbleness. Of course, cost savings on both the hardware infrastructure and the IT administrative staff are the key objectives. The ability to rapidly scale up resources as needed, and avoid the undesirable consequences resulting from over and under provisioning is another benefit. Other benefits include speedy deployment, easier back up, and disaster recoveries. All of these benefits bring advantages from both the tactical and strategic planning perspective.

Current major IaaS providers include Amazon EC2, the Bluelock virtual data center, the Google

Computer Engine and the IBM smart Cloud Enterprise. They all allocate computing, storage and bandwidth resources to customers on demand.

With Amazon's Elastic Computer Cloud service, the consumer can select the desired platform from a list of instances. Each instance offers a specific computer unit, memory, storage and IO performance. Once the option is selected, the customer can customize certain attributes. After the finalization of the selection attributes and authentication process, the infrastructure can be instantiated and immediately available to the customer with the associated charges.

PaaS

PaaS, platform as a service, is to provide client with the deployment of applications in the cloud infrastructure. It used to be very expensive, time consuming and complicated to deploy a new built customized application. IT needs to do all kinds of preliminary studies to determine hardware, middleware and software infrastructure at the company, and set up all kinds of deployment, backup and disaster recovery plans for the new deployment. A team of experts including system administrator, DBA, storage admin, network admin, application support specialist are needed to keep everything up and running. In the case of a change of the application, another cycle of development, test and re-deployment is to prolong the whole process. It can take weeks or months to have a new application added into a large enterprise's IT infrastructure.

Now with cloud computing, delivering a new application can be as fast as opening the web browser. Platform as a service (PaaS) eliminates the expense and complexity of evaluating, purchasing, configuring, managing and supporting all the hardware and software needed for custom-built applications. A customer only needs to select a PaaS service provider (Amazon virtual Private Cloud, Google App Engine, Microsoft Windows Azure Platform, EMC Private Cloud and Salesforce etc.), then an application-centric environment is created. It is to provide a great benefit for software developers and startup companies. With Microsoft Windows Azure PaaS offering, the consumer can select the OS instance, databases or the web application environment.

With PaaS, organizations can focus on creating applications that provide business value. PaaS reduces complexity, increases agility, simplifies the task of application deployment, and lowers cost, while achieving higher computing efficiency. It can provide faster services and a "plug-and play" interface. It also provides businesses with a reliable, scalable and secure private infrastructure, so that they can quickly roll out a solution, and conveniently manage applications in a central location, access to data whenever and wherever required with low TCO.

PaaS can be used for the virtual environment, integration, development and testing, application deployment and business intelligence.

SaaS

SaaS, software as a service, is a flexible software application delivery model. SaaS providers provide a hosted, web based and platform operated software application, and let end users access it all over the internet. SaaS products are usually sold via subscriptions and allow companies, especially startups to avoid large up-front licensing fees and capital costs. Customers subscribe to the service and pay per use for applications running on a cloud infrastructure, without considering licensing, installation, upgrading, also support and maintenance issues. The applications are run on servers in the SaaS provider's data center, and are accessible through the web interface from the client's desktop, tablet or even mobile devices. The consumer does not manage or control either the underlying infrastructure or the application itself. All activities are managed from remote servers in the provider's data center, explicit APIs are created for the customer to access the database, messaging, web portal, e-commerce or storage, all through the internet cloud infrastructure. Major SaaS providers include Microsoft SQL Azure, Microsoft Dynamic CRM, Microsoft Office 365, Concur and Salesforce.com.

Gartner has predicted that the SaaS market is going to be seeing 20.7% growth to generate $12.1 billion revenue in 2011. In fact, SaaS and cloud-based business application services has generated $13.4 billion revenue in 2011, and is forecasted to reach $32.2 billion in 2016, a five year CAGR of 19.1%. (Goasduff, 2013)

REFERENCES

Abdelnur, A. (2012). *Apache Oozie (incubating) 3.2.0 release.* Retrieved from http://blog.cloudera.com/blog/2012/06/apache-oozie-incubating-3-2-0-release-hadoop-workflow-scheduler/

Aginity.com. (2013). *Customer intelligence appliance (CIA).* Retrieved from http://www.aginity.com/solutions/customer-intelligence-appliance/

Ahronovitz, M., & Pabla, K. (2013). What is Hadoop? *Thecloudtutorial.com.* Retrieved from http://thecloudtutorial.com/hadoop-tutorial.html

Alfke, J. (2012). *Guide: Introduction – The REST API.* Retrieved from https://github.com/couchbaselabs/TouchDB-iOS/wiki/Guide%3A-Introduction

Amazon Dynamo, D. B. (n.d.). *Wikipedia.* Retrieved from http://en.wikipedia.org/wiki/Amazon_DynamoDB

Amazon Web Services. (2010). *How to create and debug an Amazon elastic MapReduce job flow.* Retrieved from http://aws.amazon.com/articles/3938

Amazon Web Services. (2013). *Amazon DynamoDB (Beta).* Retrieved from http://aws.amazon.com/dynamodb/

Amazon Web Services. (2013). *Amazon EC2 instances.* Retrieved from http://aws.amazon.com/ec2/instance-types/

Apache Hadoop. (n.d.). *Wikipedia.* Retrieved from http://en.wikipedia.org/wiki/Apache_Hadoop

Apache Incubator, P. M. C. (n.d.). *Bigtop - Apache Hadoop ecosystem packaging and test.* Retrieved from http://wiki.apache.org/incubator/Bigtop-Proposal

Apache Software Foundation. (2010). *Apache ZooKeeper.* Retrieved from http://zookeeper.apache.org/

Apache Software Foundation. (2011). *Hadoop 0.20 documentation.* Retrieved from http://archive.cloudera.com/cdh/3/hadoop-0.20.2+320/

Apache Software Foundation. (2012a). *What is Bigtop, and why should you care?* Retrieved from https://blogs.apache.org/bigtop/entry/bigtop_and_why_should_you

Apache Software Foundation. (2012b). *Apache CouchDB relax.* Retrieved from http://couchdb.apache.org/

Apache Software Foundation. (2012c). *Apache Flume user guide.* Retrieved from http://flume.apache.org/FlumeUserGuide.html

Apache Software Foundation. (2012d). *HCatalog table management.* Retrieved from http://incubator.apache.org/hcatalog/docs/r0.4.0/

Apache Software Foundation. (2012e). *What is Apache Mahout?* Retrieved from http://mahout.apache.org/

Apache Software Foundation. (2013). *Accumulo.* Retrieved from http://accumulo.apache.org/

Apache Software Foundation. (2013a). *HDFS users guide.* Retrieved from http://hadoop.apache.org/docs/stable/hdfs_user_guide.html

Apache Software Foundation. (2013b). *Welcome to Apache HBase*. Retrieved from http://hbase. apache.org/

Apache Software Foundation. (2013c). *The Apache HBase reference guide*. Retrieved from http://hbase.apache.org/book.html

Apache Software Foundation. (2013d). *Welcome to apache HCatalog!* Retrieved from http://incubator.apache.org/hcatalog/

Apache Software Foundation. (2013e). *MapReduce tutorial*. Retrieved from http://hadoop. apache.org/docs/stable/mapred_tutorial.html

Apache Software Foundation. (2013f). *Welcome to Apache Pig!* Retrieved from http://pig.apache.org/

Apache Software Foundation. (n.d.). *Apache PoweredBy*. Retrieved from http://wiki.apache. org/hadoop/PoweredBy

Apprenda.com. (n.d.). *Conducting a PaaS comparison*. Retrieved from http://apprenda.com/ library/paas/conducting-a-paas-comparison/

Ariker, M. (2012). *The one tool you need to make big data work: The pencil*. Retrieved from http:// www.forbes.com/sites/mckinsey/2012/10/09/ the-one-tool-you-need-to-make-big-data-work-the-pencil/

Awsdocumentation. (n.d.). HDFS architecture - Store data with Hbase. *Amazon Elastic MapReduce developer guide*. Retrieved from http:// docs.aws.amazon.com/ElasticMapReduce/latest/ DeveloperGuide/emr-hbase.html

Baranau, A., & Gospodnetic, O. (n.d.). *Apache HBase: The NoSQL database for Hadoop and big data*. Retrieved from http://refcardz.dzone. com/refcardz/hbase

Barton, D. (2012). *How to make big data work for you?* Retrieved from http://www.smartcompany. com.au/information-technology/052342-how-to-make-big-data-work-for-you.html

Borthakur, D. (2010). *Facebook has the world's largest Hadoop cluster!* Retrieved from http:// hadoopblog.blogspot.com/2010/05/facebook-has-worlds-largest-hadoop.html

Borthakur, D. (2013). *HDFS architecture guide*. Retrieved from http://hadoop.apache.org/docs/ stable/hdfs_design.html

Burns, C. (2012). *10 most powerful IaaS companies*. Retrieved from http://www.networkworld. com/supp/2012/enterprise2/040912-ecs-iaas-companies-257611.html

Chang, F., Dean, J., Ghemawat, S., Hsieh, W. C., Wallach, D. A., & Murrows, M. ... Gruber, R. E. (2006). Bigtable: A distributed storage system for structure data. *OSDI*. Retrieved from http:// static.googleusercontent.com/external_content/ untrusted_dlcp/research.google.com/en/us/archive/bigtable-osdi06.pdf

Chansler, R., Kuang, H., Radia, S., Shvachko, K., & Srinivas, S. (n.d.). *The Hadoop distributed file system*. Retrieved from http://www.aosabook.org/ en/hdfs.html

Clouds360.com. (n.d.). *Top 20 platform as a service vendors*. Retrieved from http://www. clouds360.com/paas.php

Cloudera Blog. (2013). *Flume posts*. Retrieved from http://blog.cloudera.com/blog/category/ flume/

Cogswell, J. (2012). *SQL vs NoSQL: Which is better*. Retrieved from http://slashdot.org/topic/ bi/sql-vs-nosql-which-is-better/

Columbus, L. (2012a). *Cloud computing and enterprise software forecast update, 2012*. Retrieved from http://softwarestrategiesblog.com/ category/2012-cloud-predictions/

Columbus, L. (2012b). *Why CIOs are quickly prioritizing analytics, cloud and mobile.* Retrieved from http://softwarestrategiesblog. com/2012/09/16/why-cios-are-quickly-prioritizing-analytics-cloud-and-mobile/

Conway, D. (2012). News release: Teradata big analytics appliance enables new business insights on all enterprise data. *Teradata Corp.* Retrieved from http://www.teradata.com/News-Releases/2012/ Teradata-Big-Analytics-Appliance-Enables-New-Business-Insights-on--All-Enterprise-Data/

Cooper, G. (2011). *Getting started with CouchDB.* Retrieved from http://net.tutsplus.com/tutorials/ getting-started-with-couchdb/

Couch, D. B. (n.d.). *Wikipedia.* Retrieved from http://en.wikipedia.org/wiki/CouchDB

Cutting, D. (2013). *Hadoop and big data.* Retrieved from http://www.cloudera.com/content/ cloudera/en/why-cloudera/hadoop-and-big-data. html

Daly, D. (2012). *Donal Daly on big data analytics.* Retrieved from http://donaldaly.blogspot. com/2012/10/my-perspective-on-teradata-aster-big.html

Datastax Corp. (2012). *Comparing the Hadoop distributed file system (HDFS) with the Cassandra file system(CFS)* (white paper). Retrieved from http://www.datastax.com/wp-content/uploads/2012/09/WP-DataStax-HDFSvsCFS.pdf

Dean, J., & Ghemawat, S. (2004). *MapReduce: Simplifed data processing on large clusters.* Retrieved from http://static.googleusercontent.com/ external_content/untrusted_dlcp/research.google. com/en/us/archive/mapreduce-osdi04.pdf

Dignan, L. (2010). Cloudera, EMC greenplum form data warehousing alliance. *ZDNet.* Retrieved from http://www.zdnet.com/blog/btl/cloudera-emc-greenplum-form-data-warehousing-alliance/39483

Dumbill, E. (2010). *The SMAQ stack for big data: Storage, MapReduce and query are ushering in data-driven products and services.* Retrieved from http://strata.oreilly.com/2010/09/the-smaq-stack-for-big-data.html

Dumbill, E. (2011). *Oracle's big data appliance: What it means.* Retrieved from http://strata.oreilly. com/2011/10/oracles-big-data-appliance.html

Dunning, T. (2008). *ZooKeeper – A reliable, scalable distributed coordination system.* Retrieved from http://highscalability.com/blog/2008/7/15/ zookeeper-a-reliable-scalable-distributed-coordination-syste.html

Everett, C. (2011). *Gartner predicts boom year for Saas.* Retrieved from http://www.businesscloud9. com/content/gartner-predicts-boom-year-saas/5907

Finley, K. (2010). Getting started with Hadoop and Map Reduce. *Readwrite.com.* Retrieved from http://readwrite.com/2010/11/13/hadoop-tutorial

Games, P., & George, D. (n.d.). *Smaq presentation.* Retrieved from http://cs.boisestate.edu/~amit/ teaching/555/talks/SMAQ_presentation.pdf

Gens, F. (2013). *IDC PrEd.s 2013: Competing on the 3ʳᵈ platform.* Retrieved from http://www. idc.com/research/Predictions13/downloadable/238044.pdf

Gilbert, G. (2012). Real-time query for Hadoop democratizes access to big data analytics. *GigaOM Pro.* Retrieved from http://www.cloudera.com/ content/dam/cloudera/Resources/PDF/GigaOM_ Cloudera_Real-time_query_for_Hadoop_democratizes_access_to_big_data_analytics.pdf

Globant.com. (2012). *Big data and high performance: Chukwa.* Retrieved from http://bigdata. globant.com/?p=508

Goasduff, L. (2013). Refresh your integration strategy to tackle cloud-based services. *Gartner Newsroom.* Retrieved from http://www.gartner. com/newsroom/id/2421215

Gottlieb, D. (2013). *A walkthrough of MongoDB data modeling*. Retrieved from http://architects.dzone.com/articles/walkthrough-mongodb-data

Guess, A. (2012). IBM debuts Netezza customer intelligence appliance. *Dataversity*. Retrieved from http://www.dataversity.net/ibm-debuts-netezza-customer-intelligence-appliance/

Hadoop.apache.org. (2013). *MapReduce tutorial*. Retrieved from http://hadoop.apache.org/docs/r1.1.1/mapred_tutorial.html

HadoopIntroduction. (n.d.). *What is HBase?* Retrieved from https://sites.google.com/site/hadoopintroduction/what-is-hbase

Harris, D. (2012). *IBM tunes big data appliance to retailers*. Retrieved from http://gigaom.com/cloud/ibm-tunes-big-data-appliance-to-retailers/

Henschen, D. (2011). EMC tries to unify big data analytics. *InformationWeek*. Retrieved from http://www.informationweek.com/software/information-management/emc-tries-to-unify-big-data-analytics/231601867

Henschen, D. (2012a). Microsoft adds big data to SQL server. *InformationWeek*. Retrieved from http://www.informationweek.com/software/information-management/microsoft-adds-big-data-to-sql-server-20/231900633

Henschen, D. (2012b). Oracle makes big data appliance move with Cloudera. *InformationWeek*. Retrieved from http://www.informationweek.com/software/information-management/oracle-makes-big-data-appliance-move-wit/232400021

Hurwitz, J., Bloor, R., Kaufman, M., & Halper, F. (n.d.). How to choose the right cloud computing service. *Cloud Computing for Dummies*. Retrieved from http://www.dummies.com/how-to/content/how-to-choose-the-right-cloud-computing-service-pr.html

HyperTable. (n.d.). *Wikipedia*. Retrieved from http://en.wikipedia.org/wiki/Hypertable

HyperTable, Inc. (2012b). *Hypertable architecture overview*. Retrieved from http://hypertable.com/collateral/whitepaper-hypertable-architecture.pdf

HyperTable, Inc. (2012a). Retrieved from http://hypertable.org/

IBM. (2011). IBM expands big data analytics portfolio with new Netezza high capacity appliance. *Database Trends and Applications*. Retrieved from http://www.dbta.com/Articles/Editorial/Trends-and-Applications/IBM-Expands-Big-Data-Analytics-Portfolio-with-New-Netezza-High-Capacity-Appliance-76279.aspx

IBM. (n.d.). *IBM Netezza high capacity appliance*. Retrieved from http://www-03.ibm.com/software/products/us/en/ibmnetehighcapaappl/

Intel, I. T. Center. (2012). *Distributed data mining and big data, Intel's perspective on data at the edge*. 0812/RF/ME/PDF-USA, 327826-001. Retrieved from http://www.oracle.com/events/emea/en/oracleday2012/intel-vision-paper-1878780.pdf

Kasibhotla, D. (2012). *Introduction to massively parallel processing (MPP) database*. Retrieved from http://dwarehouse.wordpress.com/2012/12/28/introduction-to-massively-parallel-processing-mpp-database/

Kelly, J. (2011). *Hadoop world: Hadoop ecosystem is exploding, says Cloudera's Olson in keynote*. Retrieved from http://siliconangle.com/blog/2011/11/08/hadoop-world-hadoop-ecosystem-is-exploding-says-cloudera%E2%80%99s-olson-in-keynote/

Kelly, J. (2013). Big data: Hadoop, business analytics and beyond. *Wikibon*. Retrieved from http://wikibon.org/wiki/v/Big_Data:_Hadoop,_Business_Analytics_and_Beyond

Knolworld.com. (n.d.). *Apache Cassandra*. Retrieved from http://www.knolworld.com/apache-cassandra/

Kobielus, J. (2012). *Big data / analytics / strategy*. Retrieved from http://www.linkedin.com/groups/Workloadoptimized-systems-Built-building-bigdata-1814785.S.171434688

Kolakowski, N. (2012). Hadoop market will hit $2.2 billion by 2018: Report. *Slashdot.org*. Retrieved from http://slashdot.org/topic/bi/hadoop-market-will-hit-2-2-billion-by-2018-report/

Melli, G. (2012). *Apache Cassandra server software: Gabor Melli's research knowledge base*. Retrieved from http://www.gabormelli.com/RKB/Apache_Cassandra_Server_Software

Menegaz, G. (2012). *What is NOSQL, and why do you need it?* Retrieved from http://www.zdnet.com/what-is-nosql-and-why-do-you-need-it-7000004989/

Microsoft Corporation (n.d.a). *Appliance: Parallel data warehouse (PDW)*. Retrieved from http://www.microsoft.com/en-us/sqlserver/solutions-technologies/data-warehousing/pdw.aspx

Microsoft Corporation (n.d.b). *Microsoft dynamics*. Retrieved from http://www.microsoft.com/en-us/dynamics/default.aspx

Microsoft Corporation (n.d.c). *SQL server*. Retrieved from http://www.microsoft.com/en-us/sqlserver/solutions-technologies/business-intelligence/big-data.aspx

Microsoft Corporation (n.d.d). *Microsoft Windows Azure*. Retrieved from http://www.windowsazure.com/en-us/solutions/

Mitchell, B. (2010). *What MPP means to SQL server parallel data warehouse*. Retrieved from http://sqlpdw.com/2010/07/what-mpp-means-to-sql-server-parallel-data-warehouse/

Mongo, D. B. org. (2013). *Mango DB manual, tutorial*. Retrieved from http://www.mongodb.org/

Morgan, T. (2012). Teradata pumps data warehouses with six-core Xeons. *The Register*. Retrieved from http://www.theregister.co.uk/2010/10/25/teradata_appliance_refresh/page2.html

Morgan, T. P. (2011). IBM fattens up Netezza data warehouses. *The Register*. Retrieved from http://www.theregister.co.uk/2011/06/23/ibm_netezza_high_capacity/

NoSQL. (n.d.). *Wikipedia*. Retrieved from http://en.wikipedia.org/wiki/NoSQL

O'Reilly Media. (2011). *Big data now, current perspectives from O'Reilly radar*. O'Reilly Media, Inc. Retrieved from http://www.onmeedia.com/donwloads/Big_Data_Now_Current_Perspectives_from_OReilly_Radar.pdf

Oracle. (n.d.). *Big data appliance*. Retrieved from http://www.oracle.com/us/products/database/big-data-appliance/overview/index.html

Productengineering. (2012). *What is Cassandra and how does it help with big data?* Retrieved from http://www.zimbio.com/SQL/articles/iVMqB-Jl15lN/Cassandra+How+Help+Data

Prompt Cloud. (2013). *Technologies we use*. Retrieved from http://promptcloud.com/how-we-do.php

Rodrigues, T. (2012). *Cloud IaaS providers compared*. Retrieved from http://www.techrepublic.com/blog/datacenter/11-cloud-iaas-providers-compared

Rodrigues, T. (2012). *IaaS provider comparison reveals market trends for the cloud*. Retrieved from http://www.techrepublic.com/blog/datacenter/iaas-provider-comparison-reveals-market-trends-for-the-cloud/5755

Salesforce.com. (2013). *What is PaaS?* Retrieved from http://www.salesforce.com/paas/overview/

Shopper, L. (2012). *HCatalog – Embrace the independence*. Retrieved from http://dataforprofit.com/?p=117

Software, I. B. M. Information Management. (2011). *IBM Netezza high capacity appliance – Data sheet*. Retrieved from http://www-05. ibm.com/il/software/netezza/pdfs/IBM_Netezza_High_Capacity_Appliance_USEN.pdf

Sterling, G. (2013). *Data and forecasts: Facebook winning app. game, where's Google maps?* Retrieved from http://internet2go.net/news/Data+And+Forecasts

Stokes-Rees, I. (n.d.). *Big data: Tools and techniques for working with large data sets*. Retrieved from http://www.slideshare.net/ijstokes/2011-08-prewttcbigdataianstokesrees

Taft, D. (2012). Teradata launches Hadoop-based aster big analytics appliance. *eWeek*. Retrieved from http://www.eweek.com/enterprise-apps/teradata-launches-hadoop-based-aster-big-analytics-appliance/

Taft, D. K. (2011). IBM launches Netezza analytics appliance to wrangle big data. *eWeek*. Retrieved from http://www.eweek.com/c/a/Desktops-and-Notebooks/IBM-Launches-Netezza-Analytics-Appliance-to-Wrangle-Big-Data-728395/

Tata Communications. (n.d.). *White paper: IaaS – Fulfilling the promise of cloud computing*. Retrieved from http://www.tatacommunications.com/downloads/whitepapers/Tata_Communications_IaaS_WhitePaper_v2.0-web.pdf

Teradata Corp. (2010). *Teradata extreme data appliance scales from 29TB to 50TB*. Retrieved from https://www.storagenewsletter.com/news/systems/teradata-extreme-data-appliance

Teradata Corp. (2012). *Big analytics appliance enables new business insights*. Retrieved from http://news.thomasnet.com/fullstory/Big-Analytics-Appliance-enables-new-business-insights-623501

Teradata Corp. (n.d.). *Teradata aster big analytics appliance*. Retrieved from http://www.teradata.com/Aster-Big-Analytics-Appliance/#tabbable=0&tab1=0&tab2=0

Turner, J. (2011). *Hadoop: What it is, how it works, and what it can do?* Retrieved from http://strata.oreilly.com/2011/01/what-is-hadoop.html

Virtual Geek. (2011). *EMC GreenPlum Hadoop*. Retrieved from http://virtualgeek.typepad.com/virtual_geek/2011/05/emc-greenplum-hadoop.html

White, T. (2012). Hadoop: The definitive guide (3rd Ed.). Sebastopol, CA: O'Reilly Media / Yahoo! Press.

Wiki.apache.org. (2011). *OozieProposal*. Retrieved from http://wiki.apache.org/incubator/OozieProposal

Wiki.apache.org. (2012). *CouchDB Wiki – Technical overview*. Retrieved from http://wiki.apache.org/couchdb/Technical%20Overview

Wiki.apache.org. (2013). *Hadoop Wiki, alphabetical list of institutions that are using Hadoop for educational or production uses*. Retrieved from http://wiki.apache.org/hadoop/PoweredBy

Wikipedia. MongoDB. Retrieved from http://en.wikipedia.org/wiki/MongoDB

Yahoo. (2010). *Yahoo!'s workflow engine for Hadoop*. Retrieved from http://rvs.github.com/oozie

Yahoo. (2013). *Yahoo! Hadoop tutorial*. Retrieved from http://developer.yahoo.com/hadoop/tutorial/index.html

Zawodny, J. (2008). *Yahoo! launches world's largest Hadoop production application*. Retrieved from http://developer.yahoo.com/blogs/hadoop/yahoo-launches-world-largest-hadoop-production-application-398.html

Section 4
Networking in the Cloud Era

Chapter 10
Cloud Computing Networks:
Utilizing the Content Delivery Network

Yale Li
Microsoft Corporation, USA

Yushi Shen
Microsoft Corporation, USA

Yudong Liu
Western Washington University, USA

ABSTRACT

Cloud Computing has the potential to trigger a major computing model transformation for the IT industry. This chapter briefly describes the business and technical benefits of Cloud Computing and explains the technical challenges in Cloud Computing, such as the network bottleneck. One of the solutions to address the network problem is the Content Delivery Network (CDN). Here, the basics of the Akamai CDN technology is digested. Then, the authors conduct a CDN experiment in the Microsoft public cloud, Windows Azure, to demonstrate the benefits of CDN integration with the cloud. The results show significant gain in large data download by the utilization of a CDN. Finally, a couple of academic research ideas are summarized for future improvements on the CDN model.

CLOUD COMPUTING OVERVIEW

Cloud computing has become a significant technology trend in the recent years. Simply put, the goal of cloud computing, in its early stages, is to achieve utility computing, i.e., the delivery of IT as a service. Cloud computing represents the third major business computing model for the IT industry, with mainframe computing being the first major model, and client/server computing being the second. Cloud computing typically involves the provisioning of dynamic, scalable and often virtualized resources as a service, to be delivered over the Internet.

From the business perspective, cloud computing is a subscription model, using services over the

DOI: 10.4018/978-1-4666-4801-2.ch010

Internet. If one can use a web browser somewhere and pay a fee online to obtain a service, then one can use cloud computing. This broad definition is well described in (Armbrust & et. al., 2009).

From the technical provider's perspective, cloud computing has a more narrowed definition. To be qualified as "cloud", certain characteristics, delivery models, and service models have to be met. For instance, as defined by the National Institute of Standards and Technology (Jansen & Grance, 2011), the five essential characteristics associated with cloud computing are on-demand self-service, broad network access, resource pooling, rapid elasticity and measured services.

OPPORTUNITIES AND CHALLENGES OF CLOUD COMPUTING

Migration from client/server computing to cloud computing is a major computing model transformation. There are great opportunities for both business and technical innovations. However, tremendous challenges are also present.

Business Opportunities and Challenges

On the business side, cloud computing is to make the business more agile, by utilizing resources more effectively to achieve lower cost of ownership. From the cloud provider's perspective (Armbrust & et. al., 2009), the following formula is used, to describe the profit model for cloud service providers:

$$UserHours_{cloud} \times \left(revenue - Cost_{cloud} \right)$$
$$\geq UserHours_{datacenter} \times (revenue - \frac{Cost_{datacenter}}{Utilization})$$
$$(1)$$

The left-hand side represents the expected profit from using cloud computing. The right-hand side represents the expected profit from using the traditional data center. Both sides perform the same calculation by multiplying profits per user-hour by the total user-hours.

Because the resource utilization in cloud computing is 100% (fully utilized), and the resource utilization in the traditional data center is less than or equal to 100% (fully utilized), the true cost of the traditional data center is greater than or equal to the cost of cloud computing. This formula reveals that cloud providers have a better control over the cost per user-hour, and therefore a better opportunity to gain more profit.

From the cloud customer's perspective, applications or services with the following workload patterns are to enjoy great benefits by the adoption of cloud services:

- **Unpredictable Bursting:** An event may trigger heavy usage of resources: normally, the customer would have to scale the design considerations to try and predict what this resource usage requirement could be;
- **Predictable Bursting:** Using Dominos Pizza as an example, the store is very busy on Friday nights. In most days of the week, demand is much less. Even though the additional load is to be maintained, it is expensive for this extra capacity, because it is under-utilized when demand is lower;
- **On and Off:** Similar to Predictable Bursting, On/Off can have seasonal or time-bounded workloads where it is either all or almost nothing processing requirements. Important enterprise workloads that are run monthly, quarterly and annually exhibit this type of behaviour;
- **Fast Growing:** This is interesting in the case of smaller start-up companies or groups in larger companies. It can also be associated with new development. How to plan for rapid capacity increase is no longer an issue in the cloud, both during de-

velopment and operations. Elasticity can be a huge opportunity for savings.

Figure 1 demonstrates the above 4 application workload patterns.

The business challenges for cloud adoption is similar to IT outsourcing. It is critical to understand how the availability, security and supportability requirements are to be met by the cloud service providers. It is also important to know the responsibility of each party, and have a formal service level agreement (SLA) and legal contract between the customer and the provider.

Technical Opportunities

On the technical side, the study conducted in (Armbrust & et. al., 2009) has summarized the ten opportunities and obstacles for the growth of cloud computing. In Table 1, the challenges are obstacles for cloud providers to delivering cloud services, and road blocks for customers to adopting cloud services. The opportunities are the proposed technical solutions, to overcome those obstacles and road blocks.

Take the first item in the table as an example, the availability of cloud service might be lower

Figure 1. Cloud application workload patterns

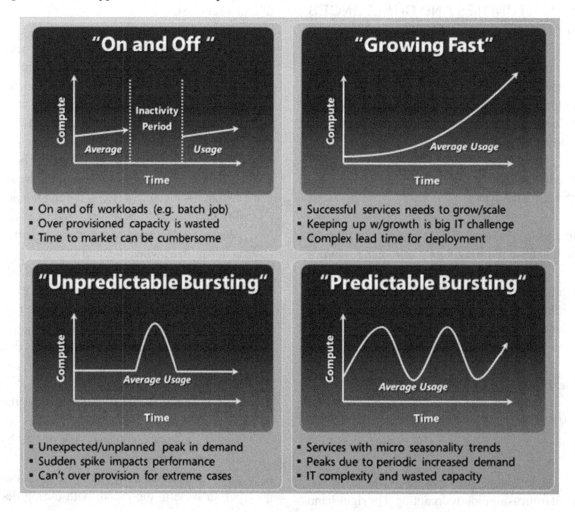

Table 1. Cloud Challenges and Opportunities being Proposed in (Armbrust & et. al., 2009)

Challenges	Opportunities
Availability of Service	Use Multiple Cloud Providers; Use Elasticity to Prevent DDoS
Data Lock-In	Standardize APIs; Compatible SW to enable Surge Computing
Data Confidentiality and Auditability	Deploy Encryption, VLANs, Firewalls; Geographical Data Storage
Data Transfer Bottlenecks	FedEx'ing Disks; Data Backup/Archival; Higher BW Switches
Performance Unpredictability	Improved VM Support; Flash Memory; Gang Schedule VMs
Scalable Storage	Invent Scalable Store
Bugs in Large Distributed Systems	Invent Debugger that relies on Distributed VMs
Scaling Quickly	Invent Auto-Scaler that relies on ML; Snapshots for Conservation
Reputation Fate Sharing	Offer reputation-guarding services like those for email
Software Licensing	Pay-for-use licenses; Bulk use sales

than traditional services provided by enterprise data centers, due to the Internet network condition, and distributed denial of service (DDoS) attacks. The solutions are a load distribution model among multiple cloud providers, and by absorbing the DDoS attacks with the power of cloud elasticity. Other challenges and opportunities are also well explained in (Armbrust & et. al., 2009), so there is no need to restate the rationales.

However, (Armbrust & et. al., 2009) overlooked an important challenge, and this issue should be mentioned or added to Table 1. We add our supplement in Table 2. Perhaps, the reason why this point is missed, is due to their focus being on the cloud side, and they have forgotten that

Table 2. Our Supplementary Cloud Challenges and Opportunities

Challenges	Opportunities
Network Congestion at Cloud Egress and Latency to Client	Integrate Cloud with the Akamai Content Delivery Network Technology

the client is another half of the entire cloud-client ecosystem.

Network Congestion at Cloud Egress and Latency to Client

For today's client/server computing model in the enterprise and business IT, the resources (e.g., applications, emails, databases and files) are typically delivered to the end user's client machines from servers over the LAN. The network congestion is not an issue because resources are highly distributed. The network hops over the LAN are also few between client and server. With the advent of cloud computing model, the resources are highly concentrated in the cloud data center. The network congestion at the cloud egress becomes an issue, because of the topology and usage patterns. Between a data center and its clients, the network hops over the Internet can increase drastically. Thus, the probability of latency due to data transmission delay, and retransmission may also increase, especially when the data center and clients are located in different continents.

Integrating the Content Delivery Network with the Cloud

One of the solutions to resolve network congestion/latency problems is to integrate the content delivery network (CDN) with the cloud computing data centers. To use an analogy, the data center is the manufacturing plant, and the CDN servers are the warehouses of the distributors. Therefore, global load balancing can be achieved with the CDN. The largest CDN in the world at present is the Akamai network which is described in this chapter. We are to demonstrate the benefits of the Cloud CDN as derived from an experiment in the Microsoft Windows Azure cloud. We also present academically proposed solutions for further optimization of the cloud CDN performance in the future.

AKAMAI CDN TECHNOLOGY

Content Delivery Network

A content delivery network (CDN) is a collection of web servers, distributed across multiple locations to deliver content to users more efficiently. When optimizing for performance, a server selected to deliver content to a specific user is based on a measure of network proximity. For example, the CDN may choose the server with the fewest network hops, or the server with the quickest response time.

A CDN service provider typically shares its CDN servers across all its clients. One drawback to relying on a CDN is that one's response time can be affected by traffic from other clients, possibly even by competitors. Another drawback is the occasional inconvenience of not having direct control of the CDN servers. For example, modifying HTTP response headers must be done through the service provider, rather than directly by the

customer's operation team. Finally, if the CDN service provider's performance degrades, one's performance degrades accordingly.

Akamai CDN Technology

The Akamai CDN (Dilley & et. al., 2002) is the most used CDN in the world. Akamai's original approach has been to sell customers a distributed content-caching service. Its goal is simply to resolve any bandwidth issues, and it has been able to solve that problem very well.

Figure 2 articulates the Akamai CDN technology and architectural design, which comprises 7 steps:

- Step 1, a client browser visits a web site, for example http://www.cbc.ca. If *cbc.ca* is integrated with Akamai CDN, the URL is mapped to the Akamai network. In this case, the *.net* root name server is queried for the name resolution;

Figure 2. Akamai CDN technology (Dilley & et. al., 2002)

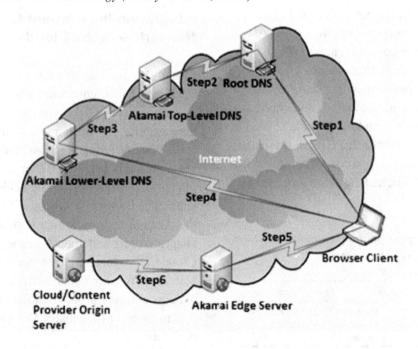

- Step 2, the *.net* root name server sends the domain delegation response to a lower level *.net* domain name server. In this process, the *.net* domain name server (DNS) returns an NS record for the *akamai.net* sub-domain. This NS record is the Akamai CDN top-level name server;

- Step 3, the Akamai Top-level DNS server returns a domain delegation, or *.g.akamai. net,* to a Low-Level Akamai name server, with a TTL (Time To Live) of about one hour;

- Step 4, the Akamai low-level DNS server returns the IP addresses of an available edge server, for example *a7.g.akamai.net.* This resolution has a short TTL (several seconds to one minute). The purpose of the short TTL is to encourage frequent refreshes of the DNS resolution. Therefore, the Akamai CDN is able to direct requests to the edge servers in some other locations, based on the network status measurements;

- Step 5, the IP address for the server *a7.g.akamai.net* domain is returned, so the browser can access the edge server URL http://a7.g.akamai.net;

- Step 6, if the requested web content is not cached on the edge server (normally the first hit only), the content is to be fetched from the origin server of the content provider or the cloud provider.

The criteria for network status measurements include service requested, server health, server load, network condition, client location and content requested. This measurement determines an edge server for client access, and finds the path from the client to the edge server.

The integration of CDN with traditional web sites and cloud services is very similar. Content origin servers are located at the customer's site or the cloud provider's data centers, and they are configured to communicate with the Akamai infrastructure and edge servers.

CDN EVALUATION IN THE MICROSOFT CLOUD

Windows Azure Overview

The Windows Azure Platform (Microsoft Corporation) is Microsoft's PaaS (Platform as a Service) Public Cloud. Customers create applications on top of the Windows Azure Platform, by using programming languages such as c#, and tools such as the Visual Studio supported by Azure. As a PaaS cloud provider, Microsoft is responsible for the Operating System (OS), network builds and maintenance.

The Windows Azure Platform is located in Microsoft's data centers. It provides a cloud operating system called Windows Azure, serving as a runtime for the applications, and provides a set of services that allows development, management and hosting of applications off-premises. The following is a detailed technical description of the Windows Azure Platform architecture and components (Microsoft Corporation), as shown in Figure 3:

- **Computing:** This is the customer's virtual machines (VM) running the Windows Server 2008 Operating System in Web Role, Worker Role and VM Role;

- **Storage:** This is the customer's scalable and persistent storage (in Blobs, Tables, and Queue forms) for large-scale needs. A blob storage container is similar to a network file drive in the cloud;

- **Fabric:** This makes up the building blocks of the Windows Azure platform. It is a collection of the network of interconnected

Figure 3. Windows Azure's High-Level Architecture

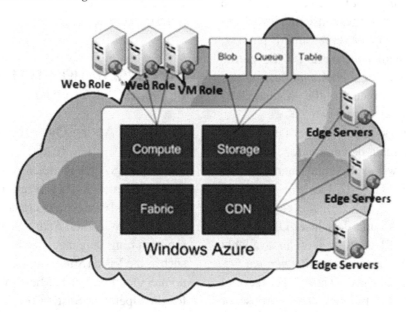

nodes consisting of servers, high-speed connections and switches;

- **CDN:** This is the Azure Content Delivery Network (Microsoft Corporation). It is based on Akamai CDN technology. It integrates with the Windows Azure Storage to provide better user experience for large file downloads. The integration of CDN with Windows Azure or any cloud service is very similar to the integration of CDN with traditional web sites.

Windows Azure has become commercially available in February of 2010. The Windows Azure CDN feature is offered as an optional service. This feature is implemented as an "Enable CDN" button in the Azure Storage service. As of 2010, the Azure CDN enables worldwide low-latency delivery of static content, from Windows Azure Storage to end-users. Microsoft has six data centers worldwide, and some of the data centers have as many as 300,000 to 400,000 servers.

The locations of the Microsoft cloud data centers are:

- North America:
  - North-central US - Chicago, IL
  - South-central US - San Antonio, TX
- Asia
  - East Asia - Hong Kong
  - South East Asia – Singapore
- Europe
  - North Europe - Amsterdam, Netherlands
  - West Europe - Dublin, Ireland

Azure CDN Evaluation

We have taken advantage of the Microsoft Free Trial, offered until June 30, 2011 for the CDN evaluation. Three Azure external storage services are created in three different data centers. Then, a public blob container *yinghua* has been created under each storage service.

The full URLs to access each public container are listed below:

- Located in US South Data Center: http:// b2bblob.blob.core.windows.net/yinghua
- Located in Europe West Data Center: http:// europe.blob.core.windows.net/yinghua
- Located in Asia East Data Center: http:// asiaeast.blob.core.windows.net/yinghua

In this experiment, a free utility called the "Azure Storage Explorer" is downloaded and installed on the PC, after creating three blob storage containers. This utility is used to upload

a large file (699 MB Ubuntu ISO image) to all three storage containers. Figure 4 is a screenshot of uploaded file in the Windows Azure Storage.

Without CDN enabled, the large file from the three cloud data centers is downloaded to a laptop

Table 3. Experimental results without CDN enabled

Data Center Location	Asia	Europe	US
1st download time	30 min 20 sec	37 min 10 sec	11 min 0 sec
2nd download time	36 min 10 sec	30 min 30 sec	10 min 50 sec
3rd download time	37 min 30 sec	31 min 10 sec	12 min 30 sec
Average download time	34 min 40 sec	33 min 0 sec	11 min 30 sec
Standard deviation	3 min 50 sec	3 min 30 sec	1 min 20 sec

Figure 4. Screenshot of uploaded file in Windows Azure Storage

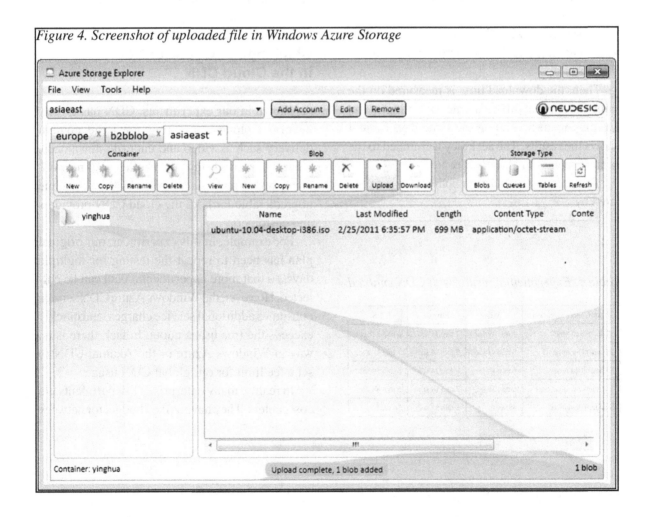

computer located in Seattle, US. Table 3 shows the download time in three measurements, made at different times (morning, noon and evening respectively) on the same day. The accuracy is rounded to the nearest 10 second by IE software.

Afterwards, the CDN is enabled in the Windows Azure Portal tool. It takes up to one hour to propagate the content from the blob storage container in the Microsoft cloud data centers to the Windows Azure CDN network globally. In the Windows Azure management tool, the authors observe that the CDN uses different URLs for content delivery of the same file. The msecnd.net CDN network is equivalent to akamai.net CDN network. The URLs are listed below:

- Europe: http://az25036.vo.msecnd.net/ yaleli/
- US: http://az25037.vo.msecnd.net/yaleli/
- Asia: http://az25038.vo.msecnd.net/yaleli/

Then, the download time is measured on the same file again at different times (morning, noon, evening, respectively) on the same day. Table 4 shows the results. The accuracy is rounded to the nearest second by the IE software.

The average (or mean) in both tables is calculated by:

$$\bar{x} = \frac{1}{n} \sum_{i=1}^{n} x_i \qquad (2)$$

The standard deviation in both tables is calculated by:

$$\sigma = \frac{\sqrt{\Sigma \left(x - \bar{x} \right)^2}}{n-1} \qquad (3)$$

Without CDN, the download speed is roughly 170% slower from the US, 350% slower from Europe and 420% slower from Asia. You can see that the Windows Azure CDN is very effective in improving the content delivery time from the cloud, particularly for cloud data centers far away from the end user's client machine.

Challenge of Cost Control in the Cloud CDN

As shown in our experiments, CDN has greatly benefited cloud computing for large content delivery such as video and data file downloads. However, it also brings the challenge of network consumption and cost control, which may become unpredictable for both the cloud CDN providers and customers.

For example, in this experiment, our original plan has been to repeat the testing for multiple days, so that more experimental data can be collected. However, the Windows Azure CDN service consumes additional service charges, and quickly exceeds the free usage quota. In fact, there is no way in Windows Azure or the Akamai CDN to set a fee limit for our global CDN usage.

In reality, many enterprise IT departments are cost centers. They have a fixed budget for network

Table 4. Experimental results with CDN enabled

Data Center Location	Asia	Europe	US
1st download time	7 min 19 sec	7 min 55 sec	6 min 34 sec
2nd download time	5 min 43 sec	5 min 34 sec	7 min 49 sec
3rd download time	6 min 43 sec	8 min 24 sec	5 min 59 sec
Average download time	6 min 35 sec	7 min 18 sec	6 min 48 sec
Standard deviation	48 sec	1 min 31 sec	56 sec

usage even if they move to the cloud. Consumers also have the same desire to limit their monthly bill when use cloud services. To satisfy customers' requirements, the cloud providers need to provide a flat-fee billing model in addition to the usage-based pricing. In order to provide a flat-fee service, a provider must be able to limit the total network usage consumption, including the CDN usage, in the cloud computing environment.

To address such issues, more improvements should be added into the CDN service in the future. In the next section, some potential solutions to this problem are to be discussed, which include implementing the Distributed Rate Limiting (DRL) (Raghavan & et. al., 2007), and its variant in the cloud CDN.

FUTURE IMPROVEMENTS FOR THE CLOUD CDN

Two possible improvements are to incorporate DRL (Raghavan & et. al., 2007) or CDN Redirection (Su & et. al., 2009) in Windows Azure or other cloud services. If the DRL is provided by the Windows Azure CDN service, network consumption and monthly bill should not be a worry after the free subscription is over. In the following, some potential solutions to this problem are discussed.

A Fixed-Cost Model for the Cloud CDN

A fixed-cost model for the cloud CDN is obviously a handy solution. This model works fine as long as the network consumption is predictable for both service providers and customers. However, such prediction turns out to be a significant challenge, in a distributed environment such as the cloud CDN. The service providers have to provide a fixed price for an aggregated global usage, and allow services to consume resources dynamically across various locations, while subjecting to the specified aggregate limit. Here we are more interested in the other two solutions.

DRL for the Cloud Control

In (Su & et. al., 2009), a good solution is DRL (Distributed Rate Limiting), proposed to address the issue. DRL is a technology to control the total usage of network bandwidth in cloud computing, whether or not CDN is enabled.

One of their contributions are the DRL algorithms. They have designed and implemented two DRL algorithms. The first algorithm is called GRD (Global Random Drop). The purpose of GRD is to approximate the number of packet drops. The second algorithm is called FPS (Flow Proportional Share). The purpose of FPS is to improve scalability.

Then they have designed a peer-to-peer limiter architecture for DRL. In their design, each limiter is not only functionally identical but also operates independently. The functionalities of the limiter are divided into three subtasks. Task one is an estimation for the average arrival rate. A standard EWMA (exponentially-weighted moving average) filter is used to cancel out fluctuations in this task. Task two is the communication for estimating the number of dynamically chosen limiters. Task three is the allocation for combining global estimates. In this task, local measurements are used to determine a limit for the local rate enforcement.

After the design, 2 limiters are implemented and then evaluated. Three metrics are developed in (Su & et. al., 2009) for evaluation: utilization, flow fairness and responsiveness. It is worth to point out that the flow fairness is described by Jain's fairness index (Jain & et. al., 1984):

$$f = \frac{(\sum_{i=1}^{k} x_i)^2}{k(\sum_{i=1}^{k} x_i^2)} \tag{4}$$

Their results show that there is good potential for DRL to work with TCP based web services, even though more work still needs to be done for the protocol agnostic DRL, due to a UPD protocol issue in the cloud. As explained in the previous section, if DRL has been used in the Windows Azure CDN, the over charges after enabling the CDN in our current Windows Azure storage service should no longer be a concern. Currently, only the CoDeeN CDN has unwillingly deployed an ad-hoc DRL solution. We highly recommend all public cloud providers to incorporate a DRL solution in their services.

Subscriber's Behavior Based DRL Solution

In the DRL solution, distributed rate limiters collaborate to enforce a global rate limit across traffic aggregates in multiple sites, which can effectively support the flexibility required by resource provisioning and accounting, in the cloud computing environment.

Based on the DRL solution, we propose a further optimization for cloud DRL – subscribers' behaviour based DRL solution. If the cloud CDN providers can leverage the knowledge of subscribers' usage habits and their network resource consumption patterns, a better estimation on the traffic demand of the aggregate at each limiter can be achieved, and capacity in proportion to that demand can be more accurately apportioned. Since the fairness between flows inside a traffic aggregate depends critically on an accurate limiter assignment, this solution can potentially benefit the flow fairness. It also allows individual flows, at different limiters, to compete with each other for bandwidth in a more intelligent way, so that it can further optimize the network bandwidth utilization and response time. Given *the consumption patterns are always changing, this solution should be made adaptive to such changes.*

CONCLUSION

Based on the study conducted in this paper, we truly believe that cloud computing is going to be a new era for the Information and Communications Technology industry. Cloud computing brings many benefits to customers, and is to dramatically increase business agility and reduce operational costs. However, there are many obstacles on this journey to the full adoption of cloud computing. One of the problems is network congestion at cloud egress and latency to clients. It is suggested that all cloud providers should evaluate and consider utilizing a CDN, to resolve this issue.

CDN has been proven a good working solution for integration with cloud computing. Microsoft Windows Azure has adopted the CDN technology and demonstrated the benefits. Our Azure CDN experimental results show significant download speed improvement, during large content data downloading. Experiments have shown that CDN is a good complimentary service, when it is bundled with cloud services. In the future, the cloud CDN service can be continuously improved with new technologies, such as DRL and the subscriber's behaviour based DRL solutions.

However, a CDN may be limited, in benefiting all types of cloud applications, such as highly transactional applications. The long term solution can be to increase the network bandwidth with new technologies, and utilize CDN as a transition step. The high speed connectivity from all clients worldwide to the Internet can be the most challenging problem in achieving the goal. Recently, a practical solution prototype has been demonstrated to resolve "the last mile", with over 100 times faster speed than the current technologies, by a Chinese company.

REFERENCES

Armbrust, M., Fox, A., Griffith, R., Joseph, A. D., Katz, R. H., & Konwinski, A. ... Zaharia, M. (2009). Above the clouds: A Berkeley view of cloud computing. Berkeley, CA: University of California at Berkeley.

Dilley, J., Maggs, B., Parikh, J., Prokop, H., Sitaraman, R., & Weihl, B. (2002). Globally distributed content delivery. *IEEE Internet Computing, 6*(5), 81–86. doi:10.1109/MIC.2002.1036038.

Jain, R., Chiu, D., & Hawe, W. (1984). A quantitative measure of fairness and discrimination for resource allocation in shared computer systems. *DEC Research Report* TR-301.

Jansen, W., & Grance, T. (2011). *Guidelines on security and privacy in public cloud computing.* Draft NIST Special Publication.

Microsoft Corporation. (2011a). *What is Windows Azure?* Retrieved from http://www.microsoft.com/windowsazure/

Microsoft Corporation. (2011b). *Windows Azure content delivery network.* Retrieved from http://www.microsoft.com/windowsazure/cdn/default.aspx

Raghavan, B., Vishwanath, K., Ramabhadran, S., Yocum, K., & Snoeren, A. C. (2007). Cloud control with distributed rate limiting. *ACM SIGCOMME Computer Communication Review, 37*(4).

Su, A.-J., Choffnes, D. R., Kuzmanovic, A., & Bustamante, F. E. (2009). Drafting behind Akamai: Inferring network conditions based on CDN redirections. *IEEE/ACM Transactions on Networking, 17*(6).

Chapter 11
Data Transfer and Storage in Cloud Computing

Yushi Shen
Microsoft Corporation, USA

Ling Wu
EMC² Corporation, USA

Yale Li
Microsoft Corporation, USA

Shaofeng Liu
Microsoft Corporation, USA

Qian Wen
Endronic Corp, USA

ABSTRACT

When network bandwidth is no longer a bottleneck for Internet applications, we still face the challenges of how to utilize the bandwidth in full when transferring data. This might sound straightforward, but it is far from being easy or straightforward. Lots of work has been done to improve the utilization of abundant network bandwidth, while maintaining the same reliability, efficiency, and fairness of slow protocols, like TCP. In this chapter, the authors introduce the background of emerging bandwidth-intensive applications, related works that are in place to solve these issues, and their limitations to make the challenges clear to the readers. Similar challenges also present for large-scale data preservation.

INTRODUCTION

The Internet can never be fast enough. As users of the Internet, we have all witnessed the Internet speed changing from 56Kbps via a modem to 10/100Mbps via ADSL or cable networks, and the new networks are being installed in hundreds of millions of homes around the world. Our utilization of the Internet has also evolved: Besides browsing simple web pages, more and more are using the Internet to watch high-resolution videos, do real-time sharing and video chatting and so on. There

DOI: 10.4018/978-1-4666-4801-2.ch011

is a clear trend on how the Internet is being used, as new network applications appear. The development of network technologies just barely meet the requirements of these new network applications, and in many cases, applications must succumb to the available network bandwidth. Although new applications have leveraged the continuous development of the Internet infrastructure, at the same time, they put great pressure on the future Internet technologies for further development. This is perhaps why we never feel that the Internet can be sufficiently fast for us. These are today's challenges, as we want to bring everything into the cloud.

As time goes on, many applications that used to appear in science fiction stories become our reality due to increasingly fast networks. Gradually, the lower-level communication modules responsible for data transfer are becoming increasingly application critical. Demands are high for improving the performance of those modules. We cannot change the trend that future applications are required to have higher network speeds and latency. We should rather think whether the potential of the current network resources has been fully utilized. More specifically, the current communication modules need to be improved, such that data can be transferred more efficiently. We believe these network communication modules should be adaptive to network applications, instead of the other way around. Since different applications may have different characteristics, communication modules need to take these differences into consideration. Communication protocols may vary between different types of network applications. The research in this section has been initially motivated by one specific type of application that emerged in the recent years: large scale digital content transfer, streaming and archiving. This is especially true in Cloud storage, where people can store and retrieve massive data whenever they need it.

There has been massive amounts of research done on optical networks in the recent years. As one example, CineGrid has led a trend of using high

bandwidth networks to transfer very high quality digital content, for real-time movie showings and digital preservation. Although many successful demonstrations of 4K video streaming have been performed over the fiber networks, we foresee the challenges in designing new protocols, which scale to applications demanding higher bandwidth and higher resolution digital content in the future. Today, ultra-high-resolution displays have become standard infrastructure in scientific research. These displays are typically built by tiling an array of standard LCD displays onto a display wall, driven by a PC cluster. There are some different types of display walls:

- The HIPerSpace uses sixty 30' LCD displays, to form a display wall with more than 200 million pixels;
- The StarCAVE uses 34 high-definition projectors to construct a 3D virtual space, where people can work with 3D virtual reality objects.

Meanwhile, high-speed research optical networks make it possible for scientists to use these ultra-high resolution displays over long distances, for such scientific applications as very-high-definition video streaming or conferencing, real-time data visualization generated by remote scientific instruments and so on. As a perfect example of the combination of display walls and a high-speed network, the OptIPuter research project, funded by the US National Science Foundation, constructed an 1Gbps-10Gbps optical network infrastructure, as well as the middleware to facilitate the interactive access to the remote gigabytes to terabytes of visualization data objects, and bring them to a visual interface, the OptIPortal.

However, scaling up visualization devices, from a single PC with a single display to a cluster of PCs with a cluster of displays, has brought up challenges on how to feed data to these display devices. These challenges are due to the limitations of traditional single data source communication model, and create the need for a new communication model with multiple-to-multiple end points, which can achieve very-high-bandwidth parallel data transfer/streaming between cluster-based display devices, while still appearing as a point-to-point communication protocol to the users.

Traditional data transport protocols have limitations that prevent their use for such multi-endpoint connections. The popular Transport Control Protocol (TCP) is slow in long distance networks, because of its window-based congestion control mechanism. Alternatives like RBUDP, UDT, and LambdaStream are the more recently developed UDP-based protocols, focusing on high-speed file transfers or real-time data streaming between two end nodes. These protocols are point-to-point rate-based, supporting one sender and one receiver. The sender controls the sending rate to minimize packets loss, and the lost UDP packets are resent. RBUDP, for instance, uses a bitmap to maintain a list of lost UDP packets and do a multi-round communication to recover lost packets, which usually takes 2-5 round trips time (RTT) to retrieve a GB file correctly. LambdaStream detects packet loss based on the gaps in the receiving time between two consecutive UDP packets, and if that gap is bigger than expected, the sender is to reduce the sending rate accordingly. None of these protocols can be scaled to a multiple-to-multiple communication model in a straightforward way.

Existing parallel data streaming protocols do not sufficiently address the synchronization issue of multiple parallel data streams, caused by unevenly-distributed packet loss. These multiple-to-multiple communication protocols tend to synchronize senders and receivers by adding a synchronization module to senders and/or receivers. This synchronization module waits until all senders/receivers have the next frame of data, and then broadcasts the command of sending/displaying to all senders/receivers. In these cases, the behavior of individual data streams can affect the overall performance, for instance burst packet loss of one data stream can slow down all the other data streams.

In addition to data transfer methods, digital storage and archiving are also critical. We are to show our preliminary research about how to use the optical network and open source software to build a scalable distributed storage platform for future digital content preservation. The article ``The Digital Dilemma'' points out that the rapidly increasing use of digital technology in the acquisition, post-production and distribution of media content not only brings significant benefits to the motion picture industry, as well as other stakeholders in the media ecosystems, but also raises serious issues on how to efficiently manage the large amount of resulting digital content, over long periods of time. Given that a single version of a movie created in ultra-high quality can fill tens of terabytes of digital storage space, current technologies for preserving large amounts of data have fallen far behind to meet the media industry's needs.

A unique feature of digital media content is its mobility. For instance, starting from its creation in the life cycle of a movie, digital media need to be moved from one system to another many times for post-production, cinema distribution, long term archiving and on-demand retrieval. Therefore, how to manage and transfer digital content efficiently becomes increasingly important. The traditional method of delivering film cans by courier has been initially adapted to deliver hard drives and data tapes. But with the increasing volume of data transfers required for modern media productions, which are themselves increasingly distributed around the world, physical delivery and physical preservation of digital media assets no longer satisfy the industry's requirements. On the other hand, large amounts of long distance fiber optical cable have been installed during the past decade, which now makes dedicated 1Gbps-10Gbps fiber connections more affordable. This trend is making it increasingly practical to transfer large digital media files to remote sites. Furthermore, a distributed storage model has the potential of unifying resources around the world to form a petabyte scale distributed storage platform for media exchange and preservation.

In this chapter, we include two research cases that are related to the Cloud infrastructure, mainly exploring how to use more efficient protocols to transfer data quickly in parallel using optical networks, and how to leverage the optical network to construct a distributed Cloud storage system that is reliable and disaster resistant. Certainly, we cannot address all application models on the current or future cloud infrastructure, and our targets are two specific research areas. Both models, we believe, address some current and future challenges in the Cloud computing.

The contents in this section are mostly composed from previous research. The problems addressed in this section, e.g. parallel data transfer, distributed storage over optical network, are similarly faced in cloud computing, under different contexts. We hope the readers can have a broader view of Cloud computing through our research findings.

RELATED WORKS

Related Research Communities

The research described in this section borders on a few related disciplines, which are going to be listed below.

Scientific Visualization

Large scale display devices with very high resolution exist in many research institutes. In the article "Visualizing Science: The OptIPuter Project" (Pieper & et. al., 2009), we have learned that visualizing large amounts of data on a display wall with hundreds of millions of pixels has become more than a convenient tool that can provide an exciting viewing experience, it is essentially needed to interpret the enormous amounts of data produced by large-scale instrumentation, experiments and stimulations. In practice, large scale display devices are typically tiled display walls, driven by a cluster of computers. Each computer in the cluster is only responsible for a small portion of the visualized data, and all computers are synchronized to refresh their images at the same pace.

However, feeding data to these huge display walls is very challenging. The dilemma is that a single data source cannot feed data fast enough to satisfy the data consumptions of a gigantic display device. Feeding with parallel data sources is hard to implement, and may cause synchronization issues and significantly degrade the viewing experience.

CineGrid

A similar dilemma exists in high resolution video streaming. CineGrid is a community that pioneered the research of how to archive, share and stream very high definition digital content over optical networks. The mission of CineGrid is to "To build an interdisciplinary community that is focused on the research, development, and demonstration of networked collaborative tools to enable the production, use, preservation and exchange of very-high-quality digital media over photonic networks." In CineGrid, streaming very high resolution video on top of gigabit optical networks provides very impressive viewing experiences. The main method to achieve this goal, however, is an ad-hoc solution: original 4K clips are compressed into a 500Mbps data stream at the sender side, and are decompressed at the receiver side in real time using dedicated hardware JPEG2000 codecs. This solution does not scale when a higher resolution image format is required in the future.

Data Grid

Data Grid is related to our research, as it provides us with tools for large scale data archiving. We use the iRODS (Rajasekar & et. al., 2010) data grid to store and manage many of the high resolution video clips held by the CineGrid community. Data grid provides a seamless way to access files in a universally distributed storage system, and also facilitate us to define workflows for content ingestion, distribution and archiving.

However, tremendous challenges remain in current data grid implementations. In the case of CineGrid, we replicate every piece of content at least three times, and distribute them into three distant locations connected by 10Gbps optical networks. We have found that synchronizing files between those locations has been extremely slow. A new file transfer paradigm is needed to boost the performance of data grid as well.

Data Transfer Techniques and Challenges

Large scale data transfer is at the core of many of the applications under study in the above listed disciplines. In this section, we briefly introduce related data transfer techniques as a basis for our further discussions in the following chapters.

Packet Switching Networks

The Internet is a packet switching network. Packet switching is "a digital networking communications method that groups all transmitted data, regardless of content, type or structure, into suitably-sized blocks," i.e. packets. Packet switching features the delivery of variable-bit-rate data streams (sequences of packets) over a shared network. When traversing network adapters, switches, routers and other network nodes, packets are queued, resulting in variable delay and throughput depending on the network traffic load. When we browse web pages, watch videos from Youtube, chat over instant messaging, and use point-to-point (P2P) software to share files, all these data are transferred over the Internet using packet switching techniques.

The research networks that we work with are implemented using packet switching as well, for example the OptIPuter project, so named for its use of Optical networking, Internet Protocol, computer storage, processing and visualization technologies, is a visionary infrastructure which tightly couple computational resources over parallel optical networks using the IP communication mechanism. For these reasons, we are going to assume that we need to base our work on packet switching networks.

Viewing from the level of network applications, we basically use the network to perform only two tasks: send and receive data. The data we want to send is wrapped in packets by the computer's operating system and sent off by the computer's network interface card (NIC). It travels through network cables, multiple switches and/or routers, and finally reaches the destination. Data packets get properly passed on by each of these network components based on their source and destination, normally represented by the source and destination IP addresses.

As robust as this data transmission process sounds, none of the participating hardware guarantees that it is not going to lose or even purposely drop any packets they handle. It happens quite regularly that all or part of the data being sent may get lost somewhere along the way. This raises the question on how this can be avoided.

Network Protocols

Network protocols describe the rules under which data is being transferred. These protocols include information which is given to the data packets before they leave the sender, and which can be used to reconstruct the original data in case of data loss along the transmission path. If there were never any packet loss, network protocols would have been much simpler than they are today. Network protocols also include data for quality of service (QoS) control, i.e. giving different jobs different priorities on the basis of their specified importance, but the major effort of network protocols is in the packet loss handling.

There are many reasons for packet loss, a fundamental reason being that packet switching networks are shared by multiple users, computers, applications, sessions and etc. Even a single user with a single computer can run many networked programs simultaneously, which need to share the network and compete with each other. For example, if a user spontaneously watches multiple videos on Youtube, each session might be noticeably slowed down, while closing some of them can make the remaining videos play faster.

The core routers on the Internet, at any given time, can manage millions of parallel sessions. These sessions compete for resources, and when a packet of one session cannot be scheduled to be delivered properly, it is to be dropped. Packet loss happens for many different reasons, e.g. collisions in a wireless network environment, switch/router buffer overflow, link errors, bit errors during transfer, receiver buffer overflow and etc. It is commonly believed that the majority of packet losses happen in switches and routers, and that it cannot be eliminated.

Packet loss does not only happen on the public Internet, but also on high-speed dedicated research networks, also known as Lambda Networks. Normally those networks, rather than being shared by millions of users, only have hundreds of users at most. Although the number of users is small, the average bandwidth per user is high, so that packet loss still happens and needs to be addressed by communication protocols and network software applications.

Although network protocols are mainly designed to cope with packet loss in shared packet-switching networks, the principles of how they work vary, and are largely decided by network settings and application characteristics.

Packet Loss Recovery

When a packet loss is detected, the network protocols react in a pre-defined way. First, the lost data packets need to be recovered, and then further action is taken to reduce the chance of future packet loss, for instance through reducing the data rate. The following is a brief overview of how existing protocols handle packet loss.

1. TCP

The Transfer Control Protocol (TCP) is the protocol used by most Internet applications. Standard TCP starts a transfer at a pre-defined sending rate, and waits for an acknowledgement for each data packet it sends. When acknowledgements are received correctly, TCP tries to increase the sending rate linearly; when no acknowledgement is received within a certain time window for a data packet, it resends the lost packet and cut the sending rate in half. All packets are identified by their unique, sequential packet numbers assigned to each TCP data packet by the protocol. In principle, TCP guarantees reliable delivery of data packets. TCP manages the sending rate very conservatively, and there exist many variations of TCP [WMJ+04, KHRlIT02] which attempt to improve the performance of TCP without losing the fairness of the standard TCP protocol. Nowadays, most network applications or higher level protocols, for instance HTTP on the Internet, are implemented based on TCP, which also means that the majority of all network traffic on the Internet uses TCP. However, TCP is not suitable for high speed data transfer on dedicated high speed fiber networks.

TCP has been used on the Internet for decades. TCP has fulfilled the mission of Internet sessions fairly well for our everyday Internet surfing. The speed of TCP is increasing gradually as Internet service providers (ISP) gradually upgrade their switching/routing equipment, so they can gradually increase the bandwidth. In the mid-1990s, it may have taken minutes to load a simple HTML webpage through a 56Kbps modem network, whereas now we can easily view high definition video clips from Youtube with our 10Mbps cable Internet service. However, the performance improvement of Internet applications is not due to the improvement of the TCP protocol, as the TCP protocol has essentially remained the same since then. Applications benefit from the evolution of network hardware technology. This shows that TCP has so far not been a bottleneck on the Internet, and the performance of TCP keeps improving as computer systems are being upgraded, network link bandwidth is going up, and switching/routing equipment are performing better. TCP has so far scaled well on the Internet.

However, when we look at future networks with bandwidths like 1Gbps, 10Gbps or more, TCP is going to break down. Here is an example: On the OptIPuter networks, we have experimented with a simple file transfer between San Diego and Chicago over a 10Gbps link. Without performance tuning, meaning using the system default settings like send/receive buffer size, data packet size, etc., TCP based file transfer speed between these two cities is below 10Mbps; with performance tuning, by increasing the send/receive buffer size of TCP, enabling jumbo frames (9000 bytes per packet instead of the standard 1400 bytes per packet), the file transfer speed between the two cities can go up to 100Mbps. Still, we can only achieve the use of a small fraction of the 10Gbps link capacity. Our investigations on the reasons for this, by using bandwidth performance tools (like iperf or nuttcp), show that the bottleneck is not the hardware, but the transfer protocol (TCP).

The TCP is to eventually become a bottleneck on the Internet, assuming that the bandwidth of current high speed research networks is to be made available for home use in a few years. The

bandwidth of the future networks is to exceed the capabilities of TCP. The way TCP handles packet loss with acknowledgements and re-transfer is unsuitable to be used with high speed long distance data transfer. Round Trip Time (RTT) is the time spent for a data packet to travel from its source node to its destination node. RTT characterizes how far two sites are away from each other on the network. RTT is governed by the network link transfer speed and the transmission latency. On typical data networks, the rule of thumb for the speed of data transfer is 200,000km/s. For example, the distance between San Diego and Chicago is around 3000km, so the RTT can be estimated as 3000*2/200,000 = 30ms. In reality, the measured RTT between our machines at Calit2 in San Diego and those at EVL at UIC is about 90ms. The difference comes from the fact that the actual length of the connecting networks between these two sites is not a straight line between them, and another factor is the latency incurred by switch/router buffering time. Theoretically, two physically co-located machines can have a long network distance if people purposely configure them that way, and two physically distant nodes cannot be close neighbors on the network regardless how they are configured, because of the physical distance between them.

TCP provides a sliding window to solve the transfer speed limits caused by a large RTT. The value of the buffer can be modified to a large value to delay the acceptance of acknowledgements of data packets, which effectively overlap the sending process and the wait for acknowledgement, so as to eliminate the idle time of TCP. The optimal value should be set equal to Bandwidth*RTT. In our case, 10Gbps*90ms = 900MB. This means the operating system needs to allocate 900MB of RAM just for using the TCP protocol. Based on our experiments, even with tuning, we only get around 200Mbps over a 10Gbps link.

2. UDP-Based Protocols

Although few applications on the Internet use UDP, on high-speed Lambda Networks many applications use UDP in the place of TCP. With UDP packets, higher transfer rates can be achieved for long distance data transfer. For example, on the OptIPuter network, we have observed that a large portion of the data is transferred via UDP. UDP-based protocols handle packet loss differently comparing to TCP, but no standard has been developed for it yet. The software engineers typically design and implement protocols which support a specific application. We are going to report on a few typical ways of handling packet loss in UDP protocols.

- **Aggregation Re-Transfer Protocols:** This type of protocols transfers large amounts of data by first dividing them into large data blocks, in the order of tens or hundreds of megabytes, and the data blocks are then sent out via normal UDP packets. But unlike TCP, rather than waiting for individual acknowledgements for those packets, the sender is to wait for a summary from the receiver specifying the list of lost packets in each of the data blocks. The sender then resends the lost packets as a whole. The successful transfer of a data block may take a few rounds, and once a data block has been correctly delivered, the sender proceeds to the next data block. Compared with TCP, aggregation re-transfer protocols are much faster when transferring very large files. But since they cannot promptly re-transfer the packets at the beginning of each data block, these protocols are seldom used for data streaming. An example for this category is RBUDP designed by EVL at the University of Illinois, Chicago.

- **Rate-Based Transfer Protocols:** In a variety of applications like video streaming, data loss below a threshold is unnoticeable to the human eyes. Taking advantage of this property, some protocols focus on controlling the data loss rate by using an adequate data sending rate, and once they find signs of packet loss, they are to promptly reduce the sending rate. The key to the success of this category of protocols is the prediction or early detection of potential packet loss, because it would be too late to wait for the receiver to report data loss, particularly in long distance high-speed data streaming. For instance, LambdaStream predicts packet loss by checking the receiving time stamp of consecutive packets. If the time gap between two consecutive packets increases at the receiver, it predicts that the queuing time in the switches has increased, indicating the packet buffers at the switches are filling up. If this trend continues, the switch buffers eventually becomes full, and packets sent to a full buffer are going to be dropped. To avoid this, LambdaStream reduces the sending rate at the sender until it detects the time gaps of consecutive packets received by the receiver start to decrease, indicating the queue buffers at the switches are getting shorter. LambdaStream cannot guarantee reliable delivery of data, but it can very well control the data loss rate under a small threshold, which makes it feasible for point-to-point multimedia data streaming.

- **Error Correction Methods:** Packet loss does not always lead to unreliable transmissions. Error Correction is a technique using redundant information to recover partial missing data. RAID is a well-adopted error correction method to recover disk failure by using redundant disk drives. In communication coding theory, a wide range of coding techniques have been invented to tolerate partial data loss. The complexities of those coding techniques vary from simple methods like parity check to complicated Forward Error Correction code like LT code, Raptor Code and etc.

Forward Error Correction

Forward Error Correction (FEC) is a mechanism of data transmission error control, whereby redundant data is added to the messages by the sender, known as error correction code. The receiver can then detect and correct transmission errors (within some bound). Since most high bit-rate transfer protocols use unreliable UDP packets to deliver data, they often use a certain type of FEC to recover lost data. FEC can correct a small percentage of random packet loss, depending on the amount of FEC data sent, but is NOT always effective for burst packet loss over a certain bound.

In recent years, a new series of FEC coding techniques have been invented, called the Fountain Code (Wikipedia), which "can generate a limitless sequence of encoding symbols from a given set of original symbols, such that the original symbols can be recovered from any subset of the encoding symbols of size equal or only slightly larger than the number of original symbols." In the network communication context, a symbol usually represents a UDP packet.

All FEC codes come with an overhead. The overhead of the fountain code is called the "erasure rate," which is defined as e, meaning if N is the number of original symbols, $(1 + e)$ $\cdot$ N encoding symbols are sufficient to recover the N original symbols. Fountain code only works for large values of N, so it is impossible to give out a simple fountain code example. But

in principle, the encoding/decoding processes of fountain code are based on a bipartite graph, in which the edges are generated by a degree distribution function (Luby, 2002). The three forms of representation of fountain codes are: the formula, the bipartite graph and the matrix. These forms are equivalent. In this section, we use the matrix representation form because it best illustrates the encoding and decoding processes. Examples of fountain code include online code, LTCode and Raptor Code.

Compared to other fountain code techniques, Raptor Codes are the first known classes of fountain codes with linear encoding and decoding time. Senders and receivers must use the same data structures to encode or decode data, including the same pseudo-random number generator, and the same coding matrices.

Will Parallel Data Transfer be the Trend?

As CPUs start to have more and more cores instead of being faster and faster, as GPUs start to integrate hundreds of processing units, we have seen a clear trend from the industry that parallelism is the right direction to break the limit of the processing capabilities of a single unit. So, from previous analysis, we also envision a parallel data transfer model in some future network applications. We do not know whether parallel data transfer is for sure the trend, but we would still like to explore the possibility of using parallel data streams to satisfy the requirements of future network applications.

In the following chapter, we explain why parallel data transfer is a hard problem, and discuss how FEC codes are helpful but not sufficient for large-scale parallel data streaming protocols. We then introduce the new Cross-Stream coding approach to perform parallel data transfer.

REFERENCES

CALIT2. (n.d.). Retrieved from http://www.calit2.net/newsroom/release.php?id=694

Castro, M., Druschel, P., Kermarrec, A.-M., Nandi, A., Rowstron, A., & Singh, A. (2003). SplitStream: High-bandwidth multicast in cooperative environments. In *Proceedings of the SOSP'03 ACM Symposium on Operating Systems Principles*. Bolton Landing, NY: ACM.

Catalyurek, U., Boman, E., Devine, K., Bozdag, D., & Heaphy, R. (2007). Hypergraph-based dynamic load balancing for adaptive scientific computations. In *Proceedings of IPDPS'07*. IPDPS.

CineGrid. (n.d.). Retrieved from http://www.cinegrid.org

CollectiveAccess. (n.d.). Retrieved from http://www.collectiveaccess.org/

COVISE. (n.d.). Retrieved from http://www.hlrs.de/organization/av/vis/covise/

Cruz-Neira, C., Sandin, D., DeFanti, T., Kenyon, R., & Hart, J. (1992, June). The CAVE®: Audio visual experience automatic virtual environment. *Communications of the ACM*. doi:10.1145/129888.129892.

DeFanti, T. A., Dawe, G., Sandin, D. J., Schulze, J. P., Otto, P., & Girado, J. et al. (2009). The STARCAVE, a third-generation CAVE and virtual reality OptIPortal. *The International Journal of FGCS*, *25*(2), 169–178. doi:10.1016/j.future.2008.07.015.

DeFanti, T. A., Leigh, J., Renambot, L., Jeong, B., & Smarr, L. L. et al. (2009). The OptIPortal, a scalable visualization, storage, and computing interface device for the OptIPuter. *Future Generation Computer Systems*, *25*(2), 114–123. doi:10.1016/j.future.2008.06.016.

DMC4K. (n.d.). Retrieved from http://www.dmc.keio.ac.jp/en/topics/071126-4K.html

Fountain Code. (n.d.). Retrieved from http://en.wikipedia.org/wiki/Fountain_code

GLIF. (n.d.). Retrieved from http://www.glif.is

Gu, Y., & Grossman, R. L. (2007). UDT: UDP-based data transfer for high-speed wide area networks. *Computer Networks*, *51*(7). doi:10.1016/j.comnet.2006.11.009.

He, E., Leigh, J., Yu, O., & DeFanti, T. A. (2002). Reliable blast UDP: Predictable high performance bulk data transfer. In *Proceedings of IEEE Cluster Computing 2002*. Chicago, IL: IEEE.

Hendrickson, B., & Kolda, T. G. (1999). Partitioning rectangular and structurally unsymmetric sparse matrices for parallel processing. *SIAM Journal on Scientific Computing*, *21*(6), 2048–2072. doi:10.1137/S1064827598341475.

Herr, L., et al. (2005). *International real-time streaming of 4K digital cinema, demonstration in iGrid*. Retrieved from http://www.igrid2005.org/program/applications/videoservices_rtvideo.html

4. KStreaming. (n.d.). Retrieved from http://www.envision.purdue.edu/4k stream/

Leigh, J., Renambot, L., Johnson, A., Jagodic, R., Hur, H., Hofer, E., & Lee, D. (2008). Scalable adaptive graphics middleware for visualization streaming and collaboration in ultra resolution display environments. In *Proceedings of the Workshop on Ultrascale Visualization* (UltraVis 2008). Austin, TX: UltraVis.

Liu, S., & Herr, L. (2008). *CineGrid exchange*. Paper presented in MSST Symposium. Baltimore, MD.

Liu, S., Schulze, J. P., & DeFanti, T. A. (2009). Synchronizing parallel data streams via cross-stream coding. In *Proceedings of the IEEE International Conference on Networking, Architecture, and Storage*, (pp. 333-340). IEEE.

LOCKSS Program. (n.d.). Retrieved from http://lockss.stanford.edu/lockss/Home

Luby, M. (2002). LT-codes. In *Proceedings of 43rd Annu. IEEE Symp. Foundations of Computer Science* (FOCS). Vancouver, Canada: IEEE.

NLR. (n.d.). *National LambdaRail*. Retrieved from http://www.nlr.net

OPIPUTER. (n.d.). Retrieved from http://www.optiputer.net

Pieper, G., DeFanti, T. A., Liu, Q., Katz, M., Papadopoulos, P., & Keefe, J. et al. (2009). Visualizing science: The OptIPuter project. *SciDAC Review*, *12*, 32–41.

Rajasekar, M. A. R., Hou, C.-Y., Christopher, L., & Marciano, R. A., Wan, M., Schroeder, W., ... Zhu, B. (2010). iRODS primer: Integrated rule-oriented data systems. San Rafael, CA: Morgan-Claypool Publishers.

Raptor Code. (n.d.). Retrieved from http://algo.epfl.ch/contents/output/presents/Raptor-Bangalore.pdf

Renambot, L., Jeong, B., Hur, H., Johnson, A., & Leigh, J. (2009). Enabling high resolution collaborative visualization in display rich virtual organizations. *Future Generation Computer Systems*, *25*(2), 161–168. doi:10.1016/j.future.2008.07.004.

Renambot, L., Jeong, B., & Leigh, J. (2007). Realtime compression for high-resolution content. In *Proceedings of the Access Grid Retreat 2007*. Chicago, IL: Access.

SAGE. (n.d.). Retrieved from http://www.evl.uic.edu/cavern/sage/index.php

Shirai, D., Kawano, T., Fujii, T., Kaneko, K., Ohta, N., & Ono, S. et al. (2009). Real time switching and streaming transmission of uncompressed 4K motion pictures. *Future Generation Computer Systems*, *25*(2), 192–197. doi:10.1016/j.future.2008.07.003.

Shokrollahi, A. (2006). Raptor codes. *IEEE Transactions on Information Theory*, *52*, 2551–2567. doi:10.1109/TIT.2006.874390.

Smarr, L. (2009). The OptIPuter and its applications. In *Proceedings of the IEEE LEOS Summer Topicals Meeting on Future Global Networks*, (pp. 151-152). IEEE. doi: 10.1109/LEOSST.2009.5226201

The Digital Dilemma. (2008). *The science and technology council of the academy of motion picture arts and sciences (AMPAS)*. Los Angeles, CA: AMPAS.

Vishwanath, V., Leigh, J., He, E., Brown, M. D., Long, L., & Renambot, L. ... DeFanti, T. A. (2006). Wide-area experiments with LambdaStream over dedicated high-bandwidth networks. In *Proceedings of IEEE INFOCOM*. IEEE.

Vishwanath, V., Leigh, J., Shimizu, T., Nam, S., Renambot, L., & Takahashi, H. ... Kamatani, O. (2008). The rails toolkit (RTK) - Enabling end-system topology-aware high end computing. In *Proceedings of the 4th IEEE International Conference on e-Science*. IEEE.

Vishwanath, V., Shimizu, T., Takizawa, M., Obana, K., & Leigh, J. (2007). Towards terabit/s systems: Performance evaluation of multi-rail systems. In Proceedings of Supercomputing (SC07). Reno, NV: SC.

Xia, H., & Chien, A. (2007). RobuSTore: A distributed storage architecture with robust and high performance. In Proceedings of Supercomputing (SC07). Reno, NV: SC.

Xia, H., & Chien, A. A. (2007). RobuSTore: A distributed storage architecture with robust and high performance. In *Proceedings of ACM/IEEE International Conference on High Performance Computing and Communications* (SC'07). ACM/IEEE.

Zoltan. (n.d.). Retrieved from http://www.cs.sandia.gov/Zoltan/

Chapter 12
Parallel Data Transfer Protocol

Yushi Shen
Microsoft Corporation, USA

Ling Wu
EMC² Corporation, USA

Yale Li
Microsoft Corporation, USA

Shaofeng Liu
Microsoft Corporation, USA

Qian Wen
Endronic Corp, USA

ABSTRACT

Transferring very high quality digital objects over the optical network is critical in many scientific applications, including video streaming/conferencing, remote rendering on tiled display walls, 3D virtual reality, and so on. Current data transfer protocols rely on the User Datagram Protocol (UDP) as well as a variety of compression techniques. However, none of the protocols scale well to the parallel model of transferring large scale graphical data. The existing parallel streaming protocols have limited synchronization mechanisms to synchronize the streams efficiently, and therefore, are prone to slowdowns caused by significant packet loss of just one stream. In this chapter, the authors propose a new parallel streaming protocol that can stream synchronized multiple flows of media content over optical networks through Cross-Stream packet coding, which not only can tolerate random UDP packet losses but can also aim to tolerate unevenly distributed packet loss patterns across multiple streams to achieve a synchronized throughput with reasonable coding overhead. They have simulated the approach, and the results show that the approach can generate steady throughput with fluctuating data streams of different data loss patterns and can transfer data in parallel at a higher speed than multiple independent UDP streams.

DOI: 10.4018/978-1-4666-4801-2.ch012

INTRODUCTION

In the recent years, CineGrid (CineGrid) has led the new trend of using high bandwidth networks, to transfer very high quality digital content, for real-time show and for digital preservation. Although CineGrid has performed many successful demonstrations of 4K video (Shirai & et. Al., 2009) (Herr, 2005), we also foresee the challenges of designing new protocols, which can scale the current solution to applications demanding higher bandwidth and higher resolution digital content. Now a days, ultra-high resolution displays have become a standard infrastructure in scientific research. These displays are typically achieved by tiling together an array of standard LCD displays into a display wall, using a PC cluster to drive it. (DeFanti & et. Al., 2009). Figure 1 a) and b) show different settings of display walls: the HiPerSpace uses fifty five 30' LCD displays to form a display wall with more than two million effective pixels; the StarCAVE (DeFanti & et. Al., 2009) uses 16 high-definition projectors to construct a 3D virtual room, where people can navigate 3D virtual reality objects.

Meanwhile, high-speed research in optical networks (GLIF) makes it possible for scientists to use these ultra-high resolution displays over long distances, in their scientific applications like very-high-definition video streaming/conferencing (OPIPUTER), real-time data visualization generated by remote scientific instruments and etc. As a perfect example of the combination of display walls and high-speed network, the OptiPuter (OPIPUTER) (Smarr, 2009) research project, funded by the American National Science Foundation, constructed a 1Gbps-10Gbps optical network infrastructure and middleware, aiming to achieve interactive access of remote gigabyte to terabyte visualization data objects, and bring them to its visual interface, the OptIPortals (DeFanti & et. Al., 2009).

However, the scaling up of display devices, from a single PC with a single display to a cluster of PCs with a cluster of displays, has brought up challenges on how to feed data into these display devices. These challenges make the traditional single data source communication model obsolete, and bring forth the creation of a new multiple-to-multiple communication model, which needs very-high-bandwidth parallel data streaming communications, between terminal display devices, while still appearing as a point-to-point communication between them. This put challenges on the traditional transport protocols. The widely adopted Transport Control Protocol (TCP) is slow

Figure 1. a) HIPerSpace, one of the world's largest display wall in Calit2, UC San Diego, has 286,720,000 effective pixels. b) The STARCAVE, a third-generation CAVE and virtual reality OptiPortal in Calit2, UC San Diego, ~68,000,000 pixels.

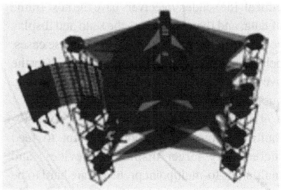

because of its window-based congestion control mechanism, particularly for long distance communications. Alternatives like RBUDP (He & et. Al., 2002), UDT (Gu & Grossman, 2007), and LambdaStream (Vishwanath & et. Al., 2006) are the recently developed UDP-based protocols, focusing on high-speed file transfer or real-time data streaming in between two end nodes. These protocols are point-to-point rate-based, which means they support one sender and one receiver, and recover lost UDP packets by resending them, and the sender controls the sending rate to minimize packets loss. RBUDP, for instance, uses a bitmap to maintain a list of lost UDP packets and do a multi-round communication to recover lost packets, which usually takes 2-5 round trip time (RTT), to retrieve a GB file correctly; LambdaStream detects packet loss based on the gap between the receiving time of two consecutive UDP packets, and if that gap is bigger than expected, the sender reduces the sending rate accordingly. These protocols, however, cannot be scaled to the multiple-to-multiple communication model in a straightforward way.

On the other hand, existing parallel data streaming protocols do not sufficiently address the synchronization issue of multiple parallel data streams. Existing multiple-to-multiple communication models (SAGE) (4KStreaming) synchronize the senders and receivers, by adding a synchronization module to the senders and/or receivers, and the synchronization module waits until all the senders/receivers have the next frame of data, and then broadcasts the send and display command to all senders/receivers. In these cases, behaviors of individual data streams can affect the overall protocol performance or data integrity, e.g. burst packet loss of one data stream.

In summary, point-to-point or point-to-multiple protocols are not sufficient to feed increasingly larger displaying devices, and multipoint-to-multipoint protocols are hard to be efficiently synchronized. In this chapter, we study the multiple-to-multiple communication model, and present a new Cross-Stream Transfer Protocol (CSTP), which focuses on the synchronization challenges of the parallel communication model. We have experimented with our protocols, and the results show that even with fluctuating network flows and unevenly distributed packet losses in the parallel streams, our approach can achieve reliable synchronized throughput.

FORWARD ERROR CORRECTION

Forward Error Correction (FEC) is:

A system of error control for data transmission, whereby the sender adds redundant data to its messages, also known as the error correction code. This allows the receiver to detect and correct errors (within some bound), without the need to ask the sender for additional data.

Since most high bit-rate transfer protocols use unreliable UDP packets to deliver data, they often use a certain type of FEC to recover lost data. FEC can correct a small percentage of random packet loss, but is not always effective for burst packet loss over a certain bound.

In recent years, a new series of FEC coding techniques, is called the *fountain code* (Fountain Code) (Shokrollahi, 2006) (Raptor Code) (Luby, 2002), which "can generate limitless sequence of encoding symbols from a given set of original symbols, such that the original symbols can be recovered from any subset of the encoding symbols of size equal or only slightly larger than the number of original symbols." (Fountain Code) In our case, a symbol represents a UDP packet.

All FEC codes come with an overhead. The overhead of fountain code is defined as α, meaning if N is the number of original symbols, $(1 + \alpha) \cdot N$ is the number of encoding symbols sufficient to recover the N original symbols. Fountain code only works for large N, so it is impossible to give a simple fountain code example. But in principle, the encoding and decoding processes are based on a bipartite graph, in which the edges are generated by a degree distribution function. The three forms of representation of fountain codes are shown in Figure 2: the formula, the bipartite graph or the matrix. In this chapter, we use the matrix representation, because it best explains the encoding and decoding processes. Examples of fountain code include online code, LTCode, Raptor Code (Shokrollahi, 2006) and etc.

In the next section, we explain why synchronized parallel data transfer is a hard problem, and discuss how FEC codes are helpful, but not sufficient for large-scale parallel data streaming protocols.

PARALLEL DATA TRANSFER CHALLENGES

To be simple, we use 4K media streaming as an example. "4K" is an ultra-high quality motion picture format. As defined by the Digital Cinema Initiative (DCI) Consortium of Hollywood Studios in 2003, 4K has up to 4096 pixels per line, and up to 2160 lines per frame. In most applications, 4K refers to a frame size of 3840x2160 pixels, which is exactly four times the resolution of 1080p HDTV. In this paper, by default, a 4K image means an image with 3840x2160 pixels. 4K images are usually captured by 4K cameras, stored in TIFF files, and shown by 4K projectors. Streaming uncompressed 4K video is very difficult, because of the high data bit-rate. For instance, the bit-rate of streaming RGBA (32bit/pixel) 4K images at 24fps is over 6Gbps, which is too high to be handled by one stream, and has to be done by multiple data streams.

Alternatively, assuming we have infinite 4K images, we can use multiple senders to stream these images to multiple remote receivers. Each of the senders sends out a portion of the images via UDP packets, and each of the receivers receives the corresponding parts of the images, and displays the images simultaneously on a display wall.

Ideally, if all parallel streams are reliably delivered, there is going to be no issues. However, in reality, UDP packet loss is inevitable in our high-bandwidth applications, which leads to synchronization problems. To our best knowledge, the UDP packet loss pattern of large scale parallel data streams over optical networks has not been very well studied. Based on our experience and experiments over the OptIPuter network, UDP

Figure 2. a) V_1-V_4 are original data packets; Y_1-Y_5 are encoded data packets. The formula and bipartite graph have the same meanings. b) Matrix element M[I,j] is marked to black iff data packet V_i is included in code packet Y_j.

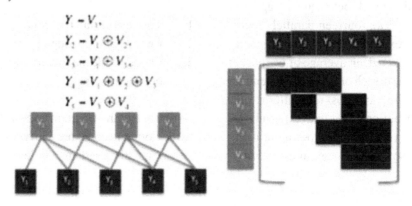

packet loss behavior is very nondeterministic, and is basically a function of many variables, including the end-node hardware configuration and real time workload, OS version, OS scheduler, NIC configurations, the switch/router scheduling, queuing and buffer sizes, and many other factors. In particular, if there are multiple streams on the same fiber link, nearly saturating the capacity of the link, we have found the following UDP packet loss behavior over the link:

1. Very frequently, burst packet loss for some individual streams may happen, and cannot be recovered by simple FEC code. We can either ignore that which leads to missing data, or we can go back to the sender to request lost packets, which is time consuming, and can keep other streams waiting.
2. Bandwidth is not evenly shared by streams due to many reasons, e.g., the UDP protocol is not fair. Switch and router scheduling may not be fair; queues in the switch/router may not be fair; end node capability may vary with time; occasional interference from other network applications may bring fluctuation to data streams and so on.
3. The overall/average packet loss rates of all data streams are stable, which means the switching capabilities are stable.

Figure 3 shows experiments verifying the packet loss behaviors, and packet loss distribution of parallel streams over CaveWave, in a10Gbps dedicated optical network between Chicago and San Diego. In Fig 3 a), fourteen parallel "iperf" tests are invoked, exceeding the 10Gbps capacity of the link. As expected, an average of 6% packet loss rate is observed in each of the five independent experiments, but the packet loss rate patterns vary a lot, and the distribution varies with experiments. Fig 3 b) is a plot of a similar experiment using video streaming software, to measure frame-by-

frame packet loss rate and to understand the burst packet loss property. It shows that burst packet loss occurs to random streams frequently.

Our experiments have verified that by using multiple data streams to transfer data between multiple senders/receivers, new challenges are being discovered. The FEC code is helpful in many cases, but not sufficient to handle burst packet loss for individual streams. In the next section, we discuss our new parallel streaming protocol: the Cross-Stream Transfer Protocol (CSTP).

CSTP: CROSS-STREAM TRANSFER PROTOCOL

Loosely coupled streams are hard to coordinate; coupling data streams bring new ideas of tolerating single stream burst packet loss. If one data stream experiences burst packet loss, the receiver does not have to fetch the lost packets from its sender, instead, it gets the data from its peers. Considering the high Round Trip Time (RTT) to fetch a bit from remote senders, being able to get it locally is a significant advantage. However, it is difficult to couple parallel data streams, because the data streams are independently carrying non-correlated data. To do that, we need to first correlate the data in the independent data streams. Therefore, we come up with the idea of using encoding methods in our parallel streaming protocol, which should be able to:

1. Tolerate certain percentage of packet loss;
2. Encode and decode efficiently;
3. Encode multiple streams to carry information between them.

We select the fountain code as the basis of our work. Fountain codes are one type of the FEC code, and is mostly used in wireless communication

Figure 3. a) Parelle iperf experiments between Chicago and San Diego. 14 streams, 750Mbps/stream (10.5Gbps) over 10Gbps optical network. b). Parallel video-streaming experiments between Chicago and San Diego.

13 streams, 700Mbps/stream (9.1Gbps) over 10Gbps optical network, the test has lasted 150 seconds, X-axis: frame serial No., Y-axis: loss rate of each frame in each stream (14% - 0%). Average packet loss rate is around 6% in all experiments. X-axis: five independent experiments Y-axis: packet loss rate of 14 streams

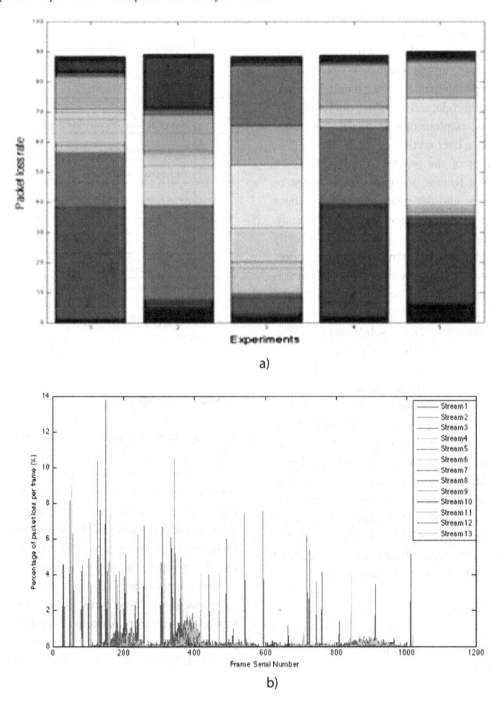

environments, where the receivers are sometimes not capable of sending back acknowledgements to notify lost packets. In computer science, fountain code has been used for high-bandwidth multicast (Castro & et. Al., 2003), the robust storage system RubuSTORE (Xia & Chien, 2007), and so on. But to our best knowledge, it has not been used in high bandwidth parallel data transfer applications to tolerate burst packet loss. We explore and analyze the problem of coupling parallel streams using fountain code, and introduce our new CSTP scheme. The implementation in detail is to be discussed in a later section.

The input of the protocol is a sequence of original data frames, for example, a series of video frames, and the goal is to transfer these data frames to multiple receivers synchronously. One original data frame is divided into S equally sized sub-frames, sent out by S individual senders to their corresponding receivers. The division is not necessarily the extra cost, if the sub-frames are acquired independently, for example, by S independent cameras. Each sub-frame is further divided into N equally sized *original data packets*, and the original data packets are encoded into *regular code packets* using fountain code. In addition to the regular code packets, we encode a certain percentage of cross-stream code packets, which are *XOR'ed* with the regular code packets from different sub-frames, which are called *pipe packets*. The senders send out the combination of both regular code packets and pipe code packets. Upon receiving those code packets, the receivers use the regular code packets to decode original data and use pipe packets to communicate between streams to help the lossy streams decode.

1. Definitions

The definitions used in our protocol are summarized in Table 1.

Table 1. Definitions of CSTP

Symbol	Definition
S	Number of data streams
N	Number of original packets for each sub-frame
α	Overhead of Fountain Code
β	Overhead of transfer protocol
N'	Number of packets (regular code packets and pipe packets) sent to each receiver $N' = N \cdot (1+\alpha) \cdot (1+\beta)$
$M_{1...S}$	Fountain Code generating matrices of S data streams, that are known to all senders and receivers beforehand
$V_{[1..S][1...N]}$	The original data packets
$Y_{[1..S][1...N']}$	The encoded code packet
d_F	*Code Degree*, the number of *XOR*'ed data packets in a regular code packet
D_F	*Code Degree Distribution*, the degree distribution function of the fountain code.
p	*Pipe Width*, percentage of pipe packets
d_S	*Stream Degree*, equals to 1 for a regular code packet, or 2...S for a pipe packet, meaning how many streams a pipe packet connects
D_S	*Stream Degree Distribution*, the distribution of d_s. For example, when S is small, we use $D_S(x) = p \cdot x^S + (1-p) \cdot x$

2. Generating M[1..S]

$M_{[1...S]}$ are pre-generated generating matrices for CSTP. Similar to the fountain code generating matrix examples we have seen in Figure 2, $M_{[i]}$ is basically a standard fountain code matrix with extra pipe packet columns. So, to generate $M_{[i]}$, we first create a standard fountain code matrix, then randomly insert pipe columns into the matrix. Each pipe column is an assembled column of multiple columns, from the S standard fountain code matrices of S streams. A sample is shown in Figure 4. A pipe packet can consist of code packets from all streams, or only consist of code packets from two streams. In the D_S function in

Figure 4. Sample matrices. The portion in the big circle marked on M2 identifies a regular fountain code matrix; the chained four small circles identified a pipe packet in M3.

S=4, N=4, N'=6, p=16.7%, X-axis: Code data $Y_{[4][6]}$, Y-axis: Original data $V_{[4][4]}$, Pipe packets (marked as red): Y_{13}, Y_{25}, Y_{32}, Y_{44}

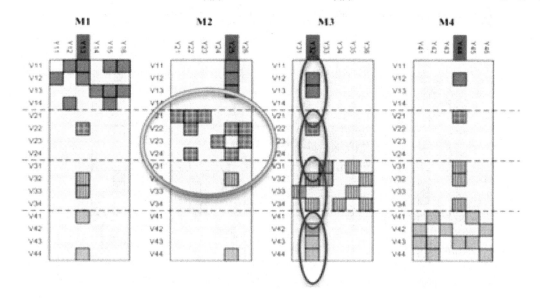

Table 1, all pipe packets consist of code packets from all S streams. We use a different D_s in our experiments. With the distribution function, 50% of the pipe packets have stream degree S, and 50% have stream degree 2. A pipe packet with stream degree equaling 2 consists of one regular code packet of its own, and one regular code packet randomly selected from other S-1 data streams.

3. Encoding and Decoding Algorithms

Figure 5 illustrates how the decoding process works, and how pipe packets can help each other to recover lost packets in one stream. Assuming receiver R1, R2 and R4 have received enough packets, and R3 has lost a big portion of the

Box 1. Encoding Algorithm

For each encoder [1…S]:
Step1: Break its original sub-frame into equal sized data packets;
Step 2: Get next column from M_p, if it's a regular code packet, XOR all packets that are valid in that column; if it is a pipe packet, fetch data from other encoders and XOR all packets that are valid in that column;
Step 3: If enough packets are generated, stop, else go to Step 2.

Box 2. Decoding Algorithm

For each decoder [1…S]
Step 1: Run a native Fountain Code decoding algorithm;
Step 2: Use pipe packet code to communicate with other decoders: if data is needed, request data from other decoders; if data is available send to other decoders;
Step3: Repeat Step2 until all data are decoded or the decoding process halts.

Figure 5. a) Assuming R_1, R_2 and R_4 have received all the packets and successfully recovered their original data (circled), but R_3 lost two code packets: Y_{34} and Y_{35} and need help. b) The decoded original data packets are distributed to each other via pipe packets, and all pipe packets columns now become regular columns of M_3. c) R_3 collects pipe packets from R_1, R_2 and R_4, and now can decode its original data.

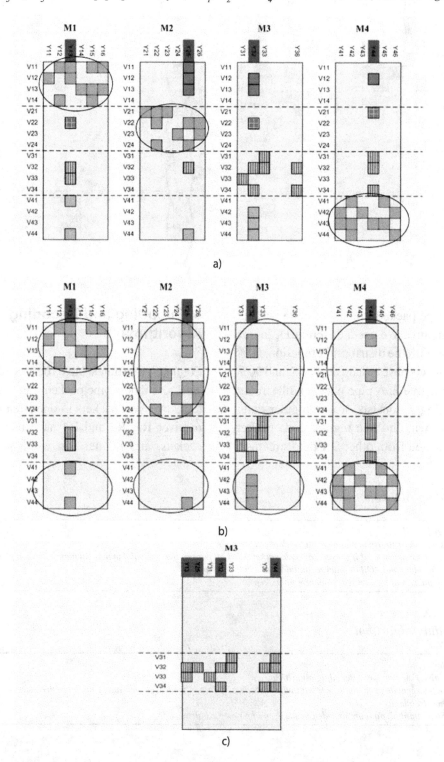

a)

b)

c)

packets, R1, R2 and R4 then can recovery their data easily by performing the standard fountain code decoding algorithm, as illustrated in Figure 5 a). When they finish the self-decoding process, all the code packets in their pipe packets have also been decoded through local communication, shown in Figure 5 b). The remaining part of these pipe packets are extra code packets for R3. These extra code packets are sent to R3, so that R3 now has enough code packet for self-decoding, as shown in Figure 5 c).

CSTP IMPLEMENTATION

CSTP has multiple senders and multiple receivers. The goal is to send sequential data frames from the senders to the receivers synchronously. Each data frame is initially divided into multiple sub-frames, and each sender sends out just one sub-frame to its receiver.

The senders keep reading sequential data sub-frames, encode them and send the encoded sub-frames to their corresponding receivers; the receivers receive the data, and do a cross-stream decoding to recover the original data. The senders and receivers communicate via a high-speed network. This topology, known as a dumbbell topology, well characterizes the connection between CineGrid nodes.

CSTP Senders

The sending process consists of three major procedures: reading, encoding and sending, which are controlled by a timer-based synchronizer. Due to the deterministic behavior of the senders, they are not the bottleneck in our protocol.

The CSTP encoding process is implemented using the coding matrix, as shown in Figure 6. The coding matrix is a two dimensional (2D) linked list, associated with four memory buffers: the DataBuf, CodeBuf, PipeBuf and ExtraBuf. Each

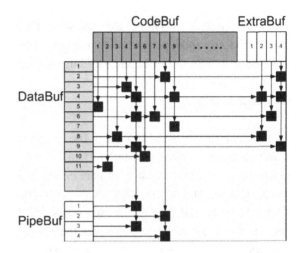

Figure 6. Code Matrix Data Structure

node (i, j) in the 2D linked list means the code packet i contains data packet j in its "XOR" list. The DataBuf stores the original data sub-frame read from the input devices, e.g. a partition of the video frame file, or input from one of multiple cameras. The CodeBuf and ExtraBuf are generated from the DataBuf using the coding matrix (Also refer to Figure 2). The CodeBuf includes regular code packets and pipe packets; the ExtraBuf includes only regular code packets for the peer senders to construct their pipe packets. The PipeBuf are regular code packets received from the peer senders. Each packet in the ExtraBuf is destined to the PipeBuf of one of the other senders.

A regular code packet, only composed of local data packets in the CodeBuf packets, are encoded immediately from the DataBuf. A pipe packet that contains packets in the PipeBuf can wait until that packet is received from the peers. Practically, the senders encode the ExtraBuf first, and distribute the ExtraBuf packets to its peer senders, so that the encoding of CodeBuf does not need to wait for the PipeBuf packets. Therefore, the encoding process is a deterministic process. Finally, the sender only sends out the code packets in the CodeBuf to the receiver, while ExtraBuf is not sent.

CSTP Receivers

The receivers have two major threads: streaming and decoding, and operate on two major data structures: a circular buffer and a coding matrix.

Circular Buffer

The circular buffer is used to buffer the received data sub-frames. It has two pointers: a reader's pointer and a writer's pointer, and are controlled by the reading and writing threads respectively. The writing thread (stream thread) reads UDP packets from the network, and saves the packet into the blocks pointed by the current writer's pointer. The reading thread (decoding thread) fetches a block from the circular buffer, and sends it to the decoder for decoding. Both threads move forward their pointers, after the buffer read and write are finished in a circular way.

Decoding Matrix

Although the decoding matrix data structure is the same as the encoding matrix data structure, the decoding algorithm is much more sophisticated. After the reading thread fetches a sub-frame from the circular buffer, it fills the decoding matrix's CodeBuf and associates with it a Mask Variable, which is an array of "Boolean", marking each packet in the CodeBuf either as "Lost" or "Received," so that only the "Received" packets are used for decoding. Because the packet loss is not known before hand, the decoding process is non-deterministic.

In the decoding process of the standard LT Code or Raptor code, the decoder keeps looking for packets in the CodeBuf, whose remaining code degree equals one, then decodes that packet by copying the code packet to the data packet, and distributes the decoded data packet to all other code packets containing that data packet, until

the process stops without any further possible movement.

In our algorithm, we first perform this standard decoding process, based on the CodeBuf and the Mask Variable using the decoding matrix. After this is done, a decoder either has recovered all its packets in the DataBuf, or only partially decodes the DataBuf due to heavy packet loss in the CodeBuf. If all the decoders have successfully decoded their sub-frames, the whole data frame is successfully received and we can proceed to the next data frame.

However, if some receivers cannot recover all the data packets, the decoders need to work together to recover the un-decoded part. The Extrabuf and PipeBuf are used to communicate between decoders, to decode that part through pipe packets.

From the PipeBuf to the ExtraBuf

Assuming receiver A has received a pipe packet

$$Y = V_{A,1} \oplus V_{A,2} \oplus \ldots \oplus V_{A,k} \oplus Y_B$$

and has decoded all it data packets $V_{A,[1..k]}$, it now can decode Y_B by doing k XOR operations on Y, and

$$Y_B = Y \oplus V_{A,1} \oplus V_{A,2} \oplus \ldots \oplus V_{A,k}$$

Y_B becomes a new regular code packet in A's PipeBuf for receiver B, so that it can be sent to B's ExtraBuf to help B decode un-decoded data packets, as if B receives one more regular code packet from its sender.

From the Extrabuf to the PipeBuf

In each decoder, the ExtraBuf is set to "zero" before the decoding process. During the first phase of the decoding process, in addition to the standard decoding process, all the decoded data packets are also distributed to the associated code packets in the ExtraBuf, and the code packets in the ExtraBuf "XOR" the data packet to itself. Therefore, for the decoders that have successfully decoded all its data packets, they also have generated the code packets in the ExtraBuf. As we have explained before, ExtraBuf are used by the encoder to encode a pipe packet during the encoding process, and are not sent to the receivers. Just as how the encoder sends the code packet in the ExtraBuf to its peers for generating a pipe packet in the peers, now, the newly generated code packets in the ExtraBuf are sent to the same pipe packet. For example, assuming a pipe packet Y is located in receiver A, and

$$Y = V_{A,1} \oplus V_{A,2} \oplus ... \oplus V_{A,k} \oplus Y_B \oplus Y_C \oplus Y_D$$

once B, C and D generate Y_B, Y_C and and Y_D in their ExtraBuf, Y_B, Y_C, and Y_D are sent to A, so that the pipe packet Y in A can be converted into a new regular code packet Y',

$$Y' = Y \oplus Y_B \oplus Y_C \oplus Y_D = V_{A,1} \oplus V_{A,2} \oplus ... \oplus V_{A,k}$$

Y' is a new code packet for A, as if A has received a new code packet from its sender.

It's straightforward to see that ExtraBuf and PipeBuf are mutually beneficial. In practice, Step (a) and Step (b) start as early as possible, overlapping with the self-decoding process, and repeat in the post decoding process.

Reliable Delivery

In the current CSTP implementation, the goal is set to tolerate unevenly distributed burst packet loss within a curtain threshold, so when significant packet loss happens for all streams, CSTP cannot

guarantee reliable delivery of data. Based on our experiments, CSTP can tolerate burst packet losses really well and is sufficient for reliable delivery. However, in case the packet loss is really significant for most data streams, and after the cross-stream decoding process, there are still unrecovered data packets, we have to retrieve more data from the senders for reliable delivery.

Two categories of issues have to be discussed: the dynamic sending rate and lost packet resending. We have not included these in the current CSTP implementation, and we are to leave it for our future work. Dynamic sending rate has been studies in (He & et. Al., 2002) (Gu & Grossman, 2007) (Vishwanath & et. Al., 2006), and in CSTP we have a similar issue. For lost packet resending, other approaches maintain a bitmap for lost packets and retransfer lost packets, which is straightforward but ineffective, because the senders have to keep all the data in the main memory to avoid disk access. For big file transfer, GB memory are used to keep the original data, like in RBUDP. In CSTP, we can only keep a small percentage of extra code packets in the senders. So when the receivers ask for more data, the senders simply send out these new code packets, which can be less expensive than saving all original data for retransfer.

Synchronization

The synchronization mechanisms are widely used in a cluster environment. In CSTP, both senders and receivers use a synchronizer to do a frame-by-frame synchronization. The synchronization scheme is simple: all senders/receivers send a "sync" message to a master node, and when the master node collects all the "sync" signal, it broadcasts a "CFM" signal to all other nodes, and all nodes proceed when they received the "CFM" signals. This mechanism is similar to other systems like COVISE (COVISE) and etc.

SCALE CSTP TO LARGE NUMBER OF STREAMS

In CSTP, both encoding and decoding algorithms incur certain communication cost among nodes within a cluster. In the encoding process, the communication is deterministic, while decoding communication is more indeterministic, because the decoding process is subject to packet loss. But on both sides, the communication cost of the CSTP is reasonably small because only pipe packets are needed to communicate among nodes. In the worst case, the total communication cost's upper bound is $(S - 1) \cdot p$, e.g., if p=0.05, S=4, the decoding communication cost is about 15% the size of the original data.

The scalability issue is more important when S is bigger. For a small number of parallel streams, the stream degree distribution function in Table 1 works well. However, for larger scale applications that use more than ten parallel streams, the communication cost increases linearly with the number of streams. We are designing and experimenting different degree distribution functions, and our preliminary results show that a constant communication overhead is achievable.

Experimental Results

In our experiments, we have evaluated the decoding performance of the most recent version of the fountain code, simulated multiple data streams using Cross-Stream coding algorithms, tested the stability of the decoding algorithm with fluctuating data flows and various packet loss rates, and compared the transfer speed of CSTP with parallel RBUDP. The fountain code we have selected is the Raptor Code, which has linear time encoding and decoding algorithms. The pre-code and LTCode we have used are those suggested in (Raptor Code):

```
Precode: LDGM + HDPC
LTCode degree distribution:
```

$$D_F(x) = 0.0156 \cdot x^{40} + 0.0797 \cdot x^{11}$$
$$+0.111 \cdot x^{10} + 0.113 \cdot x^4$$
$$+0.210 \cdot x^3 + 0.456 \cdot x^2 + 0.00971 \cdot x$$

The average code degree of LT-Code is 4.6116, and the average degree of the Raptor Code is the sum of LTCode degree and pre-code degree, which is a function of N, e.g., when N=1024, Raptor Code has an average code degree of 13. The average code degree determines the complexity of the decoding algorithms. Theoretically, assuming the packet size is fixed, the complexity of the decoding algorithm is $O(D \cdot N)$, where D is the average degree of the Raptor Code, N is the number of original data packets.

Raptor Code Decoding Performance

An important measurement is how much overhead is required, for the Raptor Code to recover the original data. Although this has been discussed in related works, we have done our own experiments. In our test, N cannot be too small since the Raptor Code is based on the probability theory, and cannot hold for small values of N. When N is around 1000, Raptor Code can recover original data with an overhead of around 6-8%.

To test the decoding speed of the Raptor Code, we run our implementation of Raptor Code (there is no open source implementation of the Raptor Code), with one thread to decode native Raptor Code, and the decoding speed is shown in Table 2. We have tested packets of 7680 and 3840 byte sizes.

The decoding algorithm is CPU intensive, and consumes significant memory bandwidth. Cur-

Table 2. Decode speed of the Raptor Code

#of Original Packets	#of Raptor Code Packets	Decoding Percentage	Decoding Speed (7680B/pkt)	Decoding Speed (3840B/pkt)
512	650	100%	2.51Gbps	3.17Gbps
1024	1200	100%	2.00Gbps	2.22Gbps
2048	2400	100%	1.68Gbps	1.82Gbps
4096	4800	100%	1.45Gbps	1.52Gbps

rently in our single thread experiments, the decoding algorithm is capable of decoding a single HD stream. The results also suggest that the cache miss rate is an important factor. As shown, when we have increased the number of original packets, the decoding speed decreases. We believe this is because the cache miss rate has become higher with a larger data set.

CSTP Recovery Performance

First, we want to understand whether streams can help each other, when one stream is losing significantly more packets than the others. We use these settings:

$$p = 5\%$$
$$S = 4$$
$$N = 1024$$
$$D_s(x) = p \cdot x^S + (1 - p) \cdot x$$

Our next experiment tests how Cross-Stream Code works with random packet loss across all streams. We have encoded 1000 frames into four sets of code packets using four generating matrices, and then simulated sending a certain number N' of code packets to each receiver. We do not assume all the packets are correctly received, but have purposely dropped some of them. Based on our network assumption, the packet loss rate of each receiver is randomly generated with every new frame. The average packet loss rate of receivers is set to 2%, 3% and 4% respectively.

We then plotted a figure with the X-axis representing N', and the Y-axis representing the possibility of successful recovery of the full frame. The result is shown in Figure 9, which proves that with a reasonable overhead, e.g. 5% to 15%, our approach can recover significant packet loss in all streams and the possibility of fully recovered frames is ~99.99%.

Burst Packet Loss Recovery

With careful control of sending rate, we are able to deliver data with only a small percentage of average packet loss. Ideally, if the packet losses are totally random and evenly distributed across all streams, simple FEC can solve the problem. But in practice as shown in Figure 3, the packet loss patterns are not uniformly distributed, and no FEC can recover burst packets. Here we compare the recovery capability of native FEC code and CSTP, under a variety of assumed packet loss patterns. We use 10 parallel data streams to do the comparison, with an assumption of Average Packet Loss (APL=7.5%). The value of APL is chosen to make the comparison more interesting. The settings of CSTP are:

$$p = 5\%$$
$$S = 10$$
$$N = 1024$$
$$D_s(x) = p \cdot (50\% \cdot x^S + 50\% \cdot x^2) + (1 - p) \cdot x$$

The meaning of $D_s(x)$ is: for the pipe packets, 50% have stream degree S, 50% have stream degree 2.

The four Packet Loss Patterns we experimented are:

1. **Unified Pattern:** All packet losses are evenly distributed across all data streams;
2. **Linear Pattern:** Packet losses of all data streams fit into a linear pattern;

Figure 7. These lines show the function of frame recovery percentage to the number of issued packets to receivers, and the lower figure is a zoomed-in version of the top-right corner of the upper figure.

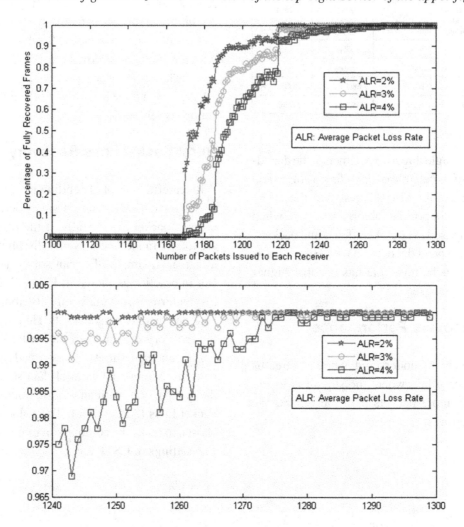

3. **Polynomial Pattern:** Packet losses of all data streams form a polynomial pattern;
4. **Random Chop:** We treat the overall packet loss as a pie, and randomly chop the pie to divide it into 10 parts.

Our experiments reveal significant advantage of CSTP over the native FEC code. In all four cases, CSTP can recover 100% original data in all 10 data streams. But the independent FEC code fails in some data streams in all cases. With packet losses evenly distributed, the FEC code only recovers about 90% of the original data in

two streams; with more unevenly distributed burst packet losses the FEC code's performance is much worse than CSTP.

CSTP Parallel Transfer Performance

We then compare the transfer speed of CSTP with a well-adopted UDP transfer protocol called RBUDP. To measure the protocol performance and avoid disk operations, we revised the RBUDP protocol by eliminating the disk I/O operations, and compare both protocols using 2-10 parallel streams between EVL in Chicago and Calit2 in

Figure 8. CSTP vs. Pure FEC (x-axis: Data Stream ID from 1 to 10; y-axis: Packet Recovery percentage)

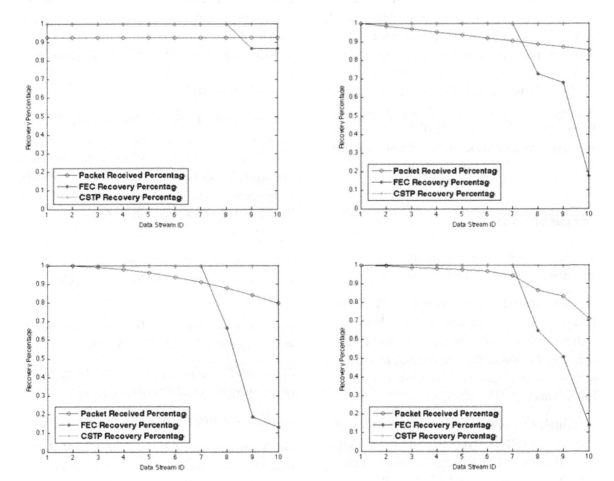

San Diego. The link between them is a 10Gbps optical network. The settings of CSTP are:

$$p = 5\%$$
$$S = 2...14$$
$$N = 1024$$
$$D_s(x) = p \cdot (50\% \cdot x^s + 50\% \cdot x^2) + (1 - p) \cdot x$$

As illustrated in Figure 9, the overall transfer speed of CSTP is about 30% higher than the overall transfer speed of the parallel RBUDP streams; the maximum throughput of CSTP is about 20% higher than that of RBUDP.

CONCLUSION

In this chapter, we have studied the problem of large-scale data transfer and streaming. Traditional point-to-point protocols are not suitable to our new cluster-to-cluster communication models in many new scientific applications, and existing multi-to-multi protocols do not sufficiently address the synchronization issue of parallel data streaming, and cannot tolerate burst packet losses. In this chapter, we propose a new Cross-Stream Transfer Protocol (CSTP), which used Cross-Stream fountain code and pipe packets to tightly couple streams and help lossy streams to decode correctly, so as to tolerate burst packet losses. Our experimental results shows that the CSTP meets our expectation in terms of burst packet loss tolerance, decoding efficiency, communication overhead, and overall data transfer throughput.

There remain many challenges to be addressed. Our future works are to mainly attack the scalability issue of the current CSTP algorithms. We also intend to add modules for reliable delivery to the current CSTP implementation.

REFERENCES

CALIT2. (n.d.). Retrieved from http://www.calit2.net/newsroom/release.php?id=694

Castro, M., Druschel, P., Kermarrec, A.-M., Nandi, A., Rowstron, A., & Singh, A. (2003). SplitStream: High-bandwidth multicast in cooperative environments. In *Proceedings of the SOSP'03 ACM Symposium on Operating Systems Principles*. Bolton Landing, NY: ACM.

Catalyurek, U., Boman, E., Devine, K., Bozdag, D., & Heaphy, R. (2007). Hypergraph-based dynamic load balancing for adaptive scientific computations. In *Proceedings of IPDPS'07*. IPDPS.

CineGrid. (n.d.). Retrieved from http://www.cinegrid.org

COVISE. (n.d.). Retrieved from http://www.hlrs.de/organization/av/vis/covise/

Cruz-Neira, C., Sandin, D., DeFanti, T., Kenyon, R., & Hart, J. (1992, June). The CAVE®: Audio visual experience automatic virtual environment. *Communications of the ACM*. doi:10.1145/129888.129892.

DeFanti, T. A., Dawe, G., Sandin, D. J., Schulze, J. P., Otto, P., & Girado, J. et al. (2009). The STARCAVE, a third-generation CAVE and virtual reality OptIPortal. *The International Journal of FGCS*, *25*(2), 169–178. doi:10.1016/j.future.2008.07.015.

DeFanti, T. A., Leigh, J., Renambot, L., Jeong, B., & Smarr, L. L. et al. (2009). The OptIPortal, a scalable visualization, storage, and computing interface device for the OptiPuter. *Future Generation Computer Systems*, *25*(2), 114–123. doi:10.1016/j.future.2008.06.016.

Digital Dilemma. (2008). *The science and technology council of the academy of motion picture arts and sciences (AMPAS)*. Los Angeles, CA: AMPAS.

DMC4K. (n.d.). Retrieved from http://www.dmc.keio.ac.jp/en/topics/071126-4K.html

Fountain Code. (n.d.). Retrieved from http://en.wikipedia.org/wiki/Fountain_code

GLIF. (n.d.). Retrieved from http://www.glif.is

Gu, Y., & Grossman, R. L. (2007). UDT: UDP-based data transfer for high-speed wide area networks. *Computer Networks*, *51*(7). doi:10.1016/j.comnet.2006.11.009.

He, E., Leigh, J., Yu, O., & DeFanti, T. A. (2002). Reliable blast UDP: Predictable high performance bulk data transfer. In *Proceedings of IEEE Cluster Computing 2002*. Chicago, IL: IEEE.

Hendrickson, B., & Kolda, T. G. (1999). Partitioning rectangular and structurally unsymmetric sparse matrices for parallel processing. *SIAM Journal on Scientific Computing*, *21*(6), 2048–2072. doi:10.1137/S1064827598341475.

Herr, L., et al. (2005). *International real-time streaming of 4K digital cinema, demonstration in iGrid*. Retrieved from http://www.igrid2005.org/program/applications/videoservices_rtvideo.html

4. *KStreaming*. (n.d.). Retrieved from http://www.envision.purdue.edu/4k stream/

Liu, S., Schulze, J. P., & Defanti, T. A. (2009). Synchronizing parallel data streams via cross-stream coding. In *Proceedings of the IEEE International Conference on Networking, Architecture, and Storage*, (pp. 333-340). IEEE.

Luby, M. (2002). LT-codes. In *Proceedings of the 43rd Annu. IEEE Symp. Foundations of Computer Science* (FOCS). Vancouver, Canada, (pp. 271-280). IEEE.

OPIPUTER. (n.d.). Retrieved from http://www.optiputer.net

Raptor Code. (n.d.). Retrieved from http://algo.epfl.ch/contents/output/presents/Raptor-Bangalore.pdf

Renambot, L., Jeong, B., & Leigh, J. (2007). Realtime compression for high-resolution content. In *Proceedings of the Access Grid Retreat 2007*. Chicago, IL: Access.

SAGE. (n.d.). Retrieved from http://www.evl.uic.edu/cavern/sage/index.php

Shirai, D., Kawano, T., Fujii, T., Kaneko, K., Ohta, N., & Ono, S. et al. (2009). Real time switching and streaming transmission of uncompressed 4K motion pictures. *Future Generation Computer Systems*, *25*(2), 192–197. doi:10.1016/j.future.2008.07.003.

Shokrollahi, A. (2006). Raptor codes. *IEEE Transactions on Information Theory*, *52*, 2551–2567. doi:10.1109/TIT.2006.874390.

Smarr, L. (2009). The OptIPuter and its applications. In *Proceedings of the IEEE LEOS Summer Topicals Meeting on Future Global Networks*, (pp. 151-152). IEEE. doi: 10.1109/LEOSST.2009.5226201

Vishwanath, V., Leigh, J., He, E., Brown, M. D., Long, L., & Renambot, L. ... DeFanti, T. A. (2006). Wide-area experiments with LambdaStream over dedicated high-bandwidth networks. In *Proceedings of IEEE INFOCOM*. IEEE.

Vishwanath, V., Shimizu, T., Takizawa, M., Obana, K., & Leigh, J. (2007). Towards terabit/s systems: Performance evaluation of multi-rail systems. In Proceedings of Supercomputing 2007 (SC07). Reno, NV: SC.

Xia, H., & Chien, A. (2007). RobuSTore: A distributed storage architecture with robust and high performance. In Proceedings of Supercomputing 2007 (SC07). Reno, NV: SC.

Xia, H., & Chien, A. A. (2007). RobuSTore: A distributed storage architecture with robust and high performance. In *Proceedings of ACM/IEEE International Conference on High Performance Computing and Communications (SC'07)*. ACM/IEEE.

Zoltan. (n.d.). Retrieved from http://www.cs.sandia.gov/Zoltan/

Chapter 13

Border Adaptive Micro–Base–Station for Wireless Communications

Henry Gao
Glocom Inc., USA

Yushi Shen
Microsoft Corporation, USA

ABSTRACT

This chapter presents a novel architecture, namely the border adaptive micro-base-station network, which can sufficiently meet the bandwidth requirements for the future wireless networks. From the three screens convergence point, the goal is to make the wireless service performance match that of the wired systems, instead of downgrading the performance of wired network applications to the wireless level. Based on the analysis of Shannon theory, the only way to build future wireless networks is to adopt this micro-base-station approach instead of progressively improving the traditional large-cell-base-station systems, such as Long-Term Evolution (LTE).

INTRODUCTION

At the present, there are two major types of wireless network systems, namely the mobile telecom (MSCBC) and the wireless local area network (LAN). The second-generation mobile telecom (2G) has been a great success; however, its descen-

dant 3G has not been as successful. The 3GPP long term evolution plan (LTE) hopes to create a new era for mobile communications. However, in the face of overwhelming bandwidth requirements, most operators have abandoned their original quality commitments, and lowered their service standards by limiting the data volume. Evidence

DOI: 10.4018/978-1-4666-4801-2.ch013

indicates that the 3GPP-LTE and other two competitors are all going in the wrong direction.

Another wireless system started from the wireless local area network, led by the WiFi Alliance (Wi-Fi), and the goal is to provide small-scale mobility. In order to expand coverage, the WiMAX Forum (WiMAX Forum) has been formed in 2001, and directly competes with the mobile telecom. However, WiFi and WiMAX are facing the same "Five-No" problems: namely, insufficient bandwidth, inconvenient roaming, weak network management, unsafe system, and no killer applications.

The main service of the 2G system is voice, and the success of 2G is based on the fact that the 2G voice quality is comparable to that of the landline telephone.

Today, both types of wireless systems have been focusing on wireless multimedia. However, the question is how can they provide wireless multimedia with comparable performance as the landline Internet? The answer is not even remotely close!

We believe that the crux of the problem does not lie in fancy applications, but in the basic bandwidth resources. Currently, the industry confines the wireless telecom market to the so-called fragmented time, which basically downgrades wired network applications to the wireless level, only to cause a serious limitation on the network economy's great potential.

This chapter presents a novel architecture, namely, the border adaptive micro-base-station network (Gao & Shen, 2012). This structure is going to be able to provide sufficient bandwidth increase (theoretically unlimited bandwidth), and thus meeting all the bandwidth requirements of the future wireless networks. The goal of this wireless system is to find the right solution, which can enhance the bandwidth and quality on demand, that is to say, to make wireless system performance comparable to that of the wired systems.

Hot spots in crowded areas, such as campus, coffee and tea-rooms, shopping malls, exhibition, stadium, airports and so on, are high-density mobile terminal regions. Once the broadband services get popular, bandwidth demand is to far exceed the capacity of the traditional base-stations. Through centralized management, the high density micro-base-stations can always split the crowd in space, and relatively reduce the number of terminals within the service area of each micro-base-station. If the space between base-stations is reduced to 10 meters or below, the gain of system bandwidth can be up by thousands of times.

In high-density residential areas, wireless signals are completely overlapped. The border adaptive micro-base-station wireless network ensures the radio spectrum management from the system architectural design. The dynamic slot and frame distribution mechanism completely eliminates mutual interference, and in the meanwhile, strictly prevents the unlawful seizure of private network resources.

In rural areas, the overlapping structure of micro and large-cell base-stations can concurrently cover both centralized and decentralized areas. If a region without sufficient bandwidth is identified, it can simply install extra base-stations. The closed-loop transmission power and antenna beam control can automatically reduce the peripheral base-station coverage, and boost up the system bandwidth capacity in the designated areas.

Along the railway and tunnels, micro-base-stations are arranged in one direction, which enables the network system to achieve high-speed vehicular communications. When the mobile terminals pass through numerous micro-base-stations at speeds of hundreds of kilometres per hour, each base-station may only send a few packets, or no packet at all. The high-speed lossless handover mechanism can ensure real-time high-quality video-telecom with a packet loss rate below one ten thousandth (0.01%).

According to the management strategy of the border adaptive micro-base-station network, in the near future, we may buy wireless base-stations in supermarkets, and install them by DIY (do it yourself) like light bulbs.

The rest of the chapter is organized as below:

- The ultimate goal of future wireless networks;
- A new angle to understanding the Shannon theory;
- Several guidelines to enhancing the micro-base-station principle to the extreme;
- A key technology in the border adaptive micro-base-station network, called CTDMA;
- An illustrative business model for the wireless network operators;
- A unique feature that provides uninterrupted wireless services during catastrophes.

ULTIMATE GOAL OF WIRELESS TELECOM: TO PROVIDE HOMOGENOUS SERVICE LEVEL COMPARABLE TO THE WIRED NETWORK

Prior to further discussion on the wireless networks, we must first clarify two basic principles, namely, the objective and methodology. The current wireless groups may have ignored this basic homework, brought out a dazzling long term evolution plan, and misled consumers by mixing up the concepts of system bandwidth with the peak bandwidth.

Here, the basic homework contains two simple questions:

- Firstly, how much bandwidth is required for the future wireless network?

- Second, how much system bandwidth can be produced based on the current cellular architecture?

As we know, the great success of the 2G wireless network comes from the support of voice communications at large scale. The next successful story, beyond 2G networks, would again be marked by high-return, large-scale multimedia applications including video. In fact, the video bandwidth is much higher than that of voice. Once video services are triggered, it is to be followed by endless troubles of image quality, expense, user-volume and customer satisfaction issues. This is a Pandora's Box. The nightmare that the Internet has experienced due to video traffic is coming again. In fact, the bandwidth of the wired Internet can be easily expanded to accommodate video contents; however, the LTE wireless network has no more bandwidth to expand. The 3GPP should not mislead consumers by promising services that LTE can never provide.

Video is a wild gorilla, and there is a great jump of bandwidth requirement from voice to video applications. Simply put, let's call this bandwidth jump a video threshold. If the network reaches this threshold, all other services can also be included. However, failing to reach the video threshold, regardless of wishful promises, any halfway efforts are meaningless. We must understand that our mission of future wireless networks is to tame the video gorilla, not to lower the consumer standards.

Now, for the first question mentioned above, the answer is simple: to achieve the objective of future video applications, the only way is to increase the guaranteed per user bandwidth by at least hundreds of times.

For the second question, no one denies that 3G is better than 2G, and of course, 4G is to be better than 3G. People can always find problems of a newly introduced network, try to improve it, and even prove that the modified system is better than its previous version. However, the issue is: what is the cost for building a new network to replace the old one? More importantly, how effective can the new system trigger the next round of new profitable applications?

After closely examining the technical documents of the 3GPP-LTE (Shen & Suo, 2008), we have reached the following conclusions:

1. One solution to increasing the bandwidth for LTE is to use more radio frequency band. Please note, this solution is also applicable to a 2G system, hence there is no real evolution at all;

2. The other solution is to increase the spectrum efficiency by 3-6 times in total. That is realized through two upgrades (or evolution stages): 2-4 times by the LTE, and 1.5 times by the LTE-A. However, the new network cannot be compatible to the old one. Hence one is required to purchase new network equipment and user terminals.

As we know, the OFDM technology can substantially increase per channel bandwidth, and seemingly, the 4G wireless system can provide peak bandwidth for several hundreds of Mbps. However, within the coverage range of each base station, the wireless bandwidth has to share with a great number of potential users, that is to say, the per user bandwidth capacity is very limited, and is not enough to support real broadband services. In other words, the total system bandwidth, or service capacity of the 4G technology has only improved a little. Obviously, without sufficient system bandwidth, the mobile cloud service is very restricted.

In conclusion, a truthful answer to the second question is that by exhausting over 15 years of efforts, the wireless industry has gained very limited system service capacity, and far from meeting the future wireless bandwidth demands.

UNDERSTANDING OF THE SHANNON THEORY FROM A NEW ANGLE

The Shannon theory (Shannon, 1949) is the guideline to the narrowband communications network design. We use "narrowband" here to emphasize that the bandwidth is the primary resource for the wireless telecom networks. In narrowband telecom networks, Shannon theory tells us that, in a noisy environment, the upper limit of the channel capacity (denoted by C) is mainly determined by two parameters: the spectrum bandwidth W and the signal to noise ratio S/N:

$$C = W \ Log \ (S/N)$$

In the field of wireless communication network, multiple technologies drastically compete with each other, which attract great attention in the industry. Such competition concerns a technology that is getting ever closer to the Shannon limit. All the competitors have forgotten the original mission of the communications network. Unfortunately, in the network marketplace, consumers do not buy technology, they buy services instead.

As the world enters the broadband era, we shall view the Shannon theory from a different angle, which includes four new interpretations:

1. The Shannon Limit on the Channel Capacity

The Shannon theory clearly states the existence of a wireless bandwidth limit. The question is, does this limit provide enough bandwidth to meet future demands? According to the demand of video applications, if the current LTE large-cell structure is maintained, the achievable bandwidth of a channel is far from meeting the real demand. Therefore, any effort to approach the limit becomes futile.

The Shannon limit clearly states that the wireless bandwidth is different from computing power. In other words, the increase of bandwidth does not follow the Moore's Law (Moore, 1965). The wireless network's evolutionary path cannot follow the pattern of the PC development, through many generations of moderate improvements, such as the 3GPP-LTE:

2. The Channel Capacities' Logarithmic Nature

The Shannon channel capacity formula is a logarithmic function. As we all know, when moving up with a logarithmic function, the gain gets smaller and smaller. No matter what powerful technologies can be applied, the resulting effects are to become less and less significant in the neighbourhood of the limit. In fact, according to the Bits per Hz spectrum efficiency, the exhaustion of the radio technology in the past 15 years improved the efficiency by only about 10 times. Currently, the two wireless groups, namely the LTE and IEEE802.11n, have adopted similar technologies of OFDM/MIMO:

3. The Importance of the Spectrum Bandwidth

One important parameter of the Shannon theory is the spectrum bandwidth (W). Restricted by the nature of electromagnetic wave, the spectrum portion that is suitable for ground wireless communications is unfortunately small. This makes such a spectrum extremely valuable public resource. Some people have suggested that FCC reassigns the band of broadcasting TV for the mobile telecom usage. It has turned out to be impractical:

4. The Importance of Signal-to-Noise Ratio

Another critical parameter of the Shannon formula is the signal to noise ratio (S/N). Assuming the noise (N) is relatively steady. According to the principle of electromagnetic field, with fixed antenna structure and radio frequency, the radio signal strength decreases as the square of distance. That means the "golden location" of wireless telecom is only in the immediate neighbourhood of the signal source.

To make it even clearer, there are only three ways to enhance the wireless bandwidth: to use more radio bands, to improve spectrum efficiency, and to increase the spectrum reuse rate. The first two methods have hit the Shannon limit. Only the spectrum reuse rate can have unlimited potential growth. Simple calculations show the gain of 3600 times in the effective spectrum resource if a 3-kilometer coverage radius is reduced to 50 meters. The continuous reduction of coverage radius, with continuous reuse of the same spatial frequencies, the wireless telecom can eventually become a close-range access method to the fixed networks.

Breaking through the shackles of traditional thinking, there is a good near field environment of the electromagnetic field for each person. Compared with personal needs, the radio bandwidth is abundant. However, for a group of thousands of users, individuals are separated or shielded by many objects. The personal radio environment gets poorer that way, while the bandwidth needs for the group are increased by thousands of times. The radio bandwidth then certainly becomes a limited resource.

In fact, Shannon has literally told us that the 3GPP LTE does not follow the aforementioned theoretical guidelines. Its activities can be summarized as an improvement of spectral efficiency near the theoretical limit. The result is analogical to the strategy of farming on desert: hard work in exchange for little harvests, and never escaping from the fate of bandwidth starvation.

Shannon has also told us that by forcing every consumer to use the remote radio band is not a good idea. It deliberately makes a simple thing complicated. The natural solution is to make use of spatial isolation. The micro-base-station structure can provide almost limitless reuse of the same spectrum resources.

Shannon has further told us that no matter how dense the user population, it is always possible to deploy enough base-stations by properly adjusting the radio transmission power, followed by separating user signals from interferences. Therefore, the wireless base-stations should act more like light bulbs. When the sky darkens, all we need to do is to illuminate the surrounding areas, instead of building an artificial Sun. By applying the same philosophy, the radio spectrum becomes rich enough around the individual users. Unfortunately, the current wireless industry stubbornly violates common sense, and by seeking what is far, they blatantly neglect what is near.

In addition, due to the reduced radiant intensity around individuals, the micro-base-station network is also a green solution with added benefits in energy savings.

Finally, the Shannon theory can promise the possibility of providing a wireless network bandwidth and performance that are on the same level as fixed wire, and the micro-base-station network is the only way to go. It is wise to start the new architecture as soon as possible, so that we can satisfy consumer demands, while avoiding precious time and resources being wasted down the wrong path.

ENHANCING THE MICRO-BASE-STATION PRINCIPLE TO THE EXTREME

The most important aspect of building the future wireless network is to select the right topological structure, instead of improving on the transmission technology. In other words, we must first determine the direction of micro-base-station architecture, followed by choosing the suitable supplementary technologies. In fact, the nature of the border adaptive micro-base-station network is to leverage the superiority of wired networks to solve the wireless puzzle (Gao, Chinese patent).

The following analysis fully expresses the micro-base-station concepts. First, we break through the traditional cellular structure, adopt centralized time division multiplexing and pre-

cise transmission power control, and thus push the spectrum reuse rate to the extreme. In addition, this approach relieves the stress of pursuing frequency spectrum efficiency. It increases the number of base stations, while at the same time decreases their unit costs. Finally, by means of precise management, it extends the ubiquitous Internet into the wireless domain.

Based on this architecture, we have derived the design strategies of the micro-base-station network:

1. The main solution of the ubiquitous network, for increasing the overall wireless bandwidth, is to sacrifice the range of coverage. Instead of increasing the total system bandwidth capacity, it is easier to increase the frequency spectrum reuse rate by a great extent. Since there is a square rule for the coverage area and radius of a base station, the potential increase on system bandwidth can be ten thousand times or more, if we make the switch from the large-cellular to micro-base-stations;

2. Since the micro-base-station network has sufficient potential for bandwidth, we only need to utilize the high quality bandwidth nearby the antennas, and take coordinated measures to prevent signal interference. It adopts the deep cross coverage of more base stations, while giving up weak signals around the edge, that is, it trades the base station coverage for high quality and short-range real-time wireless transmissions;

3. As the coverage of a single base station gets smaller, and the density of micro-base-stations gets higher, problems are surely going to arise: such as wireless signal interference, frequent handovers between different base stations, and the management cost for a large number of base stations. All these issues must be resolved from a global perspective, by taking advantage of a high performance fixed line network;

4. Since large quantities of micro-base-stations are going to be employed, meaning the base stations are very close to the users, we should install the base station in an inhomogeneous way and adjust the base station borders dynamically, so that the resource allocation adapts to the demand. In fact, the ubiquitous micro-base-station network employs precise management methods, by steering away from the traditional large cellular architecture, and dynamically adjusts the base station coverage based on demand.

By using small antennas and low power amplifiers, the base station coverage gets to consistently shrink, and the same spatial frequency gets repeatedly reused. Inevitably, the wireless networks are to become close-access doorways to the wired networks. Users can feel the presence of a wireless environment when traveling through numerous micro-base-stations, but it is in fact being supported by the underlying wired network. Conclusively, although the micro-base-station network requires certain engineering complexity, namely a substantial increase in the number of base stations, but it is the only way to overcoming a theoretical impossibility – the LTE's stranglehold being placed on the use of the frequency band and spectrum efficiency. In the result, it achieves a wireless network environment that is incomparably more efficient than the conventional technologies. Surprisingly, according to the optimization approaches in this article, and based on mature technologies, the wireless network is neither complicated nor expensive to construct.

CENTRALIZED TIME DIVISION MULTIPLE ACCESS (CTDMA)

The most fundamental issue in wireless telecommunications is how to share common spectrum resources with a large number of users: Sending mixed data to multiple users is called "multi-plexing"; Releasing personal data by occupying common resources is called "multiple access". So far, there are three fundamental types of wireless multiplexing and multiple access approaches: frequency division, time division and code division.

Let's recall the history of the development of wireless communications, and look into the future:

*   The first generation of mobile telecom (1G) initiated the cellular structure. It adopted frequency division multiplexing and multiple access (FDM/FDMA), i.e. different users use different radio frequencies to transmit and receive signals simultaneously. The core advantage of the cellular network structure is that the same frequency band can be reused, if the base stations are apart by a certain distance. Therefore, it has greatly enhanced the capabilities of the total system bandwidth. For the frequency division technology, the adjacent channels have to keep sufficient frequency intervals to prevent signal interference, causing lowered efficiency of spectrum usage;

*   The second generation of mobile telecom (2G) has mainly adopted time division multiplexing and multiple access (TDM/TDMA), i.e. different users within a cell use the same frequency to transmit and receive signals at different time intervals. Because of the inflexibility of time slot allocation, the spectrum utilization rate is also low;

*   The third generation of mobile telecom (3G) adopted code division multiplexing and multiple access (CDM/CDMA), i.e. different users use the same frequency to transmit and receive signals at the same time but with different codes. The code division technology can be visualized as a cocktail party model, namely many people communicate in the same hall, at the same time by using different languages, while other people' conversations can be treated

as background noises. Based on theoretical analysis, code-division technology is more efficient than the traditional frequency-division and time-division technologies.

Beyond the third generation (B3G, 4G), with advanced digital processing technologies, the signal phase is to be strictly controlled, and the channel spacing is to be greatly reduced. This improved frequency division technology is called orthogonal frequency division multiplexing and multiple access (OFDM/OFDMA). Since user data is decomposed into a number of low speed sub-channels, the inter-symbol interference of the wireless signal can be effectively reduced, so as to provide greater spectral efficiency. Especially when it is combined with the Multi-Input Multi-Output (MIMO) technology, it is more appropriate for large bandwidth and complex environment of the reflected waves.

The development history from the first to fourth generation indicates that wireless communications has followed the cellular structure. In other words, the base station provides independent management for each individual cell with minor coordination among other base stations. It shows that within the coverage of a wireless base station, one multiplexing and multiple access technology is utilized, however, between cells a different layer of technology is adopted. This implies the existence of a fixed cellular boundary.

In the special environment of high-density base stations, the basic technologies of wireless multiplexing and multiple access, namely frequency division, time division and code division, must be re-evaluated. For the frequency division and code division technologies, the transceiver parameters, such as frequency and coding, have to be known in advance when switching between multiple base stations. Only the time division technique, without any pre-set parameters, can seamlessly travel through the high-density base stations while ignoring the station boundaries.

Thus, the border adaptive micro-base-station network has achieved the following structural innovations:

1. Based on the traditional time division technology, it adopts the dynamic transmission power control, resource coordination among multiple base stations, and statistical multiplexing;
2. It breaks through the traditional cellular structure, by globally allocating time slots for multiple base stations, and unifying transceivers for all base stations and user terminals;
3. It dynamically adjusts the coverage boundaries of base stations, based on the terminal distribution density and communication traffic.

Indeed, the above technology presents an improved intensive time division technology, which can be referred to as the centralized time division multiplexing and multiple access (CTDM/CTDMA). Strictly speaking, the border adaptive micro-base-station network is not under the category of pure wireless technology, instead, it uses accurate management of a fixed-line network to solve the synchronization issues of numerous base stations. For the first time, it elevates the quality and capacity of the wireless network, to the level comparable to that of the wired network.

Figure 1 shows the evolution roadmap of wireless communication system. Interestingly, throughout history, it can be seen as a spiralling-shaped improvement of the wireless multiplexing technology: $FDM > TDM > CDM > OFDM > CTDM$. As the chip resource becomes sufficient, an enhanced CDM-based technology may emerge in the future, which might be called the "multiple channels merged CDM" (MCDM).

The border adaptive micro-base-station network adopts a homogeneous transceiver approach, meaning the distinction among terminals and base

Figure 1.Roadmap of wireless network structure

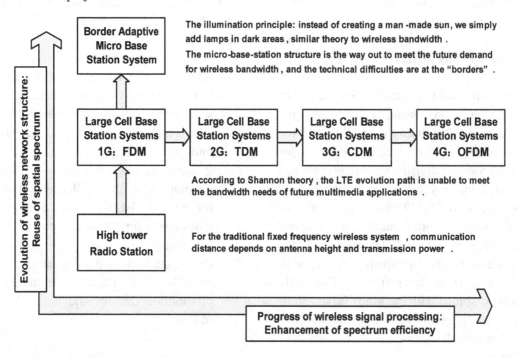

stations merely relies on the difference of each device's transmission power and time slot. From the transmission power perspective, the enhanced signal intensity may improve transmission quality, while increasing the interference to other devices. Therefore, the transmission power of each terminal and base station in the network must be adjusted to a proper level at any time. Thousands of wireless transceivers' signal connection and intervention must be analysed and calculated within several milliseconds, to identify possible links among the terminals and base stations without interfering one another. Apparently, the computational workload is much higher than the capability of low-cost micro devices. The designed wireless network adopts the algorithm of an approximation template, which greatly reduces the workload. With the artificial experience in the template design, the initial operating parameters of each base station are to optimize the template during operation, and adapt gradually to the optimal value. In comparison with the traditional mobile communications, the growth potential of

local bandwidth for CTDMA technology is unlimited. In other words, the bandwidth insufficiency is no longer going to be a concern to meet any real-world demand.

According to the network general status and dynamic coordination, the CTDMA technology mainly includes four adjustment mechanisms:

1. Multiple closed-loop control on the transmission power and antenna beam;
2. Dynamic assignment of frame and time slot;
3. Dynamic adjustment of base station boundaries;
4. High speed and lossless handover between base stations.

Please refer to more documents about the detailed descriptions of above mechanisms (Gao, Chinese patent).

Another significant advantage of the CTDMA technology is the adoption of homogeneous transceivers. Every wireless equipment, including the base station and the terminal, employs a unified physical layer technology, which represents the same frequency, encoding and protocol processes. A reliable communication link can be established among base stations, from station to terminal, and among terminals in case a certain signal-to-noise ratio is satisfied. Specifically, the differences between the network transceivers are the transmission power, the antenna beam and the time slot; similar modules are configured by different service parameters. There is a primary base station to provide such centralized control. With the aforementioned four adjustment mechanisms, the primary base station dynamically increases or reduces the level of correlation among base stations and wireless terminals, so as to automatically maintain the best signal-to-noise ratio for the entire network.

PART-TIME WIRELESS NETWORK OPERATORS

Since the wireless environment brings extra convenience to the users, the network described in this article may treat the wireless connection as a value-added service to the wired network, and collect additional fees on top of basic network services. Based on such arrangement, the border adaptive micro-base-station network may not require dedicated wireless operators, and can even use the free ISM (industrial, scientific, and medical) band. In this case, it can dramatically reduce the network operating costs. Through the ubiquitous Internet, large number of low-cost micro-base-stations can cover crowded public areas, roads, and private residential areas. A distinctive business model can be designed that any user can apply for permits to install micro-base-stations within his/her authorized regions. By the built-in automatic network access function of the micro-base-stations, users can become "part-time wireless operators," and share the revenue that is generated from the wireless access services. The network

implements a strict management and billing system to the base stations and terminals. The network can automatically record and cut off any access connections, not complying with the service agreement. In the meanwhile, any user at any location can be accurately billed for their wireless terminal connection, and the service revenue is to be credited back to the base-station provider as appropriate.

Following the plug and play (P&P) network management features of the ubiquitous Internet, the process of massive promotion is simplified technically. Actually, if one relies on the operators to deploy and maintain broad-scale wireless base stations, that can still be a protracted project. Inevitably, the business model of low-cost and high-profit "part-time wireless operators" is to become a powerful driving force for the micro-base-station network, and can deliver the services to any potential user at any place quickly.

UNINTERRUPTED WIRELESS COMMUNICATION SERVICES DURING CATASTROPHES

Wireless communications come with an inherent feature of convenience, and it can save lives especially during a catastrophe. Regarding the disaster recovery capability of wireless networks, a variety of network architectures have been developed, such as Mesh (Zhang & et. al., 2007) and the Ad Hoc (Makki & Li, 2010) network, and satellite communication technologies. However, the construction of commercial wireless networks with disaster recovery capability is very costly and difficult to deploy. It is not possible for ordinary consumers to pay for the disasters that may or may not happen in the future. So far, none of the current wireless networks have the ability to cover both the daily commercial operations and the disaster situations effectively. However, the system presented here can practically solve this problem (Gao, Chinese patent).

Traditional communication networks usually require single-point error recovery capabilities, as the chance of multiple devices failing at the same time is very low. However, when encountering major catastrophes such as earthquake and tsunami, large areas of ground networks, power supplies, and wireless base stations may be destroyed at the same time. For the wireless network presented in this article, every base station or terminal is continuously aware of the real-time network status. Once abnormal network conditions are detected, for example, wired or wireless connections breaking off, the status can be immediately reported to higher level network management. In addition, because of the deep intercross-coverage distribution of the network base stations, there are a number of potential wireless links between base stations. Once the ground connection is interrupted, the remaining base stations and terminals can quickly switch to the Ad Hoc mode, automatically extend the communication distance and maintain the smooth flow of the basic wireless services, with a reduced modulation scheme.

If a number of devices are detected to be in abnormal conditions, which may be caused by man-made accidents or catastrophes, the network management center retains a record of the network topology, and the working status of all equipment before the accident. By comparing these data with the status information collected after the accident, the system can clearly determine the range of accidents, or divide them into a number of regions with different disaster levels. According to the prevention plans, different levels of accident control processes may be selected. In fact, under the ongoing situation, and with the progress of the network repairing actions, network status is subject to change at any time. The border adaptive micro-base-station network management has the ability to respond to accidents dynamically. In other words, responding to major disasters is only one part of the failure recovery process for a typical accident. If there are blind spots of communication coverage after disaster, the system can remotely launch installation-free temporary relays, via delivery methods such as cannon eject and helicopter drop, numerous temporary relay stations can be properly oversupplied. As long as a small number of relay stations are deployed successfully, the communication connection in the blind areas can be recovered quickly.

Obviously, the ubiquitous Internet, as a daily commercial network, usually provides high-quality services to both mobile and fixed terminals through precise network management, and connects a large number of wireless base stations. During major catastrophes, the affected local network can selectively restrict part of the broadband services, downgrading to disaster communications. When faced with unpredictable disaster locations, it is an ideal choice to selectively switch a large number of user terminals into relay stations, hence maintaining uninterrupted telecom services.

CONCLUSION

We have presented a new wireless system structure, which is an alternative direction comparing to the current 4G evolution trend. This border adaptive micro-base-station network, as a daily commercial wireless network, can provide sufficient bandwidth at the same level as wired systems. Based on the ubiquitous Internet, this wireless network can be easily deployed by a special business mode, namely, the part-time wireless operators. Last but not least, this system can provide an ideal solution during major catastrophes.

REFERENCES

Gao, H. (n.d.a). *The wireless micro cellular network based on the centralized time division multiple access technology*. Chinese Patent 200910222768.2. Shanghai, China: Chinese Patent Office.

Gao, H. (n.d.b). *The wireless network and methods for both disaster times and daily commercial operations*. Chinese Patent 201110129888.5. Shanghai, China: Chinese Patent Office.

Gao, H., & Shen, Y. (2012). *IT of cloud era: The computer and network world after resources abundance*. Peking, China: Peking University Press.

Makki, S. K., & Li, X.-Y. (2010). *Sensor and ad hoc networks: Theoretical and algorithmic aspects*. Berlin: Springer.

MSCBC. (n.d.). Retrieved from http://www.mscbsc.com

Shannon, C. (1949). *A mathematical theory of communication*. Urbana-Champaign, IL: University of Illinois Press.

Shen, J., & Suo, S. (2008). *3GPP: Long term evolution: Principle and system design*. Shanghai, China: Posts & Telecom Press.

Wi-Fi. (n.d.). Retrieved from http://www.wi-fi.org

WiMAX Forum. (n.d.). Retrieved from http://www.wimaxforum.org

Zhang, Y., Luo, J., & Hu, H. (2007). *Wireless mesh networking: Architecture, protocols and standards*. Boston: Auerbach Publications.

Section 5
Appendix

Chapter 14
Impact of Cultural Differences on the Cloud Computing Ecosystems in the USA and China

Yushi Shen
Microsoft Corporation, USA

Jie Yang
Microsoft Corporation, USA

Tayfun Keskin
University of Washington, USA

ABSTRACT

The IT industry is both fundamental and strategic to a nation's economy. It continues to play a critical role in the industry's upgrade and economic development in the foreseeable future. The future of the IT industry lies in cloud computing. In the recent years, many countries in the world are responding to cloud computing with much enthusiasm. The USA, Japan, and European countries have created strategies to develop cloud computing, aiming to become the leader of the new era. The Chinese government also sees cloud computing as a historic opportunity to rebuild competitive advantages and leapfrog Western countries. Against this backdrop, this chapter compares and contrasts the evolution of IT towards cloud computing between China and the Western countries, especially the USA.

DOI: 10.4018/978-1-4666-4801-2.ch014

INTRODUCTION

Cloud computing, as it grows in popularity, is now a part of every CIO's agenda. It has been ranked #1 in Gartner's top 10 strategic Technologies for 2011. The global cloud computing market is expected to grow at a 30% compound annual growth rate (CAGR), reaching $270 billion in 2020 (Market Research Media, 2012). According to these projections, cloud computing is becoming the third revolution in the information technology (IT) industry, after the personal computer and the Internet. The cloud computing phenomenon can change the IT industry landscape and business models for all the players. The driver of this change can determine pricing schemes, market shares and the overall bargaining power of forces at play. But who is to dominate the cloud computing service? We hypothesize that the dominant forces in the cloud varies in different geographical regions, and it depends on the cultural differences that drive the business ecosystem.

The United States and China are the two most powerful countries in the world, both in terms of economy and technology. The U.S. has the biggest IT market, and China has the fastest growing market with a remarkable potential for demand. Therefore, it is important to compare and contrast the U.S. and China's respective cultures, while the cloud computing ecosystems develop within their borders.

Culture has an impact on the development of IT systems and institutions. Furthermore, the U.S. and China are very different in the cultural dimensions, such as long term orientation, individualism and power distance (Hofstede, 1981). Based on our observations, we first point out those differences in the cloud computing ecosystems, and then theorize the role cultural differences play on the bargaining power of the key players in each country. The prominent feature of our research is a comparison of the cloud computing ecosystems of the U.S. and China, from the perspective of culture, and the key players' intended roles within each culture. Specifically, we focus on trying to understand the future of the cloud architecture, and the bargaining power of the players, in order to see which party is to play the dominant role in the development of cloud services. To the best of our knowledge, our study is the first to analyze cultural differences in the context of cloud computing services.

CLOUD COMPUTING

Cloud computing is a model for enabling ubiquitous, convenient, on-demand network access to a shared pool of configurable computing resources, e.g., networks, servers, storage, applications and services, which can be rapidly provisioned and released with minimal management efforts or service provider interactions (Mell, 2011).

The conception of cloud computing dates back to 1961, when John McCarthy, an American computer scientist and cognitive scientist, in a public speech celebrating MIT's centennial, suggested that "computation may someday be organized as a public utility." A Canadian technologist and former research minister, as well as the author of several publications, Douglas Parkhill in his 1966 book: The Challenge of the Computer Utility, has thoroughly explored almost all the modern-day characteristics of cloud computing: elastic provision, provided as a utility, online and illusion of infinite supply, where he has made the comparisons to the electricity industry, the use of public, private, government, and community forms.

Despite its early conceptualization, cloud computing has not reached the critical mass until recently. The bursting of the dot com bubble, at the turn of the millennium, has introduced two important changes: first, significant increase of the Internet's bandwidth making broadband commonplace; secondly, the boom of commercial and consumer applications based on the Internet, which has created further demand.

After the bursting of the bubble, Amazon has played a key role in the development of cloud computing by modernizing their data centers. Amazon has been using as little as 10% of their capacity at any given time, just to leave room for occasional spikes similar to other IT companies. The discovery of the new architecture, which we call the cloud, results in significant internal efficiency improvements. Amazon has begun to provide cloud computing services to external customers, and thus launching the Amazon Web Service (AWS), on the basis of utility computing in 2006.

Meanwhile, newly successful Internet companies such as Google has started their effort to uproot the traditional personal computer (PC) based software ecosystem, pushing for browser based web apps and operating systems. Finally, software giant Microsoft has realized the strategic importance of cloud computing and speedily shipped Windows Azure and SQL Azure. On March 4th, 2010, during an address and live Webcast at the University of Washington's Paul G. Allen Center for Computer Science & Engineering in Seattle, Microsoft CEO Steve Ballmer has publicly announced for the first time that Microsoft is "for the cloud, we're all in."

Even though cloud computing is literally in its infancy, its future potential seems bright. It is expected to grow over $82 billion in 2016, up from $31 billion in (Rudd, Brown, & Levitt, 2012), and the global cloud computing market is expected to grow at a 30% CAGR reaching $270 billion in 2020 (Market Research Media, 2012). Just like the Internet protocol changed the whole infrastructure of the telecom industry, cloud computing is expected to change the IT industry. Today's IT networks infrastructure, including telecom, cable, internet and wireless are converging into one standard network governed by the cloud.

The essence of the cloud is to consolidate global information and data, and centrally provide for IT resources. It is the packaging of IT resources, such as computation, storage and services, as a metered service. This is a seismic shift in information technology — the kind that comes around every decade or so, which can be compared to the historic change from individual generators to centralized power stations. It is so massive that it affects not only business models, but the underlying architecture of how we develop, deploy, run and deliver applications. Once the shift is done, we are not only going to be able to enjoy cheap and stable supply of resources on demand, but also a whole new world of applications. It is to fundamentally change the way people think, live and work. The resulting opportunities are of historic significance.

The big convergence and historic shift signify the restructuring of the IT industry, which has already begun. On January 9th 2007, at Macworld Expo, Steve Jobs has announced that Apple is dropping the word "Computer" from its name to become "Apple Inc.", implying that his company is no longer only a computer company. Microsoft has quietly transformed itself from a company all about software to one all about online and devices. After claiming "all in the cloud" in March 2010, Microsoft has announced plans to form a broad strategic partnership with Nokia on February 11th, 2011. Shortly after, on May 10th, 2011, Microsoft has announced it has entered into a definitive agreement, under which Microsoft is to acquire Skype, the leading Internet communications company. Following suits, on August 15th, 2011, Google has also announced its plan to acquire Motorola Mobile. Overseas in China, from the government to the business sector, cloud computing is being developed everywhere in the country. All telecom operators have started to deploy cloud computing infrastructure to different extents.

This restructuring of the IT industry is leading the three major sectors in the cloud era, which are Cloud Server, Cloud Network and Cloud Client. The future cloud computing ecosystem is illustrated in Figure 1.

The three sectors are defined in Table 1 below. The purpose of this paper is to analyze how the

Figure 1. The illustration of future cloud computing ecosystem

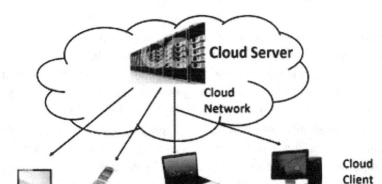

Table 1. Definitions of the three major sectors in the future cloud computing ecosystem

Sector	Definition	Examples
Cloud Server	These are the companies that store cloud data and centrally provide IT resources (computation, storage, control and etc.)	Microsoft with Windows Azure; Amazon with Amazon Web Services; Google with Google App Engine
Cloud Network	These are the companies that transport cloud data and services from Cloud Server to the Cloud Client.	AT&T with wireless broadband access; Comcast with cable model broadband access; China Telecom and China Mobile
Cloud Client	These are companies that provide terminal devices and software applications for end users.	Apple's iPhone and iPad; Lenovo and other PC manufactures; HTC and other mobile phone manufactures; software / application providers, etc.

cultural differences between the U.S. and China are to determine who is going to be the dominant player in these different sectors, in each country's cloud computing ecosystem.

CULTURAL INFLUENCES ON INFORMATION TECHNOLOGY (IT)

It has been shown that culture at various levels, including national, organizational, group and individual, can significantly influence the development, implementation and use of IT. Differences in culture can result in different outcomes of IT (Market Research Media, 2012) (Alavi, Kayworth & Leidner, 2006).

According to Schein, culture exists at three levels: basic assumptions, values and artifacts. At the deepest or core level, culture consists of basic assumptions which represent the belief systems that people use to perceive and to respond to various situations. At the next level, values represent a manifestation of culture that signify espoused beliefs identifying what is important to a particular cultural group. At the third level, culture is manifested through artifacts and creations, which are the most visible.

A fundamental mechanism has been proposed to explain the establishment and maintenance of the cultural patterns by (Hofstede, 1981), in which he has illustrated three interactive systems: origins, societal norms and consequences. A system of societal norms is at the center, consisting of value systems shared by most of the population. Its origin consists of a variety of ecological factors such as geography, economy, demography, genetics, history, technology and urban development. The consequences of the social norms are the corresponding structural, functional and social institutions, which include the family, education systems, politics and legislation.

Hofstede has also developed the original four dimensions of culture — uncertainty avoidance, power distance, masculinity/femininity and individualism/collectivism (Hofstede, 1981, 1991, & 2010), which are still widely accepted and used in across disciplines. Further studies has expanded the cultural dimensions with taxonomies such as locus of control, time-orientation, sociability, bureaucracy, markets and aggression. A relatively complete summary of these cultural dimensions has been provided in a 2006 MIS review (Leidner & Kayworth, 2006). According to these taxonomies, certain sets of values are to persist in all countries, but yet vary in their magnitude across geographic regions.

As culture has significant influences on IT, and cloud computing being the future of IT services, it is essential and interesting to study the effects of cultural differences, in terms of the determined cultural dimensions to the cloud computing ecosystem. It is especially desirable to conduct this research on the U.S. and China, which are to play the most important roles in the future world, but are with significantly different cultures. As far as we know, this paper is the first attempt to research on this topic, and our findings reveal interesting differences between these two markets.

CULTURAL DIFFERENCES BETWEEN THE U.S. AND CHINA AND THEIR IMPACT ON CLOUD COMPUTING

This research is the first phase of many consecutive steps of a larger cloud computing project, across institutions that create and use the cloud. After initial interviews, we have determined the following six cultural dimensions, to explain a majority of cultural differences between the U.S. and China. These cultural dimensions also have significant impact on shaping the cloud computing ecosystem in each country. Table 2 below summarizes the six key cultural dimensions and their impact on

Table 2. Key cultural dimensions and their impact on cloud computing

Cultural Dimension	The U.S.	China	Impact on Cloud Computing
Current IT status	Leading	Following	Who owns the core technology?
Long term orientation	Low	High	Will the ecosystem be formed through long-term planning or short-term profit?
Government driven vs. Market driven	Market driven	Government driven	What drives the development of cloud computing?
Locus of control	Internal	External	What type of companies are most likely to succeed?
Power distance	Low	High	Likelihood of Cloud Computing being built top-down?
Individualism vs. collectivism	Individualism	Collectivism	The relationships between different players in cloud computing, and between them and the government.

cloud computing. The remainder of this section elaborates on each of these dimension's effect on the local cloud computing services.

The Current IT Status

The current status of the IT industry in each country is influenced by the sociological differences embedded in their cultures. The U.S. and Chinese cultures are very different, and therefore, the current status of the cloud computing services. Most of the leading cloud computing companies are in the U.S., including cloud service companies like Amazon, Google, Microsoft, and the cloud hardware makers like IBM. Amazon is the first to launch Amazon Web Service (AWS) on a utility computing basis in 2006. In April 2008 Google has launched the Google App Engine, which is a platform as a service (PaaS) cloud computing platform for developing and hosting web applications in the Google-managed data centers. In February 2010, Microsoft has launched its Windows Azure Platform, a cloud platform used to build, host and scale web applications through

Microsoft's data centers. IBM cloud computing has emerged from the union of two of IBM's most influential technologies: mainframes and virtualization. These technologies are crucial in building the Cloud Servers.

On the other hand, China does not have a global leadership in cloud computing. The largest computer company in China in 2011 has been Lenovo Group, a PC manufacturer that ranked 450th in the Global Fortune 500. The largest software companies in China are Baidu and Tencent, but they are more application companies, and do not own core computing technologies, let alone owning core technologies to build the Cloud Server, as mentioned above. However, China has extremely strong state-owned telecom operators, namely China Mobile, China Telecom and China Unicom, which are ranked 87th, 222nd and 371st in the 2011 Global Fortune 500 respectively, and they own an enormous customer base. For example, as of January 2012, China Mobile is the world's largest mobile phone operator with about 650 million subscribers, as reported on the company's official website, which is more than double the whole population of the U.S.

The drastic differences in the IT status between the U.S. and China signify the future cloud computing ecosystems between the two countries can hardly be alike. The U.S. is likely to own the core technologies in the Cloud Server, but China is to own the largest numbers of end users.

Long Term Orientation (LTO)

LTO describes societies' time horizon (Hofstede & et. al., 2010). Long term oriented societies attach more importance to the future. They foster pragmatic values oriented towards rewards, including persistence, saving and capacity for adaptation. In short term oriented societies, values promoted are related to the past and the present, including steadiness, respect for tradi-

tion, preservation of one's face, reciprocation and fulfilling social obligations.

The United States scores 29 on this dimension and is a short-term oriented culture. As a result, it is a culture focused on traditions and fulfilling social obligations. Given this perspective, American businesses measure their performance on a short-term basis, with profit and loss statements being issued on a quarterly basis. This also drives individuals to strive for quick results within the work place. There is a need to have the "absolute truth" in all matters.

With a score of 118, China is a highly long term oriented society, in which persistence and perseverance are normal. Relationships are ordered by status quo and the order is observed. People are thrifty and sparing with resources, and investment tends to be in the long term projects such as real estate. Traditions can be adapted to suit new conditions. The Chinese people recognize that the government is also human, rather than as in the Low LTO countries, the government is influenced by God or the law. Ways of thinking sway from the bipolar full to no confidence, rather than the low LTO countries that think in probabilistic terms.

Unlike in the U.S. where company behaviors are driven by investors' expectations of quarterly results, cloud computing in China is being strategized through long-term government planning.

Government Driven vs. Market Driven

U.S. is a free market economy, while in China the government is playing a much more proactive role in not only regulating, but actually leading the economic development. This applies to the cloud computing as well. In the U.S., cloud computing is driven by the market, and therefore public clouds are more common, which can fully exploit the cost benefit of large economies of scale. In China however, cloud computing is driven by the government. Due to regulations, the Chinese government does not allow foreign companies to own data in China, and therefore none of the public clouds are currently available in China, and probably is not going to be available in the foreseeable future.

Moreover, each provincial government is trying to establish a strategic position in cloud computing so the form is more likely to be private clouds or hybrid clouds. The only potential player in the public cloud in China is going to be the state owned telecom operators, who have the best resources, control the channels and own the largest customer base, an essential monopoly.

The Locus of Control

The locus of control is a theory in personality psychology, referring to the extent to which individuals believe that they can control events that affect them. The concept has been developed by Julian B. Rotter in 1954, and has since become an important aspect of personality studies. One's "locus" (Latin for "place" or "location") can either be internal, meaning the person believes that they control their life, or external, meaning they believe that their environment, some higher power, or other people control their decisions and their lives. Individuals with a high internal locus of control believe that events result primarily from their own behavior and actions. Those with a high external locus of control believe that powerful others, fate, or chance primarily determine events.

It has been shown that in comparison with the Chinese, Americans are more internal in the attribution of their successes, but more external in the attribution of their failures. Furthermore, Americans are more internal in the attribution of their successes than their failures, while the opposite is true for the Chinese (Chiu, 1987).

Chinese companies largely rely on the leadership of the government, and do everything to comply with government policies and regulations. The relationship with the government determines the success or failure of an enterprise. State owned operators thus have competitive advantages in addition to the huge customer base and deep pockets. On the other hand, U.S. companies believe that success or failure is controlled by the company itself.

The Power Distance

The power distance is the extent to which the less powerful members of organizations and institutions accept and expect that power is distributed unequally (Hofstede & et. al., 2010). Cultures that endorse low power distance expect and accept power relations that are more consultative or democratic. People relate to one another more as equals regardless of formal positions. Subordinates are more comfortable with and demand the right to contribute to and critique the decision making of those in power. In high power distance countries, the less powerful accept power relations that are more autocratic and paternalistic. Subordinates acknowledge the power of others simply based on where they are situated, in certain formal and hierarchical positions.

According to Hofstede, the United States score low on this dimension (40) which underscores the American premise of "liberty and justice for all." This is also evidenced by the focus on equal rights in all aspects of American society and government. Within American organizations, hierarchy is established for convenience, superiors are always accessible and managers rely on individual employees and teams for their expertise. Both managers and employees expect to be consulted, and information is shared frequently. At the same time, communication is informal, direct and participative.

China sits at 80, in the higher rankings of PDI – i.e. a society that believes that inequalities amongst people are acceptable. The subordinate-superior relationship tends to be polarized, and there is no defense against power abuse by superiors. Individuals are influenced by the formal authority and sanctions, and are generally optimistic about people's capacity for leadership and initiative. People should not have aspirations beyond their ranks.

The power distance determines the influence of government officials on the directions of an enterprise, especially in the cloud computing development at this stage.

Individualism vs. Collectivism

Individualism is the degree to which individuals are integrated into groups. In individualistic societies, the stress is put on personal achievements and individual rights. People are expected to stand up for themselves and their immediate family, and to choose their own affiliations. In contrast, in collectivist societies, individuals act predominantly as members of a life-long and cohesive group or organization. People have large extended families, which are used as a protection in exchange for unquestioning loyalty (Hofstede & et. al., 2010).

The United States, with a score of 91 on this dimension, is a highly individualistic culture. This translates into a loosely-knit society, in which the expectation is that people look after themselves and their immediate families. There is also a high degree of geographical mobility in the United States, and most Americans are accustomed to doing business with, or interacting with strangers. Consequently, Americans are not shy about approaching their prospective counterparts, in order to obtain or seek information. In the business world, employees are expected to be self-reliant and display initiative. Also, within the exchange-based world of work, hiring and promotion decisions are based on merit or evidence of what one has done or can do.

On the contrary, at a score of 20 China is a highly collectivist culture, where people act in the interests of the group and not necessarily of themselves. In-group considerations affect hiring and promotions with closer in-groups (such as family) are getting preferential treatment. Employee

commitment to the organization is low. Whereas relationships with colleagues are cooperative for in-groups, and they are cold or even hostile to out-groups. Personal relationships prevail over task and company.

The implication on cloud computing is that whereas in the U.S. cloud computing is likely be dominated by individual companies, who have the best cloud computing technologies such as software companies like Microsoft and Google, as well as hardware companies like IBM and HP. In China the dominant players are likely to be the Chinese government and companies that have both great resources and close ties with the government, such as those state owned telecom operators.

METHODOLOGY

Based on the cultural differences and their impact on cloud computing, it is suspected that:

1. The future cloud computing ecosystems might be completely different between the U.S. and China;
2. The dominant players in the American cloud computing ecosystems might be the companies who control the Cloud Server;
3. A dominant party in the Chinese cloud computing ecosystems might be the companies who control the Cloud Network.

To further testify the above conjectures, we have conducted case-based interviews, and talked to a large number of people with different roles in both the U.S. and China.

Subjects

In the U.S., we interviewed 50 IT professionals, from both the public and private sectors. In the private sector, we have talked to people from all three major parties of cloud computing, namely

Cloud Server such as Microsoft, Amazon and Google, Cloud Network such as AT&T and T-Mobile, and Cloud Client such as some local application providers. The people we interviewed include both technical engineers and senior level executives.

In China, we have also interviewed 50 people, ranging from provincial government officials, employees and CEOs in some leading Chinese software companies, as well as researchers in the Chinese universities.

Instrument

We have mainly used case-based interviews around three main categories of questions. The questions focused on both the status quo and projections of the future.

The purpose of the first category of questions is to get people's direct perceptions on which party they think dominates cloud computing. In essence the two main questions in this category are:

1. Which of the three major sectors (Cloud Server, Cloud Network and Cloud Client) dominates the cloud computing ecosystem now?
2. Which sector is to dominate the cloud computing ecosystem in the next decade?

For a second category of questions, we have identified three proxies that describe the dominant sector in the cloud computing ecosystem, and asked questions around these indicators. The three proxies are (1) bargaining power, (2) total profit, and (3) profit margin. The main questions in the second category can be summarized as the following:

3. Which of the three major sectors (Cloud Server, Cloud Network and Cloud Client) has the biggest bargaining power in the cloud computing ecosystem now?

4. What sector will have the biggest bargaining power in the cloud computing ecosystem in the next decade?
5. Which sector has the biggest profit in the cloud computing ecosystem now?
6. Which sector is to have the biggest profit in the cloud computing ecosystem in the next decade?
7. Which sector has the highest profit margin in the cloud computing ecosystem now?
8. Which sector will have the highest profit margin in the cloud computing ecosystem in the next decade?

The last category of questions is around the six key cultural dimensions we analyzed in previous sub-section and their impact on cloud computing, such as the current status of cloud computing, the role of government on cloud computing development, and whether cloud computing is going to be built bottom-up or top-down.

RESULTS

Which of the Three Major Sectors (Cloud Server, Cloud Network and Cloud Client) Dominates the Cloud Computing Ecosystem Now and Future?

72% of the respondents in the U.S. have expressed that the Cloud Server companies should play a dominant role in the ecosystem both now and future. 20% have claimed that Cloud Network companies would play a leading role, and only 8% believe in the Cloud Client companies.

Almost all the people in Cloud Server companies we interviewed are optimistic about their companies' future in cloud computing. Quite a few senior managers in the leading Cloud Server companies have claimed that they "already lead the ecosystem and are confident that they would maintain the leading position going into the future."

Interviewees in the Cloud Network companies are more cautious about their future roles in cloud computing, but they said they "have ambitious plans for cloud computing too."

In China, almost all people we have interviewed agree that no companies have managed to become a major player in the Chinese cloud computing market yet. Many companies we interviewed have said they have "just started trials." But when asked who they think would likely to become a dominant player in could computing in the future, 66% of the interviewees have mentioned state-owned telecom operators (i.e., Cloud Network companies), and many of them even have mentioned the Chinese government including provincial governments. 12% of the interviewees have said that the Client Server companies would dominant, and 22% for Cloud Client companies. Also, over two-thirds of the interviewees agree Chinese companies are unlikely to become a key player in the global Cloud Server domain.

Which of the Three Major Sectors (Cloud Server, Cloud Network and Cloud Client) has the Largest Bargaining Power in the Cloud Computing Ecosystem Now and Future?

The statistical result of this question is summarized in Table 3.

Table 3. Survey result of party with largest bargaining power

% of Respondents		Cloud Server	Cloud Network	Cloud Client
American	Now	52%	28%	20%
	Next decade	68%	20%	12%
Chinese	Now	16%	40%	44%
	Next decade	20%	62%	18%

The results have shown that in the U.S., more than half of the people believe Cloud Server companies currently have the biggest bargaining power, and its bargaining power is likely to be more in the next decade. In China, current Cloud Client companies are believed to have the most bargaining power among three parties, and second are the Cloud Network companies. This is likely because the Cloud Servicer and Cloud Network are not fully established yet, but thousands of cloud applications are already available. It is strongly believed that the Cloud Network companies are to have the most bargaining power in the next decade, and only 18% of the interviewees believe the Cloud Client providers are to have the most bargaining power, which is likely because the providers for client terminals and applications are scattered and dispersed.

Which Party is Most Profitable in the Cloud Computing Ecosystem Now and Future?

Table 4 below summarized major players in the U.S. and Chinese cloud computing markets, and their total profits as well as profit margins in 2011.

Please note that many of the players are in multiple business lines and their profits are not only limited to cloud computing. As a matter of fact, most of the profits for such companies as Apple, Microsoft and IBM are not from cloud computing as of today. However, it is expected that cloud computing is to grow dramatically in the coming years. According to one analyst we have talked to, "even though right now the cloud computing unit in Amazon is small enough that Amazon doesn't report its revenue, it could well hit $1B in 2012."

The difference between the profitability of major cloud computing players between the U.S. and China as of 2011 is quite distinct. In the U.S., the companies with the biggest profit also have highest profit margin, such as Apple, Microsoft,

Table 4. Major cloud computing players in the U.S. and China markets and their profitability

U.S. Market			Chinese Market		
Company	Net income for year ending December 31, 2010	Net Profit Margin	Company	Net income for year ending December 31, 2010	Net Profit Margin
Apple	USD 25.9B*	23.9%	China Mobile	CNY 119.6B	24.7%
Microsoft	USD 23.2B*	33.1%	China Telecom	CNY 15.8B	7.2%
AT&T	USD 19.9B	17.5%	Tencent	CNY 8.1B	41.0%
IBM	USD 14.8B	15.0%	China Unicom	CNY 3.9B	2.3%
Intel	USD 11.5B*	26.3%	Baidu	CNY 3.5B	45.8%
Google	USD 8.5B	29.0%	Alibaba	CNY 1.5B	26.4%
HP	USD 7.1B*	5.6%	Sohu	USD 148.6M	24.3%
Comcast	USD 3.6B	9.6%	Qihoo 360	USD 8.5M	14.8%
RIM	USD 3.4B*	17.1%	Sina	USD -19.1M	-4.7%
Dell	USD 2.6B*	4.3%			
Verizon	USD 2.5B	2.4%			
Amazon	USD 1.2B	3.4%			
Salesforce.com	USD 64.5M*	3.9%			

* Apple's fiscal year ending on September 24th, 2011; Microsoft's fiscal year ending on June 30th, 2011; Intel's fiscal year ending on December 25th, 2010; HP's fiscal year ending on October 31st, 2011; RIM's fiscal year ending on February 26th, 2011; Dell's fiscal year ending on January 28th, 2011; Salesforce.com's fiscal year ending on January 31st, 2011

IBM and Google. These are also the companies that are either among the first movers or have shifted company strategy to enter the cloud computing market with their deep pockets, particularly in the Cloud Server space, as we have already discussed in the beginning of the chapter. In comparison, the Cloud Network companies such as Comcast and Verizon are less profitable. However in China, the most profitable companies in cloud computing are not software companies, but the three largest state-owned telecom operators, and particularly China Mobile with almost $20B profit in 2011. The leading Chinese Internet companies such as Tencent, Baidu and Alibaba, though having high profit margins, are relatively small compared to the giant operators.

In terms of projection of future profitability, more than 70% of the people we have interviewed in the U.S., think the status quo is likely to con-

tinue, indicating the Cloud Server companies are likely to be the dominant players in the ecosystem. 25% of the people expect pure cloud computing companies are to become more profitable than they are today.

In China, less than 30% of people interviewed expect China to become a major player in the Network Server space globally in the next decade. However, close to 70% of the interviewees expect the Chinese telecom operators to dominate the cloud computing space in China, where the Cloud Network companies already are as of today.

When we have interviewed people working in these telecom companies, they have indicated very ambitious plans. One senior officer in one of the Chinese telecom operators have said that Chinese telecom operators are currently "the key players in the Chinese data center market, amounting to 60% of the market share. Telecom operators own and control enormous IT infrastructure resources in China, which could effectively resolve the key issues in the future cloud computing services, such as performance, security and reliability. This gives telecom operators huge competitive advantages in cloud storage and virtualization." When asked about the cloud computing strategy, a person working in the research institute of a major telecom operator in China has said "the ultimate goal of the Big Three (a name given to the three state-owned telecom operators in China) should be to become all-service providers in cloud computing, including Server, Network and Client".

SUPPORTING QUESTIONS AROUND CULTURE DIMENSIONS

The Current IT Status

In the U.S. market, the major cloud computing players are already offerings Software as a Service, Platform as a Service and Infrastructure as a Service, deployed across Private Clouds, Hybrid Clouds and Public Clouds. In contrast, Chinese players have just started to experiment with cloud computing.

One of the cloud computing researchers in a top Chinese university has told us during the interview that "compared to western advanced countries, our study of cloud computing has started relatively late in China. Furthermore, Chinese domestic companies as well as the users have a different understanding of cloud computing, and as a result many companies right now focus more on just the concept and less on real applications. Few companies have really landed in cloud computing yet."

Long Term Orientation

We have asked about how much further into the future each company is planning for their cloud computing development. In the U.S., the larger the company, the longer they plan strategically. Only 28% of the people we interviewed have admitted, that they have had strategic plan for three years and beyond.

In China, since cloud computing has just started and companies are still exploring the concept, not many companies has figured out a clear plan yet. However, almost all the government officials we have talked to clearly indicate that the Chinese government has already a long term plan for cloud computing. One senior government official has told us that "20 cities in China consider cloud computing as a strategic development area in the 12th five-year plans of China, which runs from 2011 to 2015."

Government Driven vs. Market Driven

In the U.S., almost all companies respond that their strategic plans are driven by the market and competition, without much or even no influence from the government. One of the local government officials we have talked to said they "have already started to use cloud computing to provide more efficient public services to the citizens", but they "have no intention to guide or regulate the market."

In China, almost all government officials we have talked to say either they have already or are planning to deploy cloud computing. One of the experts in could computing has told us that "almost all local governments are actively leading cloud computing by building large data centers in their own area and demonstrating cloud computing services." One of the government officials has mentioned that "in 2011, the Chinese National Development and Reform Commission has invested 0.7 billion RMB in 5 cities including Beijing, Shanghai, Shenzhen, Hangzhou and Wuxi, as first round of cloud computing demo cities. Led by the government, we have moved from concept to application."

Another interesting point we have come across during the interviews is about net neutrality. Whereas in the U.S., everybody agrees that there should be no restrictions by Internet service providers or the governments, on consumers' access to the Internet, the Chinese views are obviously very different. One senior level manager in one of the leading Chinese Internet company has expressed their desire to "cooperate fully with the government and comply with the law," and that they would "of course not show anything the government deems inappropriate." More than one interviewee mentioned that "one of the advantages of state-owned operators is that the government has full control over them."

Locus of Control

When asked about what factors determine whether their companies can succeed in cloud computing, people in the U.S., have cited such factors as technology, service, understanding of the market, as well as competition. About 70% of the interviewees have expressed the belief that "they controll their own destinies."

Chinese interviewees have cited similar factors when asked the same question. However, almost all interviewees also have mentioned the relationship with government as one important success factor in business, especially in cloud computing. More than 90% of the people think their success in cloud computing are controlled by the government to some extent. The case of Google being forced out of China mainland has been mentioned multiple times.

Power Distance

When asked whether they think their company's cloud computing strategy defined by senior level executives are heading in the right direction, the answers from American interviewees are mixed. One of the employees in a leading software company has expressed the concern that moving to cloud would drastically shrink its company's profit margin and wondered whether it is a good idea at all.

The answers from Chinese interviewees are almost unanimously yes. "Our strategy is to work closely with the government," says one executive. Other people have expressed similar opinions. "To be successful in cloud computing, you should definitely get into the circle", mentions one manager in a key cloud computing service provider, pointing to the second pilot list from the Development and Reform Commission. "The central government has invested almost a billion RMB in the first pilot. With funds from local governments as well as from the industry, the total investment in cloud computing has exceeded tens of billions RMB. We are trying our best to get into the second pilot list."

Individualism vs. Collectivism

We have asked the interviewees whether they believe the cloud computing players in their market would be more likely to compete or cooperate.

Almost 78% of the respondents in the U.S. market believe they are more likely to compete. One senior executive of a leading cloud computing player thinks it is almost impossible for competitors to collectively work together. "We have a corporate group where people look at competition full time. It is built into our scorecard that we need to gain market share at the expense of competitors." "Of course we would form strategic alliances, just like Microsoft and Nokia did, but this is more the exception than the norm."

Only about 30% of the respondents in China believe they are more likely to compete. More people believe the most likely scenario is for each player to work with the government collectively in cloud computing. Almost all companies we talk to have mentioned they are working with either the local government or state-owned telecom operators on cloud computing to different extents.

ANALYSIS

The survey results have pointed out, both quantitatively and qualitatively, that the cloud computing ecosystems between the U.S. and China today are drastically different, where major players in the U.S. have moved into the cloud already, and own technologies to build enormous Cloud Server systems, providing both cloud storage and cloud service centrally in large scale, cloud computing in China has just started and is still mainly at the concept phase.

Today, the most profitable cloud computing players in the U.S., are the Cloud Server companies, and they are expected to remain the dominant players in the future.

Even though China has just started to deploy cloud computing, the Chinese government has put it as a strategic area in its 12th five-year national development plans, and has already invested billions into cloud computing. It is expected that cloud computing is to develop rapidly by the commercial sector and the local governments working collectively, under the leadership of Chinese central government. The state-owned telecom operators are expected to be the biggest players in cloud computing. Those in control of the Cloud Network today, are expected to reach beyond, and become the Cloud Server and as well as the Cloud Clients in the future.

CONCLUSION

Cloud computing is becoming the next revolution in the IT industry after the PC and the Internet. It has the potential to dramatically change the structure of the current IT industry. As Internet data and services continue to be centrally stored and serviced as metered utility, various players today are likely to transform into three major sectors in the future cloud computing ecosystem namely the Cloud Server, Network and Client.

There is a sharp contrast between the current state of cloud computing in the U.S. and China. Most of the advanced technologies of cloud computing are owned by the U.S. companies. China has just begun developing cloud computing. In the U.S., the dominant players in cloud computing are companies such as Microsoft, Google, and IBM, who are in the Cloud Server business. They are likely to continue to dominate the cloud computing ecosystem in the future.

In China, the cloud computing industry is less established, and it is still in the concept development phase. However, IT companies have substantial profits, and a large customer base. The control of the infrastructure is owned by organizations that have close ties to the Chinese government. The state-owned Chinese telecom operators stand to be the strongest players in the future cloud computing ecosystem. Currently, they are in the Cloud Network business, but they aim to become all-service providers in the future.

Due to cultural differences, especially along the six key cultural dimensions, the transformation of cloud computing ecosystems could follow different paths in the U.S. and China. It is natural to expect that the cloud computing development in the U.S. to be driven by free markets and competition, with competitive companies having the best technologies. In China, the development of cloud computing is being led by national and local governments, with large investments in the order of tens of billions of RMB. Almost all players are seeking support from the government and state-owned telecom operators, who have the best chance to become the dominant players in the future.

REFERENCES

Alavi, M., Kayworth, T., & Leidner, D. (2006). An empirical examination of the influence of organizational culture on knowledge management practices. *Journal of Management Information Systems*, *22*(3), 191–224. doi:10.2753/MIS0742-1222220307.

Gartner. (2010). *Gartner identifies the top 10 strategic technologies for 2011*. Retrieved from http://www.gartner.com/it/page.jsp?id=1454221

Hofstede, G. (1981). Culture and organization. *Int. Studies of Man., &. Org.*, *10*(4), 15–41.

Hofstede, G. (1984). *Culture's consequences: International differences in work-related values*. Beverly Hills, CA: SAGE Publications.

Hofstede, G. (1991). *Cultures and organizations: Software of the mind*. London: McGraw-Hill Book Company.

Hofstede, G., Hofstede, G. J., & Minkov, M. (2010). *Cultures and organizations: Software of the mind*. London: McGraw-Hill.

Leidner, D., & Kayworth, T. (2006). A review of culture in information systems research: Toward a theory of information technology culture conflict. *Management Information Systems Quarterly*, *30*(2), 357–399.

Market Research Media. (2012). *Global cloud computing market forecast 2015-2020*. Author.

Mell, P., & Grance, T. (2011). *The NIST definition of cloud computing*. Washington, DC: National Institute of Standards and Technology.

Rudd, S., Brown, A., Levitt, M., & Luk, G. (2012). *Global cloud computing services: Software, infrastructure and platform services move to the mainstream*. Strategy Analytics.

Chapter 15
Cloud Strategy Leads Innovation in China

Yushi Shen
Microsoft Corporation, USA

Ling Wu
EMC² Corporation, USA

Yale Li
Microsoft Corporation, USA

Shaofeng Liu
Microsoft Corporation, USA

Qian Wen
Endronic Corp, USA

ABSTRACT

Cloud computing is a historically significant trend in the development of information technology and applications. The cloud concept and the corresponding series of changes in technology, business, application, and service models are inevitable results of such developments in the information industry. In recent years, governments and major IT companies have introduced new IT strategies based on cloud computing, such as innovative platforms, services, and applications. More and more data and applications are migrating into the cloud, and the development of cloud computing is in full swing (Shen & Zhang, 2013).

INTRODUCTION

Today, Microsoft, Apple and Google dominate the global information industry, and thus three major ecosystems have been formed gradually. Although the Big Three are different in terms of characteristics, they have many similarities in investment and strategic layout: they tend to develop the cloud technology at the back-end in terms of cloud centers and platforms; they also develop terminal technologies at the front-end such as but not limited to mobile phone, tablet,

DOI: 10.4018/978-1-4666-4801-2.ch015

desktop, TV, game console and etc.; and they have all adopted the App Store model in terms of providing intermediary services.

With the approach of "absorbing the useful and discarding the useless", China is learning from the experience and the strategic layout of these international cloud computing giants, and actively exploring cloud strategy in line with China's national characteristics. The latest result of our endeavour is the "E-government 2.0", a new generation of e-government platform that is people-oriented and based in the cloud, and also adopting new IT trends. This may become the core engine of China's economic development, social management and services. It is to lead China's industrialization and innovation, promote the emergence of a large number of innovative application services in various fields, such as economic and social development, government's social management, public services and SMEs, narrow the gap between urban and rural areas, and provide a strong impetus for speeding up China's economic restructuring of industries and scientific developments.

A NEW GENERATION OF E-GOVERNMENT PLATFORM

Compared with the previous "E-government 1.0", "E-government 2.0" is a new generation of e-government platform. After 20 years of development, the traditional e-government has some brilliant achievements: government website systems for central, local and various industries have been generally established; the construction of a basic information base has been steadily moving forward, and a series of "golden projects" have been promoting the informatization of the core business of government, creating significant economic and social benefits. The informatization of the government stimulates the informatization of the society as a whole, and therefore has significant influence on the

modernization of China's economic system – industrial, organizational and social structures.

However, traditional government platforms have major problems in overall planning, coordinated sharing, independent innovation, unified planning and standards so on. Examples are the island data centers established for each committee, office, department and bureau of the government, which makes it difficult to share, coordinate and integrate data because of fragmentation. This prevents efficient planning, design, construction, application and management according to unified business requirements, data format, technologies and evaluation standards. This system fails to provide everyday users with intelligent on-demand services, so they often have to search in a vast sea of data.

With the vigorous development of cloud computing and mobile Internet, the information world is soon to enter an era of big data, and China is also to usher in the era of E-government 2.0. In order to seize the historic opportunity and achieve leapfrog development, China needs to accurately grasp the essence and nature of information industry's development, and learn from the international industrial giants' strategy of the three-tier framework, namely, "Cloud + Terminal + App Store", so as to formulate cloud strategies based on China's national characteristics.

In the international community, public cloud platforms are mainly invested and built by Microsoft and other social and/or private enterprises, providing services to users worldwide. But in China, the government holds the most credible power of action rather than any private enterprises, and therefore China's cloud platforms must be built, managed and operated with more or less involvement of the government. The Chinese government is undeniably the single dominating player in the entire industry.

To develop a Chinese model of cloud computing, there are two basic characteristics, namely, "independence and self-control" and "opening up and win-win". China should actively track and learn from foreign cutting-edge technologies and state-of-art operation models, while bearing in mind the reality of China. Meanwhile, China can take advantage of government policies, markets and talents to guide the forward-looking and independent innovation of cloud computing.

In the hands of hundreds of millions of users, the terminal provides all kinds of cloud applications and services as well as user experience. With the success of iPhone, the era of "whoever wins the back-end can conquer the world" has been completely replaced by Apple's strategy of the big unification of "the front-end, middle-tier and back-end." Now Google and Microsoft are vigorously pursuing the terminal market, and "whoever wins the terminal can conquer the world" has become the strategy by industry consensus.

In contrast to the "closed" Apple and "excessively open" Google strategies, Microsoft's strategy of "Cloud + Terminal" is far-reaching. Microsoft proposes to establish a joint user experience and a unified R&D experience covering PC, tablet, mobile phone, Internet TV, game console and other types of terminals. In consideration of China's large population and a variety of terminals, it seems that China can take advantage of the "Microsoft Model."

Terminal management and services are to become the basis of e-government's management and service model. The new generation of e-government develops a new "terminal" services concept: that all users can be involved in the development and services process, and such services target highly individualized needs. One specific example is the government or enterprises providing highly personalized services for citizens, such as providing the air quality and pollution information, at the place a user suffering from asthma happens to stay; and another example is providing the driver real time vacancy information of parking lots in the vicinity.

E-government 1.0 requires civilians to search by themselves for the needed information at the back-end where massive information accumulates, whether they understand IT or not, even if the needed information is just one sentence. However, E-government 2.0 is to remove this inconvenience, helping the government to automatically deliver the "one-sentence information" to its civilians. Imagine, for a country of 1.3 billion, if every citizen can receive a personalized service message from the government, the image of the Chinese government can be much improved that the government is for the people and by the people.

The core of cloud computing is the transition from products to services. The essence of the cloud service is the informatization of human social life, and the virtualization of the physical world. After the analysis of the control functions of "the cloud," and the management and service functions of "the terminal" in E-government 2.0, a more ambitious blueprint of the government driving economic development is formulated with the middle-tier "App Store."

Internationally, Apple has "Apple Store" and Microsoft has "Windows Store." Today, there are over ten thousand applications on Apple's platform, and this number is still growing at a rapid pace, bringing into existence hundreds of development companies. After the release of Windows 8 and Windows Phone 8, Microsoft is rapidly catching up. Both are typical patterns of the platform stimulating industrial innovation and market demand. The current app stores are still in the elementary stage of development, and can only support independent developers. In the future, collective development is to further address the manpower issues for the development of large-scale systems.

In consideration of China's national characteristics, one possible model is: The government leads or participates in the construction of "the cloud", and then provide its data to developers at extremely low prices or free of charge, thus further opening up government data appropriately, and encouraging all the people to participate in innovation and enjoying the benefits resulting from such innovation. The profit can be divided among the government, network or telecom operators and developers, according to certain proportion. Thus, hundreds of millions of SMEs, developers, entrepreneurs can participate in innovation at very low costs. Enterprises from big to small, such as the developer of "Angry Birds," can all be part of an industrial and information revolution! In the future software development, the development process is to change to an open model; the developers are to shift from the elite to the masses, and the development organizations are to shift from workshops to the whole community. This model integrates collective and mass R&D, elite planning and management, personalized and diversified services, which are bound to drive the industrial development, and enhance the productivity and creativity of the community as a whole.

MICRO-ENTREPRENEURSHIP AND CIVILIAN INNOVATION

The current world is undergoing great development, changes and adjustment. With the further development of world's diversity and economic globalization, the increase in global employment pressure, and the widening gap between the rich and the poor, governments are constantly exploring new development patterns which can keep pace with the era. History proves that innovative and subverting technologies are to lead to a new industrial revolution, not only greatly improving productive efficiency and expanding new markets, but also changing the organizational structure of the traditional enterprises, and the industrial structure of society as a whole. As a new generation of revolutionary technology, cloud computing is perhaps the key force in promoting global industrial change, and the transformation of China.

The importance of innovation is self-evident. Improving its ability in independent innovation and building an innovative country is an urgent need for China, to meet the challenges of a new technological revolution and the industrial evolution of the world. It is the core of China's national development strategy, and an impetus for enhancing comprehensive national strength. The key to the issue is how to guide, promote and achieve China's transition to become an innovation-oriented nation.

Innovation without entrepreneurship is like a tree without roots. Under the support of the new generation of e-government platform, combining micro-entrepreneurship with new information technologies like cloud computing is going to be an effective way for China's transition to an innovation-oriented country!

Micro-entrepreneurship is a new eco-entrepreneurship pattern, based on micro-projects in market segmentations, resource sharing and intensive management. Due to its small investment, quick results and capacity for bulk copy or expansion, it overcomes the general concern of economists and sociologists. After all, what meets the individual needs of human beings is often the "detailed and special" rather than the "large and comprehensive", and multi-function tends to sacrifice the efficiency of a single function, so the Pareto principle (also known as the 80-20 rule) in the traditional economic pattern is not applicable in the cloud era.

However, it is difficult for a disorderly sprouting of micro-enterprises to create effective business value and social benefits, or to have a competitive edge in the market. But when micro-entrepreneurship is combined with the new information technologies like cloud computing, under the support of a new generation of e-government model, a variety of individual characteristics and advantages are going to crystalize, and revealing its commercial value in the larger scope. With more and more innovators involved, the large and all-encompassing organizational structure of the traditional manufacturing enterprises is to largely disappear, while micro-enterprises with only simple functions and a focus on the segmented business is to become prevalent.

The combination of micro-entrepreneurship and cloud computing is to break the monopoly of a few large enterprises, making possible a new form of society featuring "civilian innovation." The emergence of revolutionary technologies lowers the start-up costs and enriches the resources available for entrepreneurship, and facilitates the promotion of application services. Under this circumstance, communication, sharing and self-learning take place all the time, and everyone can be an expert as well as a "property owner" in the virtual world, converting the information wealth into material wealth, and gradually narrowing the gap between the rich and the poor by wealth redistribution.

It is to be emphasized that in order to realize E-government 2.0, we need to build micro-enterprise systems and promote the transition to an innovative society, it is of the utmost importance to open up, circulate, share and integrate big data, apart from employing cloud computing and other new information technologies. The data possessed and maintained by the government is the wealth and assets of the nation, so in principle, for data not involving national security, personal privacy and business secrets, especially the data related to public affairs, we should break the fragmentation, integrate and open it up to the people or the corresponding development communities. The openness and flow of data represents the openness and flow of knowledge and wealth. Only by following the path of "public ownership of data and national innovation", can we fundamentally solve the embarrassing situation of "data explosion with poor knowledge." The government can then obtain more information scattered in all corners of the society, and benefit from the collective wisdom of the people. Of course, in reality, this is a gradual process to achieve freedom and equality, mutual promotion and common development in the whole society.

CONCLUSION AND OUTLOOK

By virtue of the government's credibility and the public data possessed by the government, to provide scientific and technological development communities with cloud platforms - the construction of which is led by the government for free or at low costs, and by taking advantage of the public clouds, private clouds and intelligent terminals, to inspire the masses to develop lots of regional and personalized information services, can be a cloud strategy with Chinese characteristics. The government's objectives of "mobilizing the masses and serving the masses", "by the people and for the people" and "from the masses, to the masses" are to enjoy a new manifestation in the cloud era.

It is of far-reaching significance to build E-government 2.0 based on the new trends of information technology, and apply it to government administration and public services, since it is to create countless employment opportunities, promote China's transition to an innovative society while still maintaining economic growth, and improve social management and services while preserving the social order.

We believe, in the near future, the new generation of e-government based on China's standards and the concept of E-government 2.0 is bound to power the rise of industries in China. This industry is going to be low-carbon, environmentally friendly and high value-added. It reflects the government's purpose of serving the people, also achieving efficient and healthy social management. By the opening up and sharing of big data, characterized by micro-entrepreneurship, this industry is to promote civilian innovation throughout all walks of life.

A powerful and fair cloud computing information ecosystem is to change the form of distribution of material wealth through technical means. In this sense, the cloud computing revolution is no longer a heroic revolution, but a people's revolution which delivers great hope for the Chinese people. In the era of cloud computing, people rather than heroes are to become the real forces creating the history. Following this major trend, with the perfection of the institutional systems, and through ideological and moral reconstruction, the great dream of common prosperity is to be gradually realized.

REFERENCES

Shen, Y., Zhang, Y.-Q., & Li, Y. (2013). *Cloud 360 - An in-depth look at cloud era by Microsoft experts*. New York: Electronic Industry Press.

Compilation of References

Abdelnur, A. (2012). *Apache Oozie (incubating) 3.2.0 release*. Retrieved from http://blog.cloudera.com/blog/2012/06/apache-oozie-incubating-3-2-0-release-hadoop-workflow-scheduler/

Accelerated Analytics. (2010). *Making sense of retail link data*. Retrieved from http://www.acceleratedanalytics.com/blog/2010/10/1/making-sense-of-retail-link-data.html

Accenture. (2011). *How big data can fuel bigger growth*. Retrieved from http://www.accenture.com/us-en/outlook/Pages/outlook-journal-2011-how-big-data-fuels-bigger-growth.aspx

Aginity.com. (2013). *Customer intelligence appliance (CIA)*. Retrieved from http://www.aginity.com/solutions/customer-intelligence-appliance/

Ahronovitz, M., & Pabla, K. (2013). What is Hadoop? *Thecloudtutorial.com*. Retrieved from http://thecloudtutorial.com/hadoop-tutorial.html

AI3. (2005). *Semi-structured data: Happy 10th birthday*. Retrieved from http://www.mkbergman.com/153/semi-structured-data-happy-10th-birthday/

Alavi, M., Kayworth, T., & Leidner, D. (2006). An empirical examination of the influence of organizational culture on knowledge management practices. *Journal of Management Information Systems*, 22(3), 191–224. doi:10.2753/MIS0742-1222220307.

Alfke, J. (2012). *Guide: Introduction – The REST API*. Retrieved from https://github.com/couchbaselabs/TouchDB-iOS/wiki/Guide%3A-Introduction

Amazon Dynamo, D. B. (n.d.). *Wikipedia*. Retrieved from http://en.wikipedia.org/wiki/Amazon_DynamoDB

Amazon Web Services. (2010). *How to create and debug an Amazon elastic MapReduce job flow*. Retrieved from http://aws.amazon.com/articles/3938

Amazon Web Services. (2013). *Amazon DynamoDB (Beta)*. Retrieved from http://aws.amazon.com/dynamodb/

Amazon Web Services. (2013). *Amazon EC2 instances*. Retrieved from http://aws.amazon.com/ec2/instance-types/

Answers.com. (2013). *How do you create VLAN step-by-step?* Retrieved from http://wiki.answers.com/Q/How_do_you_create_VLAN_step-by-step

Apache Hadoop. (n.d.). *Wikipedia*. Retrieved from http://en.wikipedia.org/wiki/Apache_Hadoop

Apache Incubator, P. M. C. (n.d.). *Bigtop - Apache Hadoop ecosystem packaging and test*. Retrieved from http://wiki.apache.org/incubator/BigtopProposal

Apache Software Foundation. (2010). *Apache ZooKeeper*. Retrieved from http://zookeeper.apache.org/

Apache Software Foundation. (2011). *Hadoop 0.20 documentation*. Retrieved from http://archive.cloudera.com/cdh/3/hadoop-0.20.2+320/

Apache Software Foundation. (2012). *What is Bigtop, and why should you care?* Retrieved from https://blogs.apache.org/bigtop/entry/bigtop_and_why_should_you

Apache Software Foundation. (2012). *Apache CouchDB relax*. Retrieved from http://couchdb.apache.org/

Apache Software Foundation. (2012). *Apache Flume user guide.* Retrieved from http://flume.apache.org/FlumeUserGuide.html

Apache Software Foundation. (2012). *HCatalog table management.* Retrieved from http://incubator.apache.org/hcatalog/docs/r0.4.0/

Apache Software Foundation. (2012). *What is Apache Mahout?* Retrieved from http://mahout.apache.org/

Apache Software Foundation. (2013). *Accumulo.* Retrieved from http://accumulo.apache.org/

Apache Software Foundation. (2013). *HDFS users guide.* Retrieved from http://hadoop.apache.org/docs/stable/hdfs_user_guide.html

Apache Software Foundation. (2013). *Welcome to Apache HBase.* Retrieved from http://hbase.apache.org/

Apache Software Foundation. (2013). *The Apache HBase reference guide.* Retrieved from http://hbase.apache.org/book.html

Apache Software Foundation. (2013). *Welcome to apache HCatalog!* Retrieved from http://incubator.apache.org/hcatalog/

Apache Software Foundation. (2013). *MapReduce tutorial.* Retrieved from http://hadoop.apache.org/docs/stable/mapred_tutorial.html

Apache Software Foundation. (2013). *Welcome to Apache Pig!* Retrieved from http://pig.apache.org/

Apache Software Foundation. (n.d.). *Apache PoweredBy.* Retrieved from http://wiki.apache.org/hadoop/PoweredBy

Apprenda.com. (n.d.). *Conducting a PaaS comparison.* Retrieved from http://apprenda.com/library/paas/conducting-a-paas-comparison/

Ariker, M. (2012). *The one tool you need to make big data work: The pencil.* Retrieved from http://www.forbes.com/sites/mckinsey/2012/10/09/the-one-tool-you-need-to-make-big-data-work-the-pencil/

Armbrust, M., Fox, A., Griffith, R., Joseph, A. D., Katz, R. H., & Konwinski, A. … Zaharia, M. (2009). Above the clouds: A Berkeley view of cloud computing. Berkeley, CA: University of California at Berkeley.

Autonomy. (n.d.). Retrieved from http://www.autonomy.com/content/Technology/what-is-big-data/index.en.html

Awsdocumentation. (n.d.). HDFS architecture - Store data with Hbase. *Amazon Elastic MapReduce developer guide.* Retrieved from http://docs.aws.amazon.com/ElasticMapReduce/latest/DeveloperGuide/emr-hbase.html

Baidu Encyclopedia. (2013). *Electronic information economy.* Retrieved from http://baike.baidu.com/view/2302817.htm

Baidu Encyclopedia. (2013). *Information economy.* Retrieved from http://baike.baidu.com/view/62984.htm

Baranau, A., & Gospodnetic, O. (n.d.). *Apache HBase: The NoSQL database for Hadoop and big data.* Retrieved from http://refcardz.dzone.com/refcardz/hbase

Barton, D. (2012). *How to make big data work for you?* Retrieved from http://www.smartcompany.com.au/information-technology/052342-how-to-make-big-data-work-for-you.html

Baunach, S. (2012). Three vs of big data: Volume, velocity, variety. *Data Center Knowledge.* Retrieved from http://www.datacenterknowledge.com/archives/2012/03/08/three-vs-of-big-data-volume-velocity-variety/

Biddick, M. (2012). Feds face 'big data' storage challenge. *Informationweek.* Retrieved from http://www.informationweek.com/government/information-management/feds-face-big-data-storage-challenge/240000958

Big Data. (2012). *Wikipedia.* Retrieved from http://en.wikipedia.org/wiki/Big_data

Bilger, M., et al. (2006). *Data-centric security.* IBM Corporation. Retrieved from http://www-935.ibm.com/services/us/cio/risk/gov_wp_data_centric.pdf

Bodkin, R. (2010). *LinkedIn's data infrastructure.* Retrieved from http://www.infoq.com/news/2010/08/linkedin-data-infrastructure

Borthakur, D. (2010). *Facebook has the world's largest Hadoop cluster!* Retrieved from http://hadoopblog.blogspot.com/2010/05/facebook-has-worlds-largest-hadoop.html

Borthakur, D. (2013). *HDFS architecture guide.* Retrieved from http://hadoop.apache.org/docs/stable/hdfs_design.html

Branddirectory.com. (2012). *Global 500 2012 – Find out what the world's top brands are in 2012*. Retrieved from http://brandirectory.com/league_tables/table/global-500-2012

Brand, S. (1987). *The media lab: Inventing the future at MIT*. New York: Academic Press.

Brenner, M. (2012). What is big data? *Business Innovation from SAP*. Retrieved from http://blogs.sap.com/innovation/big-data/big-data-what-is-it-05326

BrightPlanet. (2012). *Structure data vs. unstructured data*. Retrieved from http://www.brightplanet.com/2012/06/structured-vs-unstructured-data/

Burns, C. (2012). *10 most powerful IaaS companies*. Retrieved from http://www.networkworld.com/supp/2012/enterprise2/040912-ecs-iaas-companies-257611.html

CALIT2. (n.d.). Retrieved from http://www.calit2.net/newsroom/release.php?id=694

Castro, M., Druschel, P., Kermarrec, A.-M., Nandi, A., Rowstron, A., & Singh, A. (2003). SplitStream: High-bandwidth multicast in cooperative environments. In *Proceedings of the SOSP'03 ACM Symposium on Operating Systems Principles*. Bolton Landing, NY: ACM.

Catalyurek, U., Boman, E., Devine, K., Bozdag, D., & Heaphy, R. (2007). Hypergraph-based dynamic load balancing for adaptive scientific computations. In *Proceedings of IPDPS'07*. IPDPS.

CEBR. (2012). *Data equity: Unlocking the value of big data*. Retrieved from http://www.sas.com/offices/europe/uk/downloads/data-equity-cebr.pdf

Chandler, A. D. (1977). *The visible hand: The managerial revolution in America business*. Boston: Harvard University Press.

Chandler, A. D., & Cortada, J. (2000). *A nation transformed by information: How information has shaped the United States from colonial times to the present*. Oxford, UK: Oxford University Press.

Chang, F., Dean, J., Ghemawat, S., Hsieh, W. C., Wallach, D. A., & Murrows, M. … Gruber, R. E. (2006). Bigtable: A distributed storage system for structure data. *OSDI*. Retrieved from http://static.googleusercontent.com/external_content/untrusted_dlcp/research.google.com/en/us/archive/bigtable-osdi06.pdf

Chansler, R., Kuang, H., Radia, S., Shvachko, K., & Srinivas, S. (n.d.). *The Hadoop distributed file system*. Retrieved from http://www.aosabook.org/en/hdfs.html

China Ministry of Industry and Information. (2012). *Internet of things – 12ᵗʰ five-year development plan*. Retrieved from http://www.gov.cn/zwgk/2012-02/14/content_2065999.htm

CineGrid. (n.d.). Retrieved from http://www.cinegrid.org

CISCO. (2013). *Network virtualization solutions*. Retrieved from http://www.cisco.com/en/US/netsol/ns658/index.html

Clegg, D. (2012). *Big data: The data variety discussion*. IBM The Big Data Hub. Retrieved from http://www.ibm-bigdatahub.com/blog/big-data-data-variety-discussion

Cloudera Blog. (2013). *Flume posts*. Retrieved from http://blog.cloudera.com/blog/category/flume/

Clouds360.com. (n.d.). *Top 20 platform as a service vendors*. Retrieved from http://www.clouds360.com/paas.php

Cogswell, J. (2012). *SQL vs NoSQL: Which is better*. Retrieved from http://slashdot.org/topic/bi/sql-vs-nosql-which-is-better/

CollectiveAccess. (n.d.). Retrieved from http://www.collectiveaccess.org/

Columbus, L. (2012). *Cloud computing and enterprise software forecast update, 2012*. Retrieved from http://softwarestrategiesblog.com/category/2012-cloud-predictions/

Columbus, L. (2012). *Why CIOs are quickly prioritizing analytics, cloud and mobile*. Retrieved from http://softwarestrategiesblog.com/2012/09/16/why-cios-are-quickly-prioritizing-analytics-cloud-and-mobile/

Condliffe, J. (2012). *How Facebook uses you as part of a giant sociological experiment*. Retrieved from http://gizmodo.com/5918319/how-facebook-uses-you-as-part-of-a-giant-sociological-experiment

Conway, D. (2012). News release: Teradata big analytics appliance enables new business insights on all enterprise data. *Teradata Corp*. Retrieved from http://www.teradata.com/News-Releases/2012/Teradata-Big-Analytics-Appliance-Enables-New-Business-Insights-on--All-Enterprise-Data/

Cooper, G. (2011). *Getting started with CouchDB.* Retrieved from http://net.tutsplus.com/tutorials/getting-started-with-couchdb/

Cosentino, T. (2012). *Gaining time to value from big data.* Retrieved from http://tonycosentino.ventanaresearch.com/2012/08/30/gaining-time-to-value-from-big-data/

Couch, D. B. (n.d.). *Wikipedia.* Retrieved from http://en.wikipedia.org/wiki/CouchDB

COVISE. (n.d.). Retrieved from http://www.hlrs.de/organization/av/vis/covise/

Crump, G. (2009). *What is file virtualization?* Retrieved from http://www.storage-switzerland.com/Articles/Entries/2009/12/3_What_is_File_Virtualization.html

Cruz-Neira, C., Sandin, D., DeFanti, T., Kenyon, R., & Hart, J. (1992, June). The CAVE®: Audio visual experience automatic virtual environment. *Communications of the ACM.* doi:10.1145/129888.129892.

Cutting, D. (2013). *Hadoop and big data.* Retrieved from http://www.cloudera.com/content/cloudera/en/why-cloudera/hadoop-and-big-data.html

Daly, D. (2012). *Donal Daly on big data analytics.* Retrieved from http://donaldaly.blogspot.com/2012/10/my-perspective-on-teradata-aster-big.html

Data Structure. (n.d.). *Wikipedia.* Retrieved from http://en.wikipedia.org/wiki/Data_structure

Datastax Corp. (2012). *Comparing the Hadoop distributed file system (HDFS) with the Cassandra file system(CFS)* (white paper). Retrieved from http://www.datastax.com/wp-content/uploads/2012/09/WP-DataStax-HDFS-vsCFS.pdf

Davenport, T., & Patil, D. J. (2012). Data scientist: The sexiest job of the 21st century. *Harvard Business Review.* Retrieved from http://hbr.org/2012/10/data-scientist-the-sexiest-job-of-the-21st-century/ar/1

Davis, A. (2012). The government and big data: Use, problems and potential. *Computerworld.* Retrieved from http://blogs.computerworld.com/19919/the_government_and_big_data_use_problems_and_potential

De Luca, A., & Bhide, M. (2010). *Storage virtualization for dummies.* Hoboken, NJ: Wiley Publishing, Inc. Retrieved from http://www.hds.com/at/go/virtualisierung/download/hds_storage_virtualization_for_dummies.pdf

Dean, J., & Ghemawat, S. (2004). *MapReduce: Simplifed data processing on large clusters.* Retrieved from http://static.googleusercontent.com/external_content/untrusted_dlcp/research.google.com/en/us/archive/mapreduce-osdi04.pdf

Decision Stats. (2011). *Statistics on social media.* Retrieved from http://decisionstats.com/2011/11/17/statistics-on-social-media/

DeFanti, T. A., Dawe, G., Sandin, D. J., Schulze, J. P., Otto, P., & Girado, J. et al. (2009). The STARCAVE, a third-generation CAVE and virtual reality OptIPortal. *The International Journal of FGCS, 25*(2), 169–178. doi:10.1016/j.future.2008.07.015.

DeFanti, T. A., Leigh, J., Renambot, L., Jeong, B., & Smarr, L. L. et al. (2009). The OptIPortal, a scalable visualization, storage, and computing interface device for the OptiPuter. *Future Generation Computer Systems, 25*(2), 114–123. doi:10.1016/j.future.2008.06.016.

DHS/DOJ. (n.d.a). *Fusion center guidelines—Developing and sharing information in a new era.* Washington, DC: US Government.

DHS/DOJ. (n.d.b). *Baseline capabilities for state and major urban area fusion centers.* Washington, DC: US Government.

Digital Dilemma. (2008). *The science and technology council of the academy of motion picture arts and sciences (AMPAS).* Los Angeles, CA: AMPAS.

Dignan, L. (2010). Cloudera, EMC greenplum form data warehousing alliance. *ZDNet.* Retrieved from http://www.zdnet.com/blog/btl/cloudera-emc-greenplum-form-data-warehousing-alliance/39483

Dijcks, J.-Pi. (2012). *How to implement a big data system.* Oracle Technology Network. Retrieved from http://www.oracle.com/technetwork/articles/servers-storage-admin/implementing-bigdata-1502704.html

Dilley, J., Maggs, B., Parikh, J., Prokop, H., Sitaraman, R., & Weihl, B. (2002). Globally distributed content delivery. *IEEE Internet Computing*, *6*(5), 81–86. doi:10.1109/MIC.2002.1036038.

Director of National Intelligence. (n.d.). *The national intelligence strategy*. Washington, DC: US Government.

DMC4K. (n.d.). Retrieved from http://www.dmc.keio.ac.jp/en/topics/071126-4K.html

Duhigg, C. (2012). How companies learn your secret. *The New York Times*. Retrieved from http://www.nytimes.com/2012/02/19/magazine/shopping-habits.html?pagewanted=all

Dumbill, E. (2010). *The SMAQ stack for big data: Storage, MapReduce and query are ushering in data-driven products and services*. Retrieved from http://strata.oreilly.com/2010/09/the-smaq-stack-for-big-data.html

Dumbill, E. (2011). *Oracle's big data appliance: What it means*. Retrieved from http://strata.oreilly.com/2011/10/oracles-big-data-appliance.html

Dunning, T. (2008). *ZooKeeper – A reliable, scalable distributed coordination system*. Retrieved from http://highscalability.com/blog/2008/7/15/zookeeper-a-reliable-scalable-distributed-coordination-syste.html

Evans, B. (2012). Big data set to explode as 40 billion new devices connect to Internet. *Forbes*. Retrieved from http://www.forbes.com/sites/oracle/2012/11/06/big-data-set-to-explode-as-40-billion-new-devices-connect-to-internet/

Everett, C. (2011). *Gartner predicts boom year for Saas*. Retrieved from http://www.businesscloud9.com/content/gartner-predicts-boom-year-saas/5907

Exams, E. M. C. (n.d.). *Which data asset is an example of quasi-structured data?* Retrieved from http://www.aiotestking.com/emc/2013/01/04/which-data-asset-is-an-example-of-quasi-structured-data/

Farr, C. (2012). *These are the skills you need to be a data scientist at Facebook*. Retrieved from http://venturebeat.com/2012/08/27/these-are-the-skills-you-need-to-be-a-data-scientist-at-facebook/#G8PrucQJM7C8ORGg.99

Federal Aviation Administration. (2009). *Review of web applications security and intrusion detection in air traffic control systems*. Retrieved from http://www.oig.dot.gov/sites/dot/files/pdfdocs/ATC_Web_Report.pdf

Fehling, M. (2011). *IBM storage virtualization – Guildeline for SAP landscapes and SAP private clouds, version 3*. Retrieved from http://www-03.ibm.com/support/techdocs/atsmastr.nsf/5cb5ed706d254a8186256c71006d2e0a/3dfdbe503bafd370862577f80064e64a/$FILE/IBM%20Storage%20Virtualization%20Concepts%20for%20SAP%20landscape%20V3.pdf

Feinleib, D. (2012). The big data science behind today's most popular content. *Forbes*. Retrieved from http://www.forbes.com/sites/davefeinleib/2012/09/07/the-big-data-science-behind-todays-most-popular-content/

Fineberg, S. (2012). *Big data storage options for Hadoop*. HP Storage. Retrieved from http://snia.org/sites/default/files2/ABDS2012/Tutorials/SamFineberg_Big_Data_Storage_Options_Hadoop-v1-7.pdf

Finley, K. (2010). Getting started with Hadoop and Map Reduce. *Readwrite.com*. Retrieved from http://readwrite.com/2010/11/13/hadoop-tutorial

FireEye. (2013). *Next generation threats*. Retrieved from http://www.fireeye.com/threat-protection/

Flaster, M., Hillyer, B., & Ho, T. K. (n.d.). *Exploratory analysis system for semi-structured engineering logs*. Retrieved from http://ect.bell-labs.com/who/tkh/publications/papers/xlog.pdf

Forsyth, C. (2012). *For big data analytics there's no such thing as too big*. Retrieved from http://www.cisco.com/en/US/solutions/ns340/ns517/ns224/big_data_wp.pdf

Fountain Code. (n.d.). Retrieved from http://en.wikipedia.org/wiki/Fountain_code

Games, P., & George, D. (n.d.). *Smaq presentation*. Retrieved from http://cs.boisestate.edu/~amit/teaching/555/talks/SMAQ_presentation.pdf

Gao, H. (n.d.a). *The wireless micro cellular network based on the centralized time division multiple access technology*. Chinese Patent 200910222768.2. Shanghai, China: Chinese Patent Office.

Gao, H. (n.d.b). *The wireless network and methods for both disaster times and daily commercial operations.* Chinese Patent 201110129888.5. Shanghai, China: Chinese Patent Office.

Gao, H., & Shen, Y. (n.d.). *The cloud era information technology – A new world of computers and networks under resource rich conditions.* Peking, China: Peking University Press.

Gao, H., & Shen, Y. (2012). *IT of cloud era: The computer and network world after resources abundance.* Peking, China: Peking University Press.

Gartner. (2010). *Gartner identifies the top 10 strategic technologies for 2011.* Retrieved from http://www.gartner.com/it/page.jsp?id=1454221

Gartner. (2011). *2011 planning guide: Security and risk management.* Washington, DC: Gartner.

Gartner. (n.d.a). *In defense of silos.* Washington, DC: Gartner.

Gartner. (n.d.b). *Leveraging event and log information: A strong case for standards.* Washington, DC: Gartner.

Gartner. (n.d.c). *Overcoming silos: Evolving from stand-alone information architectures to shared-information architectures for the emerging data economy.* Washington, DC: Gartner.

Gartner. (n.d.d). *Prepare for the emergence of enterprise security intelligence.* Washington, DC: Gartner.

Gartner. (n.d.e). *Security information and event management technology assessment.* Washington, DC: Gartner.

Gartner. (n.d.f). *SIEM and IAM technology integration.* Washington, DC: Gartner.

Gartner. (n.d.g). *SIEM enables enterprise security intelligence.* Washington, DC: Gartner.

Gartner. (n.d.h). *Understanding IT controls and COBIT.* Washington, DC: Gartner.

Geer, D. E. (2008). Beware the IDs of March. *IEEE Security and Privacy, 6*(2).

Genovese, Y. (n.d.). *Getting value from big data.* Retrieved from http://www.gartner.com/technology/research/pattern-based-strategy/

Gens, F. (2013). *IDC PrEd.s 2013: Competing on the 3rd platform.* Retrieved from http://www.idc.com/research/Predictions13/downloadable/238044.pdf

Gentile, B. (2012). *Creating big value from big data.* Retrieved from http://slashdot.org/topic/bi/creating-big-value-from-big-data/Chapter 6

Gilbert, G. (2012). Real-time query for Hadoop democratizes access to big data analytics. *GigaOM Pro.* Retrieved from http://www.cloudera.com/content/dam/cloudera/Resources/PDF/GigaOM_Cloudera_Real-time_query_for_Hadoop_democratizes_access_to_big_data_analytics.pdf

Gilder, G. (2002). *Telecosm: The world after bandwidth abundance.* New York: Touchstone.

GLIF. (n.d.). Retrieved from http://www.glif.is

Globant.com. (2012). *Big data and high performance: Chukwa.* Retrieved from http://bigdata.globant.com/?p=508

Goasduff, L. (2013). Refresh your integration strategy to tackle cloud-based services. *Gartner Newsroom.* Retrieved from http://www.gartner.com/newsroom/id/2421215

Goldman, D. (2010). *Rapleaf is selling your identity.* CNN. Retrieved from http://money.cnn.com/2010/10/21/technology/rapleaf/index.htm

Google Developers. (2012). *Providing structured data.* Retrieved from https://developers.google.com/custom-search/docs/structured_data

Google Webmaster Central. (2012). *Introducing the structured data dashboard.* Retrieved from http://googlewebmastercentral.blogspot.com/2012/07/introducing-structured-data-dashboard.html

Google. (n.d.). *Data scientist job description.* Retrieved from http://www.google.com/jobs.

Gorman, S. (2009). *FAA's air-traffic networks breached by hackers.* Retrieved from http://online.wsj.com/article/SB124165272826193727.html

Gottlieb, D. (2013). *A walkthrough of MongoDB data modeling*. Retrieved from http://architects.dzone.com/articles/walkthrough-mongodb-data

Gottlieb, I. (1986). *Structured data flow: A quasi-synchronous Interpretation of data driven computations*. New York: City University of New York.

Gray, J., Chaudhuri, S., Bosworth, A., Layman, A., Reichart, D., & Venkatrao, M. (1996). Data cube: A relational aggregation operator generalizing group-by, cross-tab, and sub-totals. *Data Mining and Knowledge Discovery*, *1*, 29–53. doi:10.1023/A:1009726021843.

Graziano, D. (2012). *Google+ now home to 400 million total users*. Retrieved from http://bgr.com/2012/09/17/google-plus-stats-2012-400-million-members/

Gross, M. J. (2011). *Exclusive: Operation shady RAT – Unprecedented cyber-espionage campaign and intellectual-property bonanza*. Retrieved from http://www.vanityfair.com/culture/features/2011/09/operation-shady-rat-201109?printable=true&currentPage=2

Guess, A. (2012). IBM debuts Netezza customer intelligence appliance. *Dataversity*. Retrieved from http://www.dataversity.net/ibm-debuts-netezza-customer-intelligence-appliance/

Gu, Y., & Grossman, R. L. (2007). UDT: UDP-based data transfer for high-speed wide area networks. *Computer Networks*, *51*(7). doi:10.1016/j.comnet.2006.11.009.

Hadoop Wiki. (n.d.). Retrieved from http://wiki.apache.org/hadoop/PoweredBy

Hadoop.apache.org. (2013). *MapReduce tutorial*. Retrieved from http://hadoop.apache.org/docs/r1.1.1/mapred_tutorial.html

HadoopIntroduction. (n.d.). *What is HBase?* Retrieved from https://sites.google.com/site/hadoopintroduction/what-is-hbase

Halfon, A. (2012). *Handling big data variety*. Retrieved from http://www.finextra.com/community/fullblog.aspx?blogid=6129

Hall, A. (2012). To succeed as an entrepreneur, know your customer. *Forbes*. Retrieved from http://www.forbes.com/sites/alanhall/2012/06/14/to-succeed-as-an-entrepreneur-know-your-customer/

Hall, S. (2011). *DOT issues vulnerability report on the FAA's ATC system*. Retrieved from http://avstop.com/april_2011/dot_issues_vulnerability_report_on_the_faa_s_atc_system.htm

Hammer, J., McHugh, J., & Garcia-Molina, H. (n.d.). *Semistructured data: The TSIMMIS experience*. Retrieved from http://www.cise.ufl.edu/~jhammer/publications/ADBIS1997/adbis97.pdf

Hardy, Q. (2012). Google ventures' big data bet. *The New York Times*. Retrieved from http://bits.blogs.nytimes.com/2012/04/11/google-ventures-big-data-bet/

Hardy, Q. (2012). How big data gets real. *The New York Times*. Retrieved from http://bits.blogs.nytimes.com/2012/06/04/how-big-data-gets-real/

Hardy, Q. (2012). *Rethinking privacy in an era of big data*. Retrieved from http://bits.blogs.nytimes.com/2012/06/04/rethinking-privacy-in-an-era-of-big-data/

Harris, D. (2012). *IBM tunes big data appliance to retailers*. Retrieved from http://gigaom.com/cloud/ibm-tunes-big-data-appliance-to-retailers/

Harwood, M. (2009). *Dept. of transportation: Air traffic control systems have been hacked*. Retrieved from http://www.securitymanagement.com/news/dept-transportation-air-traffic-control-systems-have-been-hacked-005617

Haykin, S. (1999). *Neural network: A comprehensive foundation* (2nd ed.). Upper Saddle River, NJ: Prentice Hall.

He, E., Leigh, J., Yu, O., & DeFanti, T. A. (2002). Reliable blast UDP: Predictable high performance bulk data transfer. In *Proceedings of IEEE Cluster Computing 2002*. Chicago, IL: IEEE.

Hendrickson, B., & Kolda, T. G. (1999). Partitioning rectangular and structurally unsymmetric sparse matrices for parallel processing. *SIAM Journal on Scientific Computing*, *21*(6), 2048–2072. doi:10.1137/S1064827598341475.

Henschen, D. (2011). EMC tries to unify big data analytics. *InformationWeek*. Retrieved from http://www.informationweek.com/software/information-management/emc-tries-to-unify-big-data-analytics/231601867

Henschen, D. (2012). Microsoft adds big data to SQL server. *InformationWeek*. Retrieved from http://www.informationweek.com/software/information-management/microsoft-adds-big-data-to-sql-server-20/231900633

Henschen, D. (2012). Oracle makes big data appliance move with Cloudera. *InformationWeek*. Retrieved from http://www.informationweek.com/software/information-management/oracle-makes-big-data-appliance-move-wit/232400021

Herr, L., et al. (2005). *International real-time streaming of 4K digital cinema, demonstration in iGrid*. Retrieved from http://www.igrid2005.org/program/applications/videoservices_rtvideo.html

Hill, K. (2012). How target figured out a teen girl was pregnant before her father did. *Forbes*. Retrieved from http://www.forbes.com/sites/kashmirhill/2012/02/16/how-target-figured-out-a-teen-girl-was-pregnant-before-her-father-did/

Hofstede, G. (1981). Culture and organization. *Int. Studies of Man., &. Org.*, *10*(4), 15–41.

Hofstede, G. (1984). *Culture's consequences: International differences in work-related values*. Beverly Hills, CA: SAGE Publications.

Hofstede, G. (1991). *Cultures and organizations: Software of the mind*. London: McGraw-Hill Book Company.

Hofstede, G., Hofstede, G. J., & Minkov, M. (2010). *Cultures and organizations: Software of the mind*. London: McGraw-Hill.

Horowitz, B. T. (2012). Big data analytics, HIE could aid hurricane sandy recovery efforts. *eWeek*. Retrieved from http://www.eweek.com/enterprise-apps/big-data-analytics-hie-could-aid-hurricane-sandy-recovery-efforts/

Horton, C. (2012). *My smartphone told me to buy it: Big data hits mobile*. B2C. Retrieved from http://www.business2community.com/online-marketing/my-smartphone-told-me-to-buy-it-big-data-hits-mobile-0280565

Hurwitz, J., Bloor, R., Kaufman, M., & Halper, F. (n.d.). How to choose the right cloud computing service. *Cloud Computing for Dummies*. Retrieved from http://www.dummies.com/how-to/content/how-to-choose-the-right-cloud-computing-service-pr.html

HyperTable, Inc. (2012). Retrieved from http://hypertable.org/

HyperTable, Inc. (2012). *Hypertable architecture overview*. Retrieved from http://hypertable.com/collateral/whitepaper-hypertable-architecture.pdf

HyperTable. (n.d.). *Wikipedia*. Retrieved from http://en.wikipedia.org/wiki/Hypertable

I/O Virtualization. (n.d.). *Wikipedia*. Retrieved from http://en.wikipedia.org/wiki/I/O_virtualization

IBM Global Education. (2007). *Virtualization in education* (White Paper). Retrieved from http://www-07.ibm.com/solutions/in/education/download/Virtualization%20in%20Education.pdf

IBM. (2011). IBM expands big data analytics portfolio with new Netezza high capacity appliance. *Database Trends and Applications*. Retrieved from http://www.dbta.com/Articles/Editorial/Trends-and-Applications/IBM-Expands-Big-Data-Analytics-Portfolio-with-New-Netezza-High-Capacity-Appliance-76279.aspx

IBM. (n.d.). *IBM Netezza high capacity appliance*. Retrieved from http://www-03.ibm.com/software/products/us/en/ibmnetehighcapaappl/

IBM. (n.d.). *Vivisimo is now part of IBM*. Retrieved from http://vivisimo.com/solutions/bigdata.html

Inmon, W. H. (2005). *Building the data warehouse*. New Delhi: Wiley India Pvt.

Intel, I. T. Center. (2012). *Distributed data mining and big data, Intel's perspective on data at the edge*. 0812/RF/ME/PDF-USA, 327826-001. Retrieved from http://www.oracle.com/events/emea/en/oracleday2012/intel-vision-paper-1878780.pdf

Internet Marketing Solution (IMS). (n.d.). *How to use the Facebook like button*. Retrieved from http://www.adsforfacebook.com/the-facebook-like-button.php

ISE. (n.d.a). *National strategy for information sharing*. Washington, DC: US Government.

ISE. (n.d.b). *Information sharing environment profile and architecture implementation strategy, version 2.0*. Washington, DC: US Government.

Jain, R., Chiu, D., & Hawe, W. (1984). A quantitative measure of fairness and discrimination for resource allocation in shared computer systems. *DEC Research Report* TR-301.

Jansen, W., & Grance, T. (2011). *Guidelines on security and privacy in public cloud computing*. Draft NIST Special Publication.

Johnson, M. E. (2012). Hurricane Sandy: Big data predicted big power outages. *InformationWeek*. Retrieved from http://www.informationweek.com/big-data/commentary/big-data-analytics/bog-data-helped-to-track-hurricane-sandy/240115312

Kasibhotla, D. (2012). *Introduction to massively parallel processing (MPP) database*. Retrieved from http://dwarehouse.wordpress.com/2012/12/28/introduction-to-massively-parallel-processing-mpp-database/

Kavanaugh, K., & Nicolett, M. (2012). *Magic quadrant for security information and event management*. Stamford, CT: Gartner Inc..

Kelly, J. (2011). *Hadoop world: Hadoop ecosystem is exploding, says Cloudera's Olson in keynote*. Retrieved from http://siliconangle.com/blog/2011/11/08/hadoop-world-hadoop-ecosystem-is-exploding-says-cloudera%E2%80%99s-olson-in-keynote/

Kelly, J. (2012). *Big data: Hadoop, business analytics and beyond*. Retrieved from http://wikibon.org/wiki/v/Big_Data:_Hadoop,_Business_Analytics_and_Beyond

Kelly, J. (2013). Big data: Hadoop, business analytics and beyond. *Wikibon*. Retrieved from http://wikibon.org/wiki/v/Big_Data:_Hadoop,_Business_Analytics_and_Beyond

Keylock, M. (2012). *The unstructured data challenge by AdExchanger*. Retrieved from http://www.adexchanger.com/data-driven-thinking/the-unstructured-data-challenge/

Kimball, R., Ross, M., Thornthwaite, W., Mundy, J., & Becker, B. (2008). *The data warehouse lifecycle toolkit*. Hoboken, NJ: Wiley Publishers.

Knolworld.com. (n.d.). *Apache Cassandra*. Retrieved from http://www.knolworld.com/apache-cassandra/

Kobielus, J. (2012). *Big data / analytics / strategy*. Retrieved from http://www.linkedin.com/groups/Workloadoptimized-systems-Built-building-bigdata-1814785.S.171434688

Kolakowski, N. (2012). Hadoop market will hit $2.2 billion by 2018: Report. *Slashdot.org*. Retrieved from http://slashdot.org/topic/bi/hadoop-market-will-hit-2-2-billion-by-2018-report/

Kruegel, C. (n.d.). *Automated malware analysis*. Santa Barbara, CA: UC Santa Barbara, Computer Security Group.

Kurtz, G., McClure, S., & Scambray, J. (2012). *Hacking exposed 7: Network security secrets & solutions* (7th ed.). New York: McGraw-Hill.

Laundrup, J. (2008). *Detecting insider trading using automated correlation*. Adelphi, MD: University of Maryland.

Laundrup, J. (2009). *Data security breaches: An unstoppable epidemic?* Sacramento, CA: The State of California Office of Information Security.

Laundrup, J. (2011). *Implementing SIEM in the enterprise: A plan for success*. San Carlos, CA: Emagined Security Inc..

Laundrup, J., & Schultz, E. (2011). *Cloud computing security and auditing*. Seattle, WA: ISACA.

Leidner, D., & Kayworth, T. (2006). A review of culture in information systems research: Toward a theory of information technology culture conflict. *Management Information Systems Quarterly*, *30*(2), 357–399.

Leigh, J., Renambot, L., Johnson, A., Jagodic, R., Hur, H., Hofer, E., & Lee, D. (2008). Scalable adaptive graphics middleware for visualization streaming and collaboration in ultra resolution display environments. In *Proceedings of the Workshop on Ultrascale Visualization* (UltraVis 2008). Austin, TX: UltraVis.

Lewis, N. (2012). Pittsburgh healthcare systems invests $100M in big data. *Information Week*. Retrieved from http://www.informationweek.com/healthcare/clinical-systems/pittsburgh-healthcare-system-invests-100/240008989

Lewis, N. (2012). Supercomputer speeds up cancer analysis. *Information Week*. Retrieved from http://www.informationweek.com/healthcare/clinical-systems/supercomputer-speeds-up-cancer-analysis/240008817

Lippis, N. J., III. (2007). *Network virtualization: The new building blocks of network design* (White Paper). Lippis Consulting. Retrieved from http://www.cisco.com/en/US/solutions/collateral/ns340/ns517/ns431/ns725/net_implementation_white_paper0900aecd80707cb6.pdf

Liu, S., & Herr, L. (2008). *CineGrid exchange*. Paper presented in MSST Symposium. Baltimore, MD.

Liu, S., Schulze, J. P., & Defanti, T. A. (2009). Synchronizing parallel data streams via cross-stream coding. In *Proceedings of the IEEE International Conference on Networking, Architecture, and Storage*, (pp. 333-340). IEEE.

LOCKSS Program. (n.d.). Retrieved from http://lockss.stanford.edu/lockss/Home

Lohr, S. (2012). The age of big data: Big data's impact in the world. *The New York Times*. Retrieved from http://www.nytimes.com/2012/02/12/sunday-review/big-datas-impact-in-the-world.html?pagewanted=all

Lopez, M. (2012). The 4 phases of big data. *Forbes*. Retrieved from http://www.forbes.com/sites/maribellopez/2012/10/31/the-four-phases-of-big-data/

Loukides, M. (2010). *What is data science?* Retrieved from http://radar.oreilly.com/2010/06/what-is-data-science.html

Lowe, S. (2011). *Block level storage vs. file level storage: A comparison*. Retrieved from http://www.techrepublic.com/blog/datacenter/block-level-storage-vs-file-level-storage-a-comparison/3766

Luby, M. (2002). LT-codes. In *Proceedings of 43rd Annu. IEEE Symp. Foundations of Computer Science* (FOCS). Vancouver, Canada: IEEE.

Makki, S. K., & Li, X.-Y. (2010). *Sensor and ad hoc networks: Theoretical and algorithmic aspects*. Berlin: Springer.

Manyika, J., Chui, M., Brown, B., Bughin, J., Dobbs, R., Roxburgh, C., & Byers, A. H. (2011). *Big data: The next frontier for innovation, competition, and productivity*. McKinsey & Company. Retrieved from http://www.mckinsey.com/insights/business_technology/big_data_the_next_frontier_for_innovation

Market Research Media. (2012). *Global cloud computing market forecast 2015-2020*. Author.

Martinek, L. (2012). *Big data analytics*. Retrieved from http://searchbusinessanalytics.techtarget.com/definition/big-data-analytics

McDonnell, S. (2011). Big data challenges and opportunities. *Spotfire Blogging Team*. Retrieved from http://spotfire.tibco.com/blog/?p=6793

McGuire, T., Manyika, J., & Chui, M. (2012). Why big data is the new competitive advantage. *Ivey Business Journal*. Retrieved from http://www.iveybusinessjournal.com/topics/strategy/why-big-data-is-the-new-competitive-advantage

Melli, G. (2012). *Apache Cassandra server software: Gabor Melli's research knowledge base*. Retrieved from http://www.gabormelli.com/RKB/Apache_Cassandra_Server_Software

Mell, P., & Grance, T. (2011). *The NIST definition of cloud computing*. Washington, DC: National Institute of Standards and Technology.

Menegaz, G. (2012). *What is NOSQL, and why do you need it?* Retrieved from http://www.zdnet.com/what-is-nosql-and-why-do-you-need-it-7000004989/

Microsoft Corp. (2011). *What is Windows Azure?* Retrieved from http://www.microsoft.com/windowsazure/

Microsoft Corp. (2011). *Windows Azure content delivery network*. Retrieved from http://www.microsoft.com/windowsazure/cdn/default.aspx

Microsoft Corp. (2013). *Microsoft fusion framework and fusion core solution*. Retrieved from http://www.microsoft.com/industry/government/solutions/Fusion_Framework/default.aspx

Microsoft Corp. (n.d.). *Managing cyber risk in the face of sophisticated adversaries* (White Paper). Microsoft Corp.

Microsoft Corp. (n.d.a). *Appliance: Parallel data warehouse (PDW)*. Retrieved from http://www.microsoft.com/en-us/sqlserver/solutions-technologies/data-warehousing/pdw.aspx

Microsoft Corp. (n.d.b). *Microsoft dynamics*. Retrieved from http://www.microsoft.com/en-us/dynamics/default.aspx

Microsoft Corp. (n.d.c). *SQL server*. Retrieved from http://www.microsoft.com/en-us/sqlserver/solutions-technologies/business-intelligence/big-data.aspx

Microsoft Corp. (n.d.d). *Microsoft Windows Azure*. Retrieved from http://www.windowsazure.com/en-us/solutions/

Miller, M. (2009). *Cloud computing: Web-based applications that change the way you work and collaborate online*. New York: Que Publishing.

Mills, E. (2008). *What is your stolen data worth? McAfee Avert Labs finds price list for stolen bank account and credit card data*. Retrieved from http://www.news.com/8301-10784_3-9939862-7.html?part=rss&subj=news&tag=2547-1_3-0-5

Mitchell, B. (2010). *What MPP means to SQL server parallel data warehouse*. Retrieved from http://sqlpdw.com/2010/07/what-mpp-means-to-sql-server-parallel-data-warehouse/

Mongo, D. B. org. (2013). *Mango DB manual, tutorial*. Retrieved from http://www.mongodb.org/

Morgan, T. (2012). Teradata pumps data warehouses with six-core Xeons. *The Register*. Retrieved from http://www.theregister.co.uk/2010/10/25/teradata_appliance_refresh/page2.html

Morgan, T. P. (2011). IBM fattens up Netezza data warehouses. *The Register*. Retrieved from http://www.theregister.co.uk/2011/06/23/ibm_netezza_high_capacity/

Morris, J., & Lavandera, E. (2012). Why big companies buy, sell your data. *CNN*. Retrieved from http://www.cnn.com/2012/08/23/tech/web/big-data-acxiom

MSCBC. (n.d.). Retrieved from http://www.mscbsc.com

National Information Exchange Model (NIEM). (2011). *Business information exchange components*. Retrieved from http://reference.niem.gov/niem/guidance/business-information-exchange-components/1.0/

Neal, H. (2011). *Business intelligence 101 – A beginner's guide to BI software*. Retrieved from http://plotting-success.softwareadvice.com/beginners-guide-to-bi-software-1113011/

Net Forensics. (2008). *10 mistakes to avoid in evaluating security information management solutions*. Edison, NJ: Net Forensics Inc..

NetSuite. (n.d.). *What is ERP*. Retrieved from http://www.netsuite.com/portal/resource/articles/erp/what-is-erp.shtml

Nimmons, S. (2012). *CIO agenda: Big data ecosystem*. Retrieved from http://stevenimmons.org/2012/02/cio-agenda-big-data-ecosystems/

NIST. (n.d.). *Cloud computing definition*. Retrieved from http://csrc.nist.gov/publications/nistpubs/800-145/SP800-145.pdf

NLR. (n.d.). *National LambdaRail*. Retrieved from http://www.nlr.net

Noguchi, Y. (2011). *Following digital breadcrumbs to 'big data' gold*. Retrieved from http://www.npr.org/2011/11/29/142521910/the-digital-breadcrumbs-that-lead-to-big-data

NOKIA. (2012). *Mobile data challenge: Big data for mobile computing research*. Nokia Corp. Retrieved from http://research.nokia.com/files/public/MDC2012_WorkshopFrontmatter.pdf

NoSQL. (n.d.). *Wikipedia*. Retrieved from http://en.wikipedia.org/wiki/NoSQL

Nusca, A. (2012). Big data: Brainstorming the possibilities. *ZDNet*. Retrieved from http://www.zdnet.com/big-data-brainstorming-the-possibilities-7000007278/

O'Reilly Media. (2011). *Big data now, current perspectives from O'Reilly radar*. O'Reilly Media, Inc. Retrieved from http://www.onmeedia.com/donwloads/Big_Data_Now_Current_Perspectives_from_OReilly_Radar.pdf

Open Data Center Alliance. (2012). *Big data consumer guide*. Retrieved from http://www.opendatacenteralliance.org/docs/Big_Data_Consumer_Guide_Rev1.0.pdf

OPIPUTER. (n.d.). Retrieved from http://www.optiputer.net

Oracle. (2012). *Oracle information architecture: An architect's guide to big data*. Retrieved from http://www.oracle.com/technetwork/topics/entarch/articles/oea-big-data-guide-1522052.pdf

Oracle. (2013). *Oracle: Big data for the enterprice* (An Oracle White Paper). Retrieved from http://www.oracle.com/us/products/database/big-data-for-enterprise-519135.pdf

Oracle. (n.d.). *Big data appliance*. Retrieved from http://www.oracle.com/us/products/database/big-data-appliance/overview/index.html

Ou, G. (2003). *An introduction to VLAN trunking: Technology for mortals*. Retrieved from http://www.formortals.com/an-introduction-to-vlan-trunking/

Pack, D. (2011). *Using correlation rules to perform decentralized threat detection*. The DiaLog powered by LogRhythm. Retrieved from http://blog.logrhythm.com/security/using-correlation-rules-to-perform-decentralized-threat-detection/

Pant, P. (2009). *Business intelligence (BI), how to build successful BI strategy*. Deloitte Consulting LLP. Retrieved from http://www.deloitte.com/assets/Dcom-SouthAfrica/Local%20Assets/Documents/Business%20intelligence%20that%20aligns%20with%20enterprise%20goals.pdf

PCMag.com. (n.d.). *Definition of structured data*. Retrieved from http://www.pcmag.com/encyclopedia_term/0,2542,t=structured+data&i=52162,00.asp

Peretti, K. K. (n.d.). Data breaches: What the underground world of carding reveals. *Santa Clara Computer and High Technology Journal, 25*.

Pieper, G., DeFanti, T. A., Liu, Q., Katz, M., Papadopoulos, P., & Keefe, J. et al. (2009). Visualizing science: The OptIPuter project. *SciDAC Review, 12*, 32–41.

Ponemon Institute. (2013). *Ponemon institute research findings*. Retrieved from http://www.ponemon.org/

Press, G. (2013). *What's the big data*. Retrieved from http://whatsthebigdata.com

Pring, C. (2012). 216 social media and internet statistics. *The Social Skinny*. Retrieved from http://thesocialskinny.com/216-social-media-and-internet-statistics-september-2012

Privacy Rights Clearing House. (2013). *Chronology of data breaches*. Retrieved from https://www.privacyrights.org/data-breach-header-top

Productengineering. (2012). *What is Cassandra and how does it help with big data?* Retrieved from http://www.zimbio.com/SQL/articles/iVMqBJl15lN/Cassandra+How+Help+Data

Prompt Cloud. (2013). *Technologies we use*. Retrieved from http://promptcloud.com/how-we-do.php

Protalinski, E. (2012). Facebook has over 845 million users. *ZdNet*. Retrieved from http://www.zdnet.com/blog/facebook/facebook-has-over-845-million-users/8332

Provoost, L. (2010). *The structured vs. unstructured data dilemma*. Retrieved from http://www.dachisgroup.com/2010/01/the-structured-vs-unstructured-data-dilemma/

PwC's Financial Services Institute (FSI). (2011). *Getting to know you: Building a customer-centric business model for retail banks*. Retrieved from http://www.pwc.com/us/en/financial-services/publications/viewpoints/assets/viewpoint-retail-bank-customer-centric-business-model.pdf

Raghavan, B., Vishwanath, K., Ramabhadran, S., Yocum, K., & Snoeren, A. C. (2007). Cloud control with distributed rate limiting. *ACM SIGCOMME Computer Communication Review, 37*(4).

Rainmakers. (2012). *Hadoop on massive clusters drive social business*. Retrieved from http://rainmakerfiles.com/2012/07/hadoop

Rajasekar, M. A. R., Hou, C.-Y., Christopher, L., & Marciano, R. A., Wan, M., Schroeder, W., ... Zhu, B. (2010). iRODS primer: Integrated rule-oriented data systems. San Rafael, CA: Morgan-Claypool Publishers.

Raptor Code. (n.d.). Retrieved from http://algo.epfl.ch/contents/output/presents/Raptor-Bangalore.pdf

Renambot, L., Jeong, B., & Leigh, J. (2007). Realtime compression for high-resolution content. In *Proceedings of the Access Grid Retreat 2007*. Chicago, IL: Access.

Renambot, L., Jeong, B., Hur, H., Johnson, A., & Leigh, J. (2009). Enabling high resolution collaborative visualization in display rich virtual organizations. *Future Generation Computer Systems*, *25*(2), 161–168. doi:10.1016/j.future.2008.07.004.

Rodrigues, T. (2012). *Cloud IaaS providers compared*. Retrieved from http://www.techrepublic.com/blog/datacenter/11-cloud-iaas-providers-compared

Rodrigues, T. (2012). *IaaS provider comparison reveals market trends for the cloud*. Retrieved from http://www.techrepublic.com/blog/datacenter/iaas-provider-comparison-reveals-market-trends-for-the-cloud/5755

Roe, C. (2012). *So you want to be a data scientist?* Retrieved from http://www.dataversity.net/so-you-want-to-be-a-data-scientist/

Rouse, M. (2006). *Storage virtualization*. Retrieved from http://searchstorage.techtarget.com/definition/storage-virtualization

Rouse, M. (2009). *Server virtualization*. Retrieved from http://searchservervirtualization.techtarget.com/definition/server-virtualization

Rouse, M. (2010). *Virtual switch*. Retrieved from http://searchservervirtualization.techtarget.com/definition/virtual-switch

Rouse, M. (2011). *Virtual storage area network (VSAN)*. Retrieved from http://searchstorage.techtarget.com/definition/virtual-storage-area-network

Rudd, S., Brown, A., Levitt, M., & Luk, G. (2012). *Global cloud computing services: Software, infrastructure and platform services move to the mainstream*. Strategy Analytics.

Sabhlok, R. (2012). Is big data right for your business? President Obama thinks so. *Forbes*. Retrieved from http://www.forbes.com/sites/rajsabhlok/2012/11/15/is-big-data-right-for-your-business-president-obama-thinks-so/

SAGE. (n.d.). Retrieved from http://www.evl.uic.edu/cavern/sage/index.php

Salesforce.com. (2013). *What is PaaS?* Retrieved from http://www.salesforce.com/paas/overview/

SAP. (2012). *Big data for retail is flying off the shelves*. Retrieved from http://www.forbes.com/sites/sap/2012/05/11/big-data-for-retail-is-flying-off-the-shelves/

SAS. (2012). *Big data meets big data analytics: Three key technologies for extracting real-time business value from the big data that threatens to overwhelm traditional computing architectures* (White Paper). Retrieved from http://www.sas.com/resources/whitepaper/wp_46345.pdf

Savitz, E. (2012). The big value in big data. *Forbes*. Retrieved from http://www.forbes.com/sites/ciocentral/2012/09/25/the-big-value-in-big-data-seeing-customer-buying-patterns/

Scherer, M. (2012). *Inside the secret world of the data crunchers who helped Obama win*. Retrieved from http://swampland.time.com/2012/11/07/inside-the-secret-world-of-quants-and-data-crunchers-who-helped-obama-win/#ixzz2JbhjDs88

Schultz, E. (2009). *The in's and out's of SIEM technology*. Paper presented at the IX National Computer and Information Security Conference. Bogota, Colombia.

Schultz, E. (2010). *Cloud computing security: A look into the future*. San Carlos, CA: Emagined Security Inc..

Schumpeter. (2011, May 26). Building with big data. *The Economist*. Retrieved from http://www.economist.com/node/18741392

SearchStorage FAQ. (2007). *What is unstructured data and how it is different from structured data in the enterprise?* Retrieved from http://searchstorage.techtarget.com/feature/What-is-unstructured-data-and-how-is-it-different-from-structured-data-in-the-enterprise

Semi-Structured Data. (n.d.). Retrieved from http://www.dcs.bbk.ac.uk/~ptw/teaching/ssd/notes.html

Servo, T. (2008). *Boeing's new dreamliner has serious security vulnerability*. Retrieved from http://www.freerepublic.com/focus/f-news/1949826/posts

Shannon, C. (1949). *A mathematical theory of communication*. Urbana-Champaign, IL: University of Illinois Press.

Shaw, R. (2011). What is business intelligence? *Database Trends and Applications*. Retrieved from http://www.dbta.com/Articles/Editorial/Trends-and-Applications/What-is-Business-Intelligence-73502.aspx

Shen, J., & Suo, S. (2008). *3GPP: Long term evolution: Principle and system design*. Shanghai, China: Posts & Telecom Press.

Shen, Y., Zhang, Y.-Q., & Li, Y. (2013). *Cloud 360 - An in-depth look at cloud era by Microsoft experts*. New York: Electronic Industry Press.

Shirai, D., Kawano, T., Fujii, T., Kaneko, K., Ohta, N., & Ono, S. et al. (2009). Real time switching and streaming transmission of uncompressed 4K motion pictures. *Future Generation Computer Systems*, 25(2), 192–197. doi:10.1016/j.future.2008.07.003.

Shokrollahi, A. (2006). Raptor codes. *IEEE Transactions on Information Theory*, 52, 2551–2567. doi:10.1109/TIT.2006.874390.

Shopper, L. (2012). *HCatalog – Embrace the independence*. Retrieved from http://dataforprofit.com/?p=117

Simonite, T. (2012). *What Facebook knows?* Retrieved from http://www.technologyreview.com/featured-story/428150/what-facebook-knows/

Smarr, L. (2009). The OptIPuter and its applications. In *Proceedings of the IEEE LEOS Summer Topicals Meeting on Future Global Networks*, (pp. 151-152). IEEE. doi:10.1109/LEOSST.2009.5226201

Software, I. B. M. Information Management. (2011). *IBM Netezza high capacity appliance – Data sheet*. Retrieved from http://www-05.ibm.com/il/software/netezza/pdfs/IBM_Netezza_High_Capacity_Appliance_USEN.pdf

Spakes, G. (2012). Turning big data into value. *SAS Voices*. Retrieved from http://blogs.sas.com/content/sascom/2012/04/12/turning-big-data-volume-variety-and-velocity-into-value/

Statistic Brain. (2012). *Google annual search statistics*. Retrieved from http://www.statisticbrain.com/google-searches/

Sterling, G. (2013). *Data and forecasts: Facebook winning app. game, where's Google maps?* Retrieved from http://internet2go.net/news/Data+And+Forecasts

Stokes-Rees, I. (n.d.). *Big data: Tools and techniques for working with large data sets*. Retrieved from http://www.slideshare.net/ijstokes/2011-08-prewttcbigdataian-stokesrees

Storage Magazine. (n.d.). *HBAs go virtual*. Retrieved from http://www.bitpipe.com/detail/RES/1163403108_503.html

Storage Virtualization. (n.d.). *Wikipedia*. Retrieved from http://en.wikipedia.org/wiki/Storage_virtualization

Structure Data. (n.d.). *Wikipedia*. Retrieved from http://www.webopedia.com/TERM/S/structured_data.html

STUXNET. (2012). *Wikipedia*. Retrieved from http://en.wikipedia.org/wiki/Stuxnet

Su, A.-J., Choffnes, D. R., Kuzmanovic, A., & Bustamante, F. E. (2009). Drafting behind Akamai: Inferring network conditions based on CDN redirections. *IEEE/ACM Transactions on Networking*, 17(6).

Subbaraman, N. (2012). *A nosy smartphone app. wants your data*. Retrieved from http://www.technologyreview.com/view/429421/a-nosy-smartphone-app-wants-your-data/

Taft, D. (2012). Teradata launches Hadoop-based aster big analytics appliance. *eWeek*. Retrieved from http://www.eweek.com/enterprise-apps/teradata-launches-hadoop-based-aster-big-analytics-appliance/

Taft, D. K. (2011). IBM launches Netezza analytics appliance to wrangle big data. *eWeek*. Retrieved from http://www.eweek.com/c/a/Desktops-and-Notebooks/IBM-Launches-Netezza-Analytics-Appliance-to-Wrangle-Big-Data-728395/

Tata Communications. (n.d.). *White paper: IaaS – Fulfilling the promise of cloud computing*. Retrieved from http://www.tatacommunications.com/downloads/whitepapers/Tata_Communications_IaaS_WhitePaper_v2.0-web.pdf

Tate, J. (2003). Virtualization: In-band and out-of-band - What is the difference? *IBM Redbooks*. Retrieved from http://www.redbooks.ibm.com/abstracts/tips0203.html

Telecom World, I. T. U. (2011). *The world in 2011: ICT facts and figures*. Retrieved from http://www.itu.int/en/ITU-D/Statistics/Documents/facts/ICTFactsFigures2011.pdf

Teradata Corp. (2010). *Teradata extreme data appliance scales from 29TB to 50TB*. Retrieved from https://www.storagenewsletter.com/news/systems/teradata-extreme-data-appliance

Teradata Corp. (2012). *Big analytics appliance enables new business insights*. Retrieved from http://news.thomasnet.com/fullstory/Big-Analytics-Appliance-enables-new-business-insights-623501

Teradata Corp. (n.d.). *Teradata aster big analytics appliance*. Retrieved from http://www.teradata.com/Aster-Big-Analytics-Appliance/#tabbable=0&tab1=0&tab2=0

Terry, K. (2012). Health IT execs urged to promote big data. *InformationWeek*. Retrieved from http://www.informationweek.com/healthcare/clinical-systems/health-it-execs-urged-to-promote-big-dat/240009034

The Digital Dilemma. (2008). *The science and technology council of the academy of motion picture arts and sciences (AMPAS)*. Los Angeles, CA: AMPAS.

Turner, J. (2011). *Hadoop: What it is, how it works, and what it can do?* Retrieved from http://strata.oreilly.com/2011/01/what-is-hadoop.html

Twitter. (2011). *One hundred million voices*. Retrieved from https://blog.twitter.com/2011/one-hundred-million-voices

U.S. Secret Service. (2006). *U.S. secret service press release: United States secret service's operation rolling stone nets multiple arrests*. Retrieved from http://www.secretservice.gov/press/pub0906.pdf

University of Minnesota Extension. (2011). *Market analysis: Consumer survey*. Retrieved from http://fyi.uwex.edu/downtown-market-analysis/understanding-the-market/consumer-survey/

Unstructured Data. (n.d.). *Wikipedia*. Retrieved from http://en.wikipedia.org/wiki/Unstructured_data

Utz, S., & Krammer, N. C. (2009). The privacy paradox on social network sites revisited: The role of individual characteristics and group norms. *Cyberpsychology (Brno)*, *3*(2).

Vergano, D. (2012). *Big data disguises digital doubts*. Retrieved from http://usatoday30.usatoday.com/tech/science/columnist/vergano/story/2012-06-16/big-data/55628002/1

Virtual Geek. (2011). *EMC GreenPlum Hadoop*. Retrieved from http://virtualgeek.typepad.com/virtual_geek/2011/05/emc-greenplum-hadoop.html

Virtualization. (n.d.). *Wikipedia*. Retrieved from http://en.wikipedia.org/wiki/Virtualization

Vishwanath, V., Leigh, J., He, E., Brown, M. D., Long, L., & Renambot, L. ... DeFanti, T. A. (2006). Wide-area experiments with LambdaStream over dedicated high-bandwidth networks. In *Proceedings of IEEE INFOCOM*. IEEE.

Vishwanath, V., Leigh, J., Shimizu, T., Nam, S., Renambot, L., & Takahashi, H. ... Kamatani, O. (2008). The rails toolkit (RTK) - Enabling end-system topology-aware high end computing. In *Proceedings of the 4th IEEE International Conference on e-Science*. IEEE.

Vishwanath, V., Shimizu, T., Takizawa, M., Obana, K., & Leigh, J. (2007). Towards terabit/s systems: Performance evaluation of multi-rail systems. In Proceedings of Supercomputing 2007 (SC07). Reno, NV: SC.

VMware, Inc. (2007). *Information guide: VMware virtual networking concepts.* Retrieved from http://www.vmware.com/files/pdf/virtual_networking_concepts.pdf

VMware, Inc. (2007). *Understand full virtualization, paravirtualization, and hardware assist* (White Paper). Retrieved from http://www.vmware.com/files/pdf/VMware_paravirtualization.pdf

VMware, Inc. (2012). *VMware network virtualization paves the way for next generation cloud services at iland.* Retrieved from http://www.vmware.com/company/news/releases/vmw-iland-network-121712.html

von Neumann, J. (1958). *The computer and the brain* (2nd ed.). New Haven, CT: Yale University Press.

Walker, M. (2012). *Traditional BI vs. data analytics approach.* Retrieved from http://www.datasciencecentral.com/profiles/blogs/traditional-bi-vs-data-analytics-approach

Wallace, J. (2012). *How big data is changing retail marketing analytics.* Retrieved from http://www.revolutionanalytics.com/news-events/free-webinars/2012/how-big-data-is-changing-retail-marketing-analytics/

Wang, R. (2012). *Monday's musings: Beyond the three v's of big data – Viscosity and virality.* Retrieved from http://blog.softwareinsider.org/2012/02/27/mondays-musings-beyond-the-three-vs-of-big-data-viscosity-and-virality/

Weglarz, G. (2004, September). Two worlds of data – Unstructured and structured. *DM Review Magazine.*

Westerman, G., & Hunter, R. (2007). *IT risk: Turning business threats into competitive advantage.* Boston: Harvard Business School Press.

White, T. (2012). Hadoop: The definitive guide (3rd Ed.). Sebastopol, CA: O'Reilly Media / Yahoo! Press.

Whitehouse. (2010). *National security strategy.* US Government. Retrieved from http://www.whitehouse.gov/sites/default/files/rss_viewer/national_security_strategy.pdf

Whittaker, Z. (2012). Oracle's hurd: World is drowning in data, wars of overload. *ZDNet.* Retrieved from http://www.zdnet.com/oracles-hurd-world-is-drowning-in-data-warns-of-overload-7000006141

Wi-Fi. (n.d.). Retrieved from http://www.wi-fi.org

Wiki.apache.org. (2011). *OozieProposal.* Retrieved from http://wiki.apache.org/incubator/OozieProposal

Wiki.apache.org. (2012). *CouchDB Wiki – Technical overview.* Retrieved from http://wiki.apache.org/couchdb/Technical%20Overview

Wiki.apache.org. (2013). *Hadoop Wiki, alphabetical list of institutions that are using Hadoop for educational or production uses.* Retrieved from http://wiki.apache.org/hadoop/PoweredBy

Wikipedia. MongoDB. Retrieved from http://en.wikipedia.org/wiki/MongoDB

WiMAX Forum. (n.d.). Retrieved from http://www.wimaxforum.org

Woods, D. (2012). What is a data scientist? *Forbes.* Retrieved from http://www.forbes.com/sites/danwoods/2012/07/23/what-is-a-data-scientist-tom-wheeler-of-clickfox

Wuorio, J. (n.d.). *7 ways to use customer data.* Retrieved from http://www.microsoft.com/business/en-us/resources/management/customer-relations/using-customer-data.aspx?fbid=FSaxUpiCGfC

Xia, H., & Chien, A. (2007). RobuSTore: A distributed storage architecture with robust and high performance. In Proceedings of Supercomputing (SC07). Reno, NV: SC.

Xia, H., & Chien, A. A. (2007). RobuSTore: A distributed storage architecture with robust and high performance. In *Proceedings of ACM/IEEE International Conference on High Performance Computing and Communications (SC'07).* ACM/IEEE.

Yahoo. (2010). *Yahoo!'s workflow engine for Hadoop.* Retrieved from http://rvs.github.com/oozie

Yahoo. (2013). *Yahoo! Hadoop tutorial*. Retrieved from http://developer.yahoo.com/hadoop/tutorial/index.html

Yang, J. (2011). *From the Turing machine to von Neumann machines*. New York: Academic Press.

YouTube.com. (n.d.). *Statistics*. Retrieved from http://www.youtube.com/t/press_statistics

Yu-Gang, W. (2009). *Enjoy the blessings of the internet of things, but we do have privacy?* Retrieved from http://news.xinhuanet.com/mrdx/2009-06/21/content_11575947.html

Zawodny, J. (2008). *Yahoo! launches world's largest Hadoop production application*. Retrieved from http://developer.yahoo.com/blogs/hadoop/yahoo-launches-world-largest-hadoop-production-application-398.html

Zhang, Y., Luo, J., & Hu, H. (2007). *Wireless mesh networking: Architecture, protocols and standards*. Boston: Auerbach Publications.

Zoltan. (n.d.). Retrieved from http://www.cs.sandia.gov/Zoltan/

About the Authors

Yushi Shen is an outstanding scholar and social activist. He has over 15-year of research, development, and management experiences in the IT industry, and leadership experiences in various influential international and local organizations. With five books and over twenty research papers published, Dr. Shen is an internationally recognized expert in the areas of cloud computing, wireless communications, and video coding. He has served as a reviewer, associate editor, technical program committee chair/member for numerous international conferences and core journals. He is the recipient of various awards and recognitions. Dr. Shen is currently Microsoft's Cloud Business Development Government Affairs and Strategy Director in the China region. He joined Microsoft in Redmond, WA, in 2006 and worked on the design and serviceability for general Windows Media (WM) techniques and the WM platform. From 2010 to 2012, Dr. Shen served as the Chair of the Chinese Microsoft Employee Network (CHIME). Since late 2012, he has stepped up as the Chair of the entire Microsoft Asian Employee Resources Group (ERG), overseeing the 17 Asian ethnicity groups with more than 10,000 Microsoft employee members. Dr. Shen received his B.S. degree in electrical engineering from the Tsinghua University, Beijing, P.R. China, in 2001, and Ph.D. degree in electrical and computer engineering, from the Univ. of California at San Diego (UCSD), La Jolla, in 2006, and MBA degree from the Univ. of Washington (UW), Seattle, in 2012.

Yale Li is the Principal Security Architect and acting China Information Security Officer for Microsoft. In this role he focuses full time on corporate security strategy, architecture, solutions, and research of emerging technologies such as cloud computing, mobile computing, big data and machine learning. He currently serves as Board Member and Research Director for CSA Seattle Chapter, CSA APAC CISO Summit Program Committee Member, ICCSM Programme Chairman, RecordsInTheCloud.Org Collaborator, NIST Big Data Workgroup Member, and Board Member/Advisor for multiple research institutes and MS partner companies. He also collaborates on cloud security research with University of Washington, University of British Columbia, and Beijing University of Aeronautics & Astronautics. He is one of the earliest CCSKs. In his 15 years with Microsoft, Yale held various lead positions in Windows, Tools Development, and Internet Datacenter Web Platform, and contributed to Cloud Security, Engineering Excellence, Shared Source, and enterprise software/internet service management, development, deployment, and operations. Prior to joining Microsoft, he was Chief Technology Architect for an IBM company, Co-founder/CTO of multiple tech startups, and research assistant to CERN's Nobel Prize and Rutherford Medal laureates.

Ling Wu is the Principal System Integration Engineer at EMC. She has been working on database, data warehouse, and business intelligence since 2000. She has served as DBA, BI developer, Data Warehouse Architect at T-mobile, AT&T, and Washington Mutual Bank. In the last couple of years, she has focused on data warehouse architecture on SQL and Oracle solution at Visa and EMC. Now, she works in the Enterprise solution group at EMC and is dedicated to cloud storage and storage solutions for enterprise data warehouse architecture.

Shaofeng Liu holds a Ph.D. in Computer Science from the University of California, San Diego (UCSD), one of the top universities in system and networking. He holds BS and MS degrees from Tsinghua University. He is now working as a Windows CORE software design engineer on Hyper-V, a core virtualization technology supporting the architecture of future operating systems and Windows Azure cloud platforms. He has carried out research in grid computing, scheduling, parallel fault tolerance, database optimization, machine learning, large-scale data preservation and distribution, and so on. His Ph.D. work breaks through existing bottlenecks of Forward Error Correction code by parallelizing code across data sources and streams, using a creative Cross-Stream code invented by him. He is actively involved in research at Calit2, and works closely with Cinegrid research community and AMPAS to design large-scale data preservation and distribution strategies. He is now an associate board director in Chinese Microsoft Employee (CHIME), and has served as the president of Tsinghua alumni association at San Diego.

Qian Wen is an IT strategist, business leader, and enthusiast for world cultures. Her specialty areas include but are not limited to business modeling, international team dynamics and organizational behavior, strategic investment and marketing, cloud computing architecture, network communications, and doing business with China. She currently serves as the CEO of Endronic Corporation, which she co-founded with her brother in 1994. In its early days, the company did engineering consulting for AT&T wireless and Matsushita Electric Industrial on the installation of wireless communication systems for Boeing airplanes. The company specializes in IT development and strategic business consulting with the current focus being Cloud Computing Architecture, Business Modeling, and doing business with China. In 2012, Qian served as CEO for one of the top three creative marketing and business consulting firms in China. Prior to co-founding Endronic Corp., Qian worked at the Microsoft VC++ Group, and co-authored the Microsoft VC++ Reference Manuals. While at Microsoft, she facilitated department-wide customer visits that reached out to over 20,000 worldwide Visual Studio customer install bases. She coordinated the site visits and ensured that information could be quickly disseminated with the entire department, such that customer feedbacks could be incorporated into the product design in a timely manner. Qian holds an MSEE from the Department of Electrical Engineering of the University of Washington. She entered college at the age of 15, obtained her BSEE at the age of 18, MSEE at the age of 19, and became a Ph.D. candidate at the age of 20. Qian has lived in the USA for almost 30 years. She is a good English prose writer, speaker, and an expert in the Chinese culture and history. She is an accomplished Chinese calligraphy artist, and an active member of the Chinese Big Calligraphy Association in Beijing. Qian is married to Ping Jin, also a Chinese calligraphy artist and expert of the Chinese culture in Beijing, China. Ping is the 15th generation descendant of the founding Emperor of Qing Dynasty, Nurhaci. Together, they have a lovely three-year-old son.

* * *

Henry Gao is currently the CTO of Glocom and MPI. He received his two M.S. degrees in electrical engineering from the Jiao Tong University, Shanghai, in 1980, and Iowa State University, in 1982. In 1988, he funded his first company, Glocom, in Germantown, Maryland, and focused on mobile satellite telecom equipment. In 1998, he funded his second company, MPI, and focused in video Internet technologies. In 2008, he shifted his research activity into micro-base station wireless systems and cloud computing areas. He holds several core patents in video Internet, wireless network, and advanced computer technologies.

Tayfun Keskin is a Professor at the UWB School of Business. His research and teaching interests include collaborative information technologies, behavioural modelling and simulation, and the strategic management of information systems. He is particularly interested in developing a quantitative "role of information systems" theory. He has published two papers in *European Journal of Operational Research* and *Informs Journal on Computing*. He also worked for a couple Fortune 500 companies such as Procter & Gamble, Oracle, and Kraft Foods prior to his academic career. He holds a Ph.D. degree from The University of Texas at Austin, McCombs School of Business since May 2010.

Yudong Liu is currently a Visiting Professor at Western Washington University (WWU). Her research interest includes Statistical Natural Language Processing (NLP), Formal Languages, Artificial Intelligence (AI), Machine Learning, and Security. She was the only nominee from SFU for Canadian AI Association Doctoral Dissertation Award 2010. She has a series of publications in multiple well-known NLP conferences and has given talks at these conferences, and once won "Best Oral Presentation Award." She obtained her PhD in Computer Science from Simon Fraser University (SFU), Canada. Prior to joining WWU, Yudong worked as a Translation Tool Engineer for SAP, Canada, where she was mainly in charge of the software translation automation.

Jie Yang is currently a Sr. Business Manager in Microsoft Corporation, Redmond. He received his bachelor and master degrees in Electrical Engineering from Shanghai Jiao Tong University, Shanghai, China, in 1995 and 1998, respectively, and MBA degree from Ross School of Business at University of Michigan, Ann Arbor, in 2008. He worked in Ericsson R&D center between 1998 and 2006.

Index

A

B

C

D

E

F

G